A SIMPLE SAILOR

A LIFETIME AT SEA

by

Captain Mike Reeder

Grosvenor House
Publishing Limited

This book is published by
Grosvenor House Publishing Ltd
28-30 High Street, Guildford, Surrey, GU1 3EL.
www.grosvenorhousepublishing.co.uk

A CIP record for this book
is available from the British Library

ISBN 978-1-78148-651-1

This book is dedicated to the Royal Navy of the Twentieth Century, in thanks for the excellent training, and for the opportunities to visit so many countries and meet so many Highly Interesting People from so many walks of life.

CONTENTS

CHAPTERS

1	Sons Of The Sea	1
2	Korean War Additional For Training	16
3	Further Training Afloat And Ashore	44
4	Submarines	64
5	Malaya And My First Command	93
6	Cruises To Columbo, Cairo, The Canaries And The Caribbean	141
7	HMS Ganges, Mens Sana In Corpore Sano	175
8	The Wee Grey Ghost Of The Arabian Coast	189
9	HMS Kildarton, My Fourth Command	223
10	Shoresides Including Another Sea Command	267
11	Mercantile Marine Matters	298
12	Falklands And Heaps Of Hips	355
13	Nautical Nineties And Mariners Mishaps	384
14	Fings Ain't Wot They Used To Be	413

SONS OF THE SEA

My father was killed while serving with the Royal Navy aboard HMS Kelly, when she was sunk by enemy dive bombers at the Battle of Crete on 23rd May 1941. I was nine years old at the time. In my family it had been more or less understood that when I grew up I would go into the Navy, and even at that early age I knew that this was what I wanted to do – to go to sea like my father. His sad loss, although it left me fatherless and my mother a widow, did not dim the light of my ambition. On the contrary, if anything it strengthened my resolve. To a child of that age, death is not a real concept, it is something that is so far away that it could "never happen to me". So it is even possible that this traumatic event within the family to some extent powered my motivation to fulfil my dream, to get on and do the work which the adults told me I would have to do to get me where I wanted to be. Much though it went against the grain – for I am an open-air person, interested and involved in most forms of sport available to the average lad – I therefore got down to the necessary study and the rather hard work which every youngster has to do in order to be accepted by the Navy.

Four years later, in early June, we watched hundreds of allied planes flying towards France in support of the D-Day landings and the subsequent advance into Europe. By the end of the year, after much cramming and hard work on the part of the teachers, I obtained 80% in the Common Entrance Examination. This mark was sufficient to gain a scholarship into the Royal Naval College at Dartmouth, which meant my mother did not have to pay any more for my education. Before I was finally accepted I had to go to the Old Admiralty Building at Whitehall for a medical examination. No problem with that, but we then had to face the dreaded Admiralty Interview Board which somehow I also managed to pass.

The R.N. College, Dartmouth Winter 1946

Thousands of naval officers were educated at the Royal Naval College for the four years from the age of 13½ to 17½, and many have written about their time there. The magnificent red brick and white stone building is still very much in its famous position overlooking the River Dart, but not only has its name been amended slightly over the years, but also the officers being trained are doing a much wider range of courses, and are very much older. Whilst we were there it was a boarding school, where everyone except the civilian teachers wore naval uniform, and whose main object was to train us to be in command of ships and leaders of men. I was impatient for that day to arrive. Make no mistake, I thoroughly enjoyed my time at Dartmouth, especially the sport, and I will always be grateful to the Navy for giving me such a fine educational start to my climb up the ladder. I was an average product of the system and it was not their fault I was only average.

At long last, during the first week in January 1950, we joined the Cadet Training Cruiser at Devonport. She was HMS Devonshire, a three funnelled County Class Cruiser of about 10,000 tons in weight and 630 feet in length. The ship's company

2

Our last passing-out parade

consisted of 48 Officers and 560 Ratings – supplemented by about 230 of us Cadets on board for two cruises. Joining up with us were approximately 40 British Cadets who had joined Dartmouth at the age of 17, and other Cadets from the Royal Australian, Royal Canadian, Royal New Zealand, Indian and Pakistan Navies.

The first few days were spent getting us organised for working the ship. We were divided into three parts of the ship, the Foc'stle, Top and Quarterdeck. I was in the latter. At sea we would work a watchkeeping system, usually one in four, which meant you would be in the first or second part of the Port or Starboard Watch. We slept in hammocks, so we had to be instructed on how to sling them between metal bars running athwartships from one side to the other. Then, early in the morning, we also learnt to lash up and stow them sausage shape in the areas provided, known as nettings.

Every day, in spite of the fact that it was damp, miserable and very cold, was exciting. We got to know our messmates and shipmates, and particularly the "Colonials" as we nicknamed those from the "further outposts of the Empire". They would be

3

with us for a few years, they were great companions and some became close friends. We were all very happy to hear the first turn of the screw, as we slipped from Devonport on 14th January. Now we felt our careers had really started. We were part of a ship's company which included Officers, Ratings, Royal Marines and Bandsmen.

The cruise was to last twelve weeks and during that time we worked as perhaps not very able seamen, but doing our best at running the ship's routine, steering the ship, acting as lookout, manning the sea boat, lowering and hoisting it, sending signals, firing guns and cleaning the ship. One task of no great importance, other than in an emergency, was the sea-boats crew. During the night we were allowed to sleep on the job so to speak. This meant that we could kip on the wooden decks, using maybe a folded oilskin as a pillow. This taught me the ability to sleep anywhere at any time – a skill I possessed for the rest of my life! We sailed southwards away from the British winter, across the Bay of Biscay, past Gibraltar and then, once in the warmer climes, westward out into the Atlantic. A couple of days further on, a most unusual accident occurred. In not very rough weather Able Seaman Delvental was forward in the paint shop. A scuttle must have been hit by a hard floating object, because a chunk of thick glass hit him in the throat and he literally bled to death. The Navy immediately informed the next of kin, who were asked to state their choice of burial. They chose not to have his body returned to the UK, but asked for a ceremonial Burial at Sea. Lower Deck was cleared and the Padre conducted the very dignified service. Luckily this event was very infrequent in the peacetime navy, but perhaps a good experience for us to witness whilst under training. There followed the Kit Auction of A.B. Delvental's personal belongings. Everyone chipped in fantastic amounts of money, often for the most unwanted items. Things were often returned two or three times for re-auction. The proceeds were forwarded to his next of kin.

An overnight stop at Point-a-Pierre in Trinidad to refuel, and then to our first port of call, Grenada, one of the most beautiful natural harbours in the world.

HMS Devonshire refuelling at Point-a-Pierre, Trinidad January 1950

We painted the ship. This was achieved by pairs of us being lowered over the side on wooden planks. The plan, which seemed to work, was to lower yourself, on your side, by releasing a rope which was led up around a stanchion and then back down to your side of the plank. The paint pots and brushes were lowered to us on another rope. When we got to the bottom, theoretically, we hoisted ourselves back up, but it was much easier, and more refreshing, to drop into the sea and swim round to climb up the gangway.

Whilst painting the ship, so called "bum boats" hovered around, hoping to sell us all sorts of merchandise including ripe and fresh fruit, mangoes, watermelon, etc. One boat had on board a musical group we ignorantly called "The Dustbin Doodlers". They were playing the most marvellous tunes: "Island in the Sun", "Jamaica Farewell" and "Brown Skin Gal Stay Home and Mind der Babee", etc. It was the first introduction to what was to become my eternal enthusiasm for the Calypso Rhythm and Steel band music. Visits to Barbados, Trinidad and Jamaica followed. "Join the Navy and see the world" were the advertising slogans in the UK. What a start we were having, especially so soon after the war, when very few people were able to leave war-torn Great

Cadets painting ship at anchor in Grenada Harbour

Britain with its rationing. We worked hard and ate well. As far as the navy cooks were concerned curry was just another meal and like stew or roast lamb, was served up not with rice but with spuds and cabbage.

Every morning we scrubbed the wooden decks in bare feet – fine in the West Indies but not so back in freezing Plymouth. We took plenty of time on passage from one island to the next, so that we could be introduced to the practical aspects of navigation, the Admiralty chart, latitude and longitude, the nautical mile and how to find out where you were by plotting the ship's position, etc. The "shifts" we kept, known as watches, were a complete new way of life for us. We kept the 24 hour clock and we seemed to lose two minutes every day! "There is no such time as midnight or 2400 because we would not know whether it was yesterday, today or tomorrow". So the day finished at 2359 and started at 0001.

The watch system seemed completely crazy. The first watch of the day was called the middle, from 0001-0400, because it was in the middle of the night. Morning, forenoon and afternoon seemed sensible enough but in order that we kept a different watch every day, a 7-watch-per-day system was used. Therefore, 1600-1800 and 1800-2000 were called the First and Last Dog Watches because they had been curtailed! Finally the last watch of the day was called the First Watch because it was the first of the night. It all became logical in the end, but we were getting the message that you needed a sense of humour, or if you can't take a joke, you shouldn't have joined!

The occasions we did have runs ashore were for short periods, three days out of four, usually spent sightseeing, swimming from the fabulous beaches, shopping or playing sport. I played water polo for the cadets against a Bayjan under-17 side alongside a pier in Barbados. No-one had warned us, but during the game, which we lost by about ten goals to the young, fit locals, I shoved off with my right foot. Below the waterline the pier was covered with black spiked shellfish – sea urchins I think they were called. Several of these spikes were embedded in my foot, so I could only walk one-legged. The next few days were spent in sick bay whilst the spikes were slowly persuaded out of my foot. I was brought technical books to read, so there was no let up on the work which continued to be both enjoyable and instructive.

The summer cruise was to Glengariff in Bantry Bay, Ireland, Odda, Oslo and Narvik in Norway. And then up to Jan Mayen Island and back to four places in Scotland, namely Scapa Flow, Lossiemouth, Loch Ewe and Rosyth. Perhaps not such exciting places as on the first cruise but nonetheless interesting and good times were experienced by all. Glengarriff was my first visit to Ireland and what a great place it was. Very hospitable people who were always smiling and apparently happy. I was Shore Signals Party there. That meant being on the veranda of the local hotel and passing messages between the ship and those on shore – when we weren't being plied with pints of Guinness by the landlord! One message I had to pass was a challenge from the locals to a game of Gaelic football! We immediately got the Australian cadets to teach us Ozzie rules, for it was the Irish immigrants playing their football, and being copied, that led to the formation of Australia's national game. We won but only because we were reasonably fit, and they were a small town. The next day, they took us by bus to "kiss the Blarney stone". It is a block of bluestone built into the battlements of the castle and you have to put yourself into a most awkward position, lying on your back, in order to ensure you are "blessed with the gift of the gab" and "the luck of the Irish"!

The visits to Norway were excellent. The Devonshire had brought King Haakon of Norway back to the UK before Oslo was occupied by the Germans, and then returned him home after the liberation. Needless to say therefore we were Norway's favourite ship, and were made very welcome all over the country. Some of us had the pleasure of being introduced to Thor Heyerdahl, the world famous explorer, who spent much time telling us about his adventures. He had worked out that people from South America settled Polynesia in pre-Columbian times, and set about trying to prove it. He went to Peru and constructed the raft, Kon-Tiki, of balsa logs and other native materials. He set sail from Callao in April 1947 and smashed into a reef at Raroia 101 days later. Kon-Tiki was taken to Tahiti, repaired, and is now in its own museum in Oslo. Thor's book on the expedition was a best seller translated into 67 languages, and the documentary film won an Academy award the year after we were in Oslo.

The Kon-Tiki

Visits were made to Holmenkollen, the world-famous ski-jump for Winter Olympic Games, after which we were invited to a party at a marvellous restaurant at Frognerseteran. Many female students were there to greet us. They all wore red berets with a peak at the front and a line with knots hanging out the back. Apparently the number of knots indicated the number of occasions they had spent the night with a man under the midnight sun!

I was asked out for the day by one of them, Maimey Gilhuusmoe. I don't know how many knots she had! Her family was with her and we drove to a secluded beach for a pre-lunch swim. I had not brought my swimming gear with me, but that did not matter. The moment we arrived, they all completely undressed and slowly walked into the sea. There was only one thing I could do and that was to run with the herd, and I mean run!

Inevitably it was time to leave Oslo and proceed on a most picturesque voyage northwards via the fjords. En route some of us joined the Christian Radich, the Norwegian Merchant Navy training ship. She is internationally well known and appears in most Tall Ship Races. We were there for a day's sail and helped get her three masts fully rigged. She looked beautiful as we re-joined the Devonshire for the long and again picturesque voyage up Hardanger Fjord to Odda. We had an athletics match against the locals. They were so fit and healthy that they won every event. The buzz was that the Communist Party was a bit strong in the area, and we were sent there "to show the flag". Our Royal Marine Band beat retreat in the town square, very impressive as always. At the later parties, there was no sign of any of the girls being the slightest bit interested in politics.

We arrived in Narvik for a weekend. My only recollection of the short stay was taking a scenic train journey into nearby Sweden. The rail track was high up and at the head of Narvik Fjord, in the clear and very deep water, we could see two sunken destroyers with swastikas painted on their bows - no-one had mentioned the Battle of Narvik in the Dartmouth naval history lessons. We reached Norrbotten in Sweden, where a very attractive blonde called Monica signed the certificates confirming we had crossed the Arctic Circle.

Norway's sail training ship "Christian Radich", built in 1937, still looking beautiful and going strong

We cruised further north and far into the lands of the midnight sun. No darkness at all. The middle watch was unbelievable and actually enjoyable. Our Captain thought we should visit the areas where the next sea battles might be fought. We travelled to within one thousand miles of the North Pole and close to Jan Mayen Island and Iceland. The sky was blue, not a breath of wind, there was thin ice nearly covering the sea, and early morning scrubbing decks would have been fun – if we could have worn sea boots and stockings instead of bare feet.

The cruise then petered out a bit as we turned southwards towards Scotland, visiting not the most attractive places, namely Loch Ewe, Scapa Flow, Lossiemouth and Rosyth, but all with strong naval connections. We were able to catch up on the work, both theoretical and practical. Only a day or so at each of the first three places, but a week at Rosyth.

We held our athletic championships there, and who should win the hurdles? None other than John Ronald Gower, who had been the Navy champion in earlier days. You could tell by his style.

On 25th June, whilst still at Rosyth, BBC News told us that North Korean Forces had crossed the 38th parallel and invaded South Korea, thereby starting the Korean War. There had been a tremendous run down in the strength and capabilities of the forces involved in WW2. However, there were still substantial US Forces in Japan and only British Commonwealth troops in the area compared in size. The recent history of the area and the political situation involving Russia, China, Japan, Korea itself and of course the US, was all too complicated. Shortening the story, the United Nations entered the war on the side of South Korea.

Southwards towards Devonport, we were able to have our last fling in Torquay – at the height of summer, this was good. The Mayor, Aldermen, and Burgesses went out of their way to welcome us. They made a lot of facilities free, and arranged a swimming and water polo match between Torquay Leander Swimming Club and HMS Devonshire. Also a Naval Ball to which we were all invited at Torre Abbey Mansion House. It was here that I overheard one girl say to another: "Can't bear late nights. If I'm not in bed by midnight, I go home"!

Back to more serious things. The United Nations were not winning the Korean War. The British Commonwealth, heavily involved in the Malayan Emergency, were asked to help as much as possible. National Service was at its height and some reservists were called up. As regards the Navy, the aircraft carrier HMS Triumph was in the area, but although ill-prepared, was adequately filling a gap. And how did this affect us cadets in HMS Devonshire? Well, the carrier HMS Theseus was alerted to sail from Portsmouth as soon as possible, which was going to be in August. John Ronald Gower cleared lower deck and told us of the Korean situation. He said four R.N. Cadets were required to join the Theseus as midshipmen. This would mean a shortened summer leave, but any volunteers should tell their Divisional Officers immediately. To this day I have no idea how many of us volunteered, or how they selected the lucky four. All I know is my name, along with those of Chris Comins, Blair Wilson and George Vallings, came out of the bag. At the end of cruise, prize giving in Devonport, Wee Mac, the Commander-in-Chief, Plymouth, did the honours and at the end of his speech he said:-

"Get to know your men. They are worth knowing, and if you can get their confidence, they will follow you anywhere. They are the greatest single factor."

Yes, get to know your men. Who are these men referred to as sailors, Jack Tars, or Matelots, and whom collectively you hope one day to form into a happy and efficient ship's company under your command? That is what all the training is about.

"Wee Mac", Admiral Sir Roderick McGrigor, inspecting our guard.

He is a Jack of all trades and master of some. He wears a uniform and has an official number. This number is preceded by the letters C, D, or P, indicating his home port of Chatham, Devonport or Portsmouth. He refers to these ports as Chats, Guzz and Pompey. Don't ask me why, but the rivalry between these places has led to tremendous sporting occasions and the internationally renowned Field Gun competition.

He has a language of his own which has been developed over the years. A lot of it is a bit basic, nearly every phrase contains the F word and it contains much sense of humour. It is very descriptive and to the point.

Nearly everyone he meets has a nickname depending on their surname. For example Dusty Miller, Chalky White, Bunny Warren, Fanny Adams, Happy Day, Rusty Steel, Spud Murphy, Windy Gale, and Tug Wilson to name a few. He has signed on for a number of years, often twelve. Hence the frequently heard expression usually voiced within the earshot of authority: "Roll on my effing duzz". Because there is no-one so hard done by, he will continually drip and moan about his lot in life. But when the duzz is nearing completion, he requests to sign on for another ten. This in spite of his favourite saying "never volunteer for anything"!

When he is given a task about which he hasn't the slightest clue, he will set about it, but not necessarily with enthusiasm or haste. He will use a certain amount of common sense, and then flannel everyone into thinking he is expert at the work. When he has nothing to do, especially when he is ashore in a barracks (which he calls a stone frigate) he will take with him a clipboard and pencil, thereby looking occupied. He knows that if he stands still or loafs around, "That man over there report to me" is going to be shouted at him by some chief or petty officer from afar.

He always has his hair cut in working hours, often in small ships, by the ship's barber. In shore establishments there is the NAAFI (No Ambition and F-all Interest) barbers shop open all day.

"Having your hair cut in working hours?" queried an officer.

"Yes, sir. It grew in working hours," said Jack.

"It didn't all grow in working hours," said the officer.

"No, sir. That's why I'm not having it all cut off!"

He goes to a football match with the express intention of cheering on the visiting side, especially at Home Park Plymouth and Fratton Park Portsmouth. At the bull ring especially in La Linea, across the border from Gibraltar, the bull cannot believe its luck and the support it gets. One of his favourite pastimes is to start an argument in a pub, and then quietly slip away to the pub next door.

Whether he has been foreign or not, he likes to make out he has travelled the world. He uses words like Dhobi (laundry) and mufti (non-uniform clothes) and Imshi (buzz off). He refers to Guinness as "Nigerian lager", ravioli as "Italian teabags" and cockroaches as "Bombay runners". He refers to all Dutchmen as "Hertz van Rental" and when in their country goes on a "reep creep", which is the inevitable stroll down the Reeperbahn, that well known street of pleasurable activity in Amsterdam. He assures you that it's not only Dutch girls who wear Dutch caps and warns you to be careful of Welsh letters – that is French letters with leaks in them.

He is a Casanova in bell-bottoms. When seasonal leave is shortly due, he will write a quick note to his pash, with whom he is "up homers". On the back of the envelope he would write the word Burma (Be Undressed Ready My Angel) or Norwich (Nickers Off Ready When I Come Home). He has very good medical knowledge particularly centred on parts of the female anatomy, for which he has a variety of words and expressions. Some of the less scandalous are his calling Welsh rarebit a "Cardiff virgin", and his referring to coitous interruptus as "getting off at Fratton". You have to know that Fratton is the last station before Pompey on the train from London! When his pash says she has acute angina, he replies that he has known that for some time!

His knowledge of foreign languages is often good, and he will translate for you. " Illegitimum non tatum carburundum" means "don't let the bastards grind you into the ground", and excreta taurii cerebrum vincit" means "bullshit baffles brains". He calls admirals and other senior officers who are posted ashore, Whitehall Wallies and assumes they all have second jobs working for NATO (No Action, Talk Only). Undoubtedly there are far too many of them – there being more admirals than ships.

An admiral was beginning to lose his zest for life. So he went to a naval quack who could find nothing wrong but suggested he privately visited a brain specialist. This he did and was told his brain was prematurely worn out but that with modern surgery he could have a new one transplanted. The admiral enquired of the specialist as to the cost. He was told that a doctor's brain would be quite cheap but that an admiral's would be at least three times as much. Why, he asked, was an admiral's so expensive and the reply was that the admiral's was as good as new, and had never been used!

Visiting Ramsgate one day in the 80s, I walked ashore from the marina and entered the nearest visible pub called the Standard. The landlord was on duty behind the bar and within seconds of his welcoming me we both realised we were ex-navy. He had been 7 and 5; that is 7 years' service followed by 5 years in reserve. He was a Cockney, with a tremendous sense of humour and his eyes lit up as he reminisced about the best seven years of his life. He was a submariner and had reached Leading Stoker. He only remembers the good times of which there were many, in that short period of his otherwise mundane life.

KOREAN WAR ADDITIONAL
FOR TRAINING

My mother had moved from Campbeltown to Alverstoke, which was on the other side of the harbour from Portsmouth. So it was there that I spent my shortened summer leave from "Devonshire". I was now a midshipman and I had had my uniform altered by Gieves, the naval tailor – affectionately known as Thieves – in their shop situated not far outside the main dockyard gate. On my visits to them, watch was kept on HMS Theseus as she was busily being prepared and storing ship alongside South Railway jetty. I was also busy preparing myself and packing my trunk with all the necessary gear, which of course included white tropical uniform. I was ready in plenty of time as the joining instructions were patiently awaited. They arrived in the following form, very abrupt and to the point:-

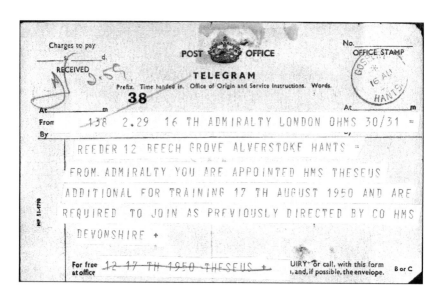

Telegram

I noticed I should join the next day, but I decided to quietly join that evening, get unpacked and settled in ready to start at the crack of dawn on the 17th. This was a wise move as Blair, Chris and George arrived shortly after me and they had much further to come. Next morning, after a very good breakfast prepared by Goanese cooks and stewards, the senior Sub-lieutenant Stubbs introduced himself as our guide for the day.

As Midshipmen of the Fleet we were known as "snotties". They used to have three buttons sewn on their uniform cuffs supposedly to stop them wiping their noses on their sleeves! A more derogatory name, which I cannot remember ever being called was a "wart". We were evidently discrepancies on the face of the earth! Our home in the ship was the gunroom, which was down below and far aft above the propellers. The Sub-Lieutenants were also billeted in the gunroom. All other officers were in the Wardroom one deck up and further forward. We midshipmen slept in hammocks in our Chest Flat; we were by now used to that sort of existence.

Alan Stubbs showed us round the ship, especially the areas which were going to be of most immediate use to us. The bridge, the operations room, the flight deck and hangars, and of course the various motor boats of which we would be the coxswains when in harbour, at anchor, or secured to a mooring buoy.

Our action stations were going to be the radar plotting room and my job was to stand (sometimes sit) behind a large twelve feet square perspex screen with concentric circles leading to tens of miles from the ship which was the centre spot. We would plot every aircraft and ship detected by our various types of radar sets. The whole ship's company would remain at action stations until the situation improved. Then we would relax a little and go to defence stations, which was one in two watches, or watch on watch off. Defence stations would be our normal routine during daylight hours whilst our aircraft were operating in the war zone. When the aircraft were all on board, we would relax to normal watch keeping of one in four, which for us meant bridge work as midshipman of the watch, understudying the OOW. The seamen were allocated a part of ship to keep clean and work when entering and leaving harbour; and so were we. I was quarterdeck.

August 18th was the day we had been waiting for since we drew the short straws on board "Devonshire". Up early, everyone smartly dressed in best uniform, most of the ship's company lined up on the flight deck, but me with my bunch of seamen on the quarterdeck ready to let go ropes and hoist fenders inboard. Our Royal Marine Band was playing stirring Gung-Ho marches, and at the allotted moment we slipped from South Railway Jetty and proceeded out of Portsmouth Harbour. "All the nice girls love a sailor" played the RM Band as we passed Point Farewell – the usual place for families and friends to gather at the Round Tower in Old Portsmouth, which was opposite Fort Blockhouse in Gosport. It was at the narrow entrance to the harbour where one got the closest view. On passing the outer spit buoy, at the end of the buoyed channel, the ship's company were told to fall out, go to stand easy and clean into the rig of the day, namely working uniform. So began our first period of eight days at sea, preparing ourselves, the ship and its aircraft and equipment to fight in the name of the United Nations?

Firstly, we four had to learn about life in an aircraft carrier. There were close on a thousand people on board this large warship. What did they all do? The ship's company was divided into departments, each with perhaps a Commander in charge, supported by a few officers of Lieutenant Commander and Lieutenant rank, some Chief and Petty Officers, and finally many Junior Ratings. We, the seaman branch, were responsible for the bridge watch keeping, the operations room, the ship's defence, the general administration, the discipline and the running of the routine. In fact, everything except the equally important engine room, electrical, medical, dental, clergy and supply and secretariat. The latter were responsible for supplying our stores, clothing, food, pay and keeping the inevitable paperwork flowing. We were all, in fact, members of a self-contained village-size team, important cogs in a wheel, rapidly turning and moving further from our homeland towards an unknown country called Korea.

Our headman was Captain Ben Bolt DSC and he was starting the process of moulding us into a happy and efficient ship.

As we proceeded south across the Bay of Biscay and towards the Mediterranean, we had flying stations practically every day. This was what an aircraft carrier was really all about. A few days before we left Pompey, the 17th Carrier Air Group consisting of 807 Squadron of Sea Fury fighter bombers and 810 Squadron of Firefly fighter reconnaissance aircraft, had embarked on board. Each had black and white stripes painted on its wings. These aircraft were in one main hangar, from which they could be taken to the flight deck by two lifts, situated one at each end. The flight deck was the runway, only about 600 feet long, from which the aircraft operated. At the fore end was a steam catapult for launching; across the after end were 10 arrester wires to pull up the aircraft on landing. Then abreast the island were two wire barriers to stop any plane which missed the wires. These arrester wires were on hydraulic rams lifted a few inches above the flight deck, and hopefully a hook suspended from the tail of the aircraft catches one of the ten wires, whilst the pilot cuts the throttle and comes to a halt. In spaces just below and on either side of the flight deck, known as sponsons, were stationed naval airmen, the able rates of the fleet air arm. As the aircraft comes to rest, these men, wearing different coloured water polo type caps to indicate different tasks, rush to release the hook from the wire, the barriers are lowered and the plane is moved forward either onto the lift to be lowered down to the hangar, or further forward to the deck park. Needless to say we were to witness this many times and it was fascinating to watch.

Eight days later, having bypassed Gibraltar, we entered Grand Harbour, Malta for a short weekend. The first day I was midshipman of one of the liberty boats. I had an able seaman as bowman, a stoker in charge of the engine and alongside me (the novice) a competent leading seaman. We were not called away very often as Malta is the island with boats called Dghaisas. For next to nothing, anyone could be taken ashore or returned aboard whenever he wanted and without having to wait for a routine boat and its restraint. The second and last day, George

Maltese Dghaisa Valetta Harbour 1950

and I went ashore for the first time as mids dressed in plain clothes. It was only for a short run ashore as we were bound to visit Malta GC many times in the years to come. We felt obliged to go down the Gut, more correctly known as Strait Street in the Old City, and pay homage to the Gyppo Queen. This sleazy hostelry was needless to say brim full of "Theseus" matelots thoroughly enjoying themselves before sailing next day. George and I had one pint of hop leaf before returning on board for our next session of training. Chinese cooks and stewards took over from the Goanese; we were getting closer to the Far East.

It was announced on the day we reached Port Said that our pay had been increased to 7/6 per day, that's 37½p! No hanging about – straight into the Suez Canal to celebrate – which was another first for most of us. Only those actually on watch and necessary to get the ship through the canal, were at work. Most others were on the flight deck watching all the goings on. Gully-

Gully Men had been hoisted in their boats by the ship's cranes onto the flight deck, so that they could sell us all the tourist traps we had missed by not stopping. Some performed the usual magical Arabic tricks. While this was going on there was much banter between our crew and the British military in the Canal Zone, who dashed out of their encampments to cheer us on our way. The incident I will always remember involved the canal pilot arriving on the bridge to guide us through. He was British and he had had a few! Ben Bolt, appreciating the situation, asked his steward to bring up some whisky, soda and ice, sat the pilot in his personal chair at the back of the bridge and conned the ship himself through to Port Suez. We disembarked the sleepy pilot and the Gully-Gully Men and set forth down the Red Sea.

It was now getting very hot, in fact the hottest most of us had ever experienced. With my fair complexion and too much time spent stripped to the waist, I got a severe dose of sunburn on my back, resulting in the formation of blisters. They began to burst, so I had to go to sick bay. The Sick Berth Tiffy covered my back in nice cool calamine lotion and told me to come back twice a day for further applications of the pink stuff. It was an offence to get so sunburnt that it prevented you from carrying out your duties. A lesson had been learnt, and it was fortunate that from then on I was still able to sunbathe, but only in moderation.

One branch or department not yet mentioned but nonetheless very important, was the Educational Branch or the "schoolies". The Instructor Lieutenant Commanders and Instructor Lieutenants were responsible for the further education of those on board, especially those wanting advancement or promotion. Also they were the Met Men, who with their own expertise and information from weather ships and other stations, were able to forecast the weather. They also provided news bulletins which were posted on noticeboards around the ship. It was about now that news was coming through that US Forces had been pushed right back from the 38th parallel. The North Koreans had been stopped as far south as Pusan. Not good news.

We reached Aden and its barren rocks on 4th September. Two days were spent there replenishing ship with fuel and stores and each watch was given one opportunity to go ashore and see the sights, such as they were. All we did was go ashore to the Gold Mahur Bathing Club for a swim in the pool. Or one could swim in the Indian Ocean protected by a shark net. Then followed the longest sea passage of the voyage with only a glimpse of Ceylon from where we received an air-drop of very welcome mail. Apart from normal work and training the dog watches were occupied in sport in order to keep, or get, everyone fit. Provided the aircraft are in the hangar, the empty flight desk is a very good sports field - metal decked though and unsuitable for some games. We had inter-mess or inter-departmental fixtures at Deck hockey, a game similar to grass hockey, using the same sticks but a rope grummet or puck. We had tug o' war competitions and other athletic events. We were introduced to a new game called volley ball played in the lowered lift wells – good when the aircraft were on deck. Without explaining the exact rules, it was 6-a-side, each team on opposite sides of a 6ft high net and you lose a point if the ball is grounded on your side. A good light-hearted game invented in aircraft carriers of the Royal Navy. It soon got ashore, so to speak, and played in many countries. Eventually it became an international sport and an Olympic event. I don't think Great Britain has ever qualified!

Singapore was reached on 16th September and it was urgent that we should arrive at the scene of operations as rapidly as possible. Therefore our stay was cut down to the minimum time required to re-fuel and take on all the necessary stores: once again, two days, and one run ashore for each watch.

On our way north to Hong Kong and with winter approaching, we went back into blues. Just as well the schoolies had warned us: we arrived in a violent tropical storm. We had a week's stay and even though the news from Korea was still no better, it was time well spent. The carrier air group were ashore at Kai Tak airport, rehearsing the technique of operating with the Army and continuing to get fully operational, it was their last opportunity. Replenishment of the usual fuel and supplies took place and HMS Triumph, whom we were relieving, arrived down from Korea on her way home. Much useful information and advice was gleaned from their ship's company.

One of the first people on board was Jenny with her side party of girls who attached themselves to our ship for the rest of our stay. Not for what you think. None of that from them. They had already helped us to secure to the mooring buoy. From now on they washed and ironed uniforms, cleaned ship, and chipped away any rust before painting the ship's side. They were charming hardworking girls. We had a make-and-mend every afternoon, unless we had our usual harbour duties as midshipman of the watch or coxswain of a liberty boat. Like Malta with its Dghaisas, there were plenty of Chinese Sampans ready, willing and able to scull you, with their single yuloh, anywhere in the harbour. Two of us hired a sampan for our first run ashore, landing at the Naval Base on Hong Kong Island. I will never ever forget shortly after going out of the base's main gate. Two matelots, who had perhaps indulged in a couple of beers, were discussing some financial deal with two rickshaw drivers. Money changed hands and within seconds the two drivers were sitting in their rickshaws whilst the two matelots pulled them in a race down the street. The local Chinese were well amused and some Europeans even clapped and cheered them on. Those were the good old days. We then went on to get the tram up to the peak and admire the fabulous view of the rest of the colony, Kowloon and the New Territories leading on towards Communist China. Then down to sea level and to look at the eye-boggling shops before introducing ourselves to Chinese chow. We had no idea how mouthwatering the fantastic local food would be. Chinese restaurants (one or two maybe in London) had not really started to appear in the UK. Other days we took the Star ferry across to Kowloon and went swimming at the Officers' Club. Then a round of golf at the Royal Hong Kong Golf Club out at Fanling, where we were honorary members. More gazing at shop windows but we were not going to buy anything until the return journey. We knew there might not be a return.

Jenny and her side party Hong Kong 1950

Never go to sea if there is a gale warning in force – unless you have to. So we were told and so we did; head on into a typhoon in the Formosa Straits. Another first for most of us. It was very unpleasant down aft in the gunroom, the whole stern shuddering as the propellers came out of the water, but the ship did demonstrate its excellent sea qualities.

Naturally with a typhoon warning in place, all the aircraft had been stowed down below in the hangar, and each one secured with a strop to its eyelets. This was before we left harbour. The next day it was announced that the hangar was out of bounds, as one of the planes had broken adrift. It could have been very dangerous as well as expensive, if it had careered around all the other aircraft, doing untold damage. Luckily, it ended up in a corner away from all the others, and the naval airmen involved were able to re-secure it to its moorings. Also in the Formosa Straits we experienced another alarm. An unknown and unidentified aircraft was picked up on the radar, and its position was plotted on the vast screen. All hands went to action stations for the first time; the plane circled the ship and then went away. Although clearly seen on the radar, no-one actually saw it visually because of the low cloud prevailing.

It was late afternoon on 5th October when we arrived in Sasebo, Japan, exactly 48 days after leaving Pompey. Our arrival was an eye-opener for us all. This long, thin harbour, like a Norwegian fjord, was full of some of the finest warships around. Most were from the US Navy which about ten years previously had overtaken the Royal Navy as the largest in the world. There was the vast battleship Missouri, known as the "Mighty Mo", the equally vast aircraft carrier Philippine Sea, known as the "Phil Sea", several other US carriers the same size as ours, and many of their cruisers and destroyers. Theseus now became the Flag Ship of the Flag Officer, Far East, who also had quite a few Canadian, Australian and New Zealand and Dutch cruisers and destroyers under this command. We were now in the Combat Zone, and we had two days in Sasebo to complete our final preparations for our first operational patrol. No shore leave was given that night.

The "Mighty Mo" Sasebo Harbour, October 1950

I was woken next morning by the following announcement made over the ship's radio, which had been tuned into the only English language station being broadcast in the area:-

"This is A.F.R.S. Kyushu, the Amurrrican Forces Radio Service Keyooshoo, Jaypan. Don't forget a blob on your nob will stop your demob."

What an introduction to the United States for a young, fairly innocent 18 year old Limey! British Prime Minister, Clement Attlee, had stated in the House of Parliament that no-one under the age of 19 was, or would be, fighting in the Korean War. Never believe a politician. If they don't tell lies, they certainly muck about with the truth.

Chris Comins and I went ashore next afternoon for our first visit to Japan. Everyone had to be in uniform and the town was heaving with sailors mostly from the US of A. Quite a few of them were carrying life-size inflated female rubber dolls back to their ships. Chris and I couldn't believe our eyes!

About 1700, after light refreshment in a café, two USA naval officers, each with a thick and a thin stripe on their uniform arms, chatted to us. "Say guys, are you both Limeys?" And before we had time to answer, they said "What are those white patches on your laypells?" "They indicate we are midshipmen in the Royal Navy" was our reply. "Gee, that's great. We're lootenants Junior Grade, and we're aviators in the Phil Sea" – the vast carrier we had already seen on our arrival, and passed in the liberty boat on our way ashore. We shook hands and introduced ourselves. They were Bob Krause and Don Loranger.

"Say, how would you guys like to come along to our club?" We accepted their invitation without hesitation and much chatting took place as we walked the mile or so to the Camp Mower Officers' Club. It was huge and extremely well done out. "What would you guys like to drink then?" We hesitated because we were only allowed to drink beer, port and sherry (no spirits) in the gunroom on board and we knew the US ships were dry. "What are you having or what do you suggest?" we shyly replied. "How's

F/PW/80

If you are captured you are required to give the enemy the information shown on the following certificate in order that your capture may be reported to your next of kin. When you are questioned, but not before, tear off the duplicate certificate and hand it to the interrogator. DO NOT ANSWER ANY OTHER QUESTIONS. ALWAYS CARRY THIS CARD IN ACTION. The interrogator may not take away your S. 1511, S. 43A, A.B. 64 or A.B. 439. It is important in your own interest that the particulars of rank should be kept up to date.

Write in BLOCK CAPITALS

BRITISH FORCES IDENTITY CERTIFICATE

SERVICE
NUMBER..................RANK..*MID RN*..........

SURNAME..........*REEDER*..........................

CHRISTIAN OR
FORE NAME(S)..*MICHAEL JOHN*..............

DATE OF BIRTH ....*30. 6. 32*..............

- -

BRITISH FORCES IDENTITY CERTIFICATE
(DUPLICATE)

SERVICE
NUMBER..................RANK..*MID RN*..........

SURNAME..........*REEDER*..........................

CHRISTIAN OR
FORE NAME(S)..*MICHAEL JOHN*..............

DATE OF BIRTH ....*30. 6. 32*..............

W.O.P. 33764

Prisoner of War Card

27

about Bourbon on the rocks?" We had never heard of it. Bourbon was American rye whiskey ((note spelling, not Scotch whisky) and the rocks were of course ice cubes. Very nice too, they were and together with the most succulent T-bone steaks – rationing was still on in the UK – we had a fantastic evening to remember. Bob and Don had been great hosts, and they were the first people from that magnificent country I met – the first of many I was to get to know over the years.

Next day we were extremely busy aboard. We were all issued with action working clothes, and extra warm foul weather gear for those going to be on watch in the open air. Winter was upon us and it was going to be extremely cold. To cap it all we were all issued with a form F/PW/80.

The very next day we left Sasebo and made for the Yellow Sea. Not many hours later we were near the west coast of Korea and our aircraft were in action. Within a day we had our first taste of the price of war. Lieutenant Stanley was shot down by Communist flak and was gallantly rescued by a US helicopter, from out of the clutches of enemy troops. Responding to Theseus's signal the helicopter hovered above Stan, trapped in his Sea Fury, whilst other planes of our squadron straffed the approaching enemy. Stan returned fire with his pistol but had to stop as he had badly sprained his wrist. In the midst of the fierce exchange of gunfire the chopper landed. Its pilot held the enemy at bay with his carbine, whilst the doctor used an axe to cut away part of the Sea Fury and then removed the wounded Stan to safety on the beach at Inchon. A launch transferred him to the US hospital ship Consolation. He was all right in the good company of female nurses and within a day or two was in a Tokyo hospital being treated for his injuries. He soon returned on board.

There followed a period of intensive operations. We were escorted at all times by at least two destroyers. To name a few there were H.M. Ships Concord, Charity, Comus and Morecambe Bay, the Canadian ships Sioux, Athebaskan and Nootka, the Australian ships Warramunga and Tobruk, the New Zealand ships Pukaki and Rotoiti and the Dutch ship Evertsen. On two occasions we refuelled from a Royal Fleet Auxiliary at anchor off Inchon. Whilst on our way to the Far East we had heard of the enemy capture of Inchon on their way southwards. However, three weeks before our arrival in the area, a UN counter-offensive started with a landing at Inchon. It was a bold move and proved successful.

The UN naval forces were split into four Task Forces which were again split into four Task Groups. Our Task Group consisted of British, Commonwealth and other allied warships and was under the command of Rear Admiral Andrews. His HQ we had seen secured to a jetty in Sasebo – it was a converted passenger ship called "Ladybird". Theseus' job was to help maintain a continuous blockade of the enemy held part of Korea. This was done by daily first-light reconnaissance to check on any enemy shipping movement and mining activity; to fly Carrier Air Patrols (CAPs) and Anti-Submarine Patrols over elements of the Task Group as required, and to provide planes for bombardment spotting and for indirect or close air support of the land forces along the battle front.

After a fortnight we returned to Sasebo for a so-called rest period. During time ashore, one day we took a bus to Nagasaki. Even though it was five years since the atom bomb had been dropped there, you could still see the vast saucer-shaped crater and the devastation both physical and human created by this terrible weapon of war. In the area desolated by the bomb there were a few shanty buildings and what was even worse, several people walking around who were perhaps "lucky enough to be alive", but had terrible burns and missing or broken limbs.

By now the land forces, which included a British Commonwealth Brigade of British, Canadian, and Anzac Battalions, had reached the furthest point in their advance towards the Manchurian border. Were we winning? Yes, by the end of this ten day operational period the requirements for an aircraft carrier in the Yellow Sea were regarded as no longer necessary. We had returned to Sasebo, and a couple of days later "Theseus" was released to return to Hong Kong. All the indications were that our mission was about over and so the Japanese shops were raided for "rabbits" – gifts for the folks at home. We were then off in high

Heavy seas, viewed from the port quarter,
pushing us back to Hong Kong

spirits towards Hong Kong. Even another typhoon in the Formosa Straits did nothing to dampen the ardour of the ship's company. It was from the north pushing us along.

We were beginning to get good write-ups in the press and there was a report on the cheering which greeted the description given of "The gallant conduct of the officers and ship's company of HMS Theseus" by the Financial Secretary to the Admiralty (Mr L.J. Callaghan) who went on to state "Ever since the aircraft carrier arrived in Korea last October the ship's company had worked in such a way that no aircraft had ever been unserviceable for more than two hours, and the ship had the remarkable record of more than 1,300 deck landings without failure or accident – an unprecedented feat of efficiency." It was a labour government and Mr L.J. Callaghan – ex Chief Petty Officer Callaghan became our Prime Minister in 1976.

Hong Kong welcomed us as heroes. "Theseus Returns after Blasting North Korean Targets; Only one plane lost in Operations" wrote the local English language newspaper. And who were the first people to greet us? None other than Jenny and her side party who helped us secure to the buoy. Life was now relaxed. The ship was full of "buzzes" (lower deck rumours) as to our future programme. Where were we going to be for Christmas, etc? Except of course for watch keepers, we had make and mends every afternoon. We did our stints as Midshipmen of the Watch, understudying and learning from the real Officer of the Watch and I was now entrusted to be in charge of any of the motor boats without the supervision of a Leading Seaman.

We had plenty of shore leave and we tried to find out as much as possible about the Colony, its people and the shops – as well as the fantastic restaurants and nightlife. One shop I found fascinating was the one that sold ivory ornaments, chess sets, back-scratchers, as well as the balls-within-balls. I got to know the owner who was charming in spite of the fact he probably realised I would not be buying very much. He had a factory at the back of his shop which consisted of a dimly lit shed and four craftsmen (sweated labour I guess) who skilfully carved away at pieces of elephant tusk to produce these magnificent objects of art.

We went to the races at Happy Valley, played golf at the Royal Hong Kong Golf Club, swam at the USRC and the ship had many sports fixtures against local Army and RAF sides. I was selected to play for the ship's rugby team against the Combined Services HK at Kai Tak, and also against Hong Kong at Happy Valley. Grossly unfit when we left Japan, we did train quite enthusiastically on our way south and on a couple of occasions in Hong Kong before the matches took place. We had a good team which included Alec Valentine, who had played for the Royal Navy, Combined Services, and Scotland. He was a very good all round athlete and threw the hammer for Scotland at the next Commonwealth Games in Vancouver.

But the news from Korea was not good. The Chinese Communists were entering the war on the side of North Korea. They had crossed the Manchurian border and within a few days had launched a major offensive. The UN land forces went into full retreat and Theseus was recalled to the west coast of Korea to render them badly needed air support. The recall arrived on the second Friday, so we had a weekend to get ourselves organised in order to sail on the Monday.

The Carrier Air Group who had been ashore in Kai Tak doing exercises with the Army and RAF, got themselves back on board by the Friday evening and a farewell cocktail party for all the kind people ashore was held in the wardroom. Needless to say the gunroom could not attend so we went ashore and ended up at the Mandarin Hotel. Many of the wardroom officers were there – well oiled – and there was an excellent dance band performing. I was standing by the bar chatting to fellow officers when a group who had been dancing came and joined us. When the music re-started, Pauline suggested it was time I moved from the bar and joined her, plus other friends, at their table. There were quite a few of our pilots already seated there. Pauline and I were soon dancing together and, as time progressed, we were dancing very closely. It seemed no time before we were doing the last waltz. As soon as it was over she said: "Come on, I must get home now." She ordered a rickshaw and we arrived down at the water front and jumped on board a sampan. She lived across the harbour in Kowloon and it was my intention to return on board as we passed Theseus, but she said: "Come home for a nightcap." Arriving at the end of her garden she asked the sampan to be there to pick her up at 0700 in the morning. Apart from her Christian name the only thing I knew about her was that she was a presenter with Radio Hong Kong. As we said our fond farewells she told me to listen to her programme at 1800 that evening. I was Midshipman of the Watch that day, but was actually off watch at the time of the programme. I heard her voice say "and for Michael on board HMS Theseus, it is with great pleasure and happy memories I play "It only happens when I dance with you". No-one of importance had seen me arrive on board by sampan shortly after 0700 – it was a Sunday – and as far as I know, no-one linked the radio request with me. Whilst I was on watch early afternoon, an aviator Lieutenant Commander, who had been at our table the night before, came up and enviously accused me of being a lucky so-and-so. "She certainly had a shiner for you," he said. He later told me that Pauline was married to a Major in the Royal Army Medical Corps and stationed with the Commonwealth Brigade up in Korea. I was only 18 and I had become a toyboy!

The next day Jenny and her side party, who during our stay had made the ship look immaculate, let go the bridle from the buoy, and we were on our way straight back to the Yellow Sea. We started operations on 5th December and we were working under very heavy pressure, particularly the aircrew. On top of that it was very cold and often snowing. Instead of anchoring close inshore to refuel we started doing so at sea, thereby being able to remain on patrol longer. Attached to our Task Group were the "Brown Ranger" and the larger "Wave Laird", two oil tankers manned by the Royal Fleet Auxiliary, an expert part of the Merchant Navy. They would top up in Japan and then rendezvous with us at the required time to provide the necessary supplies. The operation was known as RAS (pronounced RAZZ), which stood for Replenishment at Sea and it required a high level of seamanship. The oil tanker would steer the required course and speed, as accurately as possible, and it was up to the warships to keep station. Then supported by a derrick the oil pipeline would be passed and refuelling would commence. Any stores, mail or personnel would be transferred by jackstay. Often three ships could fuel at the same time, say a destroyer on each side of the tanker and us from astern.

The R.F.A. Brown Ranger refuelling 'Theseus' on her port side and the frigate 'Morecambe Bay' to starboard

'Theseus' and 'Unicorn' alongside in Kure late Christmas 1950. Anchored in the bay are the R.F.A. 'Wave Laird' and hospital ship 'Maine'

For weeks members of the ship's company had been speculating where we would spend Christmas and it was hoped that we would at least be in harbour for the festivities. Alas, it was not to be and 25th December was just another working day, there wasn't even any snow to cut down the visibility and hence flying operations. Four days later, however, instead of Sasebo, we went to Kure for the first time and we were there for a week.

Kure is on the main island of Honshu and was the British Commonwealth Forces base. It was east of Sasebo and therefore further from the Combat Zone and was not nearly so crowded with ships or people from the services. No US Forces. Note I rarely call them Americans because there were many Canadians fighting out there and they did not wish to be mistaken for their fellow continentals from North America. Kure was great. We were alongside a large pier, we did not have to run boats and we could walk ashore whenever we wanted to. It was decided we would hold our official Christmas on 31st December. It was a Sunday, the ship was decorated in the traditional manner and everyone ate enormous quantities of food. It was also, of course, being the last day of the year, Hogmanay and to herald in the New Year the youngest rating on board was beckoned to strike the ship's bell sixteen times. It would normally be struck eight times at the end of each watch (which was also the beginning of the next), then once for each half hour until the watch ended. There was the inevitable tradition behind all this dating from before the days of clocks when half-hour glasses were turned (like an egg timer). So on New Year's Eve ring out the old ring in the new it became tradition to strike the bell eight times for each. For the remaining days of our rest period we continued our festivities in the British Commonwealth Services Clubs. We were also able to visit Hiroshima where the first atom bomb had been dropped. We were presented with the same terrible scenes that we had witnessed at Nagasaki a few months earlier. Possibly the most memorable of our visits to Japan was the day spent at the sacred island of Mayijima and seeing all the beauty of the shrines, pagodas and gardens. We played two games of rugby against a university side, and all-Japan. We won both, but things are different now with Japan playing in the World Cup. Well known are Max Boyce's rugby ballads of the eighties about Japanese touring teams in Wales.

In Korea the Chinese communists launched another major offensive which drove the UN forces back to a line about one third of the way down South Korea. We were losing and a few very hard months lay ahead for us. Our thoughts were often with the armies ashore battling not only a human enemy but also extremes of cold and discomfort. Our belated Christmas and New Year rest period over, we set off for the Combat Zone once more. We

Funny money

were now known by the US Navy as the veterans and the ship was christened the "Fighting T". They sent one of their carriers, the USS Bataan, also a Carrier Vessel Light CVL) as we were described, to operate with us. Life was going to be hard and things were getting worse. There were a few incidents – luckily only minor.

The Carrier Air Group Commander was Lieutenant Commander Freddie Stovin-Bradford, a marvellous man. One day on patrol he met an enemy MIG 15, the latest Russian-built fighter. He flew his outclassed Sea Fury back on board without serious damage. He had already seen action during the war and, at the Battle of Matapan, helped destroy the Italian fleet; he had been promoted to Commander on New Year's Eve. He was a dab hand on the piano and magnificent at keeping morale high with his occasional singsongs in the wardroom. He was to become

Winter games!

Commander (Air) at RNAS Brawdy and in 1963 composed with the aid of his piano the Fleet Air Arm March.

On another occasion Lieutenant DWP Kelly had to ditch his Sea Fury owing to engine failure and he managed to warn us he was going to do so. He landed in the sea about four miles ahead of the ship, jumped out, his plane sank in about ten seconds and he floated in his "Mae West" until picked up by HMCS Sioux. Earlier the Sioux, together with sister Canadian ships Cayuga and Athabaskan and two Australian destroyers Warramunga and Bataan, had ploughed through heavy seas and snowstorms: they rescued 7,000 wounded and non-essential military and civilian refugees from the Pyongyang area. It was one of the most hazardous naval operations of the Korean War, and our aircraft provided air patrols nearby and cover overhead.

It was during this period that I asked Freddie if he could arrange for me to go on operations over Korea. I thought at the time, as did many of my mates, that I must out of my tiny mind. Here I was volunteering again. Freddie duly obliged and I was to be in the back seat, as the observer, in a Firefly. I didn't know which was going to be worse, being catapulted off, or landing on, a moving airfield. Both were a great experience, the pilot being very relaxed and kind to me. In between times with other aircraft in company we bombed a few railway trucks, one bridge and one tunnel. I didn't see any troops or civilians so hope we didn't actually kill anyone.

Four British cruisers, HMS Belfast, Ceylon, Jamaica and Kenya were in Korean waters. We didn't see much of them as they were usually closer inshore bombarding enemy targets. The Belfast in particular had been very accurate with its aim. If the US ships were missing the target, Belfast would be sent over to finish the job off. One day the US General MacArthur, the Supreme Commander of all UN Forces in Korea, requested to go on board Belfast so that he could actually witness her guns in action. He just couldn't believe what he saw. The US warships were all fully automatic, but in Belfast Able Seamen were laying and training the guns by hand and their mates were lifting and loading the shells into the barrel by hand. I nearly forgot to

The bridge destroyed by "my" Firefly over Korea!

mention that the shells did come up to the gun turrets from the magazines by lift! But everything else was by hand.

In February and March the enemy advance southwards had been stopped and then UN Forces went over to the offensive and fought back. They slowly and steadily advanced, consolidating their gains as they went along. It was after these months, at the beginning of April, that the Fighting T was asked to go and help up the east coast of Korea. With us, to form a very large striking force, were HMS Consort, the Australian destroyer Bataan, the two Canadians Athabaskan and Nootka, plus the US aircraft carrier Bataan and her two destroyer escorts, Borie and English. It was to be our last fling and we were determined to finish with a big bang. On our return to Sasebo on 29th April the following statistics appeared in the British press:- "During the past few days planes from Theseus' Task Group have inflicted the following damage to enemy forces in Korea: 120 enemy occupied buildings destroyed, 13 oil dumps, 12 villages overrun with enemy soldiers, many trucks, locomotives, railway carriages, gun emplacements and a railway tunnel destroyed, and an estimated 1000 enemy troops killed". With our help South Korea was now back in friendly hands and the UN Forces were continuing their advance north of the 38th parallel. We had returned to harbour after virtually three months of operations – only a couple of small breaks – and we eagerly awaited the arrival of HMS Glory to relieve us. We finally relaxed at last.

She arrived on time two days later. It took two days to hand over and on 25th April we left Sasebo bound for the UK. We had all saved much money – even on seven shillings and sixpence a day – and when in harbour we wanted to buy "rabbits" for relations and friends at home. And that's all we had time for because we only spent two days in Hong Kong. This was my third visit to this wonderful place and although I was to enjoy more times there, never again in a ship. So it was the last occasion that I saw Jenny and her side party. She was a doyenne who kept generations of sailors and their ships looking shipshape. She was invested with the British Empire Medal in 1980 and is alleged to have said with her gold-toothed grin: "I velly chocker. All time work in sampan. No learn to lead or lite." She died in February 2009 aged 92.

Then one day in Singapore, and half a day in Aden only to refuel. It was during this long trip from Singapore to Malta and transiting the Suez Canal that Blair, Chris, George and I did our engineering time which could have been most enjoyable had it not been during the hottest time of the whole trip. We were on watch one in four and during those watches we understudied the Engine Room Artificers of the Watch and the Chief and Petty Officer Stokers in the engine and boiler rooms. We learnt how all the systems worked, did rounds of the machinery spaces, took readings on generators and made sure there was plenty of fresh water being produced. How did warships exist for fresh water? Hopefully in harbour, we would be replenished from water barges which came alongside. But at sea, salt water was pumped in, boiled up and the steam produced went into a condenser. More salt water was pumped in, passed through tubes inside the condenser, the steam then cooled and became fresh water. Simple but in fact a very expensive method. Funnily enough the Channel Islands run short when the many visitors in the summer more than double the local population. They use the same method in what they call a desalinator.

We did all that was necessary during our Engine Room time because we realised it was extremely important that we seamen should know what goes on down below in the heart of the ship. But it was hot, and everyone seemed to spend as much time as possible in front of the intakes bringing in welcome cool air and drinking gallons of limers. Lime juice had been introduced to the Royal Navy two centuries earlier to treat and prevent scurvy. No problems these days but very refreshing it was. It was also the reason why the US Navy called us limeys.

In the evenings sporting activities were organised and apart from the usual games, parallel bars, box-horses and enormous weight lifting equipment appeared on the flight deck. Once or twice the ship stopped in the Mediterranean for "Hands to Bathe", and here's something not many people have done. Two nets were lowered by crane or derrick over the side and some of us played water polo. The game is usually played in a swimming pool where one can at times – except when actually playing the ball – stand on the bottom or hold onto the sides. Not in the deep Mediterranean. Very exhausting but fun.

The last couple of days before Malta were cooler and more enjoyable in the engine room spaces, but our time was up and we thanked the various Tiffies and Stokers who had been very kind, understanding and helpful and we returned to our normal seaman duties. On entry into Malta we were shown some very good seamanship or was it airmanship, by our Captain Ben Bolt. About a dozen planes were lined up and secured on the flight deck pointing inwards. On the order from the bridge those on the starboard side were told to start up their engines. For every action there was an equal and opposite reaction. This helped turn the ship to port or anti-clockwise, more quickly in a confined space than by only turning the ship's propellers in opposite directions. This was the first and only time I witnessed that manoeuvre. Another first was to spell out the ship's name using the ship's

*The 'Fighting T' approaches the English Channel
on her way home, June 1951*

company fallen in on the flight deck. These two things can only be done when the navy has an aircraft carrier and in the case of the manoeuvre, when it has propeller aircraft.

Next port of call! Falmouth. We arrived there earlier than expected. Those engine room guys had put on homeward bounders (extra revs). Before we anchored for the night our aircraft took off to return to RNAS Yeovilton. The crews would return to re-join us at Pompey for the celebrations. How good it was to see the coast of England again. The next morning customs officers swarmed on board. In spite of their reputation they were the most delightful people and very kind to us. In the afternoon, after everyone had cleared customs, we weighed anchor. But not before the gentlemen of the press complete with notebooks and cameras of every size and description had arrived on board. They were to accompany us for the last few miles, past the Needles Lighthouse, up the Solent and into Portsmouth Harbour for the most tremendous welcome home.

On the way home we had already received good press "HMS Theseus makes naval history" in Hong Kong and "Her log shows a proud record" in Malta. Both gave statistics, which I dislike intensely. Someone once said that statistics are like miniskirts. They give you good ideas but hide the most important thing! And now, on the day of our arrival home, before we had even secured alongside the papers said:-

"Theseus Heroes Return Home"
"Customs men win Theseus cheers"
"The happy ship that couldn't stop fighting"
"Bands and Crowds Welcome Home the Theseus"
and so on.

A message saying "Welcome Home and Hearty Congratulations from the Lord Mayor and People of Portsmouth" was received as we secured alongside South Railway Jetty whence we had sailed 285 days before. Several thousand families and friends were there whilst the Royal Marine Bands on board and ashore played their usual first class music. Then the order "Hands Fall Out" was given and all hell broke loose as guests came aboard and were able to witness the ship's company at Divisions. Admiral of the Fleet Lord Fraser, the First Sea Lord, came on board to greet us and most important of all, present the Boyd Trophy, awarded for the most outstanding air feat of the year, to our Carrier Air Group.

Now followed several weeks of celebrations, including invitations to many private parties and events. We were all due about six weeks' leave accumulated during our time away. A few days' leave is great but six weeks seemed too much. However, as my home was a stone's throw away in Alverstoke, I was able to keep in touch with the ship and partake in those events which sounded best.

We had tickets to the Test Match at Lords against South Africa. I went because they were free and I had a date in London that evening, but I was sadly disappointed with the match. I had played cricket at school and found three or four hours of it not very exciting to say the least. I couldn't understand why, when a cricketer improved, he was selected to play for his county and had to play 3-day matches and then if selected for his country, the agony was prolonged to last five days. The deadly dull goings on at Lords the day we went seemed to substantiate this opinion.

The weather was good so there was no need for "Rain stopped Play". A lot of gentlemen were asleep in their sun-drenched seats, with their heads covered with the Times or Telegraph. Every now and then there was clapping for no apparent reason. No run had been scored. Oh, he's just bowled a maiden over. Couldn't see any around; in fact there weren't any females of any sort in the ground! Then maybe after a nicked single run there would be more clapping; that was because the batsman, who had taken ages, had at long last scored his half-century. There were no centuries scored that day. And so it went on with the umpires making funny gestures every now and then. Cricket appears to be the only game that you can actively put on weight whilst playing!

We were also given tickets for the Tennis Championships at Wimbledon. That was much better, especially if your ticket was a "Rover", and you could walk around choosing the matches you wanted to watch.

Invitations to parties came flooding in and the best for me was a Summer Ball at St. Mary's Hospital Nurses' Home. The nurse I met knew how to dance and later gave me my best welcome home present. She was shortly leaving for Canada where she had been offered a nursing job with far better pay and prospects. She said she was determined to enjoy her last few days in England. To help her do so I took her out several times and on returning to the home she made a simple sailor very happy. She taught me a lot and I certainly enjoyed learning.

We left the Fighting T, our home for over a year, in early September. She did not go out to the Far East again, was put in reserve eight years later and arrived at the Inverkeithing Breaker's Yard exactly eleven years to the day after we had proudly entered Portsmouth as the Royal Navy's Ship of the Year.

FURTHER TRAINING AFLOAT
AND ASHORE

For the next three years it seems we were destined to be ashore for our further training. However, there were to be some welcome spells at sea. Firstly though there was the small matter of a Seamanship Board to pass. We had to produce a Sight Book containing twelve star, sun or moon sights. This had been done in Theseus and mine had been signed by our Snotties Nurse as being "Very Good 98%". I had actually only taken a couple of the sights myself and bought the others for two shillings each from other midshipmen! I don't know how, but we passed the Board. Maybe it was because we were smartly dressed in our uniform sporting two new campaign medal ribbons above our left breast pockets, the British one with yellow and blue stripes and the UN one with blue and white.

I joined HMS Relentless, a Type 15 frigate, for my so-called small ship training. She had been built in 1942 as an R-Class destroyer, saw little service in WW2, and was then converted into a fast anti-submarine frigate fitted with a pair of the latest mortars called Limbo. The conversion had just been completed so I merely had to "cross the road" to join her. Although still a midshipman I felt more adult and mature as I was taken into the wardroom and introduced to the other officers. There was no gunroom in small ships and I rapidly became known as "The Midshipman".

A few days later we left Pompey. "Have you checked the Gyro Compass, Reeder?" "Yes, sir," I replied to the captain thinking he meant was it clean and readable and not steamed up. "You bloody liar." A minute earlier we had passed the war memorial on Southsea Common and it had been in line (known as a transit) with St Judes Church Spire. At that moment a true bearing can be taken with the compass and checked with the chart. We were bound for Portland where we secured alongside at the Naval Base. Every day we moved out to a pier alongside the breakwater to do trials and practice firings of our new Limbos. On successful completion of these trials we sailed for Londonderry. One day in the Irish Sea fog descended and the Captain said: "Make the necessary fog signal." I went to the push button and pressed it for five seconds. Just under two minutes later I pressed it again for five seconds. "Well done, Mike." He never called me Reeder again!

On arrival at Londonderry we joined the Third Training Squadron, which was attached to the Joint Anti-Submarine School situated ashore in HMS Sea Eagle. Basically the object of the set up was to train the RN surface ships, in conjunction with the RAF in the art of carrying out anti-submarine warfare. Submarines would dive, RAF planes and RN ships would try and find them and when detected the surface ships would "kill" them. Every now and then, if their enemy weren't having any success the submariners would emit a green grenade, which would float on the surface as a green flare – to give us a chance.

Obviously it wasn't as simple as that because all the ships' companies and aircrew had to be trained up to operate the sonar, radar and anti-submarine weaponry. Yes, Squid and Depth Charges were still being used to "kill" submarines as well as Relentless's new modern Limbo. Londonderry was such an efficient setup that many navies including the US Navy sent their ships there for training.

Our Captain (F), that is the officer in charge of the whole Training Squadron, was none other than Mike Le Fanu. Of course I did not know it then, but this was the first of three occasions that I was to have the fortune of serving with this fantastic man. He was the Navy's youngest Captain, this was his first sea-going command at the age of 36 and already he was destined for the highest office. I got to know him quite well; he always had time for a word or two with me, as he did with everyone and he would come down to the wardroom and have one drink nearly every day. He invited me out to his large house overlooking the River Foyle for dinner one evening – don't dress up, "rig scruff" was on the invitation.

Life ashore was great, provided religion and politics were not mentioned. We were warned about this and there was no problem because the sailor kept his religious views to himself: he certainly had no interest in politics and disliked most politicians. Even calling the place by its shortened name of Derry had its political connotations. There were eight girls to every man, the reason being lack of good work for the breadwinner. So depending on the amount of travel money available, the man would go to Liverpool, Manchester, or Glasgow for work and help to swell the Irish communities further afield. The richer ones went to New York and joined the police department. Meanwhile the girls sought work locally and many worked in shirt factories of which there were quite a few. Our clothes went to a laundry run by unmarried mothers and we used to get little notes, containing names and telephone numbers, inserted in our shirt pockets.

The girls liked dancing. So did we and we used to climb the hill to the Northern Counties Club, which was known as the wardroom ashore. There was dancing there, with a crooner and band, at least three times a week. On one particular evening the dancing entrance fee was in aid of ex-serviceman's funds. One girl called Mary whom I had met once or twice was there. Towards the end I asked her for another dance which I thought was the Last Waltz. "You stand to attention," she said. The band was playing the national anthem of the Irish Republic and the fund to which we had contributed our admission money was, in fact, the IRA!

Even six years after the war there was still some rationing in the UK and certain items such as cigarettes and whisky were plentiful, and cheaper, in the Irish Republic. Nylon stockings and perfume were virtually unobtainable at home, so there was a great opportunity to keep in with the fairer sex. We would take a bus across the border to Lough Swilly in Donegal where there was a place called Buncrana. As always charming people, lovely countryside and a shop where we bought as much of the aforementioned goods as we wanted. We had to be a little careful not to exceed our allowance by too much when coming back through the British customs. The shopkeepers and customs officials on either side of the border were very friendly with each other and they would sometimes pass information. One

HMS Relentless leaving Portsmouth Harbour, September 1951

New Zealander called them a "bunch of bogtrotters" when he had all his purchases confiscated – they would be returned to the shopkeeper and re-sold to the next customer!

At sea was very hard work. We would leave our berth very early in the morning to do the long trip down the River Foyle to the exercise area – sometimes the far end. Often the visibility was poor. The RAF pilots would look out of their bedroom windows, decide it was too dank, and go back to bed until the visibility improved. They would then come out a couple of hours later, whilst we had been tossing around waiting for them. Yes, it was often very rough in that area. Luckily I wasn't seasick but I didn't enjoy it. The main thing, the Navy was teaching me a lot about anti-submarine tactics and warfare.

Time flew by, Christmas leave was taken and enjoyed and then on 5th February we were refuelling at Lisahally when something occurred causing a boiler breakdown. It was snowing. All very depressing and the ERAs and stokers were trying to get things sorted out without much luck. The next day it was announced from Buckingham Palace that His Majesty King George the Sixth had died. He had not been well for some time and he was at Sandringham when he suffered a coronary thrombosis in his sleep. His elder daughter had left a week earlier for a tour of Australia via Kenya. She flew back to London as Queen Elizabeth the Second.

Relentless had to be repaired. My training had to continue and so it was arranged for me to join HMS Crispin, another ship of the Londonderry Squadron. I was in Crispin for a month – not really long enough to get my teeth into the job before the Easter leave period and the next stage of our training at the Royal Naval College, Greenwich.

The purpose of us going there was to further our education, both academic and professional and to attend the Junior Officers' War Course. It was known as the Navy's University and provided we attended all the lectures, we were free to come and go as we pleased. No watch keeping or duties or work to keep us on board at the weekends or after 1700 in the evenings. Wednesday afternoons were for sport, any sort you care to mention. Possibly Egyptian PT, matelot's lingo for sleeping, in order to have a good rest before the night's activities. Our daytime activities were sometimes organised by the college and were sometimes of our own free will. We visited the Houses of Parliament, the Old Bailey, the National Gallery, Downing Street, Covent Garden, Scotland

The Royal Naval College at Greenwich – our
London home for eight months

Yard and the various museums. We went to theatre land and saw all the good musicals: "South Pacific", "Annie Get Your Gun", "Oklahoma" and a new play just on the market, so to speak, called "The Mousetrap".

Licensing laws in the UK at times were very restrictive, but not for us in London. Apart from the expensive night clubs, which we didn't frequent unless we were on a freebee, we were able to find clubs of various sorts that enabled us to legally drink twenty four hours a day. One summer's evening we were sitting on Eros in Piccadilly Circus – the days before it became boarded up. We were smartly dressed in grey flannel bags, sports coat and tie, and along came a policeman. "And what are you lads doing up there? You know it's not allowed." "Oh, sorry Officer, we are strangers here and did not know that was the case," was our reply, as we descended. There was no aggro, everyone treating or being treated, with respect. We asked the policeman if he would like to join us for a drink in a nearby pub. "You know I'm not allowed to do that whilst I'm on duty, Sirs." He joined us half an hour later for one drink on his way home after work!

The various buildings in the college were best accessed by an underground passageway system, the middle of which was called "Piccadilly Circus". Here was a labyrinth of noticeboards giving all the necessary information.

Orders were promulgated there, sports team selections, tours, and possibly of most interest invitations to many parties. Five, ten or twenty Sub-Lieutenants would be invited to balls and dances at nurses' homes and teacher training colleges, etc. and we would write our names down if we wanted to attend. Some of us went to Queen Charlotte's Ball at the Savoy Hotel. It was the traditional "coming out" ceremony when the daughters of aristocracy (virgins on the verge!) were firstly presented to the Queen at Buckingham Palace. They then attended the Debs Ball or Debs Delight. It was the beginning of the London season and their quest for potential suitors started. We certainly had no intention of falling into that bracket, we were merely making up numbers, but it was a fabulous occasion. Prince Philip called it "bloody daft" and Princess Margaret proclaimed "every tart in

London was getting in on it." It was held annually in its traditional form for only another six years.

We all had transport of some sort. A great friend of mine, Jim Trounson, had a super but by no means new Austin 7. It frightens me nowadays to see how thin the wheels were. Most of us like Jim had second hand cars, but I actually bought a motor bike – a brand new Royal Enfield 350cc. On promotion to sub lieutenant we received a uniform allowance of about £150 – enough to buy the bike – and I paid for the uniform on my Gieves account. One evening I drove it from the college to the Dorchester Hotel with David Watts as my pillion passenger. We were in our Mess Undress, kitted up for a very important naval occasion – it was the annual King George V Fund for Sailors Ball. I wish I had had a camera to snap the doorman's face! He very kindly and smartly suggested that "Sir" might like to park his bike well away round the back where, as he implied, it would not be seen by any of the Rolls Royce owners!

As always, we were very lucky in that we were being quite well paid, so we had an advantage over those say at other colleges and universities. Nevertheless, we were broke most of the time and we had the long university-type summer holidays coming up. This is where my motorbike came in handy. With £25 each – that was the maximum we were allowed to take abroad and all we could afford anyway – David Watts and I embarked on a quite fantastic fortnight's tour of France, Italy and Switzerland. We crossed the Dover Straits in the ferry to Calais, then via Paris to the Mediterranean. We were able to stop and swim at every beach and bay until we got past Genoa, when we turned northwards through Italy to the Grand St Bernard Pass into Switzerland. So far we had slept every night in a field or on the beach, except one at the home of a girlfriend, Chantal Fleury, in Paris. In the evenings we would go into a pub, buy the cheapest drink and then in turn go into the "hommes" for the best wash available. We did of course have toothpaste, bar of soap and towel with us in a shopping bag. For sleeping at night all we had was a ground sheet, but then we had learnt how to sleep rough when sea boats crew in Devonshire.

All we could afford to drink was lemonade bought from a supermarket. After a swim at Juan Les Pins I took a sip from a bottle and it slipped. As it was falling I caught it but at the same moment it hit a small rock and shattered causing blood to come from my right hand little finger. We dashed to the nearby chemist who told me to go to the doctor three doors up. In the room, where I had to wait a few minutes, were well framed photos signed "To doctor Luigi with grateful thanks from Errol Flynn", the US Admiral Nimitz and other famous people. The doctor was charming, and while he stitched my finger, with me lying horizontal on the slab, he asked me a few questions: "And what brings you to Juan Les Pins?" he asked in perfect English. "Well, we're very poor young officers in the Royal Navy, we can't afford hotels and we are camping out and touring on a motorbike," I replied. All I was worried about was not my finger but how much he was going to charge. He very kindly charged me the equivalent of only £1. Switzerland, with all its beautiful scenery and lakes, was far too expensive for us, so we escaped to Chamonix in France and then back across to Calais, Dover and home. All on £50 including the petrol. What an experience! A year or so later I read in Time Magazine that King Baudouin of the Belgians who had some bad ailment, had travelled down to Juan Les Pins to visit his (my!) Docteur Luigi.

Work hard and play hard, the Navy had told us. So on our return to the college we had the opportunity to do the former, as we started on the Junior Officers' War Course. In retrospect this was in my opinion the most important part of our very good training - to command ships and men. It taught us to think and plan things through logically. It was known as "appreciating the situation". We were told about certain aspects of the D-Day landings. All those Allied troops in Great Britain about to be embarked on an armada of ships to land on the beaches of Normandy. And yet the whole thing, its failure or success, could have depended on "appreciating the tidal stream and weather situation". It needed to be spring tides and high water at a certain time in the morning. Then the landing craft could get further up the beach. 4th June was the day chosen, but the weather forecast was terrible and all the PBI (poor bloody infantry) would be sick in their craft before they were anywhere near landing on the beaches. General Eisenhower postponed D-Day by 24 hours. The weather was just as bad on the 5th so a further 24 hour postponement. The forecast indicated slight improvement for the next day. If the troops did not land then the whole thing would have to be postponed until the next spring tide in about two weeks' time. What a decision to make. June 6th it was, and the rest is history.

Having listened to our instructors we now had to go away and do the thinking and the appreciating of several fictitious situations. You have so many ships of different sorts, so many Royal Marines and Aircraft and one submarine. The enemy is installed ashore with so many men, guns and tanks plus one squadron of fighter aircraft. We were given a small chart and map of the island and told to write our plans for invasion on several foolscap pieces of paper. During the course we were given three or four different situations to appreciate. All very good stuff.

To prove how well we had been instructed and how much we had learnt, unbeknown to the authorities we decided to "attack" our opposite numbers at the Royal Military Academy, Sandhurst. One or two surreptitious visits were made, the situation was appreciated and, at the planned time, we all dressed up as pirates, got into our cars and assembled in a pub at Camberley. It was dark and after doing final checks the attack commenced. God knows what we didn't do, but amongst the things we were successful at were pinching several mementoes, including the flag from the mast and painting with whitewash all over the balustrades of the parade ground "Thank goodness we've still got the RAF". Somehow or other we found the strength to move a very heavy gun from above down onto the parade ground. We left undetected and called in at a pub for the inevitable post mortem on our way back to Greenwich.

The next morning normal instruction continued and the message got around that we had to assemble at 1200 in one of the common rooms. We knew why! We were to be addressed by our Captain Tony Miers. He had been contacted by the not very amused Commandant of Sandhurst, who had ranted and raged about the behaviour of young hooligan naval officers who had caused considerable damage and that it was going to cost an arm and a leg to put everything back to normal. And that it would need a crane to replace the gun which we had moved by hand – or was it brute force and ignorance! We hadn't yet done our field gun training!

Our Captain, known throughout the Navy as "Crap" Miers, was a submarine hero who had won the Victoria Cross for his courageous and daring raid on enemy shipping whilst submerged in the close confines of Corfu Harbour. He had also been awarded the D.S.O. twice for other acts of bravery. He gave us a monumental blast, telling us how irresponsible and stupid we had been and finished off his tirade with a wide grin and the words "well done". He was worried about the large bill that might come our way, only to be reassured by us that we would be only too happy to foot that said expense. We did not hear any more of the incident. We were just grateful that the Navy still had senior officers like him.

Exercise and generally keeping fit was probably the one thing missing from the curriculum, although I did play for the college First Eleven soccer team. We had matches on Wednesday afternoons and I remember one game which almost had to be abandoned because of fog. To be more exact it was smog – air pollution at its worst caused by the burning of large amounts of coal in large cities, in this case London. It contained soot particles from the smoke, plus sulphur dioxide. Many people died, especially the elderly and those with heart and lung conditions. The atmosphere was simply filthy. We had to put on clean white uniform shirts every morning and change them again at lunchtime. We were quite glad to get away at the weekends, but in spite of the smog very sad to leave London after eight wonderful months.

The college itself will always be remembered mainly because of the painted hall. On occasions such as Trafalgar Night and our Farewell Dinner we were introduced to the extremely high standard of an RN mess dinner with all the traditional customs, speeches and the passing of the port. It was our dining room and every meal could be taken there. It is often described as the finest dining hall in Europe. It was designed by Sir Christopher Wren and Nicholas Hawksmoor. Its excellent wall and ceiling decorations are by James Thornhill and pay tribute to British maritime history and power. Nowadays this magnificent building can be hired for prestigious dinners and weddings.

After Christmas leave we all descended on Portsmouth for technical courses. With the addition of sub lieutenants from commonwealth and foreign navies we must have totalled about 170, so we had to be divided into groups. There is no doubt about it, the sixteen of us, including four Canadians and one Australian, who were lucky enough to be in D-Group were undeniably the dab hands! That is what the D stood for and we were to be together for what was going to be the hardest eight months of mental work in our lives. We studied strenuously for five and a half days a week and at the end of each course we had an exam resulting in a first or second class pass.

The subjects covered were in alphabetical order ABCD (Atomic, Bacteriological and Chemical Defence), Aviation, Communications, Divisional, Electrical, Gunnery, Navigation, and TAS (Torpedo and Anti-Submarine). We were also to spend some time down in Devon for an engineering course at the Royal Naval Engineering College, Manadon and with the Royal Marines at their Infantry Centre at Lympstone.

So we worked hard and played hard and as always in life one mostly remembered the good times. Firstly, there was the aviation programme at Lee-on-Solent which included the Junior Officers' Air Course.

We were doing this to learn all about the Fleet Air Arm, its officers and ratings, air warfare and how to fly a Sea Venom. After a couple of days our course officer asked us all if we had ever been on board a carrier and were we interested in joining the FAA? I told him I had been in the Fighting T and that I had a great admiration for the work done by our Carrier Air Group. It was true, but only said so that they would take interest in me and so that I might get a first class pass!

By the time the course was finished they had virtually taught us to fly – with the instructor firmly seated beside us – but certainly not solo. It was a thoroughly well run course and on completion of the exam I got my First Class pass! The FAA must have been happy because six of our group, that's over a third, became naval aviators. They were Chris Comins, Jim Trounson, Digby Lickfold and Jeremy Nichol, plus Australian Tom Dadswell and Canadian Barry Troy.

To the north of Portsmouth over Portsdown Hill is an estate called Southwick House. It had been the headquarters of the Allied Expeditionary Forces used by General Eisenhower and Field Marshall Montgomery to plan and execute the D-Day Landings. Yes, yet another stately home being provided by the Navy for us to be trained at. When we went there in May it was the RN School of Navigation, HMS Dryad. The house itself whose walls still had the large maps used in the planning of D-Day was to be the wardroom. The rest of the school was in buildings spread out over the estate. Early summer was a great time to be there and for most of us this was possibly the most important course of all. Whatever specialisation we were going to go for, we all, as Seaman officers, Officers of the Watch and hopefully future Captains of ships, had to be experts at navigation. So the instruction included all about chart work and the Buoyage System, how to allow for tides and tidal streams and how to use radar, not only for navigational purposes but also for collision avoidance. We were also taught other aids to navigation both present and future.

There was one very big and important interruption to our timetable and that was the Coronation of Her Majesty Queen Elizabeth the Second on 30th May. The Navy, as well as the other services, were very much involved in this and had been training, practising and preparing for the great day. Although none of us or any of our trainers was in any way directly involved on the day, the attention of the whole country was focused towards London.

We were given a make and mend the day beforehand. So after forenoon instruction and a couple of beers in the wardroom, we made a beeline for London picking up our girlfriends on the way. Our plans were quite clear. We were going to camp out on the grass in Hyde Park, near Speakers' Corner, and alongside Park Lane. We arrived there about 1700, found a good area, marked it out and settled down for the occasion. We had no food, a few drinks, a sleeping bag or two and the clothes we were in. Amongst our crowd were Chris Comins, George Vallings, David Watts, Jim Trounson, Dan Mainguy the Canadian and Tom Dadswell. It was impossible to keep tabs on everyone; people were coming and going especially to get provisions at a nearby shop in Oxford Street.

Shortly after dark we heard that Edmond Hillary and Sherpa Tenzing had become the first to conquer Mount Everest, all 29028 feet of it. Everyone was in party mood, ably assisted by Dan Mainguy on his squeeze box and our choral voices. It did get a bit cold in the middle of the night but we had our girlfriends plus sleeping bags to keep us warm until the sun rose. Breakfast of cups of tea and bacon and egg sarnies were purchased from a roving van. It wasn't long before the truly magnificent parade started and the full procession passed slowly along Park Lane in front of us and close by.

Monday morning produced a few bleary eyes amongst both trainers and students when we returned to Dryad and our navigational studies. The good news was that we were actually going to sea again. For a few days, in order to teach us ship handling skills and ensure we were up to scratch on practical navigation, we were going out in the sloop, HMS Starling. Each day we had to con the ship in and out of harbour – that is by giving the Quartermaster his necessary orders, e.g. Port 20, Midships, Starboard 10, Midships, Steer 120 degrees, in order to keep us on the starboard side of the channel. Then we had to plan how to anchor the good ship in a pre-determined position, by use of the compass and getting two visual objects such as a church spire and a lighthouse in transit. Having prepared the chart work down below in the chart room, we would then come up onto the bridge and hopefully proceed to anchor in the correct position. Starling had an eccentric captain. He would carry out revolver practice whilst we were concentrating on getting the ship to its allotted anchor berth. At the critical moment, he would chuck an empty tin over the side and fire his revolver at it. Trying to distract us! All good stuff.

Everyone knew that the Gunnery Branch was not only there to fire guns. It had the special responsibility for the ceremonial side of the Navy, expert evidence of this we had just witnessed at the Coronation of Her Majesty the Queen. It was the parade training for which the Gunnery instructors were particularly famous and notorious and which did not endear them to the ordinary matelot or young officer under training. If you can't take a joke you shouldn't have joined. It was very necessary to have a sense of humour and we in D-Group certainly had an overdose of that.

On the Sunday evening we quietly drove our fleet of bangers and motorbikes through the portal gates and crossed over to Whale Island, ready for whatever was to come our way. We knew that none of us wanted to be gunnery specialists, that they were a dying breed, and that they weren't over-endowed with brain cells. After all, Whale Island was called HMS Excellent and that was the cap tally worn by the matelot on the front of Players cigarette packets! The first thing that put us off was that we had to dress like navy-blue soldiers and wear blue battledress uniform boots and gaiters. We met our course officer, Lieutenant Cooper, after breakfast next morning. There he was giving us our introductory lecture, our programme for the next month and a half and very smart he was too – in normal uniform but boots and shiny black gaiters!

It wasn't long before we were down in the drill shed, being sized up tallest on the outside, shortest in the middle and fallen in in two ranks. All ready for our first inspection by the gunnery instructor who was a petty officer aged about 28. He seemed very reasonable, told us his name, and informed us that he had the doubtful pleasure of being our G.I. for the duration of our stay on the island. And so the repartee commenced. The NAAFI van arrived in the area and we were dismissed for our afternoon stand easy cup of tea and a cigarette. At the end of stand easy we strolled back into the shed and were greeted by our G.I. shouting: "Come on, come on, get fell in." We got fell in and then he said: "Never forget. Thems wots keen get fell in previous." We all cheered because one of us had won a bet as to when we would first hear that wonderful Whale Island slogan which, if understood, does make sense.

We were taught how to march, the first step with the left foot and right arm going forward. Try right foot and right arm at the same time! From now on we would have to march to and from our places of instruction, in fact everywhere during working hours. We began to realise why someone had called the place "All Gas and Gaiters". We were taught about the upkeep and maintenance of the different guns and small arms and we went on the Tipnor Range for rifle and revolver firings. They had us doing 6-inch gun drill, firstly in calm conditions and then in a turret revolving all over the place as they poured water over us to simulate rough weather. I thought back to Korea a year ago and US General MacArthur being amazed at the accuracy of HMS Belfast's gunnery. Perhaps that's why Whale Island hadn't automated like the US Navy. We trained for Field Gunning and took part in a mini field gun competition known as the Brickwoods Trophy.

Two or three afternoons a week we seemed to have a session on the parade ground. We learnt about lining the streets, state funerals and cheering ship. Inevitably there was the opportunity for the GI to send us individually or collectively round the parade ground, or if that didn't have the necessary effect, the whole island. Those gunnery people definitely had a warped sense of humour and we decided we would intentionally give them the opportunity to indulge it. One afternoon it was my shout and when he gave the order "Right turn", I turned to the left. "You, sir, with the red hair. Doubling round the Island. Go." They used to time you to make sure you did not slow down a bit and relax. What the GI didn't realise was that I did it intentionally as a method of keeping fit for rugby or any other sport. Another method of keeping fit which we employed occasionally at underground stations, near the college at Greenwich, was to run up a down-coming escalator.

Life was enjoyable at Whale Island although I really did not appreciate the hard work we were being asked to do. I could see no reason for my being taught most of their syllabus. The saying goes that the only reason why you might want to be a gunnery officer was so that you wouldn't have to serve in the same ship as another! At the end of the course, the whole of Whale Island went to Friday Divisions. Nearly every Sub-Lieutenants' Course performed some practical joke before or during their final march past the Captain. It was almost tradition with one course trying to outshine previous ones. Probably the crème de la crème took place about two years after. There was a circus in town. A few days beforehand, discussions took place with the owner, a deal was struck and early on the Friday morning an elephant appeared at the Whale Island main gate. It happened to be 1st April. When the sentry told the duty officer that two sub-lieutenants were attempting to bring an elephant onto the island, he told him to "Pull the other leg, you April fool". When the class marched past they were led by the elephant, which had been concealed behind the drill shed awaiting its turn. The Captain suffered a severe charisma bypass, threatening to court martial the culprits, and kept them worrying with a week's stoppage of leave. To make matters worse, he was asked if he would care to take a trunk call! The sub-lieutenant who organised the whole thing and led the march past, was a future submariner shipmate called Bryan Smalley. More about him later.

We did not want to give the Captain, or his staff, the opportunity of showing their lack of humour. After all we had taken part in a much greater skylark when we attacked the Army at Sandhurst. So we marched past smartly, pleased everyone so it seemed, tossed our gaiters in the dustbin and left the island on weekend leave.

The last course took place in an area bordering the harbour which, because of its location, was much coveted by the Portsmouth Council. It was HMS Vernon, the Navy's Torpedo and Anti-Submarine School. The atmosphere was great, everyone just went quietly about their business and there was none of the bull which had emanated from Whale Island. The first part of our training was the theoretical use of sonar and Asdic equipment and the associated weapons. Then we went to sea to put this into practice and actually drop depth charges and fire the anti-submarine mortars Squid and Limbo. As regards torpedoes, we did not actually fire them but learnt all about the different warheads that could be fitted and the tactical depth and range settings to be put on them. After all, these "fish" could be fired from surface ships and submarines and had successfully been used by the Fleet Air Arm, flying Swordfish, during WW2.

One evening I looked at the sports noticeboard to find out if any of us were playing rugby for Vernon on Wednesday. The answer was yes. Also on the board was a signal which said I had been selected to play for the United Services (Portsmouth) on Saturday. Obviously a selector had been watching us play in our inter-establishment games and surprisingly thought Reeder was good enough to play second-row for one of the country's better teams. I couldn't believe my eyes, went back a few times to re-read the signal, and checked with various people that it was really true. It must have been correct because the next day my name was in the newspapers.

The US ground was very close to Vernon, across the road so to speak and alongside the United Services Officers' Club, which we used to frequent in the evenings. I arrived there an hour before kick-off, feeling very apprehensive and was met by the team captain, Jock England, who introduced me to the rest of the team as they arrived in their ones and twos. The game went well, we won, and we had a few drinks afterwards but most important of all, as far as I was concerned, I was selected to play again the following Saturday. What I hadn't appreciated was that this team was chosen from not only the Navy, but also the other two services in the Pompey area. We were at the height of National Service at that time and the Army in particular had many soldiers stationed at Hilsea Barracks and there was the RAF station at Tangmere. I was given a fixture list and we were undoubtedly a first class club with matches home and away against such opposition as London Scottish, Richmond, Harlequins, Northampton, Bedford, Bristol and Bath. Unknown

*First game for U.S. (Portsmouth) which was also
a Hampshire County trial*

to me at the time this was going to have a great effect on my life,
although not my career which the Navy was nurturing.

The last working memory of Vernon was the Diving School.
We were actually dressed up in an old conventional extremely
heavy diving suit and helmet, and lowered from one of the
Vernon's jetties to the bottom of the muddy harbour. We also did
shallow water diving dressed in the correct suits with masks and
fins. Very interesting but it would have been more enjoyable if
it had been in the summer or at some tropical beach, rather than
Horsea Island at the top of Pompey Harbour on a murky, cold
October day.

Before the end of courses we paid our last visit to the Empire
Theatre at Portsmouth and said goodbye to Phyllis Dixie, the
well-known Queen of Striptease. She was born in 1914, wanted
to be a ballet dancer, was too tall and so became a chorus girl.

During the war she was a forces sweetheart, dancing at the Windmill Theatre with her ostrich feathered fans giving tantalising glimpses of the naked form beneath. After the war, with the troops going home, she was less in demand. Nevertheless she appeared at the Empire in Pompey quite regularly and did a similar act. On the stage were some completely nude ladies and the rules were that they must remain motionless. Several of us booked a box and the management not only knew there would be, but also expected, some jovialities. We had come armed with a few pea-shooters and every now and then a few peas were fired at the nearest nude. Eventually, the management had to ask us to leave, but took us to a bar where we had a few drinks and were introduced to Phyllis Dixie. She stayed chatting for some time and would only have non-alcoholic drinks. She was a delightful person, but was declared bankrupt five years later and sadly died of breast cancer in 1964 just 50 years of age.

Phyllis Dixie gave us this photo on our last visit to her show in 1952

George Vallings was, needless to say, with us at the Empire. Unfortunately, although continuing to be close friends, we were never going to be shipmates again. We had joined the Navy at Eaton Hall together and we had both drawn short straws for HMS Theseus and the Korean War. We had been trained together for a good eight years. George was slightly disorganised and prone to some minor hiccups, in early days. To start with he joined the Navy early, a day before the rest of us. He lost a few teeth boxing and playing rugby. His "falsies" fell into the Hurlingham Club swimming pool one evening when we were having a post party midnight swim. At a later date, the same teeth fell into the grave whilst in uniform and saluting at a service funeral. When entering Hong Kong in the Theseus Midshipman George was Captain Bolt's "doggie". We all whilst under training had a go as doggie, following a senior officer around the ship acting as his messenger or "go-fer". Anyway, here we are entering Hong Kong harbour and I am Midshipman of the Watch, when I hear the Captain say: "Where is the buoy?" hoping someone would point it out to him. "Here I am, sir," said George. The rest of us simply collapsed!

In spite of these events we all knew George would one day be an Admiral because of his enthusiasm and determination. He went on to be first in our term to be promoted Commander, was in command of four ships and became in turn Commodore Clyde, Flag Officer Gibraltar and Flag Officer Scotland and Northern Ireland. He was a good all-round sportsman and very successful at sailing. He skippered the Navy's "Adventure" round Cape Horn from Sydney to Rio de Janeiro in the first Whitbread Round-The-World race. He was in the British Admirals Cup Team and took part in the Fastnet and Sydney to Hobart races. What a career – sadly shortened when he retired as Vice-Admiral Sir George Vallings having been diagnosed with cancer in 1976.

We left Vernon, our sub-lieutenants courses were now over, and I went home to Alverstoke on leave. I had obtained a couple of firsts but mostly seconds at our end of course exams. I was no more than an average officer.

SUBMARINES

Blessed is he who expecteth nothing for he shall not be disappointed! On October 15th a letter signed G. Moses arrived from My Lords Commissioners of the Admiralty stating that I had been selected for service in the Submarine Branch and that I will be appointed to HMS Dolphin to date 9th November 1953. It went on to explain that the appointment in the first instance will be for 3½ years and that during this period I may apply for any other specialisation. If selected I may be withdrawn at any time after completion of two years' service in the Submarine Branch. I had expected a much better appointment and I was very disappointed. I don't know if Moses' initial G stood for God!

What can I do to get out of this? I really did not know what to do. Matelots folklore was "never volunteer for anything" and yet here I was for the first time being forced into doing something I did not want. I discussed the matter with all sorts of people including members of the US rugby team for whom I was continuing to play every Saturday. Any advice seemed to end with one of two statements: "The Submarine Service seems a very happy one" and "I've never heard of anyone ever asking to leave".

On 9th November I arrived at HMS Dolphin and joined the Submarine Officers' Training Class. Within a few minutes we had met the Officers' Training Officer, a Lieutenant Tubby Squires. He was going to be in charge of us for the next four months. Yes, another course on dry land and at the end of which would be exams.

Tubby chatted with us all morning firstly explaining why at least seven of us were conscripts and why it didn't matter whether you were a cook, an electrician, a stoker or a seaman the trade, as submariners liked to call themselves, was taking in conscripts across the board. The submarine Affray had sunk in Hurd Deep in April 1951 and not only had the entire ship's company been lost but also the OTC who were on board at the time. Evidently they were snorkelling and the mast cracked, allowing water to pour in.

Twenty five officers were lost; I knew one of them, Lieutenant Johnnie Blackburn, who had been a shipmate of mine in the Devonshire and a member of the Alverstocracy; he lived like many other naval officers, especially submariners, in Alverstoke.

In the afternoon, to make sure we were fit to be submariners, we all had to visit the Quack. How could I have the temerity to say I suffered earache or claustrophobia? That night we stayed on board and got settled in to wardroom mess life. Our cabins we reckoned were by far the worst we had experienced in the whole of our training. We were sure they were the converted horse stables from the original Fort Blockhouse and I made sure Tubby knew our feelings in the morning. They were so small, there was just about enough room for the bed, us, and our gear, plus a tiny fire for which we were allowed a small bucket of coal per day. It was so cold at that time of year that we only used the cabins for sleeping; we lit the coal fires just before retiring to bed. Quite warm in the morning.

The fact that most of us were conscripts, the bringing home to us of the Affray Disaster, having to have a medical and the miserable cold cabins, did not put some of us in a very good frame of mind for the second day on course. Tubby was there to greet us all, smiling and cheerful. He explained the Submarine Command, its set-up, the different classes of submarines S, T, and A boats, and that at that time there were six squadrons in the Navy. There was one here at Dolphin, others at Portland and Rothesay, and three more overseas in Malta, Sydney and Halifax, Nova Scotia. Apart from Sydney I wasn't too impressed with their choice of bases. The rest of the day we were told about submarine history and warfare, famous submariners, and our programme for the rest of the course. The next day, Wednesday, we were going to be shown round in detail the compartments of an A Boat. In the afternoon I had been selected to play rugby for Dolphin. I approached Tubby to inform him of this and I could see straight away he was not enamoured with the idea. This was the first time I had sensed any opposition to sport in the Navy. However, I knew that if there were any problems I had one ally right here in Dolphin. He was Captain Harry Browne, the Navy rugby selector, who was on the Staff of Flag Officer, Submarines. I kept this up my sleeve as a card I might have to play at a later date.

I found the visit to the A Boat to be good and I appreciated it, when we were told we would have to learn every bit of equipment in that boat by the time we were qualified. I played rugby for Dolphin in the afternoon, we won and the next morning I told Tubby that I would need to miss Saturday morning's instruction as they had selected me to play for US (Portsmouth) away at Bath and the coach would be leaving the ground over in Portsmouth at 1030. One easily forgets that in the 50s everyone in the UK worked a 5½ week. From now on poor Tubby was resigned to the fact that I would probably be playing for Dolphin every Wednesday and every Saturday, home or away, for US Pompey. Possibly quite incorrectly, I was of the opinion that the only exercise he took was a social game of squash! After all, why did he have that nickname!

Training progressed and it was entirely to my liking, getting to know every part of the boat in case in an emergency you were the nearest member of the crew to a valve or sea-cock which needed to be open or shut: or a motor or switch which needed to be turned on or off. There was a maze of pipes containing air, water, hydraulics or fuel, etc. They were painted different colours to aid identification and we had to know them all. We went to sea several times to put all our learning into practice.

When submerged a submarine was usually driven by batteries, which of course needed charging. This was done by diesel engines, which needed air which could only be obtained when on the surface or through the snorkel mast when dived. So we had to know all about the electrical systems and the dangers involved when gases were emitted at certain stages of charging. In fact we had a very instructive few days in Manchester as guests of Exide Batteries, learning more about electricity than we had in the whole dreary course at HMS Collingwood, the Navy's electrical school at Fareham. An extra freebee was being put up at the Piccadilly Hotel in Manchester. The rooms had central heating so we didn't have to ration ourselves to a bucket of Dolphin coal!

Shortly after our return a very relaxing day was spent on a visit to the 100ft tank for our submarine escape drill. The idea was you opened the outside door of the escape compartment, shut it behind you and then turned a valve to allow water in from the tank. Just as the water got up to your chin and the pressure had been equalised, you took a deep breath, opened the inside door, entered the tank and gently popped up to the surface, releasing the air from your lungs as you did so. There was an escape compartment at 30ft, 60ft and at the bottom of the tank at 100ft. You worked your way downwards as you gained confidence. For those of us perhaps a bit worried, they had shown us a film of a donkey in a straw container doing it. To ensure the donkey took a deep breath before entering the tank it was given a good kick in the genitals. "Ouch!" "If a donkey can do it, then even you submariners can"!

The four months slipped by quickly – I think because it had been an extremely interesting and well organised course. Tubby seemed to enjoy telling me I had been successful at the exams and that I had passed. I was now a submariner, albeit a conscripted one, and proud to be so.

After a couple of weeks' leave I joined the Andrew in the Third Submarine Squadron at Rothesay in the Isle of Bute. The familiar journey back to the west coast of Scotland involved trains as far as Wemyss Bay where there was, I am sure, the longest pier in the world. It certainly seemed so when carrying trunk and suitcases from the train down to the Rothesay ferry. Then from Rothesay pier out to the submarine depot ship, HMS Montclare.

The Montclare was an ex-passenger ship built by John Brown (further up the river at Clydebank) for the Canadian Steamship Company. Her maiden voyage had been in 1922. She was requisitioned by the Admiralty at the outbreak of WW2 and converted into an Armed Merchant Cruiser, then in 1942 converted to a Destroyer Depot Ship and in 1944 yet again converted, this time to a Submarine Depot Ship. So thirty years after her maiden voyage I climbed her gangway – to all the lack of comforts she had to offer.

I found my cabin, put on my uniform and went straight down on board the Andrew. There in the wardroom was Lieutenant Commander David Scott, who was to be my new Captain. After the initial formal introduction: "What age are you, Mike?" "Twenty one, sir," I replied. "I had already had my first command by then," he said with a smile. I appreciated that so many submariners had been killed during the war that those lucky enough to survive had been given command opportunities at an earlier stage. David was First Lieutenant of the submarine Seraph when it landed US General Mark Clark on a secret mission in occupied North Africa and then returned him to Gibraltar. The Seraph also landed in neutral Spain "the man who never was" a corpse disguised as a Royal Marine Officer carrying secret papers, which misled the Germans about where the Allies would land in Europe. For a short while, after leaving Andrew, I was spare crew in Seraph. I therefore knew why above the heads door was a brass notice, always well-polished saying "General Mark Shat Here". David's first command was a former German U-Boat which was commissioned in the Royal Navy as HMS Meteorite and carried out experiments in the use of High Test Peroxide as a fuel. Prior to my joining the Andrew, David had snorkelled her across the Atlantic by a diesel submarine. I was indeed lucky to have as my first submarine CO such an experienced and capable officer. I served the last four months of the commission as Navigating Officer and put into practice what I had learned in the OTC at Dolphin.

The first new lesson learnt was that we were in a boat not a ship, and that the ratings cap tallies had HM Submarines, not HMS Andrew, on them. This I thought was fairly significant in that within the trade, it tended, intentionally or not, to encourage loyalty towards the Submarine Service as opposed to individual submarines. Watchkeeping on the bridge of a submarine was not as pleasant as on a surface ship; especially in the colder rougher conditions of the west coast of Scotland and off Northern Ireland, which was to be our patch. You had to dress up for the occasion with warm waterproof gear, climb the conning tower and take over the watch. Your only company would be the lookout similarly dressed and to communicate with anyone down below you shouted down a voice pipe. If nature calleth there was the Pigs Ear, which looked like a voice pipe – you lifted the flap and your offering went down the pipe inside the fin, but outside the boat and into the sea. Otherwise, apart from the fact it was uncomfortable compared with the relative luxury of a surface ship, actual watch keeping was the same.

HMS Andrew, the first diesel submarine to cross the Atlantic submerged. I joined her as navigating officer.

But down below in the Control Room when dived at periscope depth it was a completely different ball game. As the name of the space might suggest you were hopefully in complete control. There was a helmsman steering the boat and a planesman maintaining the correct depth. Navigation was all worked out by knowing your course and speed and taking the tidal stream into consideration. If you wanted to take a visual fix in order to check your position, you raised the periscope and lined up the ship's head on, say, a lighthouse. If the course was 110, you said "Now" to the helmsman, he confirmed that the heading was 110. From the periscope, which had no compass, you checked the relative bearing of the lighthouse. If it were Red 23 (for port side) you would subtract making the true bearing 087. If Green 44 (for starboard) you would add making it 154.

For a radar fix, the radar mast, almost similar to that of the periscope, would be raised and the Radar Plotter would give you the necessary information. David would be keeping an eye on me and if I had any doubts or problems he was very close by in the wardroom which was next door – forward of the control room.

I enjoyed a few quiet runs ashore in Rothesay. As it was summer time and we were quite busy, there wasn't any time for sport. As far as I was concerned there were these months to continue being instructed as junior boy, fourth hand, and still a sub-lieutenant. As I was no longer "under training" I would start being reported on in the normal naval manner. The form S206 was the report written by the captain when he or the officer concerned left the ship. The officer was not shown these confidential reports but he was given a thin piece of paper, aptly called a flimsy, summarising the salient features. It was now August and the end of Andrew's commission. David passed me my first flimsy and it read that I had conducted myself to his entire satisfaction and that:-

> I was a cheerful and loyal officer who has worked hard, and who with more experience will make a very useful submarine officer.

Will make, not should or might!

David returned to Rothesay in the early sixties to command the Submarine Squadron and the depot ship HMS Adamant. He had several important appointments as a "Whitehall Wallie" and also in the United States. He commanded the missile destroyer HMS Fife, and during his time they circumnavigated the world. He retired in 1980 as Rear-Admiral Sir David Scott. A fine officer and a super shipmate, who taught me a great deal in the short time I was aboard his happy and efficient boat.

I joined my second submarine, HMS Scotsman, in Devonport Dockyard and what a dismal situation that was. Dockyards are depressing enough places at the best of times and tucked away at the far end was Submarine Reserve Group F – a bunch of submarines being repaired, worked upon or modified. Scotsman was an S-Class boat, but she was being completely converted into a Trials Submarine. Both engines had been removed, to be replaced with additional batteries and two A-Boat motors. The gun and torpedo tubes had gone and the hull had been streamlined – all to give us a high underwater speed. A single engine would be used to give us a maximum speed of 8 knots on the surface.

The first five days filled me with gloom as there seemed to be nothing very much going on. The First Lieutenant Hugh Tregellis, and second hand, Alan Turvill, had already joined before me. They seemed able to pass the time of day before going home in the early afternoons. During the week I stayed in digs outside St. Levans Gate and went home to Alverstoke most weekends. In the afternoons, I made myself available to play any game going and was chosen to represent the Reserve Group at both soccer and hockey every week, with one or two chums from the other boats and we got to know the area quite well. Our favourite haunt being the Plymouth Sailing Club, known to its regulars as the Groin Exchange.

Luckily this routine didn't last all that long as one day our captain joined. He was Lieutenant Commander Harvey Dutton, a small man with an infectious smile – what an eccentric he turned out to be. It was good to know we would be leaving Devonport Dockyard and the Mateys, very soon. They did very little work: they simply hid in various compartments or went round in ever decreasing circles passing the time of day. They knew their schedule and would pace it out so that the job would be finished just in time. They were in fact very good tradesmen; in times of stress or when the country really needed them, they would turn up trumps.

At the Groin Exchange I had occasionally met Virginia, who was a big blonde girl, about 5 feet 9 inches tall. She was very interested in amateur dramatics and she enjoyed classical music. She lived in digs where the landlady insisted all visitors were out and the front door locked by 2300. On the occasional evening I went there, we snuggled together in her bed, but all the time she vowed she was, and wanted to remain, chaste. We probably met twice a week over a period of about two months; and then Scotsman's departure for Rothesay was upon us. I asked her if she would like to spend my last weekend in a hotel and she said it was her 20th birthday on the Friday. She doubted if she could get away before the Saturday evening so I reserved a room for two nights in a hotel overlooking the Hoe and Plymouth Sound.

She phoned through before lunch on the Friday to say that she had chatted with her female doctor, who was in her drama group; it would be quite safe for us to start our weekend that evening. I didn't know what she was talking about, but it was going to add an extra night to what would certainly be an enlightening experience for me. On our arrival at the hotel we went straight to the bathroom and slowly undressed. Before throwing it away, she showed me a slightly blood-stained pad and cuddling up to me said: "I won't have to wear those any more". I opened a bottle of champagne which we indulged before getting into bed. She sat astride me, gradually I could feel things getting deeper and deeper and as we rolled over together onto her back she said: "Now that you have so tenderly picked my cherry, let's have some cream!" Whilst enjoying each other's company, I thanked her profusely for allowing me to be the favoured one.

I woke up to a lovely spring morning and there, blissfully asleep, was this beautiful nubile blonde. She had been through a very emotional time and I knew she would enjoy a full English breakfast. When it arrived we sat at the table and watched the comings and goings in Plymouth Sound. She talked about how wonderful her doctor had been with the guidance, advice, and special cream – all helping to make everything painless. We got back into bed and she told me when I was ready for more, all I had to do was gently pull the piece of white string!

Later we looked out again at the splendid view; we reflected on the fact that in 1588 Sir Francis Drake was playing bowls on the bowling green below us. When warned of the approach of the Spanish Armada, he remarked that there was plenty of time to finish the game and still beat the Spaniards. In 1620 the Pilgrim Fathers had set sail in the Mayflower for America; they landed later that year in what is now known as Provincetown. As the sun began to set, we walked across the Hoe and down to the Barbican, the attractive olde-worlde part of Plymouth – and stood on the Mayflower Steps from where the Pilgrim Fathers had departed.

Captain James Cook had sailed in the Endeavour three times from Plymouth for the Pacific Ocean. During these voyages he achieved the first recorded contact with the eastern coast of Australia and the first circumnavigation of New Zealand. In his last voyage in 1799 he was killed in Hawaii during a fight with the islanders. Plymouth is certainly a famous naval port, steeped in history, and it is estimated there are at least forty places in the world named after the city.

After a hearty fish meal, we returned to the hotel and had a nightcap or two. Before popping into the bath, I helped her take off her new dress, which was still in immaculate condition. She sat down alongside me on the bidet, which she had already used a few times. I hadn't seen one before – they didn't have them at Dartmouth or on board any of the ships I had served in! She went on to explain why it was so useful for her at that particular time of the month. After all, she wanted to be as clean as possible for her man, who I think had better call me "Ginny" from now on!

We couldn't resist the late Sunday breakfast overlooking our favourite view and the sea beyond. I was beginning to wonder how Ginny and I had got ourselves into this intriguing situation. We knew very little about each other and we seemed to have very little in common. This comely female who three days ago was a teenager, had changed her mind about chastity and was now a woman of the world. She was very appreciative of the attention I was giving her but, come tomorrow morning, and we both went our different ways, would we ever see each other again? Only time would tell. On board Scotsman everyone seemed happy, probably because they had had a good weekend and we were off to sea again. The boat had been given a good clean-up by those on board and at 1100 we sailed leaving behind:-

> *The Dockyard Mateys children*
> *Sitting on the dockyard wall*
> *Watching their fathers doing f.... all*
> *When they grow older they'll*
> *Be Dockyard Mateys too*
> *Just like their fathers with f... all to do!*

The passage to Rothesay, about 400 miles at 7 knots, took over two days, but it gave us time to get to know the boat and its equipment, but most of all our shipmates with whom we were probably going to live and work for the best part of two years. On arrival in the bay, we went straight alongside HMS Adamant which had replaced the Montclare as our depot ship. Adamant's onboard facilities were to make her technical support for submarines much better.

*HMS Scotsman in her berth alongside HMS
Adamant on the port quarter*

Rothesay was going to be our base and as we only had a week
before we went off on our first trials, we started to acquaint
ourselves with the town we were going to get to know very well
over the years. It was not the best run ashore in the world and its
travel advertisement image as "The Riviera of Scotland" did not
say very much for Scotland. There were plenty of pubs and the
wardroom ashore was the Victoria Hotel. Going in there was
similar to entering the wardroom in Adamant, except everyone
was in civvies and therefore more relaxed and less rank-conscious.
Probably the first thing I noticed, and my one real memory of
"The Vic" was the motto above the bar: "He who hoots with the
Owl by night shall soar with the Eagle by day." Occasionally the
Glenburn Hotel was visited. Rich Scottish businessmen would
bring their families down for a few days. On Saturday evenings
there would be a dinner dance (black tie of course) and their
womenfolk, known as the "Glenburn Harriers", would be on
parade. It was a bit upmarket for us!

More frequently used were the fish and chip shops or
restaurants, all of which seemed to be owned by the Zavaroni
family. We got to know Victor quite well as, apart from selling fish
and chips, many of his relations and friends were musicians, great
providers of accordion-type music. Twenty years later Victor's
daughter, Lena, at the age of ten was to win Hughie Green's

"Opportunity Knocks" a record five times with her hit song "Ma He's Making Eyes At Me". Victor's chippies were probably used later at night on the way back to the pier to catch one of the last liberty boats to the depot ship.

Scotsman's task was to work with and for the boffins from the Admiralty Research Laboratory at Teddington. All the trials were related to noise which could be made by motors, generators, fans, pumps, radio equipment and even boots clumping around on the metal decks. All the training at Whale Island marching up and down in boots and gaiters – we knew it was wasted time! We were all issued with gym shoes – much better. Probably the most important trials were with different propellers – trying to get one of the right patterns, which would make Scotsman go as fast as possible, when dived, without making any noise and the minimum amount of cavitation. These trials would take us to several very attractive quiet little spots bordering on the River Clyde.

First place was Loch Goil a very attractive tributary of Loch Long. Situated ashore in the Trials Base was George Cousins, the head boffin. As he was in charge, he stayed ashore listening to Hydrophones which were attached, below the waterline, to rafts in the middle of the loch. Any noise emanating from the submarine would be measured and recorded. These first trials were carried out with Scotsman secured between two mooring buoys. It only needed about a third of the ship's company on board to dive the boat down to periscope depth, and turn different bits of equipment on and off whilst the boffins got on with it. Those of us not required on board went fishing in the loch, climbed the nearby mountains, played the locals in Lochgoilhead at football and helped to drink the local pub almost dry. All a bit boring after a couple of weeks or so, and all this inactivity could well lead to the morale of the crew going downhill fairly rapidly if something wasn't done about it.

Accommodation on board, which had been no more than reasonable in Andrew, was terrible in Scotsman. That is why we were paid Hard Lying money over and above submarine pay, but this wouldn't compensate for the lowering of morale that could well occur. There were not enough bunks on board so some of the crew had to hot-bunk or sleep in the main companionway or engine room decks. Our bunks in the wardroom were the sofa seats used during the day. It was like a fourth class railway sleeper. We had to turn in, and get up, at the same time. This was annoying as we usually had to wait until Harvey had finished his night cap or two. Then in the morning, it was marmalade and blanket fluff for breakfast! It was alright when we were back alongside the depot ship, but we were going to spend much time away on these trials.

Give Harvey his due. He quickly started getting things organised – aided by the inevitable liquid hospitality needed to persuade those in authority to oblige. The first acquisition was an ancient barge which appeared from the Greenock area. It had some bunks fitted and a space for any spare gear. It had to be towed by a tug to wherever we were operating and it very soon became known as "Harvey's Ark". Loch Goil did have an advantage or two over the other quiet places from which we were due to operate. George Cousins had two or three civilian drivers, naval utilicons and one motor boat at his disposal. We were therefore able to get ashore and get a lift if it was too far to walk. What would happen when we went to our next trials area up Loch Fyne?

With the aid of similar liquid bribery Harvey obtained a large motor boat, open at the stern, but it had a well-covered forward compartment with a coal burning stove. This is when everyone in the Clyde area got to know Leading Seaman Golding, our Second Coxswain. We already looked like a bunch of pirates when we were away from Rothesay and now "Scratcher" as any Second Coxswain of a submarine is known, looked the part as skipper of this addition to Harveys Fleet. A very experienced submariner, seaman, and delightful rogue with his bushy beard he looked the real sailor in his boat, which became known as "Scratcher's Sampan"!

Now the fleet departed for Inverary at the top of Loch Fyne. The ark had been towed directly from Loch Goil. When we arrived, with the sampan in company, we were all secured to the mooring buoy a quarter of a mile from the pier. Loch Fyne was very deep and ideal for the type of trials we were about to carry out. It was a new experience for us all and especially from my point of view as navigating officer. We would be doing runs of a

HMS Scotsman in Loch Goil

maximum four miles at different depths and different speeds; so that the boffins could find out the noise levels made by our propellers.

We would start from near a marker ashore on Strone Point, and run down on a south westerly course towards another marker on the eastern side of the loch, south of Strachur. We would dive, do a fast run, surface, turn round, dive for another fast run on the reciprocal course and surface again off Inverary. It was all stop-watch navigation requiring the accurate steering of the necessary course. Dived and stationary at periscope depth Harvey would line us up on the far marker and then give the required depth and speed for the run. I would start the stop watch and X minutes and seconds later I would say "Y seconds to go sir," and Harvey would give the orders to slow down, return to periscope depth and surface. We did hundreds of those runs.

On one north easterly run, we perhaps surfaced a second or two late – very close to Strone Point and its shoreside road. A policeman passing by got the shock of his life. On seeing us surface he thought the Loch Ness monster had arrived in Loch Fyne! The stories vary as to whether he fell off his bicycle or whether he was in a police car to which he did do considerable damage! Because we were going fast runs, speeds obtained were secret at the time – our batteries were very run down at the end of the day. So there was another addition to Harvey's fleet in the form of an A-Boat which would come up from Rothesay to charge our batteries overnight. We would secure alongside her, electric cables would be passed over and by the next morning we would be topped up and ready to go again.

Scratchers Sampan was used to ferry any of the two submarine crews who wanted to visit the dim lights of Inverary. The wardroom ashore was the posh bar in the George Hotel, whose proprietor, Donald Clark, had represented Scotland at Curling prior to the war. He, together with his wife, son, and daughter proved to be great hosts and friends. Mark you, when we first arrived at Inverary the George was an average Scottish village hostelry. By the time we finally left, it was much wealthier looking and many future visits by submariners almost turned it into The Ritz!

On most of our visits to Inverary the Duke and Duchess of Argyll, but never the twain, would come aboard at the end of the day's trials for a drop of the malt. Harvey would oblige with Laphroaig, which was almost our staple diet – his anyway. Margaret, Duchess of Argyll, was a London socialite and basically came up to Inverary for a rest. She was never there at the same time as Ian, the Duke. Whoever was in residence at the time came on board and often asked one or two of us back to their 18th century Gothic-style castle. The only entrance to Scotsman was down through the forward hatch and it had a vertical ladder. When they came down, the crew would rush to help. If it was Margaret it would be for normal reasons and she obliged by always wearing a skirt, never slacks! If it was the Duke, it would be to check if he had anything on under his kilt. Evidently Annie Laurie had once asked Hamish, when he collected his prize for Tossing the Caber at the Balmoral Highland Games, whether there was anything worn under his kilt. He replied: "I can assure you my wee lassie, there is nothing worn under my kilt. It is all in perfect working order"!

We got to know Margaret and Ian very well – individually, they hadn't lived together for some time. He had married three times, she had been married to Charles Sweeny, the US golfer, and had had numerous inter-marital romances and affairs during her other marriages. It all came to the attention of the world when, in 1963, after many scandalous stories and salacious photographs, they were divorced.

In late May we were given a great break lasting three weeks. Leaving the Ark and Sampan behind, we left Rothesay for a cruise to the South of England and Belgium. Our first stop was Bristol. Entering at Avonmouth close to high tide, we proceeded up the river under the spectacular Clifton Suspension Bridge, and through the first lock into Cumberland Basin. The swing bridge was then opened and we slowly negotiated the last mile to secure alongside the harbour wall opposite a pub right in the city centre. We spent four days carrying out one of the Navy's most important non-operational tasks called "Showing the Flag". It means pay-back time to the tax-paying public, when they can come aboard their ship, walk around, and ask as many questions as they like. This is when the ship is open to visitors, possibly two or three times during the ship's stay. Then, one afternoon, there is a children's party when the crew dress up as pirates (normal for us!) and provide plenty of sticky buns and sweets – plus fun and games. It is all, in fact, a recruiting drive.

Across the other side was a shop with our captain's name above the door. It was Harveys Bristol Cream, whose staff looked after us extremely well every day of the visit.

We had to call in at Perranporth, a tiny harbour on the north Cornish coast. There was an Admiralty Noise Range there and we were required to do several runs over it. On our approach we detected on the radar and then we visually saw, a large trawler fishing close inshore. She came out of the three mile limit as we approached. She was French, there was nothing we could do about it. She knew that and offered us a large basketful of fish. We accepted the kind offer and passed him a few bottles of the good stuff. Fellow mariners and sons of the sea. Poor Chef! He really did have to look up Mrs Beeton on how to produce Lobster Thermidore, Dressed Crab, Moules Mariniere and Cod Mornay, etc. He did a grand job for a few days.

On to Portland and alongside the depot ship HMS Maidstone. It was the 17th June and a very sad occasion. At 0825 the previous morning the submarine Sidon had had a "hot run" on one of its torpedoes: it had been embarked to go to sea for trial firings. It had no warhead but did have the new very volatile hydrogen peroxide propellant. A mate of mine, Julian Rycroft, who had joined the Navy a year before me, was the Torpedo Officer; he plus two other officers and ten ratings were killed. Needless to say no-one was interested in anything but the accident and investigations as to its cause. So we left early and caught a glimpse of Sidon bows down as we went eastwards towards HMS Dolphin where we arrived in the afternoon. I spent both nights we were there enjoying the luxuries of home in Alverstoke. During the day I was getting the necessary charts for our 210 mile passage to Terneuzen in the Westerschelde, Holland and then the 20 miles up the canal to Ghent in Belgium. We were on what the Navy called a "jolly" – a visit abroad to once again "show the flag". Most ships stationed in home waters hoped to get one of these each year. They were in fact very good for foreign relations – undoing all the bad work created by the politicians!

First night in at Ghent the usual wardroom cocktail party for the Mayor and his team, plus local businessmen and servicemen – usually people who have been kind to previous naval visits in the area. Similar to Bristol, the ship was open to visitors and we gave a children's party. The crew were invited to visit various places of interest including the local brewery and some of us went to Brussels thirty miles away and even further on to Radio Luxemburg.

On the last day, a Sunday, Harvey, Ken and I were asked out to lunch. Harvey had had a tot or two and as we walked back to Scotsman we passed a demonstration. As quick as a flash Harvey had joined up with the happy crowd, borrowing one of their boards with the saying: "Wu Zijn Geen Tweederangs-Burgers". We were told it meant "we are not second class citizens" – or words to that effect! Ken and I joined in, all good fun, and the demonstrators obviously enjoyed our company, whatever the cause. A further party on board that evening, after which it was necessary for Alan and I to turn Harvey into his bunk. He

Scotsman entering Portsmouth Harbour, June 1954

was very, very happy, not in any way drunk, but he had to take us to sea the next morning.

After our one and a half thousand mile round trip, we arrived back alongside Adamant. The usual glum faces at the sight of Scotsman, but a warm welcome for the crew. On the sports notice-board were details of the Third Submarine Squadron swimming championships to be held in the Rothesay Baths in a fortnight's time. Yes, Rothesay, in spite of its size, did have a very substantial swimming pool. Although not to Olympic specifications it was more than adequate for swimming races, diving and water polo. It was correctly called Baths because also in the building were baths for the use of those unfortunate people who lived in houses without them. I rustled around and found four or five of the crew who had taken part in competitive swimming, albeit at their training establishments, and took them for some training swims.

I told Harvey that I considered we had a good enthusiastic bunch of swimmers and that I wanted to enter them in the championships. He contemplated. Scotsman was leaving for Loch Goil the day before, because the trials were once again going to be stationary between the two mooring buoys. He agreed provided Ken Evans was happy for this Chief ERA Phil Toms and one stoker, Biscuits Crawford, to be away; and provided I got the team back to Loch Goil the morning after the event. The swimmers were on board Adamant to wave goodbye to our shipmates leaving for the loch and in the afternoon we won three events and picked up a few points in others – ending up with the inter-submarine trophy. A few celebratory drinks in a couple of local pubs – then back on board to see if the early morning arrangements I had made to get us up to Loch Goil worked. Quite simple really, Adamant's motor boat had been organised to leave us at Innellan pier by 0800 where one of George Cousin's vans was going to meet us. The shortest route was a grand 40 mile tour of Argyll, up to the Rest and Be Thankful, and then down to Lochgoilhead. You could sense a good boost to morale when those on board learnt that Scotsman were the champions. Harvey had an immediate celebratory tot!

The naval sporting facilities in the island of Bute, although existent, were the worst I have ever seen or experienced. If you were chosen to play football for your submarine, you put the sports gear on before catching the boat ashore, you then waited on the pier some time for a blue naval lorry to arrive (if you were very lucky it might be a bus). You got as comfortable as you could on the rickety wooden benches and if you weren't quick you might have to stand the whole journey of at least four miles along a narrow winding road to the Navy sports ground at Etterick Bay. This faced the south west and gave no protection against the rain or prevailing SW gales. The sports shed (it might have been called a pavilion) had no showers or washing facilities, it was merely there to leave your few belongings and go to the loo. After the game, you waited in your wet, filthy sports gear for the lorry to arrive and start the dismal journey back to Rothesay pier. There you probably had to wait for the boat to take you back to Adamant's very welcoming bathroom – and a pint of beer. After two visits to Etterick Bay I thought to myself "never again." No wonder there was very little enthusiasm for sport amongst submariners.

Perhaps my reputation for having had a rugby trial for both Hampshire and the Royal Navy had preceded me, but I was selected to play for the Royal Navy (Scotland). There were only four fixtures a season, two against Perthshire Academicals and Edinburgh University before the inter-services matches versus the Army (Scotland) and the RAF (Scotland). The only thing I remember about these games were that they were played on Wednesdays, they were all played away, the tremendous travel involved, and that I was the only submariner in the team. During my time in the Trade, I only knew of one submariner who achieved anything in sport. He was Barry Wallace who played rugby for the Royal Navy, Combined Services, and Hampshire. A few years later, there was Rodney Pattisson, who spent so much time training and participating in World and Olympic sailing that he resigned from the navy in 1968 aged 25. He was born in Campbeltown and during the war his father had been in the Fleet Air Arm at Machrihanish. Having to travel across in the ferry to Wemyss Bay, then train to Edinburgh, or Perth, and return after the match was a labour of love. It was good to get a break from submarines and enjoy a higher standard of sport and sporting facilities.

It was not actually possible to get back to Rothesay the same day, as the last ferry from Wemyss Bay was at about 1800. There was an RNVR club in Glasgow and here's a bit of maritime history.

The club was the Carrick, a fast clipper ship built in Sunderland in 1864 as "The City of Adelaide". Every year between 1864 and 1887 she transported passengers and goods from London to Adelaide. On the return she carried passengers, wool and copper back to London. Over the years she played an important part in the immigration of Australia. Commissioned in to the Royal Navy in 1928 as HMS Carrick, she was then decommissioned in 1948 and became the RNVR Club moored on the River Clyde in the centre of Glasgow. A very satisfying place to spend a quiet evening with hospitable sailors enjoying a meal and a few drinks. The only slight problem – the original bunks in the tiny cabins, although comfortable, were very small.

They didn't build six-foot sailors in those days! I did have the pleasure in staying there at least four times. Carrick was a lovely vessel of a bygone era and sadly no-one seemed able to provide the finances for her upkeep. Twice she sank at her moorings in the Clyde and in 1993 was moved to a slipway alongside the Scottish Maritime Museum in Irvine. In 2010 the Scottish Parliament discussed her future and there is a chance she could be returned to the place of her original name, the City of Adelaide. In the meantime she is still at Irvine – deteriorating.

The nearest first class rugby team of any consequence was Greenock Wanderers. I telephoned the secretary, Donald Steel, and asked if he had a vacancy in the team for a stranded sailor in Rothesay. "I'll get back to you Mike," was his reply. Sure enough, within a day, he got back and asked me if I could play for the first team at home on Saturday. He had obviously made a few enquiries and the selectors chose me to play in the back row. The problem was getting back to Rothesay on a winter's Saturday. For home matches Donald would drive me to nearby Gourock Bay for the 1800 ferry. For away matches I could stay on for the post match festivities and Donald's family very kindly put me up at their home for the night. After a good Scot's breakfast he put me onto the first ferry and so back on board to work.

The first year of trials had passed and there is no doubt Scotsman was the most disliked boat in the squadron. Every time we moved for another set of trials it meant extra work and inconvenience for many people. An A-boat and its crew had to accompany us for battery charging duties – usually overnight. A tug had to move the Ark and an MFV had to patrol to the south of us in Lochs Goil and Fyne in order to keep other vessels away. Harvey and his bunch of pirates were, however, always welcomed wherever we went be it Lochgoilhead, Inverary, Rothesay or even on board the Adamant. It was Scotsman, the boat itself, that was bottom of the popularity league. Sometimes on our return to Rothesay we went into the floating dock across the bay at Port Bannatyne. This would be to fit different propellers for the next set of trials.

Come Easter time the demand for our services seemed to become more varied. We went to Londonderry as they wanted a fast submarine to practice on. I had been there before as a midshipman, but this time I would be below the waves as opposed to above them. Little did I ever imagine then that I would be a conscript submariner. In Londonderry we went alongside HMS Stalker, a clapped out tank landing ship which had been converted to accommodate submarine crews. We had no "ark" or "sampan" but there was an A-boat there to charge our batteries.

On the Monday we went out of the River Foyle to the exercise areas and dived at the allotted time. For some of the exercises we were restricted in what we could do in order to give the surface ships, and the RAF, a worthwhile chance. In the evenings we would go alongside an A-boat at anchor for the inevitable charge of batteries. The anchor berth was a mile from Moville in the Irish Republic, opposite a pub called the Smuggler's Inn. We couldn't go ashore, but strangely that did not bother us as the work was very tiring and demanding. We went back alongside Stalker once for what they called a "wash-up" in HMS Sea Eagle, the Navy's Anti-Submarine School. There, senior officers, captains, navigators and pilots of the craft involved would discuss what had gone on during the week. After about an hour and a half most of us left, whilst only the more senior, including Harvey, stayed behind. Immediately afterwards I had one of the most interesting and educational hours in my life. I was sitting in our naval car, waiting for Harvey, and listening to the civilian driver giving his unbiased views on the situation in Northern Ireland. He was a Roman Catholic, in a strongly Nationalist area, working for the British government. I was, and still am, a simple sailor who believes politics and religion should never be discussed in public: and never in Ireland. I just listened very attentively to this extremely loyal Ulsterman. It was over ten years before Bloody Sunday occurred in Londonderry.

The couple of nights we were there I was duty officer, and I really didn't have any desire to briefly repeat previously very happy runs ashore. We sailed early because the next and final exercise was a big one covering a large area. We travelled awhile on the surface and then dived, steering towards the Isle of Man, when close to its western shores we lay on the seabed all night. We were in silent routine and we quite often heard those above us searching back and forth, but they didn't find us. About an hour before the exercise was due to finish we let off a green flare so that they knew where we were. We sped at different depths and speeds so that they could play with us until the game was over, and we surfaced. Bidding the opposition farewell we proceeded at our usual slow speed of about seven knots towards Campbeltown where we were to be for two nights.

Campbeltown is my birthplace. I didn't let anyone know this and I decided to keep a low profile whilst we were there. I had heard that most sailors considered the place to be the best run ashore in Scotland. As soon as a Navy vessel was seen to be entering harbour, the flags would come out, the bar hours would appear to be extended and probably most important of all a dance would be arranged in the Temperance Hall. There was nothing temperate about the goings on at those dances. Everyone seemed to have a flask or a bottle of VP wine tucked away, and girls never seen in town (since the last dance) would appear from nowhere.

My fellow officers had looked out for me when playing sport so I was duty officer all the time we were there, except for three hours of the last evening. I nipped ashore to visit my grandmother in the house where I was born, and where I lived until I joined the Navy. She had her sister, my great aunt staying with her, and they were both very pleased to see me and cook a wee meal. I told them I had to get back soon as we were leaving early in the morning. The latter was true, but I wanted to get back so I could do duty officer and let my fellow officer get ashore to the delights on offer in the town. Next morning as we sailed past Davaar Island, I heard a couple of stokers rendering the well known Scots ballad:-

"Four and twenty virgins came doon frae Inverness
And when the dance was over there were four and twenty less."

I was beginning to think of my future. Did I want to continue in submarines? Frequently on board the Adamant, I would meet

John Fieldhouse, the spare crew commanding officer, who was awaiting his first command. He seemed very happy on occasions to come up and chat with me about what we had been up to in Scotsman. I twigged that he didn't have too much admiration for Harvey and that he obviously felt sorry for me. On at least two occasions he asked me if I would like to join him in the Acheron when he took command. What an honour. At last someone seemed to want me! I was now at the stage where I could leave submarines as I had completed two years, provided I applied for another specialisation. I did not want to do that, as I wanted to remain a "Salt Horse" thereby hopefully getting a much greater variety of appointments. I thanked John very much indeed for his tremendous offer, but I reaffirmed that I was a conscript and, as such, would probably finish the commission in Scotsman and then leave the trade.

I always respected John Fieldhouse and every submariner seemed to have a great admiration for him. After several very good appointments, he went on to become Flag Officer Submarines, then First Sea Lord at the time of the Falklands War, and finally Chief of the Defence Staff as Admiral of the Fleet Lord Fieldhouse of Gosport. What a man and it was great to have served with him at an early stage in his fantastic career.

On our return from Londonderry there was a change of scenery in the wardroom in the form of Lieutenant Bryan Smalley. He was like a breath of fresh air, and he had a most infectious sense of humour to go with it, developed I'm sure before and while he was coming "aft through the hawsepipe". He had joined the Navy as a boy seaman in 1947 and through hard work and determination serving as an Able Seaman and Leading Seaman in several different ships he was selected as an Upper Yardman. He had undergone a four month preparation course at "Vicky B", namely Victoria Barracks in Portsmouth, followed by a year at HMS Hawke. Hawke was a stone frigate a short walk down the hill from the RN College at Dartmouth with its own buildings and completely separate routine. I thoroughly enjoyed Bryan's company and I learned a lot about him and his past. He was promoted Acting Sub lieutenant and had gone through the same training as the rest of us at Greenwich and Portsmouth. He had shown his true leadership when he was one of the instigators hiring the elephant to lead the march past at his passing out parade at Whale Island. The week's stoppage of leave preceded by the threat of a court martial from the humourless captain certainly did not affect Bryan's career. As soon as possible he volunteered for, and joined, the trade exactly two years after our OTC at Dolphin. Here he was in his first submarine, the Scotsman.

Trials continued in Loch Goil and at Inverary, but also a new area, Kilbrennan Sound, the stretch of water between the Kintyre peninsula and the Isle of Arran. I well remember one day when we were dived, I was Officer of the Watch and raised the periscope for a routine check. There "a few yards ahead of us" was a fishing boat. I was about to give the order "Flood Q" and of course alert the captain when I realised the periscope was in high magnification. I quickly turned the handle so that vision was normal and there was the fisherman a safe distance away. Whooo! Q is a tank well forward in the submarine which could be quickly flooded so that our depth would increase rapidly, thereby hopefully avoiding a collision.

In the evenings we secured to the Admiralty mooring buoy in Lochranza at the north west top of Arran, were taken ashore by Scratcher in his sampan to the local pier at the head of which was a very hospitable pub. One weekend the Brodick Highland Games were in progress and we were encouraged to enter as many events as possible including the race up Goat Fell, a well-known conspicuous hill known as the "sleeping giant" because from a certain direction it looked like a giant with its head resting on a pillow. The athletic standard of the games was not very high so we won quite a number of events including the tug 0' war. The star of the post sports event was undoubtedly Harvey, who with the Dowager Duchess of Hamilton, chose Miss Brodick 1956. The Duchess lived in the local castle and she came on board for tea one afternoon. We really were mixing in high Scottish society. What with the Duke and Duchess of Argyll and now the Dowager Duchess of Hamilton, not to forget the young sixth Marquess of Bute, John Crichton-Stuart, and his wife Nicola, who quite often came on board Adamant for Sunday night cinema in the wardroom.

Decision time was getting much closer and much Greenwich-taught appreciation of the situation had already taken place. It was obvious that the submarine fleet would reduce in size and withdraw from Canada, Australia and eventually the Mediterranean but that it would always be in the west coast of Scotland. I saw no point in continuing to exist in a cigar tube based within fifty miles of where I was born. "Join the Navy and see the world" was the slogan and the only place outside the British Isles I had seen in three years was Ghent situated twenty miles up some canal in Belgium. I had hardly been out of Scotland.

There was no doubt about the heavy drinking culture amongst submariners and together with their disinterest in sport, all these things made the scales weigh heavily in favour of my returning to General Service as they called the real Navy. After a few days living in his boat you could smell a submariner as he came on board his depot ship or walked ashore. We reckoned all the extra submarine pay and hard-lying money was needed to pay the dry cleaning bill to get rid of the smell of diesel and other odours.

I don't know whether it was written by someone in General Service or the trade but there was a submarine motto which went as follows:-

> We come at dawn
> We come unseen
> We go at dusk
> We go unclean

The submarine service had a marvellous wartime record and they quite rightly thought they had an equally marvellous esprit de corps. But they weren't the only ones. There were plenty of other small ships in the Navy and I wanted to be in one of those. Strange though it may seem I requested to specialise in Physical Training and this turned out to be a very good decision.

Before my departure we had one other change of scenery, which involved us going to Troon Shipyard so that we could be slipped out of the water for some repair work which could not be done in the floating dock. The locals were extremely friendly and we were able to play a few rounds of golf on some of the internationally known courses in the area and we challenged the locals to a game of football. We ended up playing at Rugby Park against the Scottish First Division side Kilmarnock. It was only a training session, they gave us a good run around and we lost count after they had scored ten goals.

We left Troon and the captain let me manoeuvre Scotsman alongside Adamant on my last day at sea in the Submarine Service. In my flimsy he said: "He has conducted himself to my entire satisfaction. A thoroughly likeable officer who has the interests of the service and his ratings at heart. Physically strong, energetic and courageous; he has all the qualities of a first class sportsman. Very keen to specialise in P.T. Not a great wit or intellectual but absolutely straight, good-humoured and loyal." It was countersigned by Norman Jewell, the Captain of the Third Submarine Squadron, who had been in command of the Seraph for the "Man Who Never Was" episode in which David Scott, my captain in Andrew, was First Lieutenant. Also whilst Captain of Seraph Norman had surreptitiously recovered French General Giraud from a beach west of Toulon. The General refused to be saved by the Royal Navy after they sank some of the French fleet – to prevent it falling into German hands. Norman hoisted the Stars and Stripes, temporarily lowered the White Ensign, and called his submarine USS Seraph. When the General arrived on board, everyone in close proximity talked with an American accent and the operation went smoothly. Norman was awarded the Legion of Merit. I wish I could have got to know him better.

A researcher evidently wrote this epitaph about HMS Scotsman ten years later:-

"And so ended the life of a small submarine that with its crews and the various boffins contributed so much to Royal Navy submarine and anti-submarine technology from the vital early cold war years up to the advent of the nuclear submarine."

I soon joined the Royal Navy School of Physical Training at Pitt Street in Portsmouth. No way was I going to specialise in P.T. as I had told my submarine bosses. I wanted to remain a "salt horse" and I would keep my eyes and ears open for any seagoing opportunity that cropped up. It was whilst doing the Officers' PT Course that the golden opportunity did occur. An Admiralty Fleet Order was asking for lieutenants to apply for loan service with the Royal Malayan Navy based in Singapore. I immediately applied, the Admiralty forwarded my name to the Malayan High Commission in London, where I was asked to go for interview on completion of the P.T. course. The Malay army officer who sounded me out was charming. He obviously knew most of my details from their Lordships, and I cannot really remember all that he said because I was so galvanised at the prospect of helping to train the RMN – for three years. I do remember him being interested that I had been in the Korean War, that I was a salt horse and keen on sport. He appreciated that team sport was an essential ingredient for team spirit – leading to a happy and efficient ship's company.

He gave me the short history of the RMN. At the end of 1948 the Communists started their insurgency against the British Colonial Government. The Malayan Naval Force was formed and based at the ex-RAF radio station at Woodlands. It was within the British Naval Base near the causeway across to Johor. This became the barracks known as HMS Malaya, where as he put it I would be based. Now I knew I had passed the interview and been accepted. He went on to explain that HM The Queen had in August 1952 bestowed the title of Royal Malayan Navy on the MNF and that the barracks was now His Majesty's Malayan Ship in respect to the King of Malaya who was known as the Yang di Pertuan Agong. So having served one king and one queen plus country, I was now about to serve another king and country – but all within the British Commonwealth of Nations. On saying goodbye and wishing me the best of luck he told me it might be a few weeks before I would be required to go out there.

It was during this period, as well as before the P.T. course, that Freddie Stovin-Bradford contacted me to help organise three different naval rugby tours. If I got myself fit again, I could perhaps play! This was the usual cheerful Freddie sharing my view about the lack of sport in submarines. From the Royal Naval Air

Station at Brawdy, where he was Commander (Air) a short tour of Wales was arranged with matches against Carmarthenshire and Pembrokeshire. After the match suppers there was always a good party and perhaps a small cabaret (sod's opera!) I particularly remember the second one when a Welsh woman got up and after singing a couple of slightly bawdy songs said:-

> "I've just come up from the Rhondda
> After spending the night with a conger.
> My friend down in Deal
> Asked "How did it feel?"
> I said "Just like a man only longer!"

Then he got me to organise a local tour from RNAS Yeovilton with matches against Weston-Super-Mare, Taunton and Bridgewater and Albion. And finally a substantial tour to Dublin with games against Clontarf and Old Belvedere, and last but no means least, a match at Lansdowne Road against Dublin Wanderers. It seemed we spent more time drinking Guinness at the very hospital brewery (and elsewhere) than playing rugby. What a good drop of fortune it was to play rugby at Landsdowne Road a few days before leaving for three years in Malaya.

The Royal Navy team versus the Wanderers at Landsdowne Road, Dublin 25th October 1958

MALAYA AND MY FIRST COMMAND

The aircraft landed at Changi Airport in Singapore a few minutes before midnight and I was met by the familiar face of Lieutenant Commander Bill Hughes who was "old ships"; he had been the TAS Officer in Crispin up in Londonderry when I was a midshipman. On stepping out of the plane I was hit by the heat and humidity of the island, which is only 80 miles north of the equator. We had a couple of very welcome and refreshing drinks and then, in his car we drove along the Buketimah Road to the RMN Barracks. It was about 0200 in the morning and I was amazed at the number of wild dogs running around and crossing the roads. Bill explained that they had been normal domestic pets but had been left behind – abandoned by British servicemen returning home. Every now and then the Singapore police had a shoot to cull the spread of the poor beasts who lived in secondary jungle during the day and came out at night time to scavenge any dustbins they could find.

Souvenir Programme

Reaching the barracks Bill showed me the flat which was going to be my home for the next three years and then his own flat nearby. He then introduced me to Anchor and Tiger beers which would be the staple drinking diet. All the time, since clearing customs, he had been filling me with information and my programme for the next few days. Basically but not in order of events I had to get rid of my (non-existent as far as I was concerned) jet-lag, check the inventory of my flat and then go shopping for all sorts of things including white tropical uniform and other clothes. It was all very cheap and the expert Chinese tailors would have it all made and ready within three days. Until I was settled in, he would be looking after me and driving me around. Also I would have to buy a car and he knew a good place for that. He gave me the keys of my flat and I retired for the night. What luxury – clean white sheets, air conditioning and mosquito nets. My thoughts went briefly to Scotsman and all those submariners on Hard Lying Money!

At some leisurely hour Bill arrived and the process of getting settled in began. The first event was a very unexpected surprise when my Chinese amah arrived. Very necessary to keep the flat spotlessly clean but also all my tropical uniforms and party clothes pressed and immaculate. Her services were virtually free in that I was paid an allowance and employed her during the day on a weekly wage. If I wanted to entertain with a substantial meal, she would organise the cook boy. I would discuss the menu with him and the shopping and cooking of the meal would be expertly carried out by him. Each morning breakfast started with a Paludrin tablet (anti-malaria protection). Officers were trusted to take them but ratings were "force fed" in that they were given them at morning parade. Salt tablets were available in plenty for those who sweated a lot. Having checked the flat's inventory and found no discrepancies, off we went to shop and explore the delights of Singapore. Bill knew exactly where to go.

There were shops all over the place including the world famous Change Alley. It was here that I immediately learnt never to pay the asking price; always bargain. If you paid the first price offered the retailer assumed you were a nut case! I remembered

HMMS Sri Perak, my first command

the Change Alley lesson for the rest of my life wherever I was to be – even in London and the south of England. Having been measured up for uniforms and having bought some super raw silk shirts, we went for lunch at the Singapore swimming club. In the afternoon I opened an account at the Chartered Bank and started car hunting. This settling in process went on for four or five days. Although I met a few fellow officers socially, I had not yet been introduced to my senior officers.

Then the day arrived and at 0900 Bill took me along, all tarted up in my new Lieutenant's tropical uniform, to meet my immediate boss, the Staff Officer Operations, a Kiwi-born Commander, George Graham. Here beginneth the next amazing bit of news. The Commodore had decided to appoint me as Captain of HMMS Sri Perak, a seaward defence motor launch – one of the RN's 200th Patrol Squadron which had been given to the RMN. She was a 72ft patrol vessel fitted with twin 20mm Oerlikons and twin Vickers Machine Guns and had a total ship's company of 12. George then took me to meet the Commodore Dudley Norman who was in charge of the RMN and directly responsible to the Malayan Defence Secretary, Dato Abdul Razak, who was also Deputy Prime Minister. He congratulated me on my appointment and gave me a good fatherly chat about what was expected of me in my new job. George then told me to join my ship at 0900 tomorrow, meet my ship's company and go off to sea for the day. I walked out of his office, went home to my flat, and quietly thanked the Royal Navy for the magnificent training given to me and enabling me at the age of 26 to be the first of our term to be in command of a warship. It was probably the smallest warship in the world but that made me very happy. Bill called round to take me down to the Officers' Club for a celebratory drink and a prawn curry.

Sri Perak was alongside a Tank Landing Craft called HMMS Pelandok berthed at Ruthenia jetty. I arrived down there in my newly acquired second hand Hillman Minx at 0858, walked along the jetty, over the Pelandok, and was piped aboard my first command HMMS Sri Perak at 0900 on the dot. It was one of my proudest days. Head of the piping party was my coxswain, a senior Malay Chief Petty Officer who quietly spoken and in perfect English introduced himself then the other ten members of the crew. They consisted of one petty officer, one leading seaman, one radio operator, four able seamen, two stokers and the all-important chef. I was the only officer and the only European, and it was now my job to mould them into a happy and efficient crew.

We left Ruthenia jetty and slowly made our way eastwards passing all the British warships in the naval base. The coxswain was in charge of everything including the discipline and was in fact my right hand man. We had left the jetty in a good seamanlike manner and so I had a chat with the stoker P.O. who was Indian, enquiring about our two 152hp Gardner engines capable of giving us 12 knots. He knew I couldn't go down for a look as I couldn't leave the bridge whilst at sea but he assured me everything was in good shape. We manoeuvred to a pre-determined position on the chart and anchored for lunch. The crew did the cable work efficiently, the radio operator hoisted the black anchor ball without being told and we had a delicious chicken curry provided by the chef. We then weighed anchor and on our return to base I cleared lower deck and informed them of the great honour it was

Some of the crew. On the left the radio operator, Chua,
and the second coxswain "Scratcher" proudly
wearing his Royal Malayan Navy cap

for me to be their captain and that I was pleased with what I had
seen today. I told them a bit about my past in the Navy, that I was
keen on sport, and that in addition to being their captain, I was
also their divisional officer. As such I would be speaking to each
one of them individually when we were on our first patrol starting
in a couple of days' time.

The instructions from George Graham were to go off and
patrol the west coast of Malaya, get to know the area, spend the
nights in Malacca Port Swettenham and Penang returning to base
in about eight days' time. Fairly relaxed orders, but I must get the
crew trained up and make sure they know what's going on. We
sailed at 0800 and I sent the normal departure signal with our
destination and estimated time of arrival, to HMMS Malaya.

Malaya was independent but like the other commonwealth navies from Australia and New Zealand we were under the overall control of the C-in-C and he would be kept informed of all our movements and whereabouts in case we might be needed. The Malayan Emergency which started in 1948 was still on and the main task of the RMN was to stop communist terrorists from receiving supplies from the sea. That therefore was the reason for our being on patrol.

It was quite late in the evening when we arrived in the harbour of Malacca, just time to have a shower before a curry supper and a quiet stroll ashore. We had to be in harbour every day so that the coxswain could go shopping for fresh provisions. We did have a small deep freeze cabinet fitted on the after deck but it only stored enough supplies for a dozen people for a few days. At 0800 the next morning we held the normal morning colours ceremony after which the coxswain, who had already returned from his shopping, asked me if I would like to watch the "slaughter of today's lunch". Three chickens had been brought on board alive in a straw cage. In accordance with Muslim custom the chickens were in turn laid out on the after deck, whilst their throats were cut with a sharp knife and a prayer was said to Allah. I was beginning to learn local culture and the curry for lunch was excellent. I had already decided to spend the day in port so that I could go ashore to meet the harbourmaster and a few other local people.

Malacca was probably the most Malayan of all the towns visited. It was originally a small fishing village and it had the culture of all the peoples who made it into the well-known trading port it now was. The Portuguese were there in the sixteenth century and the Dutch took over a century later, before handing over to the British in Napoleonic times. It was full of history. It was, however, too small to take the normal sized merchant ships. So they anchored off whilst barges brought the cargo ashore. Amazing was the fact that some of these barges were still being rowed by teams of men; though most were motorised.

On to Port Swettenham which was the main harbour for KL as the capital Kuala Lumpur was known. This would probably be the port we would visit most, so it was important that we were seen and that we got to know the locals. We had our own special berth alongside the office of the Harbourmaster who was a British ex-Merchant Navy officer. He was very welcoming and requested I went to see him every time I was in port and assured me that if there was anything I needed he would be only too pleased to help out. I had a few things in the back of my mind but next time perhaps. At lunchtime I walked into the small station bar which, as the name implies, was there to provide refreshment for those using the railway to and from KL. The two Chinese staff were welcoming but also very inquisitive as to why a naval officer in uniform should not only be in Port Swettenham but also in their hostelry. I told them and also enquired as to a possible light snack to go with my Tiger beer. They suggested Mee Hoon Soup and a bread roll. I ordered one and that became my regular lunch when there.

Life as a captain could be very lonely at times and so I was beginning to find out. Naturally I didn't go ashore with my crew, although sometimes I met up with two or three who might show me a place of interest or a good restaurant where I could meet some locals. The Malayan people consisted of Chinese, Indians, with a sprinkling of Portuguese, Dutch and British, but mostly indigenous Malays. The latter were charming people, courteous, dignified, and quiet living. Perhaps indolent, but they had no need to be anything else. The Malay man was a gentleman, calm and untroubled by his way of life within the small patch of rubber or padi field. Or perhaps fish were around, nearby in a pool or in the sea. My Chief Petty Officer Coxswain was Malay. He was a very experienced seaman and I knew I could trust him with the running of the routine and the discipline. The stoker PO was Indian, and likewise he was entirely trustworthy. The others, apart from the radio operator who was Chinese, were all Malay. I wanted to learn Malay and I suppose during my three years I became quite competent at Bazaar Malay. But I received no help from my crew: they needed to improve their English to advance and succeed in the RMN and used me as their teacher – quite right too.

Penang was a super island – probably the most popular place amongst the ex-pats in Malaya. There were a lot of Australian servicemen there because of the RAAF air station at Butterworth opposite on the mainland. I met the harbourmaster who once again was ex-British Merchant Navy. In the evening ashore I was strolling through the town and there sitting round a table were some of the crew who insisted I joined them. They wanted to introduce me to Ronggeng which was Malay folk-dancing and they also insisted I danced with their very attractive Malay girlfriends. The music was nice and slow and the dancing non-contact as one would expect amongst Muslim people.

By the time we left Penang for home via Malacca on the way, I had interviewed all the crew. From the very beginning I told them that the rig could be extremely relaxed once we were out of sight at sea. Most wore swimming trunks. The member of the crew I remember most was Leading Seaman Abdullah, the Second Coxswain who was a smart young and enthusiastic lad with very good English. I told him straight away that the Second Coxswain in the RN was called Scratcher and because there were too many

Malays enjoying their Rongengg

Abdullahs on board, I intended calling him that. He hadn't heard of this before but he rushed and told his mates and was determined to be known as Scratcher from then on.

Our return to Ruthenia Jetty was after dark and Bill was there, ready to dash along to the club and very anxious to hear how I had got on. I was at George Graham's office next morning, told him everything I had done and he seemed pleased. I made two suggestions. The first was that, not necessarily after each patrol, but certainly once a month, I would like to forward a Report of Proceedings like all captains in the RN did. Then everything would be down in black and white – not just verbally spoken about. He agreed. The second point was that we had sufficient liferafts, but that Sri Perak did not have a sea boat. I suggested an inflatable dinghy with an outboard engine. He said he would look into it. In the meantime he told me to spend the next few days finding out about the barracks and the rest of the RMN.

The strength of the small navy was about thirty officers, about 600 ratings and 10 ships. In the barracks was a commodore, three commanders, several lieutenant commanders and many chief and petty officers, mostly on loan from the RN. The junior ratings were trained within the barracks but their artificer apprentices went to technical school in the naval base. Their young officers were going to the RNC at Dartmouth at the age of 18, then to the Dartmouth Training Squadron for sea training both as cadets and midshipmen. In fact the first young Malayan called Thanabalasingham had returned to Malaya a few months before my arrival. Everyone called him Thana, he was of Ceylonese origin, was extremely popular, smart and enthusiastic obviously destined to be the RMN's most senior officer provided he didn't blot his copybook. There were also a few ex-RN officers on contract to the RMN and one I particularly remember was Brian Hyde-Smith who had been a couple of years ahead of me at Dartmouth. He had met a Malay girl, converted to the Muslim faith, married her and was now known as Lieutenant Ibrahim bin Abdullah, RMN. He looked the part as he went off home to his kampong, dressed in Malay clothes and wearing his songkok.

The ten warships, all a gift from the RN, were one coastal minesweeper, the Mahamiru, two inshore "Ham" class minesweepers and seven SDML's. All except Mahamiru were named after states which I remembered from my stamp collecting days to be Johor, Kedah, Kelantan, Malacca, Negri Sembilan, Pahang, Penang, Perak, Perlis, Selangor and Trengganu.

Port Dickson had a small harbour and was the HQ of the Federation Army. We as a crew wanted to get to know our fellow servicemen, and spent most of a day there being talked to and shown around in a relaxed but very instructive way. Although Malaya had become independent more than a year before, the Malayan Emergency was still on-going. Basically it was a "guerrilla war" fought between Commonwealth Armed Forces and the Malayan National Liberation Army (MNLA) – the military arm of the Malayan Communist Party. It had started in 1948 when the communists, mostly ethnic Chinese, attacked estates and plantations in Perak. If it had been called a war the losses of any rubber plantations and tin mine industries would not have been covered by Lloyds Insurers. We had the largest army since WW2, national service was at its height and regiments came from the United Kingdom, Malaya, Australia, New Zealand, Rhodesia and Nyasaland, as well as the Gurkhas, the Fijian Regiment and Sarawak Rangers. By now we were winning and much of the country was free of the CTs (Communist Terrorists). The liberated areas were called white ones, but there were still black areas near the Thailand border, particularly in Perak and Kedah. The Korean War, with American involvement, had eclipsed much of the Malayan Emergency.

That is why we went to Alor Star, the northernmost port on the west coast. It was a quiet pleasantly backward harbour. In the club ashore I met a couple of planters who invited us to go up river to their plantation where they had their own jetty. I had no chart but the harbourmaster gave us a land map showing the river, plus plantations, and he assured me there was plenty of water; it was regularly used by quite large vessels and tugs towing barges. We accepted the invitation for the morrow and challenged their team to a game of 8 or 9-a-side football. We couldn't provide a full eleven and I don't think they could either. The visit further up river did us all a power of good as we got to see how rubber was produced and to hear first-hand about the terrible experiences they suffered during the emergency. They were very generous with their hospitality and the football exercise, just before sunset, was good for us all. As we left next morning they made us promise that we would return; we assured them we would.

For the next couple of months or so we got well worked up as a crew, visiting some of the smaller harbours and navigating rivers we hadn't visited before. We wanted as many people, as well as those in Port Swettenham, Malacca and Penang, to know and see they had a Navy. I was convinced that the major factor in keeping your crew happy, when they were away from home, is to prevail upon them that they are doing a worthwhile job. Sometimes difficult in times of peace – when the media and politicians give all the wrong messages. Everywhere we went the locals seemed to enjoy meeting the crew and the crew seemed

'Sri Perak' alongside in Alor Star Harbour

103

to give the impression that they were relishing their chosen way of life.

On return to Ruthenia Jetty one day the ever faithful Bill was there to meet me and said the Commodore wanted to see me at 0900 the next morning. All that Bill would say was that I was not in for a rollicking or going to have my horoscope read! I arrived at the appointed hour, he told me he was more than satisfied with my performance so far and that I was appointed Captain of HMMS Sri Johor, he shook my hand and told me to see George Graham who would give me instructions. Sri Johor was ex-HMS Altham, an inshore minesweeper just over 100ft in length with twin Paxman diesel engines giving a speed of 14 knots. She had just been recently handed over from the RN and had come out of refit. Bill, who was her captain, would take me out for a couple of days' handover. I asked George if I could take my Sri Perak Coxswain and Second Coxswain with me and he indicated he would try to arrange this.

Sri Johor was in very good nick; Bill had made sure of that. My accommodation was at the stern of the ship and consisted of

'Sri Perak' open to visitors

HMMS Sri Johor, my second command 1959

three compartments – a cabin with a bunk, a small shower and toilet, and the wardroom where any others would be accommodated. As there were no other officers, I had the whole area to myself – certainly more comfortable than a submarine. Bill took the ship away from Ruthenia Jetty and then virtually left it all for me to do what I wanted. He showed me all the gear and how it all worked as I navigated our way to Malacca for a one night stay. He showed me to the Malacca Club, which I had not yet visited and where many British ex-pats, plus serving military officers, were enjoying their evenings off. He introduced me to a Chinese woman whom he had evidently met at the club once before. Her name was Mary and she had been married to a Scottish planter. He had retired back to Scotland, but she had preferred to remain in Malaya. We had a meal together and then she drove us back to the ship and came down to the wardroom for a nightcap. Bill said he was feeling tired so went to bed for his last night in the captain's cabin.

Mary and I had a couple of drinks and talked about places in Scotland where she had been once with her husband. I could quite understand why she preferred to stay behind in Malacca where she had many friends about whom she talked copiously. It was the first time I had been in any conversation with a Chinese woman and I think we were both enjoying each other's company. Eventually she got up and asked if she could pay a quick visit to the toilet. When she came back she had hung up her few lightweight clothes and put my towel around her small beautiful

My Malay coxswain was with me in both Sri Perak and Sri Johor

body. She had jet black hair, and was very generous in her welcoming of me to Malaya. When we got to her car, I thanked her very much and she said she hoped to see me the next time I was in Malacca – but only on board the ship. I replied that it would suit me fine, and she could come down early and we would have dinner on board.

Returning to base next day Bill and I went to see George Graham and I told him I was more than happy to take over from Bill; the three of us went to celebrate my second command. George told me that the two crew I had requested would be there next morning and that the inflatable dinghy, plus outboard motor I had suggested, would be with us in a week's time. Ask and ye shall receive! The coxswain and Scratcher appeared delighted to see me next morning and after piping me aboard, we settled down to virtually the same routine as we had organised in Sri Perak. In April the monsoon changes. The winds had been north-easterly for the previous six months, this made it untenable for small ships along the east coast of Malaya. Now with the change to the south-westerly monsoon we would be able to visit this beautiful, though slightly undeveloped, part of the country.

It wasn't long before this change of scenery and a plum job came our way. We were asked to go to Pekan and take the Sultan of Pahang to the island of Pulau Tioman for a state visit and return him to the mainland the next day. I had been told it was all very informal, but I couldn't believe my good fortune and as far as Sri Johor was concerned it was going to be a royal visit. The coxswain and crew seemed remarkably pleased to hear the news even when I told them they would have to wear their best uniform – but only whilst the Sultan was on board. I ordered new charts for the east coast and the Pahang state flag to be flown at our mainmast. I arranged for a Malay journalist called Ralph Modder to be on board, and finally asked my amah to make sure my best uniform plus sword and medals were in top-top condition. We left the naval base in plenty of time and anchored close inshore off Pekan the evening before.

At the crack of dawn, with my crew smartly at the ready, the Sultan and his consort approached in a police launch and came aboard. I took them to the wardroom and invited them to make themselves at home. I got my steward and Scratcher to look after them and suggested they might like at times to come up on the bridge. It took about five hours to complete the sixty mile passage to Pulau Tioman and then a beautifully simple ceremony took place. A police launch came alongside, embarked the Sultan and consort, and took them close inshore to the beach – there being no harbour in Tioman. Watching through binoculars I saw eight men wearing songkoks wade out to the launch and carry the two in a yellow sedan chair on to the land. There a line of school children in their blue and white uniforms, with other islanders smartly dressed in their colourful best, greeted their Sultan Abu Bakar. We were invited ashore to join in the celebrations but as it was very much a Malay occasion I stayed aboard as did my Chinese and Indian crew members. I was blissfully happy to get out of my uniform and go for a swim in the beautiful turquoise waters surrounding the ship.

The next day everything was in reverse. Sultan and consort in yellow sedan chair, police launch out to Sri Johor and the five hour return trip from Tioman to the mainland. The Sultan was very

Sultan Abu Bakar of Pahang and his consort, being carried ashore from HMMS Sri Johor in a sedan chair

happy chatting to the crew who had enjoyed the ronggeng and other festivities the night before. On arrival at Pekan he quickly disembarked into the police launch and we immediately headed for home. George was there to meet us and he congratulated us all on our successful missions. The RMN had received a very complimentary message of thanks from the sultan and there had been good reports by Ralph Modder in both Malay and English language newspapers. I was back in time to accompany Bill to Changi Airport the next day. He was returning to the UK and I was very grateful for all the assistance he had given me during my early days in Malaya. Unfortunately, I have not met up with him again.

It was not long before we went up the east coast again and as we now knew, it was completely different from the west. For six months of the year the shoreline was pounded by the NE monsoon stirring up the South China Sea. This pounding produced the most beautiful beaches including the so-called "Beach of Passionate Love" near Kuantan which was one of the many we visited and where we put landing parties ashore. The harbours were few and small (mainly used for fishing), as all the rubber and tin, the country's main industries, were exported from the harbours we had visited in the Malacca Straits. The population was sparse, but mainly Malay. The few policemen around, in addition to their normal work, performed the duty of registrar of births, deaths and marriages, provided first-aid and doubled up as wireless operators. It was through them that we arranged our landing party practices. We didn't want to upset the locals, yet at the same time we wanted to be seen by them as an aid to the civilian population in case of any emergency. There was always at least one stoker and an electrician in the party so that they could be of help in restoring any power or machinery problems. One night a police corporal took us in his Landrover to a beach to witness turtles coming ashore, slowly crawling up the sand, laying their eggs, and then departing back into the sea again. To me the eggs were not very exciting – a bit like eating white squash balls and very salty!

After that very agreeable change of scenery up the east coast we returned to our usual patrol area in the west and a weekend in Port Swettenham. On the Saturday I wanted to arrange a couple of things I had been contemplating for a while. Firstly, to the harbourmaster to ask him if there were any small ships or barges in the area on which we could practice off-loading our boarding party. The other was to ask the manager of the Missions to Seamen if he could borrow or temporarily acquire, on our behalf, any swings or roundabouts etc so that we could give a party or two for underprivileged children. Both these requests were to be favourably acted upon when we returned in about two weeks' time.

After lunch on the Sunday the coxswain told me that the Tunku was over there on the pier. I quickly put on my uniform and went ashore and approached Tunku Abdul Rahman, the first Prime Minister of Malaya. I saluted him and said: "I am Captain of one of your warships, Sir, would you like to come on board?" He accepted the invitation with alacrity. He was going fishing, a thing he did on occasions when his ministerial duties allowed. He seemed in no hurry, wanted to chat with some of the crew, and when asked if he would like a drink replied: "brandy ginger ale, please." But he also asked for a fresh orange juice to be well visible in case of any prying eyes! All very informal and I had the good luck to meet him in similar circumstances three or four times. He even called me Mike on the last occasion.

The Tunku was the seventh child of the Sultan of Kedah and had been to England several times before the war. He joined the civil service in Kedah and became a District Officer – a position he

Tunku Abdul Rahman

held throughout the Japanese occupation. After the war he went back to England and then to Cambridge University where he qualified as an advocate and solicitor. He then worked for the state legal advisor in KL, but found the work routine and dull. He then entered politics and by 1951 was unanimously voted President of the United Malay National Organisation (UMNO), and at his inaugural speech demanded that independence should be granted as soon as possible. By sheer hard work and with his charming personality, he was able to unite the other parties, particularly the Malayan Chinese Association and the Malayan Indian Congress, into the Alliance Party. He became Chief Minister in 1955 and Malaya became independent in 1957. He was actually more fluent in English than he was in Malay. He possessed charisma and a tremendous sense of humour with an infectious laugh. It was indeed an honour to have met him and to have entertained him a few times.

Final of the Singapore Cup 1959 Combined Services v Civilians played on the Padang amongst the palm trees and heat of the Equator

The rugby season was the same as in the UK, but it was much harder work playing near the equator, games were often confined to thirty minutes each way, and kick-off was as late as possible in the afternoon – sunset always being between 1800 and 1830. When the ship's programme allowed I played for the Naval Base side. George organised everything around the Navy's fixture list. I think he had been persuaded by the selector, a certain Captain Southwood DSC! During the rugby seasons I spent in Malaya I played not only against the Army and RAF but also for Combined Services Singapore. I remember a Maori Stoker in the New Zealand frigate Pukaki. His name was Henry Houia and he was an ace at scrum half. His ship arrived in Singapore the day before the Army game and he had gone ashore to sample the bright lights, got sozzled and ended up in Detention Quarters. His own ship couldn't sort things out so I as captain of the Navy side, was sent along to persuade the officer-in-charge of the DQ's to release him. He agreed for the duration of the game only and provided he was returned immediately afterwards. These kiwis, even when they're only half sober, can still play a blinder! For Combined Services we reached the final of the Malayan Rugby Union Cup and played against Perak at the Merdeka Stadium, Kuala Lumpur. This was the national football stadium and the game was played under floodlights; a very unusual thing to play rugby under the lights in those days and it was certainly a great experience. The Pipes and Drums of the 5th Battalion the Royal Malay Regiment played before, at half time, and after the match, and the Deputy Prime Minister Tun Abdul Razak presented us with the cup!

The week before Christmas we were in the Port Swettenham area. The harbourmaster had arranged it for us and we were able to practice putting our boarding parties on a few different sized barges. They used the rigid inflatable dinghy and if the vessel being boarded was a bit high out of the water, they had a Jacob's ladder which could be hooked on to a guardrail or similar piece of metal. All the crew had at least one go, except the Coxswain and myself – we manned the Bren gun on the bridge in case of opposition from those boarded. On the last afternoon we gave our first children's party. The manager of the Missions to Seamen had

SELANGOR RUGBY UNION
PROMOTING ON BEHALF OF
The Malayan Rugby Union

RUGBY FOOTBALL
H.M.S. MALAYA CUP FINAL

SINGAPORE COMBINED SERVICES
VS.

PERAK

at

The Stadium Merdeka, Kuala Lumpur

on

Saturday, 16th January, 1960

Kick Off 5.10 p.m.

THE H.M.S. MALAYA CUP
TO BE
Presented to the Winners by
THE HON. TUN ABDUL RAZAK BIN DATO HUSSAIN, D.M.N.
Acting Prime Minister
of
Federation of Malaya

The Pipes and Drums of the
5th Battalion The Royal Malay Regiment
will be in attendance
by kind permission of Lt.-Col. Mohamed Noor.

Final of the Malayan Cup 1960

113

acquired some swings and roundabouts which were transported down to the jetty alongside us. The manager certainly turned up trumps in organising also sweets and refreshments and for the children to come down in groups of twenty at periodic intervals. I thanked him for his able assistance and reimbursed him out of as yet a non-existent fund. We agreed the operation should be repeated again soon.

Undoubtedly for most of the crew Malacca was the favourite run ashore, and so we called in there on the way back. I asked Mary on board for a Chinese meal prepared early by the chef – so that he could get ashore to join his mates. We had the gear for keeping the five course meal hot: we could then take a long time over eating it, as is the Chinese custom. I learnt about her life as a planter's wife up north in Perak, and the terrible times they had been through during the Emergency. She had been born and brought up in Malacca and that's why she had returned to live there amongst her childhood friends. They hadn't approved of her marrying a European and that's the reason she shouldn't ask me to her house. The first time she had been on board she was wearing what I call the typical Chinese pyjama suit. This evening she was wearing a long-slitted dress and as the meal progressed it became more and more obvious that it was the only item of clothing she had on. I moved over beside her and asked if she was ready for her Christmas present. With a yes-look in her eyes she said she had one for me as well and would like to give it to me before going home.

In the New Year I was going on a nine day rugby tour with the Singapore Combined Services to Hong Kong. It had all been arranged behind my back, George having agreed for me to be absent for that period of time. I suppose it looked good for the Navy to have one representative in the side. Firstly though the small matter of Christmas which was to be my second in Malaya and with Korea my third away from the UK. I was asked by several kind families to join them in the evening. I cannot recall who drew the long straw, or was it the short one? Anyway, the one thing that very much comes to mind was the fact that we sat down to the traditional meal of turkey, roast potatoes, sprouts, Christmas pud with liberal quantities of brandy butter, port liqueurs and Tiger beer, plus of course crackers, funny hats and corny jokes. All this in the heat and high humidity of Singapore!

Two days later we took off Per Ardua ad Astra (the RAF motto) for Hong Kong. Within a short while, a few miles to the east of Kuantan, and below us, we could see through the crystal clear water, the wrecks of HMS Prince of Wales and HMS Repulse. They had been despatched, without any air cover, on 10th December 1941 to ward off any possible sea attack on Malaya by Japanese warships. They were spotted and eventually attacked by waves of Japanese aircraft carrying bombs and torpedoes. Sitting targets, which sank with the loss of 850 men. The battleships still lie there in 30 fathoms – protected as a war grave. Another 500 miles and we landed at Saigon, the capital of South Vietnam, presumably to refuel. We were at a USAF base and were allowed into the PX shop for a quick refreshment and shop around. Back on board the plane, and 800 miles further on we landed at RAF Kai Tak in the New Territories. My home for the week was the extremely comfortable RAF Officers' Mess and it was great to be back in Hong Kong again after eight years.

Being the only Navy member of the side and not having much in common with the rest of the team, other than rugby, I told the team manager that I would naturally be there for all the training sessions, the matches themselves and the after match entertainment. Otherwise I would be off to meet up with any naval mates ashore, or in the ships in harbour. The first match was a Far East Air Force one on 30th December so I did not play: I did in the last two on January 2nd and 4th against a Hong Kong Selection and finally against the whole of Hong Kong. We won both these games which were played under floodlights at the National Football Stadium in Happy Valley. On January 3rd the English language newspaper reported: "With Hong Kong leading 11-6 just before half time their hopes were short-lived as Ranguia (one of our Maoris) broke down the centre and booted the ball up to the Hong Kong line. Reeder following up eluded Brown and scored near the posts." And all this less than two days after Hogmanay!

It was good to be back home again at Woodlands, even if only for one day's respite before more patrols and training in the Malacca Straits. There was a lighthouse a few miles out in the open sea from Port Swettenham which we visited every now and then. The keepers, predominately Chinese, used to do monthly shifts, and they had thriving little businesses going. Instead of just keeping their domain spotlessly clean and in good working order and passing the time of day reading or gambling, they would fish and then dry their catch in the hot tropical sun. These fish they would box up and take ashore to sell when the relief boat arrived. Also they would do timber carvings or construct models from rubbishy wood which floated onto the rocks on which the lighthouse stood. A thriving industry. My suggestion of similar activity by British keepers when I returned to the UK was met with a cool reception!

At the barracks, pleasant evenings used to be spent just hopping in the car and driving the short distance across the causeway to the market in Johor Bahru. There we would have deliciously tasteful satay washed down with a bottle of Tiger or Anchor beer. If we wanted a more luxurious evening out, it was always Singapore where the choice of different ethnic restaurants was out of this world. One evening we went for a Nasi Goreng in an Indonesian club and there in a corner were three or four guys singing round the piano: "Won't you come home Bill Bailey, won't you come home?" We knew the words and went along to join them. The pianist stopped playing and introduced himself as The Bill Bailey about whom the song was written. At our incredulous looks he went on to explain that he was a remittance man, he was the black sheep of the family, who obviously intended to loaf around at home without actually getting any work. His parents had paid for his transportation to the Far East and remitted an allowance for him. It's amazing whom you meet on a quiet run ashore!

Every now and then, when they had a few days off, the Europeans as well as Malayans used to enjoy the cooler and less humid atmosphere of Frasers Hill or the Cameron Highlands. They were two to three hundred miles north of Singapore –

Frasers being the closer – and they both had Government Rest Houses which were available to us at a fantastically reasonable price. On one occasion Harry Lee Kuan Yew, the Prime Minister of Singapore, was there having breakfast on his own. I apologised for interrupting and introduced myself. He was very welcoming and we chatted a little. Then he had to dash off to meet someone and suggested we meet up again later in the day. The pleasure of listening to such an intelligent and successful man was a great experience. During the war and the Japanese occupation of Singapore he had operated a black market business selling tapioca based glue. His knowledge of the Japanese language was so good he interpreted Allied war reports for them and acted as English language editor for the Japanese Propaganda Department.

After the war he briefly attended the London School of Economics before moving to Cambridge University where he studied law and graduated with double starred First Class Honours. He returned to Singapore in 1949 to practice as a

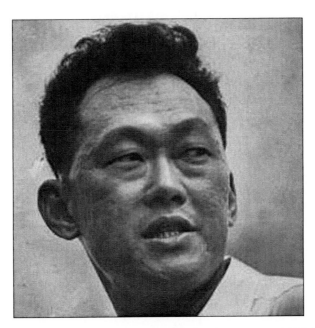

"Harry" Lee Kuan Yew Prime Minister of Singapore 1990-2004

lawyer and within four years was also legal advisor to both the Trade and Student Unions. In 1954 he formed the socialist People's Action Party and he became their Secretary General. Another five years and here he was the first Prime Minister of Singapore. I knew most of this before our meeting and at no time were politics or politicians mentioned. After all I was only a simple sailor, he was on holiday and his shrewd brain had worked that one out.

Apart from Malaya and Singapore, in that area of south east Asia there were other members of the British Commonwealth also going through their independence procedures. I refer particularly to the large island of Borneo which was mostly Indonesian but also included Sarawak, Brunei and British North Borneo. The politicians in the Commonwealth and Foreign Offices made life very difficult and complicated, but the idea was for these three territories to join up in a sort of Malayan Union. It was around this time that the RMN decided to do a cruise to these places.

In August the squadron of HMMS Mahamiru (Lieutenant Commander Mike Roden), HMMS Sri Perlis (Lieutenant Commander Nobby Mant) and HMMS Sri Johor (me the junior boy and therefore tail end Charlie!) left Ruthenia Jetty on their maiden foreign cruise not only to Borneo but also the Philippines.

Labuan in North Borneo was our first port of call. We stopped there for one day merely to fuel up on our way to the Philippines. There was time for a stroll ashore in the afternoon and some of us visited the Labuan War Cemetery. It had been established in 1945 and in it lie those who died while prisoners of war in northern Borneo during WW2 and those who paid the supreme sacrifice in the liberation of British territories there. It was beautifully maintained by the Imperial War Graves Commission who are in charge of all our war cemeteries throughout the world. On our way out we signed the visitors' book. That evening a Mr L C Jordan stopped by the ships and got into conversation with Nobby and me. He told us he was a member of parliament for New South Wales and was on some sort of fact finding mission for the Australian government. He was very interested to hear about the RMN and we had a thoroughly good evening, which ended in him taking us out to dinner at the Labuan Rest House where he was staying. I still have his address in West Ryde, Sydney but unfortunately time takes its toll.

It took us three days of very rough weather to get to Manila. Nobby told me that during one of our rolls he saw the whole of our ship's hull. It was good to arrive in the protection of the island of Corregidor and enter harbour at 0900 with a recording of the Royal Marine Band playing "Colonel Bogey", "Sons of the Sea" and "Hearts of Oak", etc. Unbeknown to the other two ships I had taken on board my rather large, as they were in those days, tape recorder purchased in Change Alley. The electrician had wired it up to the tannoy system on the ship's mainmast and I made sure he did not play "Rule Britannia"! That year the Philippine Navy was celebrating its 21st anniversary. Their uniform was similar to the US Navy and as ropes were passed you almost heard them say: "look at those goddamn Limeys in Brit uniform," whilst our crews were saying: "look at those Yanks." Guess who won the smartness trophy!

We had a thoroughly successful three days in Manila and certain things stayed in my memory. On the second day the Philippine Commodore Jose Francisco gave an incredible stag luncheon which seemed to go on all day. In the events we were entertained in the local restaurants by some of their naval officers. We were all in civvies and they had shoulder holsters with loaded revolvers at the ready. We were discouraged from walking alone day or night. That's life in Manila. The last binding memory was the island of Corregidor which we had passed on our way in, and which covers the entrance to Manila, the finest natural harbour in the Far East. In 1942 US General MacArthur for six months held onto this tiny island bastion, while surrounded by the Japanese invading armies, thus denying them the use of the harbour.

With the recording of the Royal Marine Band being played once again, we departed Manila. The weather we knew was going to be bad for our return trip to Borneo. Sure enough, the seas were strong on the beam and my crew were very sea sick. During the second night the coxswain and I were the only two fit and able; we took it in turns steering the ship with the one off watch keeping the other company. Nobby again saw our complete hull and I have a newspaper photo and report to prove it!

Jesselton, the capital of North Borneo and three days respite to allow the weather to subside, was a very welcome haven. Football, hockey and badminton matches were played against local sides. Trips of interest were arranged for our ships' companies and we in return opened our ships to visitors on two of the afternoons. The three captains were often occupied in official visits from district officers, heads of constabulary and the president of the municipal council and all these calls had to be returned. This being my first time in Borneo I found all these people very interesting to meet and it was intriguing to learn all about the way of life in this delightful country.

The most riveting call on board was that of His Excellency the Governor of British North Borneo, Sir William Goode. Born in 1907 he was one of the last real Colonial Officers and had spent most of his time east of Suez. He had been imprisoned by the Japanese and forced to work on the Death Railway in Thailand. After the war he had been Chief Secretary and Acting Governor of Aden, and Acting Governor of Singapore. Bill Goode had got to know about us because he had become the last Governor of Singapore in 1957 and as such was Commander-in-Chief of the RMN until he transferred control to the Malayan Government on 12th July 1958. Here he was showing great interest in his old navy as the local Governor in Jesselton. He was a most likeable man who had risen to the top everywhere he went and he invited us to lunch at Government House the following day.

Kuching, the capital of Sarawak, was our last visit of the cruise and virtually a carbon copy of the events at Jesselton. Sports fixtures with the locals, tours to places of interest including Radio Sarawak and ships open to visitors all preceded of course by the official cocktail party for fifty guests on the first evening in. At this party I met a District Officer who next day very kindly drove me out in his Landrover to the rainforest area and showed me the associated logging industry. The native people are mostly Iban and we saw some of their longhouses in which they lived. It was enchanting to see some of the Iban and Dayak ladies in their various attires ranging from sarongs to rattan corsets with brass rings and filigree adornments, sometimes topless. They would work at weaving and fishing.

His Excellency the Governor of Sarawak was as imposing as Bill Goode, but completely different. We hadn't even heard of him before, but he was Sir Alexander Waddell. Nick as he was locally known was a Scot who had been educated at Fettes, and had joined the Colonial Service in 1937. These men all had exhilarating lives – none of your stay at home dull existence of a nine to five office job in London or other big city. Nick's first appointment had been to the British Solomon Islands and he had a commission in the Royal Australian Navy Volunteer Reserve. Shortly after the Japanese invasion in 1942 he was put ashore by the US submarine Grampus on one of the Solomon Islands called Choiseul. He was to be a coast watcher and his job involved reporting shipping, rescuing American airmen and harassing the Japanese garrison of four thousand troops. He told us that he and the rescued airmen formed the "Ancient Order of the Rubber Rafters of Choiseul" dedicated to inebriation on the anniversary of each man's rescue.

Iban women in Sarawak

As soon as he found out I was born in the same country, even though on the west coast opposite that of his native Angus, he became even more forthcoming. After the war he was Resident Commissioner in the Solomon Islands before being posted to the Malay Civil Service in North Borneo. Then to Africa, first as Colonial Secretary in the Gambia and, secondly, as Deputy Governor of Sierra Leone. He had helped greatly in the self-government of the west African colonies. A much travelled man, he had only left Africa a month before we arrived in Kuching, to be the last Governor in Sarawak. After the cocktail party and his official visit on board, it had been great to meet him again when we were invited to lunch at Astana, the Government House. Astana had been the palace of the White Rajah of Sarawak and that's another captivating colonial story in itself!

It had been a thoroughly successful cruise. Four young Malayan officers fresh back from their training in Britain had accompanied us, as had a reporter and photographer from the Malay language newspapers. Thus, the RMN had been introduced to the art of showing the flag, a very important part of the Navy's job in peacetime. We received good press, both in Borneo and at home, our crews had been convinced they had a worthwhile job to do and they had visited some far away foreign countries. All good stuff.

One thing beginning to rear its ugly head was Indonesian piracy. God knows (or was it Allah?!) where they came from, but they had very fast boats and inflatable dinghies, and we in our minesweeper were no competition. Sweepers by the very nature of their job do not have to be fast and Harold Wilson had once said in the House of Commons that, used as patrol vessels, they were the backbone of the Navy. All we could do was keep a good lookout and report their exploits to the police inspectors ashore. The Malayan Marine Police at that time did have a launch and the Chinese skipper did work well with us when we were on his patch around Port Swettenham. Lee was his name and he enjoyed coming on board for a Tiger beer, often giving me some intelligence information. I would keep him informed of any news of use to him.

Astana the government house in Kuching where
His Excellency entertained us to lunch

Talking about police, I had been sent a notice for speeding near Kluang in Johor. I showed it to Lee and within a week I received an official letter:- "With reference to your speeding offence I am not taking the matter up any further. Therefore ignore the notice served on you by me and treat the incident as warning." It was signed by B. Munusamy, Officer i/c Kluang Police District. It's not what you know, it's who you know that counts!

Our official visit to Borneo and the Philippines had been such a success that the powers that be in KL were in the throes of arranging another one. This time it would be to Thailand and Burma. Diplomatic clearance came through remarkably quickly and it was no time before we were off again with new charts and smartly pressed uniforms. There were only two ships this time the Mahamiru and Sri Johor.

The first night's stop for fuel was at Penang and most of the crews stayed on board to save money and strength for the foreign countries. I took a stroll ashore and on passing a restaurant two of the crew, one of whom was Scratcher, came and beckoned me in saying: "Sir, come in and meet Saloma". Before I knew what was going on I found myself sitting beside and being introduced to this attractive Malay girl who was obviously a celebrity. After a brief spell she went off up to the bandstand, was given the microphone and she sang a couple of Malay songs. She certainly had a melodious voice. We listened to other music, chatted a little, had a few eats and drinks and had a relaxed evening. The crew informed me that Saloma, who re-joined us frequently between her visits to the bandstand, would like to come on board some time. I said not this visit, because it would cause too much of a stir with Mahamiru in company and the press on board but maybe next time we were in Penang. I left them and returned to the ship to prepare for the morrow.

This cruise turned out to be equally successful, but completely different from the previous one. The same routines, but the contrasts were no visual signs of the Royal Thailand or Burmese Navies, and no-one spoke Malay. Some English was heard during the official calls, when the ships were open to visitors and on the sports field in Phuket – guess how the crews pronounced that word – which was our only stop in Thailand. Although not all that big, it is the largest island in the country and its industries are tin, mining and rubber. Lovely beaches and exotic seafood have since made the place into a tourist trap of international renown.

Continuing our way northwards up the Andaman Sea we reached the capital of Burma, Rangoon. The country was very poor. It had been war torn by the Japanese and had asked for independence, which was immediately granted by the Clement Attlee government in 1948. They had a small navy but the only visual sign was a liaison officer or two who very capably organised our visit. The main attraction was the fabulous Shwedagon Pagoda, built over two and a half centuries ago and which Rudyard Kipling described as a golden mystery and a beautiful winking wonder. The first night in we had hosted the usual cocktail party for about fifty guests. In return the next evening we were at a party where we were shuffled around and introduced to naval and military attaches and diplomats from many countries. Burma was neutral in its diplomacy and had no treaties or pacts aligning them to the east or west. One memory is of the Chinese Communist and American representatives there. The two countries did not, and would not, recognise each other, so they childishly kept as far apart as possible, namely at opposite corners of the room. The Americans were friendly to the Chinese Nationalists, whilst the rest of us mingled and chatted happily with anyone.

The three evenings we were there our liaison officers took us out to dinner. There were only a few reasonable places to eat, and the visible poverty of the country was there to behold. The black market was in full swing, to the extent that some of us were able to have a good time, do some shopping, pay for a few snacks and still come away from the place with more money than we had when we arrived. This was achieved by changing Malayan dollars for twice the normal amount of kyats at the local Missions to Seamen and then handing back what we had left through the RMN.

We called in at Alor Star for refuelling. Mahamiru went back to base the next day, whereas we went further up river to revisit our rubber plantation friends and play them a game of six-a-side football. It was very restful there as by now the communists had been virtually defeated. Eight thousand of them had been killed or captured and the few remaining had fled across the border into Thailand where their leader, Chin Peng, resided for the rest of his life. The Malayan Emergency was the only war the West won against communism and we in the RMN were all very proud of the part, small though it was, we played in it. Over one thousand Malayan troops and police were killed as were three thousand civilians. Also over five thousand British Commonwealth personnel were lost in the cause.

Penang was our next port and shortly after our arrival Scratcher reminded me of our recent visit. He said three or four of them were going to be at the same restaurant with Saloma and would I like to join up with them later? I said I would and thanked him very much. In the meantime I made a few enquiries as to who this Malay celebrity was. She had been a singing sensation since the age of thirteen and had more recently been the star in several Malay films. She was, in fact, the pioneer actress in her country – not easy in those days for a Muslim. I went ashore later on and there as expected she was with some of the lads. She spoke just enough English but with my miniscule of Malay and great help from my shipmates, we all had an entertaining and relaxed evening. She went up to the stage every now and then to sing some of her lovely Malay melodies. As the evening appeared to be coming to a close, I asked her if she would like to come on board Sri Johor. She said she would but could not do so until she had done one more song. It was "Once in a While", the only English one she knew and I had a feeling it was for my benefit. In the wardroom we had a nightcap or two. She said she was enjoying learning English through our conversations and that hopefully we would meet up again soon.

We had to be back in Singapore by the weekend as one of our stokers was getting married. There was time for a quick visit to Port Dickson before an overnight passage back to Woodlands. I wasn't able to appreciate what was going on at the wedding as it was all in the Malay language and in accordance with Muslim faith and tradition. Everyone was as helpful as they could be in explaining what was happening. I was the only European and non-Muslim at the ceremony, very honoured to be asked, and it was for me not only a first but a great experience.

Driving along to the Officers' Club one day I was sure I recognised someone walking on the side of the road. It was the new Flag Officer Second-in-Command Far East Fleet, my old shipmate from Londonderry days, Rear-Admiral Mike Le Fanu. He was in scruff order as he called the very relaxed kit he liked to wear when he was out of uniform. I hopped out of the car, said good afternoon and he recognised me all right, but couldn't remember my name. I re-introduced myself and we walked and talked for a good mile before returning to the car and saying farewell. The marvellous stories about this man followed him everywhere. On his recent arrival in Singapore he evidently introduced himself to the Prime Minister in the following way:- "You Lee Kwan Yew Prime Minister of Singapore. Me Lee Fan Yew British Admiral". He was for evermore known as the Chinese Admiral. He visited practically every ship in his fleet as soon as

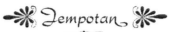

❊ Jemputan ❊

Dengan hormatnya dijemput tuan kerumah saya

21 Kim Keat Avenue, Singapura, 12

pada hari Ahad 5. July 1959

bersamaan dengan 29 Djul-Hijjah 1378

kerana hendak menyempurnakan Perkahwinan anakanda

Saya Abdullah bin H. Sujah dengan Hadah binte Idris

Atas kehadziran tuan dan puas terlebih dahulu
kami uchapkan ribuan terima kasih wassalam.

Jemputan lelaki dari 7.30 hingga 9.00 p.m

„ perempuan „ 7.30 P.M „ 9-00 p.m

Alhakirin

Haj. Sujah b. H. Abd.Rahman
Rokiah bt H. Yahaya
M. Noor bin Ismail

Wedding Invitation

Member of the ship's company getting married

127

possible after taking over his appointment. Stories abounded of his escapades such as dressing up as an able seaman and joining the queue as rum bosun and in another ship as a royal marine to collect his lunch at the galley. In the aircraft carrier Albion, on passage to Hong Kong, he liked to stroll up and down but he invited anyone to join him. These were his methods of getting to know his men and what made them tick. Very few of them had ever talked with an Admiral before. He was a real morale booster.

The usual places were visited on our last patrol before the festive season. In Penang Saloma was not working for the couple of days we were there. She took me on a trip around the island, telling me the names of all the beautiful flowers adorning the houses, such as blue jacarandas, scarlet poinsettias and frangipani. The Malays used the same names as the English. Then to her home for a delightful Malay lunch.

Afterwards, seeing how hot I was in the afternoon heat, she asked if I would like a shower. Handing me a towel, she led me into her bathroom and slipped off her sarong to reveal I think the most beautiful body I had ever seen. She had black hair and lovely olive skin; it wasn't long before we were beside each other in her fresh, cool bed. Later, I watched her put on a splendid Malay dress and we drove back to the ship where I had arranged a curry supper for her. She really looked stunning as I helped her aboard and I immediately arranged for a photo call. As far as I was concerned the photo of her taken in the bows established her as the best figurehead in any Navy! As we had supper she told me more about herself and her ambitions as an actress and being Malaya's number one songstress. She told me she was 25 and that her next birthday was in January. She added she would be in Kuala Lumpur on the day and I responded by assuring her the ship would be in Port Swettenham.

With the turn of the year it dawned on me that there were only three months before I was due to pay off Sri Johor into refit and complete my time in Malaya. So, on the first patrol of the year we went as far north as possible, a little past Alor Star, to an island called Langkawi. It was rumoured the RMN might construct a base in this beautiful but remote island. We anchored off a beach for what the RN called a banyan. There was no sign of life on this

Saloma, the best figurehead in any Navy!

particular part of the island which was situated on the Malaya-Thailand border. Then southwards to Lumut where it was almost certain the main RMN base would be once the Ministry of Defence could organise the closing down of Woodlands and Ruthenia Jetty, but that was still a long way off.

Near Lumut, which was on the mainland, was a lovely island called Pulau Pangkor. The whole area gave the appearance of being Shangri-la. There was no jetty: we ran our dinghy up on the beach and met the small population who seemed to be running a shop, a restaurant and a hotel. It seemed a pity that these two wonderful places might be spoilt with the construction of naval bases, but for better or for worse, it would bring security to this prosperous emerging nation.

A local Malay government official came down to see us and very early next morning drove me the thirty odd miles southwards to Telok Anson where the last serious communist resistance had ended in surrender. It was now six months since the government had stated the emergency was over. We drove a little further inland and then started walking into the jungle; there we caught a

Sakai with his seven-foot blowpipe and poison-tipped darts

glimpse of aboriginal Sakais before they disappeared barefooted with their seven feet long blowpipes (and poison tipped darts) to drug their prey. These people, who had acted as jungle guides and helped the Allies track down the Japanese during the occupation of Malaya, wore scanty loin cloths. The women were naked to the waist and wore only a sarong made of cloth or bark. Some had paint smeared on their faces and a matchstick thrust through the piece of flesh below and between the nostrils. All were smoke-stained and unwashed.

We then came to a Sakai house ten feet off the ground. When the women saw the Malay official they did make a brief appearance but no way were they going to descend the ladder! Their staple diet was padi and tapioca augmented with fish they would have caught in a stream, or the meat of an animal – probably a monkey

Sakai House and Sakai women dressed in sarongs

which they sometimes dry in the sun until it is bone hard. What a very interesting day that was, and extremely kind of the Malay official to let me accompany him on his rounds.

At Port Swettenham we stayed in harbour for several days in order to celebrate the New Year with another long awaited for children's party and an opportunity for the ship to be open to visitors. Also I went up to Kuala Lumpur for a couple of nights primarily to visit the Ministry of Defence and meet for the first and last time the Defence Minister. The Tunku had suggested I do this.

Abdul Razak had been Defence Minister at the taking over ceremony of the RMN in July 1958. He, like most Malays, was charmingly polite. He had joined the Malay Administrative Service in 1939 and had organised a resistance movement against the Japanese in his native Pahang. After the war he went to England to study law and by 1950 had received his degree and qualified as a barrister at Lincoln's Inn. He appeared very interested to hear of my experiences in the RMN and asked my views on future bases; I told him we expected to return to Lumut

Sakai shinning up a pole after his prey – probably a monkey!

to do some surveying. He remembered in conversation that we had been to the possible future bases in Borneo – and that we had actually met before when he presented the cup to the Malayan Rugby Union Champions! He gave the impression that he shared my opinion that the Royal Navy Commodores had passed their sell by date. I'm sure he was the instigator of the Royal Australian Navy's lending Bill Dovers to be the next Commodore of the RMN. Bill was probably the finest naval officer and seaman the

RAN ever had, and he was an inspired choice for the job. I thanked Abdul Razak for his time and said goodbye to someone who was obviously destined to be a future Prime Minister of Malaya. He became so in 1970 but sadly died from leukaemia six years later.

Because I had travelled up to Kuala Lumpur by train, the MOD had booked me in for two nights at the Railway Station Hotel, an interesting place with an attractive Islamic exterior, but inside it resembled a typical Victorian English building. I had arranged for Saloma to meet me in the coffee bar there at seven o'clock, as tomorrow was her birthday. It was just as well she came up to me as I don't think I would have recognised her. She had a huge beehive shaped wig on and her face was extremely ashen. She looked terrible, poor girl, and seeing she couldn't even enjoy some fresh fruit juice, I took her up to the room and gently put her to bed. Next morning as I was getting ready she seemed in no hurry to do anything but rest. She wanted to stay in bed; I told her I would only be a couple of hours and, putting a do not

Government buildings, Kuala Lumpur

disturb notice on the door, I returned to the Ministry of Defence.

I had to check with a couple of departments the procedure for my return to the UK. The government would pay the air fare from Singapore to London but if I wanted to travel by any other route or means then it was up to me to make my own arrangements and pay any excess due. As I hadn't had any seasonal leave during my time in Malaya I would be entitled to about eighteen weeks leave when I got home. They would be paying me for the full three years and all monies due would be paid in Malayan dollars before I left the country. It was a lovely surprise, when I returned to the hotel, to find Saloma still in bed, but looking much, much better. She had had a shower and the sun was shining on her olive brown skin to great advantage. She apologised for feeling so awful the previous day, said she didn't want to go out at all and her best birthday present would be to spend our last twenty four hours together simply enjoying each other's company.

Travelling in the train back to Port Swettenham, I know not why but I spared a thought for those poor submariners in their boats off Rothesay in the Isle of Bute! The two Chinese in the Station Bar were surprised to see my unusual means of travel but nevertheless produced my usual lunch of Tiger beer and Mee Hoon soup, plus a couple of rolls. This time on our return to base we called in at Shell Island in Singapore harbour. It was the Shell Company's main depot there and as they had done on one previous visit, the employees made us very welcome. They had a very spacious club and they challenged us to games of darts, snooker and ping pong, etc. or we relaxed at their swimming pool.

I started the ball rolling with one of the travel agents. I would have been bored out of my tiny mind with eighteen weeks leave, so I had decided to take a slow boat back and asked them for suggestions. It was Chinese New Year and I was invited to a very fine dinner dance in the Chief and Petty Officers' Mess. Every meal or party now seemed to be a farewell occasion and I was beginning to feel a bit sad. I did realise, however, that I must get home and rejoin my own Navy. As I had said to Abdul Razak, we did return to Lumut for a couple of days surveying of the area. With the aid of the ship's echo sounder and a lead-and-line from

My farewell dinner for Sri Johor's ship's company.
Pulau Pangkor restaurant, 1961

the dinghy in the less accessible areas, we were able to produce some worthwhile results. Actually we made it last three days and on the last evening I was able to invite the crew to a meal in the quiet little local restaurant.

Patrols during these last few months had revealed more Indonesian activity especially in the Malacca Straits. Warships similar to ours were occasionally seen in the distance. I would log them down and give the details to George when I got back. Also the intermittent sightings of speedy pirates continued to be noted and reported to the police. From our point of view it was all rather crazy as the Indonesian ships used to refit alongside ours in Singapore civilian dockyards and the crews speaking similar languages were friendly with each other – all sons of the sea. Politically the union of Malaya and Singapore with North Borneo and Sarawak into one country known as Malaysia was due to happen in 1963 and Indonesia was opposed to this. In 1962, only a year from now, they began armed military aggression, which became known as the Confrontation.

*Some of the wives and girlfriends at the farewell party
I gave in Johor Bahru, May 1961*

*The Officers' Club, Singapore Naval Base, where I enjoyed
my first and last runs ashore – plus many in between*

It was now the month of May and on our last patrol we paid a final visit to Malacca. Mary came down for a meal and was very kind. She said her opinion of Scotsmen had improved since parting from her husband and meeting me. She said she had enjoyed our fleeting visits and gave me an extremely pleasurable present before disappearing into the distance. Flying our paying-off pennant we made our final return through the British Naval Base to Ruthenia Jetty where Sri Johor was due to start her refit in a fortnight's time; but I had only eight days in which to do my leaving routine.

Two evenings later I asked every sailor, totalling thirty two, who had served with me in Sri Perak and Sri Johor, plus their wives and girlfriends, to a meal in a Malay restaurant over the causeway in Johor. It wasn't very expensive as Malays didn't drink alcohol when at home near their women and hajis. They made up for it when away in their ships! I don't think any of the women spoke other than very quietly amongst themselves. They all joined in the Ronggeng whilst I was very happy to chat with and listen to the lads.

My last full day in that wonderful country duly arrived. I visited the Commodore's Office and met for the first time the Great Bill Dovers who had arrived up from Australia. What a breath of fresh air he was. Commodore Luard had left a couple of weeks earlier and before leaving on our last patrol he had handed me a brown envelope, thanked me for all I had done for the RMN and bade me farewell. By lunchtime I had been paid, sold my car, handed over the flat, said goodbye to the Amah, paid all my bills and received all the necessary documentation including my ticket from the travel agent. Then a couple of Tiger beers and a prawn curry with some chums before having a monumental siesta.

Freshly rested and dressed in tuxedo, I arrived on board Sri Johor for the farewell party given by the two ship's companies. The coxswain had organised the whole upper deck to be orientally decorated and all my Malayan shipmates were assembled, some of them in their very smart Malay dress. "Would you like to go down to the wardroom for a few minutes, sir, as we want to arrange something for you?" Down I went and there, well and truly encamped, was the greatest possible surprise. Sitting there on her own, looking radiant, was none other than Saloma. I thought this was supposed to be a stag party. I took her back up on deck and the party commenced. There was canned music, eats, including my favourite satay, and plenty of the local Tiger and Anchor beer, as well as non-alcoholic drinks. Many of the boys had not met Saloma before and they were only too anxious to meet Malaya's top actress and songstress. I made tentative enquiries as to why and how her appearance at my farewell stag party had been arranged. They were not very forthcoming and merely said: "Farewell surprise for you, sir." As soon as a microphone was rigged up and, to the accompaniment of a squeeze box and a couple of stringed instruments, she sang some of her Malay songs. The boys all loved that and gave her every encouragement to sing several times. Towards the end the coxswain gave a farewell speech which was far too flattering and presented me with a Malay Kris, which I still treasure to this day. Then Saloma sang Malaya's number one pop song, which was to become their national anthem "Negaruku", which I am told means "My Country". Finally, she sang "I'm in the Mood for Love". The cheek of it: the last time I'd met her she only had one English song in her vocabulary, now she had rehearsed and become fluent at another! The party was over and I shook everyone by the hand as they left and thanked them for their friendship, support and loyalty.

Saloma had disappeared down to the wardroom for our final night together. The first time in Kuala Lumpur we thought it might be and this time we knew it was. The next morning she told me she was going to marry P. Ramlee. He was Malaya's top actor, director, songwriter, singer, composer and producer – everything in the entertainment world. She was not going to marry him until he had divorced his second wife, who was a member of the Perak royal family. I congratulated her on the good news and thanked her for delaying the announcement until now, thereby not spoiling our final meeting. She gave me a Salangor pewter beer mug with an engraving of a bullock cart and driver passing some palms. It

Selangor pewter mug and kris. Farewell gifts from Malaya

was a lovely reminder of the times in Malaya. Saloma, whose real name was Salmah Ismail, died at the young age of forty eight, and later in honour of her contributions to the Malaysian entertainments industry, they opened in Kuala Lumpur's Golden Triangle, the Saloma Bistro and Theatre Restaurant.

That afternoon, I embarked on the M.S. Falstria, a Danish cargo-passenger ship of the East Asiatic Company. I had chosen this method of travel because I did not particularly like flying and anyway I had plenty of spare time with all that accumulated leave. It was going to take five weeks to get from Singapore to London and was due to call at several interesting places on the way. There were about sixty passengers aboard. There were cargo-passenger ships which took only twelve passengers but I reckoned that was too few, especially if two or three were not on the same wavelength. Whereas with sixty hopefully you do find some kindred spirits. All my belongings were with me when we sailed at 1700 and in my last minute bag were three things: the Malay Kris from all my crews, the pewter beer mug given to me by Saloma and the brown envelope from the RMN. I had already quoted part of my flimsy to my Coxswain but as I sipped a cool lager I took it all in again:-

"Lieutenant M.J. Reeder has conducted himself to my entire satisfaction. A competent and enthusiastic young Commanding Officer, first of an SDML and then of an IMS. His ships have always been amongst the best in the Squadron. An officer of considerable promise."

Medals

PINGAT JASA MALAYSIA

THIS MEDAL IS AWARDED TO THE PEACEKEEPING GROUPS AMONGST THE COMMUNION COUNTRIES FOR DISTINGUISHED CHIVALRY, GALLANTRY, SACRIFICE OR LOYALTY IN UPHOLDING PENINSULAR OF MALAYA SOVEREIGNTY DURING THE PERIOD OF EMERGENCY AND CONFRONTATION.

CRUISES TO COLOMBO, CAIRO, THE CANARIES AND THE CARIBBEAN

"You are not in the British Navy. You are in the Royal Navy and should be extremely proud of the fact it is the best Navy in the world and the only one which does not name its nationality". This minor reprimand was administered by Captain Larsen, the Master of the Danish cargo passenger ship, to whom I was trying to explain the reason for my being with him en route from Singapore to London. I was aged 28 and homeward bound after completing my second commission as captain of a warship.

The East Asiatic Company obviously knew I was a government official and so at 1930 I had taken up what was to be my usual seat at the Captain's Table. All other meals were completely informal and were taken at any table during normal restaurant hours. Captain Larsen was much older than me and a very experienced seaman. He was big and had huge hands – every finger a marline spike. But most important of all he had a marvellous sense of humour and was a true sailor. He frequently asked me up to the bridge and we formed a worthwhile nautical debating society.

The Indian Ocean was flat, calm and azure, and everyone seemed to be enjoying having nothing to do. There were the usual deck games, which could be played all day long. Also table tennis and badminton in a couple of areas which the crew had screened off from the breeze. If the outside sun and fresh air became too much then there were dominoes, chess, Monopoly and card games available in the lounge. There was always the swimming pool, certainly the ten or so children seemed to spend most of their time there. One could just read or relax. Watching the sea pass by was a favourite pastime of mine. The great danger was to over indulge the bar products and the fantastic Smorgasbord served at lunchtime. My one set routine was a drink in the bar at about

M.S. Falstria "slow boat" Singapore to London

1900 and then sit down for dinner and await the arrival of other guests plus Captain Larsen. Who suggested if you've time to spare go by air?!

It seemed no time before we were mooring up in Colombo. We would be there for one night and two days and as I hadn't been to Ceylon before I joined up with the organised bus tour and visited Buddhist and Hindu temples, a Muslim mosque, the zoo and probably the place of most interest, the National Museum. Captain Larsen hadn't recommended anything of great interest in the place so I returned on board early. Not to forget a quick visit to the nearby bazaar the next morning before sailing at lunchtime.

Every other evening after dinner the officers arranged extra entertainment in the form of horse racing, quizzes, bingo and even dancing. Occasionally, sitting at our table was Nina, the attractive wife of a Danish diplomat who was still in Bangkok. I hadn't really been aware of her, as she seemed to spend most of the time with her two kids, as well as having most meals with them. After Colombo she seemed to be having more evening meals at the Captain's Table and Captain Larsen said he thought she had a soft spot for me and added jokingly that life could get dangerous, she had a maid with her to look after the kids in a separate cabin! Three nights out of Ceylon a dance was arranged by the ship's officers. Nina and I enjoyed dancing together and when the party finished she asked me to her cabin for a drink. I suggested she come to mine but could she give me ten minutes or so to have a shower and cool off? She agreed as she wanted to do the same. Within three minutes she was standing beside me saving water! We found we were very compatible and well suited. After getting dried, we had a drink or two and later as the sun's rays began to come through the porthole, I was aware of her creeping away to return to her cabin.

Nina appeared at our table the next evening in a new frock looking more resplendent than ever. The dinner as always was first class and the conversation was lighthearted and cheerful and, as occasionally happened, we tried a few liqueurs. Most people got up to leave early and as Captain Larsen said goodnight to us, there was a twinkle in his eye. He knew something was afoot. After our shower I asked her about her husband. She told me he had to stay on in Bangkok for a week or so and was then going on a golfing holiday. He would however be in Copenhagen to meet them when they got back. She enjoyed being with, and looking after, the two kids during the daytime but could she please be with me the rest of the time as we seemed to get on so well.

A fabulous tour was arranged when we arrived at Port Suez. Whilst Falstria was transitting the canal those in a bus were taken to the great pyramids at Giza and then the great Sphinx nearby. While having a ride on a camel, I remembered my earlier rugby days and being introduced to the bawdy version of the Eton boating song:-

The sexual urge of the camel is greater than anyone thinks
Rumour has it at Oxford it has gone and b------d the Sphinx
Now the Sphinx's anal passage is twice the size of the Nile
Which accounts for the hump on the camel and the Sphinx's inscrutable smile.

Camel

A reasonable lunch in the desert preceded a visit to the Mohammed Ali Mosque in Cairo and the number one tourist attraction – the Tomb of Tutankhamen, the Boy Pharaoh. The tomb and its treasures remained undiscovered for four thousand years. The day was certainly the most interesting and fascinating tour I've been on. Re-joining Falstria in Port Said in time for our departure and dinner, it was interesting to hear of everyone's experiences. Some had gone to different places, at different times, by different means of transport. One person who happened to be of the Jewish faith, was the only one to stay on board for the passage through the Canal. He was too scared to step ashore in Egypt.

Our next port of call was Genoa, the largest in Italy. It was a vast place with oil refineries, steelworks and massive shipyards. It formed an industrial triangle with Turin and Milan, but of more interest to the sailor, it was the birthplace of Christopher Columbus. It was to be our last stop before England and so I took a stroll along the foreshore. But that was enough, as I don't particularly like large towns, cities or harbours – especially industrial ones. The weather was getting a bit cooler and we settled down for the last week cruising. Probably a late breakfast, then a couple of hours with Captain Larsen on the bridge followed by Smorgasbord lunch. In the afternoon some reading or preferably siesta (I knew Nina would be having one with or without the kids). A game of ping pong or deck quoits would be expected of you after tea.

The dinners were always first class, three courses eaten slowly and Captain Larsen dispensed the wine. Then he would suggest the occasional liqueur with coffee whilst the other ships' officers set up the evening's entertainment which was always fun, if a bit crazy. Everything was usually finished by about eleven when the lights would be dimmed and the restaurant closed down for the night. Our last night arrived all too soon and as Nina and I said goodbye in the morning she told me it was her thirty second birthday and that the family weren't flying home to Denmark till the next day. Would I like to have a meal with her in the evening and she gave me details of the London hotel where she would be. Poor girl, she had been frightened to ask me until the last minute because she thought I would say no. The look in her eyes when I told her I would be there at eight o'clock was out of this world.

I had had very little sleep so had a late brunch and joined Captain Larsen on his bridge for the final few miles up the Thames estuary. He told me we had to be alongside at Tilbury by 1500 otherwise they wouldn't accept us until the next day. We arrived half an hour early, the stevedores, dressed up in lounge suits, picked up our ropes with their gloved hands and very carefully placed them over the bollards before shoving off home. We were back home from Malaya where we had won the only war fought against communism! When I arrived at the hotel for my promised evening meal, there on a table for me from Nina with love, was a golden bottle of Akvavit, the traditional Danish snaps. As the night progressed this exceptionally beautiful Dane gave the impression she was determined for it to be her best birthday ever. We had grown very fond of each other. But it was not to be because in another room were her two sleeping boys and there was a husband waiting for her in Copenhagen.

Later that morning I went to see the Appointments Officer in the Admiralty to find out my next job. He told me I was going to HMS Wizard as Cadet Training Officer in the Dartmouth Training Squadron. What a cracker, I thought. Not only have their Lordships trained me up to have command of two warships, but now I was getting another job at sea and it was to train young naval officers. They obviously thought more of me than my mother who gave me a severe reprimand when I arrived home next day, took a bottle of beer from the fridge and proceeded to drink it mid-afternoon in the garden! I was twenty nine years old but as far as she was concerned, home drinking hours were 1200-1400 and any time after 1800. She had asked me "what terrible habits had I picked up in Malaya"!

I joined the Wizard during the longish period between the summer and autumn cruises 1961. There were no young officers under training at the time but the ship was carrying out some extra tasks allotted such as escorting the Tall Ships Race, visits to Falmouth and Fowey, and taking sea cadets to sea during their summer holidays. The Navy had changed and also the entry system for young officers, since we were in Devonshire eleven years beforehand. Our only battleship, the Vanguard, as well as the Devonshire, and many other large men-of-war, had been scrapped and we were becoming a small ship Navy. The Wizard was a W Class destroyer built in 1944, which had been converted to a Type 15 Frigate in 1951. She had also been adapted for training purposes along with the other three or four similar frigates which constituted the D.T.S. (Dartmouth Training Squadron).

Everyone on board these frigates was to some extent involved in the training but in Wizard my specialist helpers were the Navigating Officer, Paul Payne, the schoolie Geoff Fosberry, plus the Chief GI, the Chief TASI and the Yeoman of Signals. The trainees would be cadets and midshipmen (known as M&C) who had probably been in the squadron a year earlier as cadets. In addition, there would be Royal Marine Young Officers, plus midshipmen from other Commonwealth and foreign navies. Both the midshipmen in their gunroom and the cadets in their mess deck would sleep in hammocks. In addition to these two areas, there were two extra compartments on deck for use as instructional spaces or classrooms. Each frigate could accommodate up to thirty cadets and thirty midshipmen, and the squadron for the first cruise consisted of the leader, Urchin with Captain Terry Lewin in command, us in Wizard, commanded by Commander David Farquharson, and Vigilant.

The M&C joined during the last week in September and we sailed a few days later for the autumn cruise. We would be at sea for nine days, during which time the cadets would settle down to mess deck life as able seamen – watchkeeping, cleaning ship and working the ship's sea routine. No scrubbing of decks as the navy no longer had wooden ones, but they very soon learnt the lower deck attitude of "if it moves salute it and, if it doesn't, paint it". The midshipmen would be understudying the OOW, learning practical navigation and spending some time in the engine room spaces. As often as possible they would be put in charge of cadets, particularly when exercising the sea boat. The boat would be lowered by midshipmen and coxswained by them, for transferring men or stores to the other frigates. Also for recovering a lifebuoy (practice man overboard) and then finally hoisting the boat back on board. After some rough weather in the Bay of Biscay, when quite few of the crew were seasick, we got into calmer seas off Portugal and Gibraltar before arriving at Las Palmas in Gran Canaria.

First night in the traditional wardroom cocktail party to which half a dozen midshipmen were invited. The cadets had already rigged the awning and flags on the quarterdeck and the duty watch of cadets served the drinks and small eats. The Canary Islands were advertised as being in the 70s all year round and so many swimming parties were arranged together with island tours, visits to the local brewery and sports fixtures. The Spanish hospitality was excellent and dances were arranged for the M&C who found the Spanish girls to be most attractive but the dominant influence of Madre y Padre would not allow them to stay out after

2230. Not nearly so discouraging were the Swedish women who swarmed along the Muelle Santa Catalina as soon as they saw the white ensign flying. They were all apparently married and had plenty of money to spend on having a good time, whilst their husbands were on separate golfing holidays. I don't think the Royal Navy let them down. I was still very much remembering a Danish wife whose husband went on a separate holiday.

The five days at Las Palmas were followed by four at sea cruising slowly around the different Canary Islands. Plenty of opportunity for the cadets to do anchor work after the midshipmen had navigated the ship to their pre-determined positions. Lowering and hoisting of sea boats so that every midshipman had the chance to prove his ability to give precise and correct orders. Then each evening there would be MOW manoeuvres which would be done by voice; also by flag with the mids acting as Yeomen of Signals hoisting and lowering the flags. A cool head was required as things moved fast. A great strain on everyone, especially the supervising officers, but also great fun and very instructive.

All this followed by four days alongside at Santa Cruz, in Tenerife. The Wardroom Cocktail Party, the bus tours, sports fixtures, swimming at beautifully clean beaches, all a carbon copy of the Las Palmas visit, even down to the Swedish wives swarming along the muelle! One afternoon on a run ashore I heard my name being called from above and I looked up to see waving from her hotel veranda Mrs Clark from the George Hotel in Inverary. She, with her husband George, were on holiday spending all the profits made from submariners. It was a good five years since I had seen them so we spent a very enjoyable couple of hours chatting and cutting down on their profit margin. The cruise had only started, so to speak, but you could sense that everyone was reasonably happy with the progress being made as we left Santa Cruz for Gibraltar.

We called in at Gibraltar primarily to pick up the band of the Somerset and Cornwall Light Infantry, who were accompanying us to Seville. Also joining us was a Gibraltarian called Frank Carreras who was a Major in the Gibraltar Regiment and whom I was to befriend over my next few visits to the Rock. Seville was to be the highlight of the cruise. The seventy mile trip up the River Guadalquivir was rather unimpressive, and anyway everyone was at classroom instruction. Things were to change after lunch when David Farquharson announced: "This is your Captain speaking. In an hour's time we will go aground!" He briefly explained the intentional grounding in mud that was going to help us turn 180 degrees in the narrow river. When a quarter of a mile from our jetty in Seville we put our bows into the mud on the port side of the river and let the incoming tidal stream swing the ship anti-clockwise and the stern upstream. When turned the half circle, we went astern into our berth, pointing down river all ready for our departure in five days' time.

Parties did not occupy all the shore-going time. Nearly everyone visited the great Santa Maria Cathedral which is believed to be the third largest in the world. It is also the burial site of Christopher Columbus, so in the space of a few months I have been to his birthplace, Genoa, and have seen his tomb in Seville. The visits to Jerez (from which the English word 'sherry' originates) and the bodegas of Harvey and Pedro Domecq's were very popular and oversubscribed – possibly due to some going on more than one visit!

HMS Wizard alongside in Seville

Seville proved to be the big sporting occasion of the cruise and as Sports Officer I had no trouble in organising rugger, soccer, hockey, basketball, athletics and even rowing against the locals. It was not pleasant playing rugger mid-afternoon on a very hot day in Seville, even though it was on the super Real Betis Spanish first division soccer ground. As winners we were presented with a small cup and, as captain of the team, I tried a few words of thanks in Spanish! Our band, that of the Somerset and Cornwall Light Infantry, did sterling work ashore with several public performances and of course Beat Retreat in the main city square at sunset on our last night. It was the first and last time I had seen a light infantry band march at their incredibly fast speed of so many steps per minute. It was very spectacular but it didn't seem normal to us simple sailors and it wasn't the same as the good old days of Devonshire with our own Royal Marine Band.

As far as the citizens of Seville were concerned the highlight of our visit was the children's party for fifty little girls from the San Luis Orphanage and fifty boys from the City Orphanage. This was arranged on the last afternoon and the M&C pulled out all the stops for a fine show. They were expertly dressed as one-eyed pirates, some with parrots as they operated swings and roundabouts and provided boat trips up and down the River Guadalquivir. There was an aerial ride from the bridge to the bow with strategically placed men to ensure the kids were safely delivered to their destination and rewarded with sweets. No problem leaving next day at high water with a nice ebb tide to help us on our way down river and on to Gibraltar where, from the ship's point of view, we were to be for ten days self-maintenance. For the trainees it still meant a lot of classroom work during the day and some activities in the evenings and at the weekend.

There were two night time expeditions when half the trainees landed on the Rock to attack the signal station, while the other half defended. Then next night vice versa. MFV trips to Ceuta, the Spanish Colony twelve miles south in Morocco were very popular and good for navigation, anchoring and boat handling practice. Tours around the Rock to review the military enclaves, tunnels and armament stores, etc. For recreation, sports fixtures were organised against those ashore in HMS Rooke, the local naval base. There were the inevitable visits to the night life across the border in La Linea and of course a bullfight to support the bull in his efforts against the matador!

Frank Carreras was a great friend to me. I had got to know him during the visit to Seville and on many of the runs ashore he had acted as interpreter and explained the history and workings. On the last Sunday in Gibraltar he took me across the border into Spain and we drove eastwards beside the Mediterranean. It was a fairly narrow seaside road and we stopped once for a beer and then for lunch at a tavern on the beach. The meal was simple but delicious; a good sized dorado straight from the sea and cooked in wine with herbs and onions. It cost next to nothing – I knew because I had paid, being determined to repay Frank's excellent hospitality whilst I was in Gibraltar. We continued along the attractive country road and when we had travelled about sixty miles from Gibraltar we came upon a place called Torremolinos. There were many notices indicating urbanisation. Frank explained to me that this was the beginning of the Costa del Concrete and that it won't be long before every inch of the journey we have covered today looks like Torremolinos and no more will we be able to drive out to these little tavernas. It will all be concrete seaside towns, villas and apartments joined up by an inland motorway.

That evening he took me shopping in the main street. Just like Change Alley in Singapore you were expected to bargain for everything, the only difference being the traders were mostly Indian as opposed to the Chinese in Singapore. It was the last opportunity before Christmas to get unusual presents for home. I did notice a couple of midshipmen being persuaded to buy Cossif panties for their girlfriends. The Indian shopkeeper was explaining why they had the intentional gap in the crotch: "Cossif she's wearing them, you won't have to take them off," he said grinning from ear to ear! The next evening, our last there, Frank invited me as his special guest to a Gibraltar Regiment Mess Dinner. It was all done in the true tradition of the Army and all the time he was telling me about the history of the Regiment. It was, in fact, a weekend or part-time organisation, perhaps the same as the very fine Territorial Army. I said farewell, and many thanks, to Frank that evening, but assured him we would be back in the New Year on our way to the West Indies.

Sure enough we did but it was only for a two day stop. There is no doubt the spring cruise to the West Indies is, and was, always the most popular with everyone. Hence no-one was sorry to leave Devonport and call in at Dartmouth to pick up the new lot of M&C and sail southwards from the miserable British winter. A two-day stopover at Sao Vincente in the Cape Verde Islands and we slowly made our way across the Atlantic. The weather was great and the sea was calm – plenty of opportunity for worthwhile instruction.

Replenishing at sea, fuelling by the abeam method and simultaneously transferring stores by light jackstay. To the right of the oil tanker's stern another frigate fuels by the astern method

Apart from those four days at the Rock and Cape Verde Islands we were going to be at sea for a total of three weeks since leaving England and arriving in the Windies. Nothing unusual about that as we had a new batch of M&C who had to be instructed in the same syllabus. It never appeared routine as it was exciting because every intake was slightly different and a new challenge. Cadets learning to be capable Able Seamen with midshipmen taking charge of them. More MOW manoeuvres, station-keeping, flag hoisting and sextant work. Inevitably man overboard and sea boat drills ad nauseum to the extent one midshipman was heard to say on the last day across: "the sea boat has been going up and down more often than a whore's drawers on boat race night"!

At last Bridgetown in Barbados, that island in the sun. Although I had been there once before as a cadet in Devonshire our leave had been so restricted that I didn't really know it. However, Geoff Fosberry was by now on his third visit there and knew all the right people. As soon as we had got everything on board organised he, Mike Askew the Doc and I went ashore. We met Tony and Bob who worked in a recording studio for Radio Barbados (shortly to become the Caribbean Broadcasting Corporation) and their friend Betty who was divorced from someone up high in the Barbados and West Indian cricket organisation. All three were born in Barbados, were older than us, were young at heart and were to be very good friends in introducing us to the Caribbean way of life.

It was now carnival season with all the calypsonians and steel bands practising their art for the competitions leading up to Mardi Gras (Shrove Tuesday). Every evening Tom, Bob and Betty would take us to a party where a steel band was drumming out its wonderful rhythm and introduce us to various different rum punches. We were due to be there for nine days so I was determined that firstly the training programme would be thoroughly well organised and then get ashore and find out as much as possible of the West Indian culture. Tropical routine was being worked which meant starting at 0600, having light breakfast at 0800-0830 and then working through till lunch at

1400. This was a good routine, just as much work was done in the cooler hours of the day and it meant you could have a good long siesta during the hot afternoon.

A dance had been arranged for the M&C at the Royal Barbados Yacht Club. Also there were visits to sugar factories and plantations. Plenty of cricket but I think most people, once the day's work was over, were happy to enjoy their time in the sun and watch the lead-up to carnival. The Windies cricket team were not on tour but there were plenty of inter-island matches being played. When Barbados were playing all the shop assistants would be listening on the radio and the customers would have to wait until the end of the over to be served. Betty told me this because she worked every now and then in a dress shop which I think she part-owned. Cruise ships came in every other day but only for a few hours during which time the prices would go up in the shops and the passengers would be taken on a quick tour of the island. Everything returned to normal as the liners slipped their moorings to disappear over the horizon.

On the fifth day Betty picked me up after lunch and took me to her house for an intended swim at the beach. As I was about to change into my swimmers, she stopped me and said I was looking very tired. She undressed me, led me to her bed and slipped in beside me. She knew how to make me very happy and together we fell into a very deep and lovely sleep. It wasn't until very late in the evening that she woke me to say it was time for carnival.

It turned out to be a fantastic all night party, mainly along the streets or as the West Indians called it "jump up on dee road". It was the dancing that kept you awake and sober and at some time Betty said that on the Saturday she would like to give a party. Would I like to help out and stay the weekend? I said certainly and thanked her for being so wonderfully kind to me. As the night progressed we were diverted into many people's houses, introduced, and offered drinks. Then back on the road again and more dancing to the exciting rhythm, which was being played all over town. All good things must come to an end and as the sun was beginning to rise we said goodbye to our good friends and agreed to meet up again later in the day.

As we were walking cheerfully along the jetty, the duty officer came to meet us with the words: "I don't know what you lot are all looking so cheerful about, because we're sailing for British Guiana at 0800. Tension was mounting in BG, the trades unions were calling a general strike for tomorrow Friday and the Colony's Prime Minister, Cheddi Jagan, had asked the British government for assistance. Wizard was to be the first ship to sail and we moved at 0800 round to the fuel jetty and topped right up. We would be rendezvousing with HMS Troubridge which was the sole frigate on the West Indies station. She was coming from elsewhere, probably her base in Bermuda and the other three frigates of the DTS would follow if and when necessary.

Our visit to Barbados had been curtailed by four days and nights, Geoff had managed to get a message ashore to our three friends and we were about to partake in a perfect example of aid to civil power, which the Royal Navy was particularly good at in times of peace. You could call it gunboat diplomacy. Apart from running the ship and normal watch keeping the M&C training as such came to a halt. In fact we in Wizard were going to get the best training of the lot, and we prepared for this on our four hundred mile passage to BG. Departmental officers with their chief and petty officers were allocated so many M&C to do whatever may be required and they had twenty four hours in which to get organised.

On our way we heard that the General Strike was, in fact, happening and that riots were taking place in the capital. We had rendezvoused earlier with Troubridge and as we approached the estuary we could see black smoke billowing skywards. We had no idea what we were in for, as there had been no communication with Government House. Together the two frigates entered Georgetown and there ahead of us was the cause of the black smoke. The rioters had set alight to warehouses and oil storage tanks on the piers and also several barges. Our first task – to put the fires out – was achieved by two methods. Firstly, with all fire hoses manned on the port side, we extinguished those fires on Sprostons Wharf as we secured alongside. Secondly, the M&C manning our sea-boats dealt very bravely and efficiently with the barges, which had been released by the rioters and were now floating freely around the harbour. Finally, we put a fire party ashore to deal with other fires in the harbour area.

Having put all the fires out we then sent a landing party ashore primarily to guard and maintain the power station but also to patrol the town itself. By this time the rioters had gone home and the streets were lined with friendly Guianese people waving Union Jacks and their own national flags. The main job had been completed in a couple of hours and communication had to be set up with the outside world. We now had to ensure local facilities such as power stations, generating stations, the hospital, the ambulance services, the schools and the fire services were kept going with the necessary assistance if required. We were working

The sight greeting us on arrival at Georgetown, British Guiana

in close liaison with the police and political party leaders. We reviewed the situation late that first evening and before turning in, we decided everything had been well set up ashore and that it was a job well done, especially by the young, enthusiastic M&C. How long we would have to stay depended on how long the Army took to arrive and get settled in to maintain the order which we had quickly restored.

The next day was to be the start of one of the better and most interesting weeks in my life. I was told I had been appointed ADC to the Governor of British Guiana, Sir Ralph Grey, and that I was to get along to Government House as quickly as possible – in fact, there was a police car waiting to take me right now. Sir Ralph, who met me at his front door, was charming in his thanks for my willingness not only to be his ADC but also his personal bodyguard, armed with a service revolver drawn from the armoury. He showed me to my quarters, told me to be at ease at all times and not to stand on ceremony. He told me briefly about the situation in BG, that we would be spending most of our time with the prime minister and other politicians and that he would leave me to form my own opinions. As I lay in the extremely comfortable double bed that night I thought of the weekend I was missing at Betty's but appreciated how lucky I was to be involved in this most interesting work and what a privilege it was.

Cheddi Jagan had been the Chief Minister of British Guiana since 1953 and had been Prime Minister for a year. He was the son of an ethnic Indian sugar plantation worker and studied at the Harvard University Dental School in Washington DC qualifying as a dentist in 1942. He had had to work during his time off university studies, and became very involved with the poor workers. His eyes were opened to the condition of Afro-Americans and the segregation in the south and he followed closely the struggle of the Indian Independence Movement and the work of Ghandhi. He married Janet, a qualified American nurse and former member of the Communist Youth. On his return to Georgetown in 1942, he opened his dental practice with Janet as his nursing assistant, and he was shortly to assume leadership of the sugar, rice and woodworkers unions who were mostly of

Asian origin. In 1950 he became leader of the People's Progressive Party on its foundation, with Janet as Secretary and Forbes Burnham as Chairman.

Lindon Forbes Burnham was the other political leader I was to meet over the next four days. He received a law degree from the University of London in 1948, and having formed the PPP with Cheddi two years later was to split up in 1958. He then founded the Peoples National Congress. His father was headmaster of the local elementary school and Forbes, an Afro Guianese, was always politically active. He had been President of the West Indian Students Union in London and was a delegate at the International Union of Students, both in Paris in 1947, and again in Prague the next year. He also had strong leftist leanings.

Now what about BG itself? It had been a British colony since 1831, and was the only English speaking country on mainland South America. Demerara sugar, rice farming and forestry were the main exports and it had the first railway system on the continent. Famous amongst philatelists, their first stamps issued in 1850 are some of the rarest and most expensive in the world. An 1856 Magenta stamp, costing one cent, sold in 1980 for one million dollars.

That was the political situation into which a simple sailor found himself thrust in a small country three thousand miles from his home. It was fascinating to be a neutral witness to the comings and goings of these politicians and their advisers. They were attempting to wheel and deal, and like most of their profession, they rarely told a lie, but were expert at mucking about with the truth. President Kennedy of the USA was paranoid about Cheddi Jagan and the fact that he was a Marxist. I found Cheddi to be an extremely good man. His views on life were quite understandable considering his poor upbringing and it was in the United States that he developed his Marxist views and married a communist. Forbes Burnham was okay. He was brought up in less poor conditions, and he was the man the Americans wanted to be in power. In my opinion they backed the wrong horse and their influence helped the weak British government into doing the same thing. By political and electoral wheeling and dealing Forbes

Burnham became Prime Minister in 1964 and two years later, after independence, he established strong relations with Cuba, the Soviet Union and North Korea.

I was looked after extremely well in Government House, ably guarded outside by M&C from the Wizard. The staff did my laundry and fed me very well. Dinner every night, without dressing up, was most enlightening as I learnt all about my host and his wife, Esme. He was a Kiwi and she a Scot. He was educated at Scots and at Auckland University where he read law, being called to the NZ bar in 1932 and spending four years as a judge's associate or legal factotum. Quoting his own words he became tired of the limitations of NZ society and was accepted into the Colonial Administrative Service. He was first posted to Nigeria and remained in Africa not only throughout the war but until 1959 when he was appointed Governor of BG.

I returned to Wizard on the Wednesday evening to incessant teasing about the quiet number I had had whilst they were doing all the work. I didn't argue with them. Their work had included all the very necessary stuff to keep the peace and show the flag, such as the usual sports fixtures, children's parties and the ships of which there were now five (Troubridge and all four DTS frigates) all open to visitors. The Hampshire, East Anglian and Duke of Edinburgh's Royal Regiments had all flown in to Atkinson's Field and were strategically encamped around Georgetown. They took over the task of keeping the peace and we sailed the next morning.

Within an hour we had received the following signal from the Governor of British Guiana:-

1. The swift arrival of the ships under your command, the exemplary conduct of your platoons in restoring and maintaining order, the great help given by your boats and junior officers during Friday night's fires and the assistance given by your technical departments are deeply appreciated by the Government and people of British Guiana.
2. I hope that the interruption in your training programme has been outweighed by the lessons learnt in the last few days.
3. Thank you. Bon voyage.

Next afternoon we secured alongside the oil refinery in Point a Pierre, Trinidad. We had transferred over one hundred tons of fuel to Troubridge in Georgetown, so we really needed to take on a large quantity. The officials there welcomed us as minor heroes, and organised unscheduled visits for the M&C to the refinery next morning and also the use of their club, swimming pool, tennis and squash courts. We asked half a dozen of the officials and their wives on board for informal drinks in the wardroom. That was an eye opener. All the couples were British except one Dutch and their main object seemed to be for the men to drink as much of our booze as possible while their wives flirted with us. The Dutch couple asked me round to their home next morning, saying a refinery car would pick me up and later return me to the ship in time for our departure at 1400. When I arrived I found the husband was at work at the refinery, the nanny had taken the two young children off for the morning and I was confronted with a scantily dressed Dutch lady sitting between the open patio doors of her bedroom and their small swimming pool. There was no escape!

At late lunch on board Wizard, as we sailed the short distance to Port of Spain, the conversation revealed that several of us had received exactly the same pleasurable treatment during our morning at the refinery! That evening the official Cocktail Party on the quarterdeck turned out to be the most successful I ever attended. The local British Naval Attaché, or Resident Naval Officer, had asked on our behalf local businessmen and government officials and their families to the party. As hosts we were supposed to circulate and make sure everyone was enjoying themselves – adequately supplied with drinks and small eats. It was only human nature that the girls would receive the most attention. About halfway through the party I noticed a local Trinidadian Police Officer standing on his own. I wandered over and introduced myself. He was Superintendent Clive Sealy and he couldn't have been a nicer or more interesting person to talk to. He appreciated my interest in his country to the extent that he acted as my guide for the whole weekend that we were in Port of Spain.

Just as in Barbados, Trinidad was warming up for the Lenten Carnival due to finish on Shrove Tuesday at midnight. Trinidad was the birthplace of the steel band, calypso and limbo dancing, and Clive made sure I, and one or two of my mates, would be completely indoctrinated by the time we left. He took me out to dinner that Friday evening and he made sure there was a police Landrover, with driver, available for me (not the Captain!) on the jetty any time I wanted it. By early Monday morning he had entertained us to dinner, again on Saturday and Sunday evenings at the best restaurants in town. He showed us special steel band and calypso sessions, as well as organising some limbo instruction. We were very sad to leave the pulsating island of Trinidad, but at the same time looking forward to a quieter week cruising the Caribbean with a weekend stop at the Virgin Islands.

It took us five days to navigate the short distance to Road Town in Tortola, which was the main island in a group of about sixty small isles known as the British Virgin Islands. And navigation is exactly what we did do, weaving amongst the different Windward and Leeward Islands plus MOW manoeuvres and the yo-yo sea-boat drills. Apart from the four days lost in Barbados, the only actual training time lost due to the BG riots was in fact practical sea training and we would be able to catch up on that by the time we reached the UK. The weekend in the British Virgin Islands was spent with most people just enjoying the super Caribbean beaches and the equally super rum punches. I managed a quick call to Betty who said she hadn't arranged the party as it would have been no fun without us and that she would be in England in August, so hoped we could make up for lost time then.

After leaving on Monday we rendezvoused with the other three ships of the DTS who, since we last saw them in BG, had been on separate visits to different islands. Together we continued to catch up on the training missed whilst at BG. The seven hundred miles passage northwards was in the open sea and out of sight of land, so the navigation involved sextant work and the use of the sun, moon and stars, plus an introduction to navigational aids. We did manage to journey safely through the

Bermuda Triangle and arrive on Friday alongside the Flagpole on the main jetty in Front Street, Hamilton, the capital of Bermuda. The crowds which came to greet us were mainly from the United States and Canada, and we were to be the object of much attention during our five day visit. They were able to see the comings and goings as official visits were exchanged between the Captains, the Governor, the Mayor and other dignitaries.

The first evening, the Governor, Sir Julian Gascoyne, gave a cocktail party at Government House and a dance at which the superb Esso Steel Band played. The following evening the official cocktail party was held on board all four ships side by side. After work each day visits were made to the Naval Dockyard, the rum distillery and the almost pink beaches and of course there was the usual full sports programme. Bermuda has a highly developing business economy and is an exporter of financial services, insurance, re-insurance and investment funds, and there are business offices all over the place. All a bit dull perhaps for the normal tourist. Most people travelled on motorbikes, driving on the left hand side of the road and sometimes directed by policemen dressed as London bobbies. A thoroughly good place for our final stop before the two and a half thousand mile passage across the Atlantic to the UK.

Every week each midshipman had to write up his journal, which became his personal record of his training and the cruise. Each week he had to include a sketch plus items of national and international importance occurring in various parts of the world. In order to make him even more aware of these events, I started up a Twenty Questions quiz every Friday lunchtime. Reading all the journals and correcting the quiz papers was a lengthy task in itself but very interesting and a good guide as to how the overall training was progressing.

Scandinavia from May to mid-June, followed by France and Germany in July was described by many in their journals as being fabulous. And so it was. The first port of call, Copenhagen, was arranged to coincide, and be part of, the Home Fleet visit to that fair city. The Commander-in-Chief, Admiral Sir Wilfred Woods, flew his flag in HMS Jutland, and it led the way into the Langelinie followed by the usual four frigates of the DTS Urchin, Wizard, Roebuck and Vigilant.

The Royal Danish Navy had arranged a magnificent programme for the visit. The first event was an athletics match between their naval college and our M&C. The match contained all the normal track and field events and was closely won by the Danes. That evening forty Danish Midshipmen were entertained in the gunrooms before everyone went ashore presumably to the Tivoli Gardens. The outstanding ceremonial event took place on the second day when the C-in-C laid a wreath at the Nyhaven Memorial. Led by the Band of the Royal Marines, the Cadet Guard marched through the city to the memorial, and their smart appearance, marching and drill, created a very favourable impression.

A "run ashore" with Kelly Lowe at Tivoli Gardens

Early on Sunday morning King Frederick came alongside the Langelinie near us and from his Royal Yacht witnessed the C-in-C inspecting the M&C at Sunday Divisions, after which they all walked through the park to the Church of St. Alban, Admiral Woods read the second lesson and the sermon was preached by the Squadron padre. King Frederick came to lunch with the Admiral and at a reception beforehand I had the great opportunity of speaking with him, along with the senior midshipmen.

Whenever a Royal Navy ship visited Copenhagen the first two people racing up the gangway were the Carlsberg and Tuborg representatives to invite the total ship's company to at least a couple of visits to their breweries. They knew the average matelot wasn't the slightest bit interested in how the stuff was made, but very much enjoyed tasting a pint or two. Apart from the breweries, visits were made to Danish Royal Porcelain, to the Danish Naval Museum, the Burmeister and Wain Shipyard, the House of Akvavit, and of course Tivoli Gardens. The first night in the British Community organised a dance for the Ship's Companies of the visiting ships. I thought I would give that a miss as I meet enough British people in the UK. However, I did put on my Mess Undress for a supper dance given by the C-in-C of the Royal Danish Navy on the second night in – that was great. Every midshipman's journal I read after our visit seemed to contain Danny Kaye's overworked cliché "wonderful, wonderful, Copenhagen".

We returned through the Kattegat, and the swept channels of the wartime minefields and then made our way through the Skagerrak to navigate the delightful Norwegian fjords, ending up at Bergen for a short weekend. The visit was low key in that nothing official was organised. There were plenty of private invitations from the charming and very hospitable Norwegians to visit their homes. For the next few days the ships split up again for individual training sessions in different fjords before returning to Denmark and three days in Vejle for Wizard. Again this was supposed to be low key, but this didn't stop massive invitations coming our way for the M&C to visit local families and attend dances and dinner parties. There were two successful wins at sport. The soccer team beat the veterans of Vejle FC, whose main team had only a few weeks beforehand beaten Ipswich Town in a European Cup match. The M&C beat the local Rowing Club at coxed fours by two and a half lengths. The day before we left, a four-hour luncheon party was given by the Town Council of Munkeberg which proved to be a befitting end to yet another successful visit.

Two days later we're alongside in Gothenberg, the second city of Sweden. So much had been organised for us that formal instruction as such ceased. Not to worry, we had the rest of June to catch-up. We were moored in probably the best berth in the harbour and much attention was being paid to the visiting ships, especially by flaxen-haired young ladies. At a reception held in the City Hall, the Vice-President of the City Council quoted a Swedish folk song which describes the arrival of English ships at the sandbar off Gothenburg. The local maidens adorn themselves to greet the sailors, whilst the menfolk sulk in jealousy. "Times," he said "don't appear to have changed judging by the amount of female attention being accorded to your ships here this week, and the popularity of the visit."

The submarine Porpoise had joined us for the visit and during working hours was more than willing to take M&C for instructional tours. I had served my sentence in the Trade, so kept well clear. Their ship's company joined up with those of the four DTS frigates in going to what was described as the finest foreign visit dance imaginable. It had been organised by the Consul General and the talent available was reported as being out of this world. The Swedish Navy gave a full Dinner Dance in honour of the visiting officers, midshipmen and cadets, which started at 1930 and did not finish till well after 0100 in the morning. Visits were organised to the Volvo Car Factory and the world famous ball bearing works S.K.F. In town was the British Heavyweight Boxing Champion, Dick Richardson, to defend his European title against the former world champion Ingemar Johansson. Both boxers invited us round to their pre-match training gymnasia and came on board for a look around and chat and signing autographs for those interested. The Swedes did not like the comparison, but in

Gothenburg is the Liseberg Gardens, as good, but not so well known, as the Tivoli Gardens. We all had free entrance to this most popular evening rendezvous.

The end of the Scandinavian part of the cruise arrived, and we had twenty days including a week and two weekends at Devonport before visiting France. The ten days in Guzz were for the ship's maintenance period but provided plenty of classroom time for the M&C. Terry Lewin had asked me to organise the Squadron Athletic Championships whilst we were there. He was a keen sportsman and had been a Navy sprint champion. He was often seen at the various sports encounters in foreign ports, but he would quietly go about his business – usually on his own. I had gathered in the PTIs from all the frigates. Together we set about organising the programme of events, the necessary officials, the medals for each event and the prize giving. The Sports Day, as it was called, would also include some comedy events such as the egg and spoon, three-legged and wheelbarrow races. These were primarily for families and children who may have been watching and for those less athletic members of which there were quite a few.

The event was held at the Devonport Command sports field at Brickfields and the ground staff there had everything ready for the track and field events plus the hurdles. Also the bits and pieces such as shots, discus, javelins and relay batons. Apart from a very complimentary signal and letter after the finish, Terry Lewin asked me to an informal dinner on board Urchin two evenings later. I had been in his squadron now for about ten months and this had been the first opportunity to really get to know him. He was a charming man who never raised his voice and who had a marvellous sense of humour. He had joined the Navy at the beginning of the war and he was soon to be a sub lieutenant in HMS Ashanti on some of the most hellish jobs escorting Arctic convoys. On one of these convoys he had manned a small boat in an attempt to rescue the crew from their sister ship HMS Somali which had been torpedoed and was sinking in the freezing sea. In 1942 when escorting a convoy to Malta, fourteen merchant ships were sunk. All the others got through but were seriously damaged.

His war service was remarkable and as a very junior officer he was awarded three mentions in despatches and a D.S.C. It was great to talk with such a fine officer who was obviously destined for the top.

More seamanship training on our way to the River Loire estuary. We passed St Nazaire where the German U-Boat pens had been rammed during the war by HMS Campbeltown, and enjoyed the forty mile trip up the river to Nantes. A weekend there with visits to vineyards top of the agenda, as it was the heart of Moselle. The Germans did us proud and the fabulous visit to Bremen was top of the league, equal on points, with Copenhagen and Gothenburg. We did all the same things we had done in the other two ports as we were still on top of our game, and the Germans gave us tremendous press to prove it. Three high profile visits in the space of two and a half months was probably enough, so it was good to start winding down a little even though the M&C still had another three weeks.

More practical instruction down the North Sea, along the English Channel and into Portsmouth for the weekend, before meeting up with Her Majesty the Queen on board the Royal Yacht Britannia. We escorted her into Dartmouth at 0900 on Friday 27th July and it was an impressive sight to see the Royal Yacht and all the DTS moored in the harbour. The Queen was there for the day to review the college's passing out parade. The squadron officers had an invitation to attend and I found it difficult to believe that it was a little over twelve years since I was last there as a participant in the parade. On her return to the Royal Yacht, we escorted her out of Dartmouth, and with these duties over, we proceeded overnight, through the Chenal du Four, to anchor off Morgat, a beautiful little seaside town tucked away in the south of the Rade de Brest.

It was traditional in the older days, whenever the fleet was gathered together in the summer time, to hold a regatta. As we were detached and not part of any fleet, it had been decided to hold the squadron regatta during our three days at Morgat. Each ship had a whaler and there would be an inter-ship whaler race between the stokers, electricians, wardroom, ERAs and supply &

sec, as well as the M&C. The whalers would be in use all day long as each department and several M&C crews trained for the big event on the last day. There were only two forms of gambling allowed in the navy. One was tombola, which would probably be played every evening when at sea and the other was Regatta Day.

The midshipmen who were to become electrical officers all went to Cambridge University after their initial naval training. It is interesting to note that Peter Hall of our term rowed in the Cambridge eight, and the coach said he would have liked all his crew to have been naval officers who had had experience of rowing in heavy clinker-built naval cutters or whalers. I enjoyed rowing as a sport, but two-horse races like the Boat Race leave me cold. The only excitement is when one of the boats sinks or Henry Carpenter the BBC commentator, as I once heard him, say: "Ah, isn't that nice, the wife of the Cambridge president is kissing the cox of the Oxford crew."

Our return to Devonport at the beginning of August heralded the end of another cruise. It was my third, completing a year of helping to train the future officers of several Commonwealth and Foreign navies. Maybe each cruise we were instructing the same syllabus, but it was so rewarding to see the change for the better being shown in their knowledge and officer-like qualities, as the cruises progressed and the days of departure arrived. David Farquharson left, and was relieved by David Jenks as our Captain. Without any M&C on board we spent the month employed on less arduous tasks such as being guard ship for the start of the International Sail Training Race from Torbay to Rotterdam and showing the flag at various regattas and carnival days in south Devon and Cornwall.

We spent some days at Falmouth with sea cadets on board, but I was looking forward to Betty coming down at the weekend. After her timely arrival at the hotel, she suggested that we carefully and slowly opened the present she had brought me all the way from Barbados. She had wanted to give it to me that weekend of the BG riots and assured me she kept it well and truly wrapped up since then. It was exquisite and I felt she was enjoying it too. Breakfast in bed consisted of one of Betty's delicious rum punches.

As we lay there I told her we were indulging in a modern version of "sucking the monkey" – a practice conceived by sailors during the War of American Independence. Women were asked to bring on board with them coconuts from which the milk had been drained and replaced with rum!

Then taking a stroll along the esplanade we saw Wizard moored off the Royal Cornwall Yacht Club where we went in to have the most monumental roast lunch. She then suggested we had a siesta back in the hotel. I asked her if she would like to stay on a day or two longer but her counter proposal of coming back down to Plymouth, where the ship would be next weekend, won the vote. She returned to her home in Barbados on the Monday.

The sea cadet training was easy going for us as they brought their own instructors down and had the run of our boats when in harbour. For our trip round to Plymouth via Fowey we had our own adopted unit, the Training Ship Wizard, from Wood Green and Tottenham, on board. The Captain, the gunnery officer and myself on different occasions were to visit the unit at White Hart Lane – needless to say being so close to the great football club they were all Spurs supporters. I went up to inspect them on one occasion and on another to present them with the rugby cup we had won in Seville. It was to be known as the Wizard Cup and would be presented to their outstanding Cadet Sportsman of the Year. Sea cadet training was probably the best form of recruitment the Navy had.

My second year with the DTS started late September with the Mediterranean cruise to Las Palmas, Malta and Gibraltar. The M&C were as always very determined to do well at all the usual aspects of their practical instruction. Yes, the Swedish wives were there on their own in Las Palmas, the Gyppo Queen in the Gut at Malta was visited and much Christmas shopping for Cossif pants, etc was done in Gibraltar. Frank Carreras was as always his usual kind self and took me across the border into Spain for a number of simple but very enjoyable meals.

Leave and the New Year was very cold in the UK so to depart in January 1963 for the Canaries and the West Indies was indeed a great thrill for everyone in the DTS. We missed out on Las Palmas as we had been there on the previous cruise and went straight to Santa Cruz in Tenerife. It seemed crazy that many of us climbed the famous Pico de Teidi, which was snow-capped, as we had spent much of our Christmas leave clearing snow from our footpaths.

I had now reached the not-so-dizzy heights of Lieutenant Commander, in fact I had been so for a few months, but only had the opportunity to get my uniform changed during the Christmas leave period. We were crossing the Atlantic once again with new faces lowering and hoisting the sea-boat and executing MOW manoeuvres. Amongst these new faces I was delighted to see three from the Royal Malayan Navy. Without any fear of being accused of favouritism I paid special attention to them. I was able to use a few choice Malay words if, but only if, they weren't up to scratch. They usually were.

The US naval station at Chaguaramas was our port of call in Trinidad. It was a vast base that had been leased by the British government in 1940 and at times during WW2 had as many as thirty thousand US sailors stationed there. Now it was running down and I think was only being used as an early warning radar site and for missile tracking. There were however a visiting US cruiser and two destroyers alongside nearby and they were only too happy to have batches of our M&C on board for instructional visits.

It was probably better to be in Chaguaramas rather than amongst the hustle and bustle of Port of Spain, which was no more than five miles away. Close enough for Clive Sealy to be there with his usual kind invitations to evening entertainment and for the Police Landrover and driver to be alongside for my personal use. Yet again it was carnival time and the first evening ashore Clive introduced us to Lord Kitchener who had been the world's number one calypsonian – a tremendous character. He had been born Aldwyn Roberts in Trinidad, had done well as a youngster at carnival times and resolved to become a calypso singer. He adopted the name of Lord Kitchener and in 1948 sailed for Great Britain in the Empire Windrush. On arrival at

Tilbury he was seen dressed up in double breasted suit and trilby hat, accompanying himself on the guitar, singing his latest calypso "London is the place for me".

He remained in England for fourteen years during which time he ran calypso recording sessions chronicling the West Indian experience in the country, the parlous state of the economy, but a ringing endorsement of the Festival of Britain. Also less enthusiastic songs on British cuisine, climate and landladies, but naturally the triumphal calypso "Victory Test Match" celebrated the Windies' first ever victory in England. He was a professional and social success and rumour has it that Princess Margaret ordered a hundred copies of his song "Ah Bernice". In 1958 he opened his own club in Manchester and had recently returned home to Trinidad for carnival but more importantly independence which had been granted the previous year.

We were to be in Trinidad for six days and every night Mike Askew the doc and I went out to dinner and places of interest with

"Lord Kitchener" the world's number one calypsonian

Clive. We even met members of steel bands who were practicing for the carnival competitions and they kindly tried to teach us how to play their pans. Mike being very musical was able to latch on more easily and by the end of our stay Clive had organised for us to get five second-hand pans to take back on board. It appeared as though there was no limit to the places we could go or the things Clive could arrange for us. He was, after all, a very generous superintendent of police and in naval parlance a splendid grippo.

On the last night we were introduced to Slinger Francisco who had come to Trinidad at the age of one having been born in Grenada. He was known as the Mighty Sparrow and was the Calypso King of the World. Probably his best known calypso was "Jean and Dinah", the one he composed in 1956 about the dilemma of the prostitutes in Trinidad after most of the Yankees had gone home from Chaguaramas. This together with previous good performances by Harry Belafonte and Lord Kitchener helped to make him the Calypso Monarch, and win the Carnival Road March. He was to win these awards many times. It was great to have been here once again at the most exciting time of the year and many thanks to Clive for yet another unforgettable jump-up.

We needed the ten days change as we slowly navigated the beautiful Caribbean islands with one night at St Kitts and three at St Vincent. Everywhere we went the beaches were clean and inviting for beach parties and banyans large or small. Sometimes we used them for serious instruction and put landing parties ashore. These of course ended in a recreational swim and we made sure we left them as clean as they were when we arrived.

As we were leaving St Vincent we received a request from the local police to go to the island of Bequia where Lord Avon, formerly Sir Anthony Eden, had suffered a heart attack. Bequia was one of the Grenadines group of islands and the only way of his calling for help was through the police wireless to St Vincent nine miles away. We had been asked to pick him up and take him to hospital in Barbados, about a hundred miles away. On arrival at Bequia, my captain asked me to go ashore to pick him and Lady Avon up in the ship's motor boat which was coxswained and crewed by M&C. The two were approaching the jetty from their holiday home as I walked ashore to meet them and introduce myself. The present Lady Avon was Clarissa Spencer-Churchill, the niece of Winston Churchill. As Prime Minister, he had done the country no good in 1956 at the time of the Suez Crisis, and within a year he was out of office.

We left Lord Avon in the hands of the doctors at Barbados and continued our training around the islands until being called back a few days later to return him to Bequia. He and Lady Avon didn't even have the courtesy to acknowledge my crew when we first picked them up and he only discussed, with the local and national press, his health and what the doctors had to say about him. He undoubtedly took the Wizard and the Royal Navy for granted and as a convenient means of inter-island transport, so I found myself something more important to do when they had to be transported ashore at Bequia.

None of this delayed our arrival at Barbados for our scheduled ten days' maintenance. Betty welcomed me with open arms. After all it was six months since those two weekends in Falmouth and Plymouth and now I was up-homers with her in her lovely house down at Christchurch in the south of the island. We got a topsy-turvy schedule going to coincide with the ship's tropical routine. We would start partying at about ten thirty at night after which she would deliver me back to the ship for my day's work starting at 0600. I would have lunch on board, she would pick me up about 1430 and would go back to bed, and be sufficiently rested for the next night's jump up on the road. The programme seemed to work very well and we had a lot of fun. We didn't party every night but it appeared that the nearer it got to Shrove Tuesday the happier and most uninhibited everyone became. At Sunday lunchtime Betty gave a drinks party for me and after liberally dispensing her usual magnificent rum punches, we had an exceptionally long siesta. We had become very attached to each other but were determined not to let the impending farewell spoil the fun.

Four days in Bermuda and with another Atlantic crossing under our belts we arrived back in Dartmouth on April 4th. As the last M&C disembarked to re-join the college, yet another fantastic period in my life at sea came to a close. I officially said farewell to my Captain, who handed me my flimsy, and as I left I asked him to my party in the wardroom that evening. The flimsy read that:

> "The M&C Training Officer has conducted himself to my entire satisfaction. He has taken a keen and active interest in all aspects of his duties and has produced a good training organisation. As a watch keeper he is conscientious and reliable and as Sports Officer he has done well in maintaining the interest of the ship's company. An extremely pleasant person and a most loyal and conscientious officer who gives of his best at all times."

The only other person, apart from my messmates invited to the party was Terry Lewin. I was highly privileged in that not only did he want to come but also he was able to do so. I knew within my bones as I said goodbye to him that evening that I was speaking to a future Admiral of the Fleet. He went on to command HMS Hermes, and after several very good staff jobs, became First Sea Lord. He was Chief of the Defence Staff during the Falklands War and persuaded Margaret Thatcher to order the sinking of the Belgrano. He was Margaret's right hand man throughout the war and there couldn't have been a better man for her to lean on.

HMS GANGES MENS SANA IN CORPORE SANO

As I had had probably more than my fair share of sea time, I reckoned I was bound to be shore-based for my next appointment and was amazed when I received the news. It was again to help train but now it was the turn of the young ratings of the Navy at their vast training establishment at Shotley, near Ipswich. In 1866 HMS Ganges was a Boy Seaman's Training Ship moored in Falmouth harbour but in 1899 she moved to Harwich. There were about five hundred of the lads under training in those days and slowly over the years they moved ashore to Shotley where the present day training establishment grew brick by brick. During WW2 it was used for Hostilities Only New Entry Training. Ian McKersie, a cousin of mine from Campbeltown had been there and became a Royal Marine for the duration. It reopened as a Boys Training Establishment in October 1954 when the number of trainees was two thousand and in the early fifties they became known as Junior Seamen.

In earlier days Ganges had the most terrible reputation. The experienced chief and petty officer instructors were no mollycoddlers and the officers frequently seemed remote and far from approachable. Generations of young lads separated from parents and home for the first time, first met up with the Royal Navy at this place. Many of them found it hard to take in the routine and way of life. Many had hated it.

I saw no evidence of this while I was there and I'm sure the reason was the person whose photograph was in the "Rogues Gallery " of previous captains. I refer to the man I had served with in the Londonderry Anti-Submarine Training Squadron and in my opinion the number one Twentieth Century Naval Officer, Mike Le Fanu. I just knew that when he took over as Captain in 1955 he would have done everything to get rid of the Whale Island all gas and gaiters method of training, and also the gulf that existed between the staff and the juniors. He would have got up in his not very smart plain clothes, chatting to them and by using other methods he had successfully employed elsewhere to make his team feel at ease. Also in that gallery of captains was none other than John Ronald Gower, our first Divisional Officer at Eaton Hall who had left Ganges and the Navy the previous year. I am sure he would carry on the good work started by Mike Le Fanu and I knew that Godfrey Place would.

To help me help the captain keep this training happy and efficient, I had the largest and best physical training staff in the Navy, totalling twenty three. There was another qualified PT officer, Doug Leach, a staff chief petty officer Bill Mitchell, another chief petty officer Prior (in charge of our fantastic swimming pool) and twenty more PTIs, all experts at their particular skills. This staff exceeded in number the Ships' Companies of each of my two ships in the Royal Malayan Navy. On first being introduced to them I made it quite clear I wanted everyone to be happy and cheerful in everything they did. There was to be no shouting or bullying, verbally or physically, and I wanted every junior to have good memories of his time in the PT world at Ganges.

Also of great help were the acres of level playing fields, two gymnasia, the swimming pool and a full-sized en-tous-cas type athletics track. Put all together we had better sporting facilities than any school in the UK, probably the world, and they were used most days morning, afternoon and evening. The first event of the day was probably in the swimming pool, with many of the nozzers not being able to swim let alone pass the test. Nozzer was the name given to a new entry, evidently called after an instructor of earlier days who had an extremely large nose. In the bad old days, if you couldn't swim, it was almost treated as a punishment that you had to attend Backward Swimmers at the crack of dawn every day until you passed. Now it was held at a more leisurely hour, the PTI instructed in a more sympathetic way and with the necessary encouragement they all passed well within their year at Ganges.

The ship's company consisted of several hundred chief and petty officers, and leading seaman who were responsible for the general administration and wellbeing of not only the trainees but everyone at Ganges. There were over a hundred officers, thirty five seamen, seven supply and secretariat, five doctors, six dentists, four chaplains, one matron and four nursing sisters. But the greatest number was forty five schoolies. So there was no doubt the other priority was the further education of these lads. The school was just outside the main gate and many of these young officers, although they may not have been to sea in a ship, were expert at their job and furthermore were to be of great help to me in coaching and officiating at the multitude of different games that were played.

The nozzers were divided into twelve divisions, all named after favourite admirals. Each division had a divisional officer and an assistant DO, the latter was usually ex-lower deck and if possible an ex-Ganges boy. There were divisional chief and petty officers and each one had to make every one of his charges feel at home and come to terms with his new life and routine. And the two things that were going to occupy them most were PT and sport, and their schooling. The inter-divisional competitions were all organised by the PT staff. Doug Leach would lock himself away for a few days in order to produce the Green Monster which would contain the terms inter-divisional sport, as well as all the Ganges fixtures. The divisional staff would train and select all the teams and arrange all the officials. And to help them would be one PTI who would make himself available as much as his other duties allowed.

The person who had worked in the PT office the longest was a civilian called Roy Moore, who was the secretary, the telephonist, the typist and the experienced guy who day after day made sure we got the paperwork right for all the events which we were organising. We were not at sea but we were training youngsters to become part of an efficient team known as a ship's company. So those were the two priorities, to maintain the high efficiency of the PT staff and make sure everyone went about their work in a happy smiling way. The emphasis was always to be on the team and not necessarily the individual.

A typical day in the office would start with a jocular quip from the Chief Bill Mitchell, followed by a cup of tea delivered from the staff dressing room opposite. Roy Moore lived in Harwich and he would arrive in the office at 0815 on the dot. "Morning Moore" would be the Chief's thunderous welcome and another day of occasional civilian teasing began. I once heard him get his own back by saying he had done more sea-time than the Chief had ever done – through his daily return to and fro Harwich and Shotley in the naval pinnace. Roy also said that my sense of humour was of the first order as indeed it had to be to put up with the Chief. Throughout the day the office was a hub of industry with the constant traffic of PTIs, divisional officers and divisional instructors coming in and out with their sporting queries. Everything appeared to be working well, everyone frequently complimented me on the efficient staff I had and never were there any complaints.

The main event of the year was, as always, in the summer, the Mast Manning on Parents' Day. Every morning before their school started and sometimes in the evening, there would be

The best team of physical training instructors in the ....?

juniors manning the mast and the physical training display team practising in every corner of the parade ground. There were one hundred and twenty juniors in the display team and eighty mast manners, plus the Royal Marine Band, whose expert beat and timing made everything easier for the teams. This was my first term and the way things were going I was sure it was best to let the efficient roller keep rolling in the same way. I got to know all the staff and gave them every encouragement. The only one I had met before was Petty Officer Jelley who had been with me in the Royal Malayan Navy.

Always taking an interest in everything that was going on was our Captain Godfrey Place who had won the VC for his extraordinary deeds of valour in attacking the German battleship Tirpitz in Kaafjord, Northern Norway, in September 1943. He was a submariner in U and V Boats and had won the DSC. He volunteered for midget submarines and was Captain of X7 which successfully sank the Tirpitz at her moorings, thus putting her out of action for many months. Whilst placing the limpet mines, he had been detected and considering there was no means of escape he surrendered. After many hours of interrogation he spent the rest of the war in Marlag-Milag Notd POW camp. He was a quiet deep-thinking man, not easy-going, and he was convinced he was always correct – he probably was. He did not suffer fools and was tough towards those who did not live up to his expectations After the war he did not go back into submarines – I don't blame him! Instead he trained as a pilot in the Fleet Air Arm, and in 1952 flew a Sea Fury from HMS Glory during the Korean War. I joked with him that we had already won the war a year earlier in the Fighting T!

With outside activities tending to be centred around the parade ground and mast manning, I concentrated for a while on the swimming pool. Chief Petty Officer Prior and his regular team of Petty Officer Speake plus Leading Seamen Drage and Splain seemed a very efficient close unit but it seemed not too many of the other PTIs were too interested in swimming as a sport. It was arranged that every member of staff would partake in the ASA National Personal Survival Scheme and it was expected that they would all get the golden award. There was plenty of good water polo played amongst the juniors and there were regular inter-divisional competitions. However, none amongst the ship's company. So an Establishment Water Polo competition was started. I organised the wardroom team but played for the PT staff against at least six other teams and it seemed to be successful in providing much enjoyment.

The first week in July and Parents Day were soon upon us and the combined mast manning and physical training display were impeccably performed by every one of the juniors partaking. The Inspecting Officer was Rear-Admiral Sir Ian Hogg, the Flag Officer Medway and he presented the Button Boy with his medal. Afterwards he sent the following signal:-

Your display this evening was superbly carried out and I have never seen a better performance in the Service. Heartiest congratulations.

The standard of athletics was particularly good amongst the juniors. They would have their inter-divisional matches but within a week of Parents' Day, we would have our athletics companionships. All the equipment was for the youth age-group of events but at the same time events were held for the oldies in the form of a normal sports day. It was an all-day occasion involving many heats and the organisation was quite substantial. But we were ably assisted by the divisional staff and the usual team of schoolies providing officials, timekeepers and judges, etc. The first two in each event usually went on to the RN Youth Athletic Championships at Portsmouth or Devonport. There was no money spared on any sporting event. Every junior was issued with blue and white sports shirt and shorts, plus the necessary footwear and when they played for their division or Ganges, smart team colours were issued to them. Petty Officer Jelley had all the gear locked up in a sports store at the back of the main gym. It was called Fort Knox because of the high value of it all, and the fact no-one could get past PO Jelley who had the keys.

Every Sunday, after divisions, Church would be held in the main gym. Known as the Church Wardens, the staff had to keep reasonable order, but it was easy to see that the juniors were up to the same old tricks that we were up to when we were their age. Miniature packs of cards were sneaked in, money would change hands on the number of the next hymn and you could almost hear the roar go up when the duration of the sermon was forecast correctly. Compulsory religion is a difficult one. We had all been through it under training.

Summer in Constable country, as that part of East Anglia was known, was extremely pleasant. Shotley itself was on a fork between the Rivers Stour and Orwell and there were a few nice pubs and restaurants in the immediate area. Often because we were working till quite late in the evenings we would be tired and

Mast manning display

wouldn't want to travel as far as Ipswich. To sit at the "Butt and Oyster" at Pinn Mill on a nice summer's evening seeing the Thames barges at their moorings and watching the shipping going up and down to Ipswich was a pleasant way of spending the time with a jug of ale on the table. Travelling a little further afield, the best times were probably at the Maybush Inn overlooking the River Deben at Waldringfield. Carl Giles, the well-known cartoonist from the Daily and Sunday Express, would regularly zoom up in his Aston Martin and was always full of amusing stories. Every person in his cartoon, especially the grandmother, the nurses and the policemen, he copied from real life in the Ipswich area – or so he said.

One of my best friends I met in the area was John Cobbald. He went to Eton, saw service with the Welsh Guards in Palestine and by the time he was twenty one he was the youngest director in the Football League – of Ipswich Town FC. The whole family, headed by Lady Blanche Cobbald, were eccentrics and owned the local Tolly Cobbald Brewery. Lady Blanche was President and John the Chairman of Ipswich Town throughout its most successful years in the sixties and seventies. In the football world they were possibly best known for patriotically releasing Sir Alf Ramsay and Bobby Robson, both doing very well at Ipswich, to become managers of the English national team.

Much more adult sport was played in the winter months and those in the Ganges soccer, rugby and hockey teams played their matches on Wednesdays and helped coach and officiate at juniors' games the rest of the week. It could get bitterly cold in the winter, especially during the early months of the year. At times we reckoned there was nothing between our sports fields, wonderfully maintained by our superb ground staff and Siberia.

The sick bay and hospital staff were a great bunch, consisting of a surgeon captain plus four surgeon commanders or lieutenant commanders, a matron and four nursing sisters. Because I was keen on sport, John, one of the actual surgeons, asked me one day if I would like to watch a knee cartilage operation. He started giving me instruction, so to speak, even before he had used his razor-sharp knife. I had no idea who the patient was, because the only part of his body visible under the green sheet was his knee. I was fascinated by the teamwork involved in the whole operation and the way the theatre sister, Jane, knew exactly which sterilised instrument was required and the exact moment to produce it.

In January John Cobbold phoned to ask if his soccer team could use our gym for training as their outdoor facilities were too boggy or frozen up. I said certainly provided the usual disclaimers were legally cared for. Every now and then, usually in the mornings, about fifteen of their players would by arrangement appear in one of our gyms and start training. Jackie Milburn, a tough Geordie, the former Newcastle United and England International was their manager at the time. Doug Leach was the captain of the Ganges team and he would get a few of them along for mutual benefit and possibly some five-a-side games. I had an open invitation to go to any of their home matches. I could never manage on a Saturday but did go to an occasional midweek evening game. John Cobbold would be there to guide me to the Directors' Box but often didn't see too much of the game because of the ever present bottles of malt whisky. Frequently banned from driving for alcoholic reasons was no problem for John. His chauffeur merely had to drive his car more often. It was perhaps after an away rugby match that we would drop off at the Swan in the centre of Ipswich for our post match celebrations that some of us would go to Portman Road to watch the soccer – and relieve John of some of his malt!

As I had behaved myself on the first occasion, I was invited back to the operating theatre this time to watch an appendix and hydrocele being expertly attended to by the team headed by John and Jane. Knowing them proved very useful on at least one occasion. At the end of the rugby season I had been asked to the Ipswich Rugby Club annual dinner. During the skylarking afterwards, I was accidentally upended, cut my left eyebrow on landing and it was obvious a stitch or two would be required. It was late on a Saturday night so I phoned the Duty Doctor at Ganges. Jane answered the phone and told me to come round to the sisters' quarters and she would organise John to be there by the time I got back.

Entering the out-of-bounds ivy-covered house known as the sisters' quarters seemed strange. As promised, John was there. He had a quick look at my eyebrow and administered a couple of stitches before dashing off back home. As Jane dressed the small wound, she told me that matron and the other nursing sisters were away for the weekend and that she was alone as duty gal. She obviously realised that we both wanted the same thing and, after giving me a cup of coffee, disappeared for a few minutes. I could hear her checking that the front door was bolted and she had taken off her starched uniform to keep it in pristine condition in case she was called out. Instead she had put on her alluring night attire which revealed much more than it concealed. She was very gentle with me, she wasn't called out, and it ended up being the best possible finish to a rugby club annual dinner and the start of a fine friendship.

Twice each term an Olympiad, or Games Weekend, would be held against other training establishments such as HMS St Vincent, HMS Fisgard, the Royal Marines at Deal and the Army's Junior Leader's Regiment at Nuneaton. Each place would take it in turns to be at home and in the wintertime busloads of competitors due to play football, rugby, hockey, basketball, shooting and cross country would go off on the Friday evening, do battle on the Saturday and again on the Sunday before returning home in the evening. In the summer time it would be athletics, cricket, swimming, water polo and even archery. Jane drove me down in her car to the summer one at Deal. Whilst I was occupied during the day with the games she drove around and did some shopping or whatever and then for the rest of the weekend we stayed in a country pub enjoying our quiet spell away from Ganges.

The Ganges Physical Training Display Team was the most sought after in East Anglia, if not the whole country, but because of other training commitments, we had to curtail the number of performances to six in the summer term. Over my three summers we went to the Cheshire Homes Fete, the Braintree Carnival, the Essex Show, Witham Carnival, Norwich Cathedral, the Shell Gala, and fetes at Brightlingsea, Hemingstone, Billericay, Claydon and Great Cornard. Every year we were invited to perform at the Festival of Remembrance at the Albert Hall on the Saturday before Remembrance Sunday, but that would have meant extra training in the autumn term. The summer term was always that much harder work but nonetheless very enjoyable. And the summer leave period was always very welcome, especially this time as Jane had asked me down for a few days to her family home near Cirencester.

Boxing was a sport very much encouraged at Ganges and each winter term we had the inter-divisional championships, the winner at each weight receiving a small cup. They progressed to the RN Junior Championships and the winners of that went on to the Inter-Services. We had the boxing ring and facilities to hold all these events and the PT Staff were always able to produce a fine spectacle on the night. The matches were held in the evening after dinner and everyone turned up in Mess Undress or dinner jacket and to me it all rather stank of Daniel in the Lion's Den.

Personally I had quite strong views about amateur boxing and the professional version was definitely no go. There were about two dozen Juniors in our team at any one time. Many of them had been boxing well before they were ten years old and were extremely enthusiastic. My experience of the so-called sport was winning and losing a few bouts at Dartmouth and then getting into the final of the Cadet Heavyweight Championships in Devonshire. I was just inside the heavyweight division and my opponent Davie Dalton, who was a mate of mine from the Royal Australian Navy was nearly twenty stone in weight. He hit me many times without really hurting me and I retired from the ring after receiving my loser's medal. How can such a sport where a competitor's main aim is to hit his opponent's head as hard and as often as possible be good? Some of our team were already showing signs of being "punchie", and I advised as many as possible to retire on leaving Ganges.

The season 1964-65 was to be my last rugby season as a player and a great one it was to be. It started off well in that the Navy chose me to go to the central Council of Physical Recreation at Lilleshall to attend the first Coaching Conference ever organised by the Rugby Football Union. This I did with much enthusiasm and then helped the Royal Navy Rugby Union organise its first ever Coaching Course at Portsmouth two weekends later.

The Course Directors were two people with whom I had close ties. There was Vice-Admiral Ronnie Brockman who had become Secretary to Lord Louis Mountbatten after my father had been killed in the Kelly, and he was still his secretary. The other was my old Theseus shipmate Freddie Stovin-Bradford, now Captain RN. Together we managed to assemble a strong team of Royal Navy International players to help. There was Squire Wilkins and Richard Sharp of England, Malcolm Thomas, Terry Davies, Derek Main and Dewi Bebb of Wales, and Tremayne Rodd of Scotland. I was fortunate enough to have played with all these guys and after the daytime work on the pitch, many rugby stories were exchanged and ballads sung.

This was the fourth time I had joined up with Freddie since Theseus days. Since I last met him he had been on two years exchange service with the Royal Australian Navy and had so enjoyed the country that as soon as he retired from the Royal Navy in 1966 he emigrated there. Within days of arriving he received the CBE from the Governor of New South Wales. He regenerated the Australian Barbarians Rugby Club and became their Chairman in 1970. A tremendous character and a fine man, he died four years later aged only fifty five.

The Ganges rugby team was great fun and we travelled all over East Anglia playing Wednesday fixtures against Army and RAF asides. Our team consisted of a mixture of ship's company, PT staff and schoolies most of whom seemed to be Welsh – or perhaps it was because they did the most talking! We ended up inter-services champions of the area not having lost a match. We did however lose to the local club, Ipswich RFC. For the first time we entered the Navy Cup and lost in the final to HMS Collingwood. The match was played at the United Services (Portsmouth) ground and I think everyone had forgotten about Ganges being so far away from Pompey up in Suffolk. Anyway we put up a good enough show for three of us to be selected to go on the United Services Easter Tour of Northern Ireland with games against Malone and Ballymena. What a thrill it was to play my last game of rugby against, and meet, the young Willie John McBride, who was already an Irish International and was to become captain of both Ireland, and the victorious British Lions in New Zealand.

Jane had continued to be a very good friend for many months and we had a lot of fun, including an Olympiad Sports weekend down in Plymouth. I was able every now and then to breach the ivy-covered wall and keep her company when she was alone on duty at the weekends. But eventually all good things come to an end. I was sad when she left but very happy for her, as life would be much more enjoyable at the Naval Hospital in Malta. Also she would be able to continue the very fine work she had done as a theatre sister in every Naval hospital worldwide. In a couple of years she married a naval doctor and it was great to meet up with them, and their young family, at a party in Alverstoke six or so years later.

In my last term we were asked to put on our display for the two days of the Suffolk Show in Ipswich. In addition, for the visit of Her Majesty Queen Elizabeth the Queen Mother, Ganges was asked to provide a Grand Ring Working Party, Royal Route Liners, and our Royal Marine Band. The show was organised by the Suffolk Agricultural Association and I had the privilege of lining up with Mr H J Bird, and several other members, to be presented to the Queen Mother. The success of the Ganges participation is best summed up in an extract from a letter sent by the Association to Godfrey Place:-

> Everyone thought the physical training display was quite outstanding, the assistance given by the Grand Ring Working Party was most efficient and the Royal Marine Band and Royal Route Liners did excellent work in connection with the visit of Her Majesty Queen Elizabeth The Queen Mother.

I should have mentioned that this term I had persuaded my staff to add the Sailors Hornpipe to our display. This entailed much more instruction to an additional sixty Juniors in the team. As always they rose to the occasion and produced excellent results.

About three weeks of the autumn term saw the end of my time at Shotley and all I had to get my teeth into, so to speak, were farewell parties. I handed over to my relief but I knew there were no problems there as the excellent PT staff would support him just as they had done for me. One evening Bill Mitchell organised a bus for all twenty three of the staff to dine out at a restaurant in Clacton-on-Sea. It was the only time I have ever been to that seaside resort, but it was an excellent evening out and everyone was most kind to me. I still treasure the gold cufflinks they gave me.

For the second time Godfrey Place and his wife Dorothy asked me round to dinner at the nearby Captain's Tudor residence, Erwarton Hall. A very enjoyable meal it was and a couple of days later I officially said goodbye to him. In the flimsy he wrote that I had conducted myself very much to his satisfaction. And then:

"A cheerful and very energetic officer who has led the PT world with fine example and contributed much to the establishment by his enthusiasm and courage."

Yes, courage, and that from the holder of the Victoria Cross! I'm sure he had much to do with my next appointment to be Captain of my third warship, HMS Calton based in Aden.

THE WEE GREY GHOST OF THE ARABIAN COAST

The British sponsored Federation of South Arabia was formed in 1963 and there was considerable opposition from the people of Aden and other states further inland and to the north east. Two rival nationalist groups emerged, the National Liberation Front (NLF) and the Front for the Liberation of South Yemen (FLOSY). These two parties began an armed struggle and on 10th December 1963 a grenade was thrown at a gathering of British officials, one of whom was killed and fifty injured. A state of emergency was declared and two years later I was in a British United Airways VC10, which did an emergency landing at RAF Khormaksar. The pilot was aware of possible undercarriage problems and I had been invited to accompany another loan passenger, an Army wife plus infant child, down the shute. All ended well and I had arrived in Aden to take over my third command.

HMS Calton was a coastal minesweeper, known as the South Arabian Patrol Vessel and was the only warship based in Aden. Her First Lieutenant, there to greet me, was Lieutenant Bernard Houghton, whom I had recently known when he was one of the divisional officers at Ganges. He was a Special Duties Officer, a bosun, la crème de la crème of the Seaman Branch and it was great to know that he was to be our Number One. Within twenty four hours I had met the Staff Officer Operations, Commander John Bingham, who was to be my only boss apart from the Admiral himself.

There I was holding the keys to the safe which contained all the confidential books and the medical documents of all the ship's company, plus the morphine, and yet another fantastic part of my life at sea was about to unfold. Lower Deck was cleared and I told them that I had always been in happy and efficient ships, two of which I had captained and I assured them that Calton was going to be the same. I promised to keep them informed of everything

The crew of HMS Calton

that was going on, and I assured them that they would be doing a worthwhile job, of which they would be very proud, in this rather godforsaken part of the world.

Calton's berth was alongside the concrete jetty known as Admiralty Jetty at HMS Sheba, the Navy's shore establishment at Steamer Point. The very next day the Commander-in-Chief of all three services in the Middle East was making his farewell visit to the Royal Navy. He was General Sir Charles Harrington and determined though he was to meet up, he could not find time in his busy schedule to come on board. I was equally determined that he should meet the crew of Aden's only warship, so we went ashore to meet him in Sheba. In the end he stayed with us for nearly an hour and enjoyed having an unscheduled beer and chatting with the crew whose morale had now undoubtedly risen a few points.

General Sir Charles Harrington, Commander-in-Chief of all British forces in the Middle East, is persuaded to take an unscheduled welcome stop on his farewell visit to the Royal Navy in Aden. November 1965

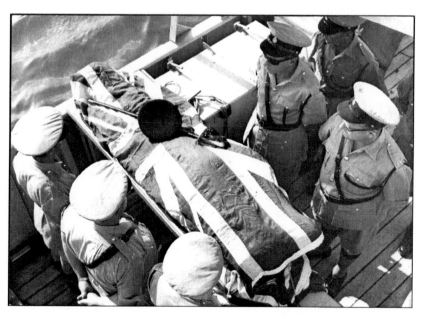

Burial at sea of a British Officer in the Aden police

No time to relax and in a couple of days we were burying some poor soul at sea. A British officer in the Aden police had requested in his will that, cometh the day, his body should be buried in the sea off Aden and Calton was asked to carry out the ceremony. I had witnessed this once before as a cadet in the Devonshire and I knew what had to be done to ensure the body remained in the canvas bag and sank to the seabed. Bernard knew the routine and checked that the Aden police, who were doing all the arrangements, and providing the chaplain, were doing all the right things. The service was conducted in a very suitable and religious manner.

I was rapidly learning that things as Captain of a coastal minesweeper were a bit different to my two ships in Malaya. Out there I had been the only officer and not only did I have to be on watch all the time at sea but I was very much involved in their training. Now I had an experienced seaman as First Lieutenant and three young enthusiastic officers to be trained, but acting, as watchkeepers. The sub lieutenant had finished his training and the two midshipmen had completed their time in the Dartmouth Training Squadron. I had quite a large cabin of my own but shared the shower and heads with the other four. In larger ships the captain has a steward of his own and eats in his day cabin. In my case I had a steward whose prime job was to look after me, but at meal times he looked after all five of us in the wardroom. The one chef cooked for the whole ship's company but able seamen took it in turns to help in the preparation of the food which was always good and none of us went hungry.

As I had found out in Malaya, being captain can at times be very lonely, not so when at sea in Calton but certainly so when alongside in Aden. The Army, and not the Navy, proved to be my saviour. We had a kind of twinning arrangement with the 16th Air Despatch Squadron of the Royal Corps of Transport, who were based in Normandy Lines at Khormaksar. Their second in command, Major Colin Doland was an ace and anything we wanted, particularly in the form of transport, he would arrange. Colin and his gorgeous wife Delia were truly marvellous friends and we spent much time together when off duty.

Now the moment I had been awaiting – to get away out to sea and do my first patrol. John Bingham had told me that our task was to search all small ships, particularly dhows, entering South Arabian waters. Any big ships would be dealt with, once they were at anchor or alongside, by the Royal Marines or military. I asked him if there were any instructions for the boarding and searching of shipping and he indicated that I should use my initiative. This item had not been included in my training as the Navy had not previously been confronted with this sort of predicament in the Indian Ocean. We were not at war with anyone, but we did want to stop arms and ammunition getting into the wrong hands and being used against British troops in Arabia.

It was a five day patrol going east and west from the port of Aden. Bernard had done this a few times without any tangible success. So we started making a few rules and guidelines. The first overall impression we wanted to leave with these seafaring people, whose vessels we were searching, was that we were friendly and that we were trying to ensure that they were likewise and not inadvertently transporting arms to anywhere. We had a job to do but we did not intend damaging their vessels or upsetting them in any way. We would never go alongside them and always used the dinghy. The boarding party would be led by the sub lieutenant with one leading seaman and four able seamen, all smartly dressed and wearing gym shoes, and if carrying arms they would not be loaded. Most important of all the boarding party would never be out of our sight, in fact it would only be a couple of hundred yards away. In case of any unfriendly actions by the vessel being boarded, there would be a loaded Bren gun on the bridge manned by a gunnery rating or myself.

Most of the vessels searched were in fact dhows plying their trade usually in an anti-clockwise direction, possibly from India, along the Arabian coast and then down the east African coast. They were often full of stinking smelling goats, sheep or shoats as the cross-breed was called. They also carried cargo and passengers whom you could see sometimes discreetly washing themselves from a bucket. The lavatory, known as the thunder box, was a

*Possibly the worst and smelliest task in the Navy – searching
a dhow full of people, sheep, goats and shoats!*

little shed hanging over the port quarter. The occupant sat over
a large hole which had nothing between it and the sea several
feet below. It was for that reason that our boarding party went
alongside the starboard side.

Every day we saw and searched four or five dhows and we
dreamt up a competition with a reward for the team who found
the most items. I don't know whether it was coincidence but the
very next day some things were found. As this was our first few
days away from base I was most interested in getting to know the
ship and, more importantly, the crew. The Chief Engine Room
Artificer Childs, or the Chief Tiff as he was traditionally called,
had in his expert care twin Mirrlees Diesel Engines, which gave us
a maximum speed of fourteen knots. He had a team of two stoker
petty officers, one leading stoker and four stokers. I think they had

posher names than that – like Mechanical Engineers – but no-one ever called them that! The petty officer electrician had three electricians and three radio electricians to help him keep everything electrical going. We were fortunate to have such a good technical team and we were confident we could rely on them.

Our first port of call was Mukalla, the capital of Qu'aiti State in the Hadramaut region of the East Aden Protectorate. The first person to visit us was James Ellis, who only a few months earlier had become British Resident Advisor. He was born in Berwick-on-Tweed, educated at Fettes and had volunteered to join the Army. This was so that he wouldn't be sent down a coalmine, which had happened to a cousin.; He went out to the North West Frontier in India and was later contracted as a Captain in the Pakistan Army for three years. He then returned to the UK but by 1951 he had started his great affection for Arabia. This brought him many tasks which he was ably equipped to do, with his fluent Arabic and other eastern lingos and his seasoned political skills. He had

The reward from some of those searches

a very clear mind, was unflappable and had a huge physique, probably gained in the Fettes and Army rugby fifteens. He was a super guy, and became a great friend, as well as a tremendous help in educating me about the intelligence and political situations in South Arabia.

Although occasional temporary visits from Aden would increase his staff, he was one of only three Europeans in Mukalla, the other two being his wife Joanna and a middle aged nurse. I asked him to bring half a dozen or so of his team on board for an informal drink that evening. It was important to get to know the local Arabs and even more important that all twenty thousand of the population of South Arabia's second port should know that we were around. It was hard going with the Arabs but with James I knew everything would work out well in our joint efforts to win the day.

He and Joanna had to dash off for a dinner date and after one more drink the nurse asked me if I would like to go ashore for a meal. As this was my first visit to Mukalla and I had no idea what happened ashore, I agreed it was a good idea. Getting into her Landrover, and manoeuvring the main street, it soon became obvious there was no restaurant – only local Arab cafes – so we bumped up a rickety hill to the block of government apartments. As we arrived in her luxurious little flat she asked me if I would mind replacing the bulb in her bathroom as she might want a shower later on. It involved moving the glass shade but she had the necessary screwdrivers. By the time I had fixed her light she had undone her chignon and there awaiting me was this shapely brunette. She was very comforting and knew how to look after a simple sailor back from the sea.

As she drove me back to the ship next morning she pointed out where she worked in the medical clinic next door to the Advisor's Residence and told me she had been in Arabia for about six months. Smartly dressed in her nursing uniform, she looked very much the Florence Nightingale of the East Aden Protectorate, as we shook hands in a very formal goodbye.

One day on patrol the radar showed a contact close inshore and we went to investigate. It was a large Greek trawler. She had her trawls out and was therefore fishing within South Arabian territorial waters. I asked Bernard to be in charge of our boarding party as he was experienced at fishery protection duties and to report back by radio the result of his investigations. He found that their fishing nets were all within regulation size and that the only problem was the area in which they had been fishing for some time. I now had to make the big decision. I knew the Admiral had many more real problems on his plate and would not be too concerned about a Greek trawler. I told the Greek captain that, if we ever found his vessel fishing in these territorial waters again, he would be arrested. He went on his way rejoicing – after we had turned down his offer of fish. The full details of the incident were signalled to the Admiral.

It wasn't long before my fifth Christmas away from home was upon us and Bernard had got the wardroom looking as festive as possible. We even had a Christmas-type tree secured to the mast. Traditionally the officers serve dinner to the crew shortly after the rum issue at midday and we certainly had no intention of breaking

Boarding the Greek fishing trawler 'Thetis', South Arabia 1965

with that long established custom. Afterwards many of them went ashore to swim or enjoy time with their naval or military friends. In the hot climate most families had their meal in the evening so many of us had two Christmas dinners, in my case with Colin, Delia and their son Jaunty.

Colin and Delia were great in showing me all over the area. Aden itself was a highly modern seaport which had all the usual facilities. Nearby to Steamer Point, in an area called The Crescent, were the Marina, Crescent, Victoria and Rock Hotels, at least two banks the National and Grindlays and many shops leading along Maahla and eventually to RAF Khormaksa which was the military base and the civil airport. Due to the Emergency, many restaurants had closed down; at night most people kept to the secure areas or remained in their homes. Also close by to Steamer Point was the Gold Mahur Beach which I had visited fifteen years earlier when in Theseus. The only change was that the Club and Pool had now become the Officers' Club where we were to spend much of our off duty time.

The Officers' Club at Steamer Point with swimming pool,
cinema screen and Indian Ocean to the right

The next patrol was short, making sure we were back alongside Admiralty Jetty for Hogmanay. There was no doubt life was hard for those ashore in Aden. Apart from the Infantry battalions and ourselves, most of the other people, if they had families, lived with them in comfortable accommodation, most of which was under guard. They were restricted in what they did, there were many out of bounds areas and their children went to military schools in buses suitably guarded. So it was good to see everyone being able to let their hair down for the Christmas and New Year parties. As regards Hogmanay, there seemed to be one going on everywhere with people darting between one event and the next. We on board were open house for any of our friends who wanted to be with us and it was pleasing for me that Colin and Delia spent well into 1966 on board.

I could see one very serious problem looming for my crew and that was the lack of female company. There were anything up to thirty thousand British servicemen in South Arabia and apart from, say, twenty unmarried females who were Army or RAF nurses, or who worked in the High Commission, the others were wives accompanying their husbands. The Infantry batallions (every regiment in the British Army came out) were there for three months. We were due to be there for at least a year. If my crew spent too much time on board and lacked the charm of the opposite sex, you could sense much bickering going on and there would be strong arguments about the most stupid of subjects. Morale which we were slowly building up would then go downhill rapidly. I was beginning to formulate my plans which hopefully meant spending less time alongside in Aden.

Half the distance from Aden to Mukalla, but in the opposite direction, was in what used to be French Somaliland, the large port of Djibouti. There was no State of Emergency there and when ashore our crew would be able to roam freely and enjoy local hospitality. It was, after all, known as the Singapore of the Arabian Sea. By now I had got to know the Flag Officer Middle East, Rear-Admiral Peter Howes DSC and he had said that every time I called to see John Bingham, he would also like to see me at the same time. I proposed to him, in John's presence, that we should call in at Djibouti for two days at the most, it would be called what is termed a non-operational visit and it would be no distance if we were suddenly required back in Aden. Peter Howes thought it was an excellent idea and immediately got the diplomatic wheels in motion – not much of a problem as France and Great Britain were NATO allies.

So our first patrol of the year took place in Djibouti. When we arrived, there was only one French warship in harbour, a destroyer on her way from France to Tahiti. The French Navy has many friendly sons of the sea, but as a unit it has disliked and been jealous of, the Royal Navy since Trafalgar, but in particular since we sank their warships in North Africa during WW2 – to stop them falling into German hands. The French Foreign Legion were not too enamoured of their Navy and therefore it was not surprising we were looked after by them when we were in their port. Good naval training at Dartmouth had included French and this was to prove useful because our courteous liaison officer, who was very attentive, could speak only a little English. He told us that we were welcome to go anywhere in town, that there were no out of bounds areas and that we could use the Foreign Legion's NCO's club facilities which were open twenty four hours a day.

Their club turned out to be the first solution to the crew's welfare, and morale problem, which I had been worrying about. It was similar to any serviceman's club one might find in Singapore or Hong Kong in that there were restaurants, bars, and all the indoor games such as darts, snooker and table tennis, and also outdoor boules. But there was one difference in that there were Somali hostesses to socialise with and to help you enjoy your time in the club. All was above board and these Jungle Bunnies, as they were called in Lower Deck lingo, were very nice girls. If, however, you wished to spend the night with your chosen lady, this could be arranged and a room booked. A section of the club was, in fact, a legalised bordello, supervised and subsidised by the Legion. All this was confirmed by a couple of the crew, as we were sailing out of Djibouti, and I could sense that all was well on board.

I became an honorary member of the Thirteenth Battalion
of the French Foreign Legion! And received my kepi!

I told Colin Doland about the NCO's club at Djibouti the day after we got back and he quoted a similar problem and solution when he was in Korea with the Royal Army Service Corps. At their HQ in the south they had a laundry firm operated by Korean girls from the local village. When his troops returned from the front line for a night or two's rest, they could relax in their makeshift club with these girls acting as bona fide hostesses. Later at night any arrangement made with the Korean lasses was considered to be of benefit to all.

A few days on patrol after Djibouti proved rewarding and it was good to see that there was no aggro with any of the dhow skippers. They were well mannered and apparently did not know that they were carrying these rifles and ammunition because they were all boxed up. They were very helpful because all they wanted was for us to get the search over and done with so that they could quickly get on their way. What was upsetting was some of the ammunition was not even a year old and had been date stamped as being made in Birmingham in March 1965. How on earth had it travelled from middle England to a dhow in the Gulf of Aden in that short space of time?

When in harbour I had virtually nothing to do on board the ship – possibly an hour's paperwork after the signalman had brought me the Daily Emergency Report outlining all the incidents that had taken place in the Federation. The daily running of the routine and the ship's husbandry, was in the very capable hands of Bernard, the Number One, and so I spent every available opportunity ashore meeting up with the Army and their intelligence officers to keep in touch with what was going on both locally and up country. One morning I was in Sheba and a very senior officer came up to me. It was none other than the Chinese Admiral, my old shipmate, Mike Le Fanu. I insisted and pleaded he came on board even if only for five minutes. When he agreed, I asked a sailor to nip along the jetty to Calton and inform Bernard of the impending visitor while I accompanied the Commander-in-Chief slowly towards the gangway where the side party had been assembled ready to pipe him on board.

He insisted everyone carried on with their work and loved the impromptu informality of the visit. He was able to talk to many of the crew and see the results of their labours when the captured arms and ammunition were laid out for his inspection. It was Shrove Tuesday and he agreed to be photographed with some of the crew tossing pancakes quickly prepared by the Chef. He was also seen to accept a very small sip of rum. He had recently taken over from General Sir Charles Harrington, whom we had met in November, as Commander-in-Chief of all British Forces in the Middle East, from his HQ in Aden he was responsible for an area which stretched form the Persian Gulf to Southern Africa and included the islands of Mauritius and the Seychelles plus the about-to-become-independent countries of Swaziland, Bechuanaland and Basutoland. We were the first naval ship he had visited since his arrival in Aden and the crew, whose morale took another leap, really appreciated the opportunity of speaking to such an approachable and fine naval officer destined, in everyone's opinion, to be top of the Navy one day soon.

The new Commander-in-Chief Middle East, my ex-shipmate,
Admiral Mike Le Fanu, on an informal visit much appreciated
by the ship's company. Being shown a box of ammunition
captured less than a year after manufacture in Birmingham

The Navy's PR man in Aden was a retired Royal Marine Captain called Bill Curtis and we became friends early on. His job was obvious and he wanted any information or publicity we could give him to pass on. He knew about our arms discoveries and the press had been informed. One day he came on board for a lunchtime drink and to tell me that Victor Blackman, the well-known Fleet Street photographer was in Aden and that he would like to come out with us for the day. My reply was that we were leaving tomorrow for a five day patrol and if he could be on board by 0800 we would be delighted to take him out and that we could drop him off, here in Aden, before proceeding eastwards up the coast.

Victor was obviously one of the country's best photographers. He was most interested to hear all about what we were up to and within two hours we were about to board a dhow. He wanted to go as well, but I apologised for the fact that I couldn't permit that. Then I relented a little and said he could go provided he stayed in the dinghy. He was working for the Daily Express but in an article

Bill Curtis, our PR man in Aden

204

he wrote for his own Cameravaria he said this dhow had fifty nine people on board and no fewer than seven hundred goats and that never in his life had he encountered such a stench. He was glad to have remained in the dinghy, and he sent us some excellent photos of the occasion. Within a week or so some of the crew were getting mail from home which enclosed newspaper cuttings along with boarding party pictures. Nothing could boost morale more than to know that their efforts were being recognised in the British press. The morning we had Victor on board I heard some more good news but decided not to let anyone know until the day we got back to Aden.

The next morning we cruised the full length of Mukalla, as close inshore as possible, so that everyone could see us or be told about us. James Ellis got the buzz and was on board within one hour of our arrival alongside in our usual berth. Mukalla was an impressive looking town from the sea, with all its Islamic buildings, but ashore it was a ramshackle place with dirty, dusty shops and market places. It was no place for the crew, who didn't

This photograph given to me by Victor Blackman

want to go shore there and preferred to stay on board and save their hard-earned money for better runs ashore later.

James apologised for the lack of facilities for the crew and appreciated why we were only staying one night. He had to get back to the office so I went with him to glean any information I could. With wall maps and large scale photos I was able to appreciate a lot more. As far as he was concerned, nothing much had changed since we were last in Mukalla two months ago and he was still very unhappy with the politicians at home, particularly Denis Healy who was our Defence Minister at the time. He apologised for the fact he couldn't entertain me that evening but he was sure the nurse would be only too happy to do so.

She came down to the ship about six o'clock and after a couple of drinks we mounted her Landrover for the inevitable dodging of pot holes en route to her flat. This engaging woman did enjoy talking, she was full of interesting stories about her life as a midwife, and she had some very amusing tales to tell. She also had this rather insatiable appetite which we both enjoyed satisfying. As she made up her chignon in the morning I didn't

Mukalla the capital of Quaiti state and the second largest town in South Arabia. A view we were to see many times.

consider it inappropriate to ask her how she had survived six months in Arabia before we first met and she produced an electrical toy from a drawer. I had seen them for sale in Japanese shop windows, sixteen years beforehand, during the Korean War. She did, however, say that it was no substitute for the real thing, which we had experienced together. British women abroad, like their foreign counterparts, seemed happy to exchange views on relationships with their male friends. Whereas those at home seemed to be more prim and secretive and gave the impression the whole thing was a bit taboo.

After searching three or four dhows, which we caught up with en route back to Aden, I told the crew that the Admiral had asked us to represent the Royal Navy at the annual passing out parade of the Ethiopian Naval College in Massawa. I added that you don't refuse the asking of an Admiral, that it would be a new run ashore for them and that we would call in at Djibouti on the way back. We took a couple of days in Aden getting the ship looking spick and span and making all the other preparations ready for the official visit. It took us a little over a day to do the four hundred miles of calm southern Red Sea. We didn't see any dhows and anyway, once in that area, they were out of our jurisdiction. The visit was low-key and all the pomp and circumstances was provided by the Emperor and the Ethiopian Navy. An excellent band greeted us with all the usual tunes, which was not very surprising, as we later met their tutor who was a retired Royal Marine bandmaster.

The Emperor Haile Selassie came on board and although I was told French was his chosen language, he spoke perfect English. After all, when Italy under Mussolini invaded his country in 1935, his family fled to Djibouti. A Royal Navy cruiser took him to Haifa, and then another a short while later to Gibraltar. After a short spell in the USA he went to Great Britain for most of his five year exile. He started telling me all this while having a cup of tea on board Calton. The next day was a great occasion for me because as the senior RN Officer present I was asked on board his exotic Royal Yacht. I hadn't visited such a glamorous vessel before and haven't done so since.

*Emperor Haile Selassie, perceived as a messianic figure
by the Jamaican Rastafaria Movement of the 1930s*

He was obviously very pro-British and pro-Western. When
he was in Great Britain for his years of exile, which also covered
the first two years of WW2, he bought a huge estate near Bath,
called Fairfield House and after the war he was to give it to the
City of Bath. Italy's entering the war on the side of the Germans
gave him the opportunity to recover his country, which he did
with the aid of British and Free French troops – plus his own
patriots. Being by no means the only person on board I was
not able to monopolise him and his extremely interesting conversation, but the most momentous few minutes was the light luncheon we were all served on gold plates. On our departure, after the
exotic meal, we were told there was nothing more required of us
and a liaison officer offered to take me up to Addis Ababa to see
the countryside and the sights of their capital city whilst the rest
of the ship's company enjoyed a different run ashore without
the restrictions of Aden. The most impressive thing about the trip

up to Addis was the number of viaducts along the hilly route, a credit to Italian civil engineering. The crew enjoyed Massawa but not as much as the two days in Djibouti.

Back in Aden, the afternoon before we were due to sail on our next patrol, I felt terrible, alternately sweating and shivering. Trying to sleep it off with aspirin but with no success, the RAF doctor was called in. He took one look and said I must go to hospital and that I would be there for at least a week. I told him I couldn't because we had to go on patrol tomorrow. His reply was that he couldn't order me to do so but that he would immediately report to my Admiral that I was medically unfit to go to sea and it would be far better if I did the contacting. I now knew that I was on a hiding to nothing because Peter Howes would ask me one question and if I answered in the negative he would not be pleased. The question was: "Are you happy for your First Lieutenant to take the ship to sea?" I answered: "Yes, Sir." If I had answered no, it would have been my lack of supervision or training which would have been at fault. As it was, I was really delighted to lose my command to such a deserving officer, especially as it wouldn't be for long. He was due to leave the ship in two and a half weeks' time to return to the UK.

By the time I had arranged a few things for my arrival at the RAF hospital up on a hill overlooking Steamer Point and Calton, it was quite late. Allowing me to keep my valuables, they took my clothes away – I think they thought I would try and escape – and that was me settled in the officers' ward for God knows how long. Life was very comfortable hell. They looked after me extremely well, recovery was good but slow, I missed my ship terribly and within five days I was feeling fine. The doctor came to see me every day, told me that I had jaundice, and when I asked the reason he said I had been working too hard and that I had probably had a few worries. He said I needed a rest and that he was going to send me on a week's recuperation leave to Mombasa. Wow! But he said: "You are not to have any alcohol for six months," and he meant that very seriously. When I complained bitterly, he relented and told me I could have half a pint of beer a day and no more than that.

The doctor told me the RAF would fly me down to Mombasa tomorrow, I would stay at the Silver Sands Hotel for six nights, it would cost me nothing and provided everything was okay with my health on the day I flew back, I could go straight back to my ship. The RAF Transport Command had planes flying there every other day, usually taking servicemen who had been in Aden over six months, but I would have priority as I was on sick leave!

When we arrived at Mombasa airport there was a reception party of British servicemen of all ranks and I was grabbed by a naval schoolie whom I had known in my last appointment at Ganges. He was part of the RN Training Team on attachment to the Kenya Navy and one of his extra-mural activities was to meet the very occasional naval officer who flew down from Aden and make him feel at home. He took me in his own car out to the Silver Sands Hotel and made sure I got settled in all right. He had been informed of my impending arrival and as we were "old ships" he had another naval couple and two young ladies were there and I started my six months of non-alcoholism by drinking super fruit juice concoctions – and no beer. A thoroughly enjoyable first few hours in Mombasa and one of the young ladies drove me in her car back to the hotel. I asked her to stay for dinner. I already knew her name was Penny, that she was a nurse in a local hospital and she asked if I would like to be shown round Mombasa, go for a swim and she would pick me up tomorrow at about midday.

I had a nice long lie in and a huge breakfast before getting to know the layout of the hotel. Penny arrived a bit late but apologised on the grounds that she had wanted to get a few things organised before coming to get me. We set off on the grand tour driving through the world famous Mombasa Tusks, which had been built shortly after the Queen's visit in 1952 and to all the other obvious places of interest. We stopped for a long and happy light lunch in a restaurant overlooking Kilindini Harbour and she then said she would like to show me her place of work, namely the Katherine Bibby (pronounced Bee-Bee) Hospital.

We seemed to be getting on well and enjoying each other's company. She parked the car near the hospital main entrance and disappeared for quarter of an hour leaving me to read various brochures we had picked up earlier on. Chucking a grip and a couple of shopping bags into the boot, she jumped into the car and off we went down to the beach. There, on the lovely white sands, was a small rattan-covered beach lodge on stilts and she told me it belonged to the hospital and that she had borrowed the keys. We dashed in for a swim before settling down for a refreshing drink, as Penny pottered around and organised a barbecue. She had brought some succulent steaks and we set about cooking and feasting on them. All the while she was telling me that she had arranged to be on holiday for the rest of the week and that if I wanted to go on safari, or up to Nairobi, she would enjoy being my guide. I agreed that it would be great fun and as we were both on holiday we might as well spend all the time together. Getting off to a fine start, she led me upstairs to the neat little nest she had obviously prepared as I was having my non-alcoholic sundowner earlier on.

Late next morning, before an even later breakfast, it was truly wonderful to be swimming all alone with this golden girl au natural in the Indian Ocean. Later, she did some organising on my behalf, and managed to arrange a couple of friends to help show us around the Tsavo National Park tomorrow morning and then we could drive up to Nairobi where we had been invited to stay the night with a couple of other friends. She wasn't able to arrange it earlier so that meant we could spend another night at the beach lodge. Terrible!

The visit to Tsavo was great and just as I had expected with plenty of giraffes, lions, elephants, rhinos and antelopes, etc, all apparently running free – a tremendous sight to behold and I was very grateful for the opportunity A quiet evening in Nairobi where Penny's friends were very welcoming. We chatted quite late in to the night and it was strange, but very nice, to snuggle up under a blanket. She had alerted me to this, as the city's elevation is about two thousand feet above sea level. It was even known for the inhabitants to have log fires in the evening, but certainly not necessary the night we were there.

Nairobi, as the capital city of Kenya, had all the obvious offices and buildings. It was the railway junction between Mombasa and Kampala in Uganda, it was the centre of the

Tsavo National Park

coffee, tea and sisal industries, it had a large stock exchange and many United Nations offices. After a long lie-in and a full monty breakfast our hosts showed us around the city before Penny drove me the two hundred odd miles back to our little nest on Nyali Beach.

The next morning she left me for a couple of hours at the Kenya Navy HQ at Mtongwe, so I could meet the boss man, Commander Max Walker, RN. The Kenyan Navy had been established in 1964, one year after independence and had only one ship, the HMS Nyati, ex-HMS Aberford an SDML donated by the British government. But later this year to arrive from the UK were three brand new Simba Class patrol vessels built by Vosper Thornycroft. Max Walker was obviously enjoying himself as the first Commander of the Kenyan Navy and we agreed it would be a good idea if Calton could pay a visit to Mombasa and carry out some exercises with them. This was another plot in the scheme to get my crew away from Aden and now I had a personal reason. She was waiting outside for me so that we could go and enjoy our last twenty four hours together. As we had our final very close skinny-dip in the Indian Ocean the next morning, we both agreed that a future meeting should be high on our priority list.

On the plane back to Aden I reminisced about many very recent episodes in my life and thought to myself yet again that it was only due to the Royal Navy that I found myself in this part of the world and about to continue the job for which the training had been so expert. There alongside at Admiralty Jetty was the present love of my life, HMS Calton. People often used to say that, amongst their many problems, some naval officers were married to their ship and the sea! Bernard had obviously enjoyed his experience, the fortnight had gone well and now he and several of the crew were due to fly home.

The next meeting with my Admiral Peter Howes lasted a good half hour and proved very beneficial. I told him that I felt fine after my spell in the hands of the RAF medics and that I had visited the Kenyan Navy in Mombasa. I mentioned that quite a few of my ship's company were being drafted home and asked if it would be a good idea, when the changes were complete, to have a Commissioning Service? He was all for it and said he would get the Commissioning Order sent when I had got the programme organised. I was getting to know his personal assistant, Patricia Curtis, quite well. She was Australian and the wife of Bill Curtis the PR man, and together they were proving to be very good friends, both professionally and socially. They were, in fact, my only two naval friends. Apart from the two Admirals, the rest of the navy ashore seemed to be either waiting to draw their pension or get back to the UK, or both. Anyway, I told Patricia about the Commissioning Service and she said she would get the ball rolling at her end.

Sub-lieutenant SD(B) Andrew arrived on board a couple of days later and took over from Bernard as First Lieutenant. Like Bernard, Andy was a first class seaman, a bosun, and had risen through the ranks from Boy Seaman. He was given a further couple of days to settle in and then we went on patrol westwards towards Djibouti. We searched four dhows in all and in one we did find one box of ammunition. It was good to do so on Andy's first trip with us.

Djibouti was its usual good rest cure and the French Foreign Legion as helpful as ever. I only ever went ashore there when accompanied by one of their Majors called Charles and his family – it was for the occasional swim at their Officers' Club. All their officers were French, but only about twenty five per cent of their troops, most of whom came from all over the world and some were hardened criminals and a formidable lot. There were evidently quite a few British but we were not knowingly allowed to meet them. It was only April but Charles told me I should try and be in Djibouti for the Bastille Day celebrations on 14th July. I thanked him for the idea, promised nothing, and noted the date in my diary.

The main oil refinery in the colony of Aden was to the west in an area called Little Aden. Many tankers called there to discharge crude oil from the Persian Gulf so that it could be processed by BP for bunkering ships on passage to the East or westwards to transit the Suez Canal. It was the only purpose of the place, so the terrorists did not bother to interrupt the peaceful life of the employees and their families. Or it may have been peaceful because the Royal Marine Commandos were protecting the area. We called in there because I happened to know an old shipmate of mine from the Dartmouth Training Squadron called Ray Roberts, who was the padre, and I was wondering if he would be good enough to conduct our Commissioning Service. He agreed and suggested we remained alongside for the night so that we could all use the excellent staff recreational facilities which included a sand golf course.

On 5th April I received the Commissioning Order directing me to commission Her Majesty's Ship Calton at Aden on Thursday the seventh day of April 1966. I had asked Colin if he could organise some music for us and he came up trumps with the band of the Royal Northumberland Fusiliers. Everything had been arranged for the big occasion and by lunchtime a very successful ceremony was being celebrated with drinks for a few of the ship's special friends. It was the one and the only Commissioning Service I was to attend.

By Peter Norris Howes, Esquire, Distinguished Service Cross, Rear Admiral in Her Majesty's Fleet and Flag Officer Commanding the Middle East Station and ships employed and to be employed on that Station.

H.M.S. Calton — Commissioning Order

The Admiralty Board of the Defence Council having directed that Her Majesty's Ship CALTON is to commission at Aden, you are to proceed forthwith to commission her on Thursday, the seventh day of April, 1966 and to prepare her for foreign service on the Middle East Station.

From the date of commissioning, Her Majesty's Ship CALTON will come under my full command.

You are to bring to my notice immediately any reason you may have for dissatisfaction with the general state of the ship or with any part of her. Similarly, you are to bring to my notice any other matters of importance, in particular those relating to the welfare of your Ship's Company.

May God's blessing be upon the ship and company hereby entrusted to your command and your joint endeavours to uphold the highest traditions of the Royal Navy in the service of Her Majesty the Queen be crowned with success and happiness.

Given over my hand, this fifth day of April, 1966

Rear-Admiral
Flag Officer Middle East

To: Lieutenant Commander M.J.Reeder, Royal Navy

H.M.S. CALTON

Copy to:- Second Permanent Under-Secretary of State (Royal Navy)

HMS Calton – Commissioning Order

Reading the Commissioning Order to the Ship's Company.
Padre Ray Roberts to my left

At the party Peter Howes whispered to me that he had a trip up to Bahrain, which he thought Calton might like. He told me to come and see him tomorrow and he would divulge all. The squadron in the Gulf had been given a week's break, or jolly, to go to Pakistan and India and he wanted me to look out for them during that time. It would mean being away from Aden for about three weeks – six days to get there, another six to return plus the week's patrol in the middle. I should let him know which fuel stops I wanted. I had enjoyed the post-commissioning drinks party as I was able to have Peter Howes to myself for a while and being out of the office he was completely relaxed. I admired him and I knew he trusted me. He had been senior ADC to Lord Louis Mountbatten when Viceroy of India and again Naval Assistant to him ten years later. He had been Captain of HMS Vigilant and the Dartmouth Training Squadron and also of the Guided Missile

Destroyer HMS Devonshire immediately before coming out to Aden. He was no slouch.

It was a good one and a half thousand miles to Bahrain and a great opportunity for Andy to establish himself as Number One. He had Sub Lieutenant D. Gooding to help him as Gunnery Officer whilst one Midshipman K. Collins was the Correspondence Officer and the other Midshipman P. Mazzeo was the Navigating Officer. We settled down to a steady watch keeping routine and stopped at Muscat to take on fuel. Then as we approached Bahrain the four ships of the Gulf Squadron passed us on their way to Karachi. I signalled Peter Howes to say I had arrived in the Gulf and taken over security duties. We were all very proud and delighted to receive the following signal from him:-

You lead the league and must explain to your Opposite Numbers in the Persian Gulf your art of being in the right place at the right time. Well done.

Me and my Admiral!

A ship could not receive a better boost to morale than that message from the Admiral and the crew were informed straight away. I was determined we would continue the good work in the Gulf, but at the same time this could be the first and only time for many of us to visit these places. After all, there was no State of Emergency, we weren't at war with anyone, everyone appeared friendly and we had been told to "join the Navy and see the world". We spent two nights and one day in Bahrain. The Emirate was a very rich oil well, in fact an island joined to Saudi Arabia by a causeway. It was very much Arabic and I enjoyed my one afternoon's stroll ashore there. At the Kasbah I purchased for next to nothing three Persian coffee pots caked in dry mud. Over the years careful slow cleaning has produced beautiful patterned copper work. Returning towards the ship a young boy approached from behind tinkling a brass object. I gave him a quarter of what he asked for, which I think came to five shillings, and he dashed away very happy. It was a pestle and mortar, which cleaned up very well.

During the week in the Gulf we searched dhows every day without any luck or success. It must have been very depressing for the local ships but my guess was that there were simply none there. We spent nights alongside at Abu Dhabi, Doha and Dubai before our last night in Sharjah. Everywhere we went there was evidence of British troops slowly building up in preparation for the withdrawal from Aden. Most evidence of this was in Sharjah, and we were all very amused to see one large shop where the troops obviously did most of their purchasing. Above the door, with Arabic writing either side, painted in perfect English was the proudly adopted name of the Arab owner, Robin Bastard!

It had been a busy week but a great break for the crew who had enjoyed the runs ashore everywhere we went. After buying some souvenirs from Mr Bastard we rendezvoused with the local squadron on their return from Pakistan and after passing through the attractive Straits of Hormoaze, we moored up for a night in Muscat, a final run ashore and top-up with fuel before our return to Aden.

A couple of nights later when the radar plotter reported an echo close inshore to the OOW, I was called so that we could go and investigate. It was a Russian fishing vessel and as we approached she switched on her navigation lights and started trawling. It was most suspicious. It was midnight and we were close inshore to the Omani Western Province of Dhofar, not far from the port of Salallah. The only people fishing to any great extent in the area were, in fact, the Russians. But they kept together well out to sea in a gaggle with a vast mother-ship and a fleet of trawlers. Mother would take their catches on board, an army of fisherwomen would process all the fish and by the time the mother-ship had returned to Vladivostock, they were boxed up and ready for marketing. In the meantime, another empty mother-ship would have arrived in the Arabian Sea. The trawlers appeared to stay there forever.

So, what was the Russian trawler doing at midnight without any navigation lights on and not trawling, one mile off the coast of Oman? I knew and it became more obvious because they started trawling as soon as we arrived on the scene. I immediately signalled FOME and told him the name, number and position of the said vessel, and requested instructions. In the meantime we went to action stations and carried out our very limited orders known as Rules of Engagement, which we were instructed to carry out when finding a foreign fishing vessel actually fishing in territorial waters. These rules terminated with us firing one Bofors 40mm round across the Russians' bows. FOME was kept informed and we had still heard nothing from him. Relations between our two ships were amicable. They slowly did what we asked by getting out of territorial waters but I knew that as soon as our back was turned they would go back again. They had a job to do and so did we, but the last thing I wanted was a cold war international incident. We manoeuvred Calton so that we couldn't be rammed if this very large trawler felt like sinking us.

Time passed and at 0130 there was still no answer from Peter Howes. I knew what he was going through because at this unearthly hour of the night, he would have to be getting some politician to make a decision and that's not easy at the best of times. Eventually, at 0200, two hours after our first report and request for instructions, the reply arrived:- "Leave them alone and come home. Peter Howes was never able to divulge what talks had occurred in Aden that night or with whom, but I should think the matter was handed over to the local military in Oman. Next stop Mukalla, purely for an overnight's stop as we had been up most of the previous night with the Russians. I didn't meet James as he was away. It was a pity as I would like to have discussed the Salallah incident with him. When Florence Nightingale came down, I explained that I was not drinking and she said it was just as well as she had nothing to drink in her flat but plenty to eat as she was hungry. Oh no, not again! The imploring look in her eyes could not be refused and I needed some tender love and care after the Russians had caused me a bit of worry.

Now for the next surprise in that we were told that we had to take Calton back to the UK to be put in reserve. This was all part of the Ministry of Defence planned withdrawal from the Far East as well as the Middle East and it meant a minesweeper from the Singapore Squadron would come to Aden as ships of the RN moved westwards towards the UK. This would obviously be great news for everyone on board, but most had not been out in Arabia very long. I went to see Patricia and asked to see Peter Howes as soon as possible. I told him my crew thought it was great news to be going home but that I personally was very much enjoying being at sea off Arabia and that I was a bit upset that my time in command was being curtailed to six months. I also pointed out that none of us had blue uniform, as we had been air transported out with the intention of returning to the UK by air when our time was up. He sympathised and said he would do what he could. Three days later he beckoned me to say that I must take Calton home to Portsmouth but that I would shortly be appointed to command HMS Kildarton on its arrival from Singapore, and that subject to various permutations some of my ship's company could join me.

We wasted as little time as possible getting home, straight up the Red Sea, but had to anchor in the Bitter Lakes to allow a south-bound convoy to pass, and then on to fuel at Port Said. The

Farewell to HMS Calton as she leaves Aden for the last time.
Most of the crew returned to join HMS Kildarton

last time I had been through the Suez Canal was in 1951 in the Theseus. In 1956 it had been nationalised and everyone in Great Britain said the Egyptians had no idea how to run a canal and that it would be chaotic. I still had memories of Captain Ben Bolt placing the sozzled British pilot at the back of the bridge and conning the Theseus himself without the aid of the said pilot. Now ten years after nationalisation I was witnessing the Egyptians doing it smartly, politely and efficiently as I'm sure they had been doing since 1956.

One night in both Malta and Gibraltar for runs ashore, and then for the most fantastic welcome in Portsmouth. Firstly we were the first ship ever to enter Portsmouth in tropical kit and our arrival had been preceded by a signal from FOME to the C-in-C Portsmouth:-

> We know that white is not quite right
> But hope you'll excuse her lack of blues
> It's not because they've got too tight
> But merely that we're travelling light.

Admiral Sir Frank Hopkins, who had been a shipmate of mine when he was a Commander in the Theseus replied:-

> The weather here is hardly fit
> For sailors in a lightweight kit
> But Calton's plight has left me moved
> I can but say herewith approved.

Wearing tropical kit as HMS Calton enters Portsmouth Harbour

HMS KILDARTON – MY FOURTH COMMAND

I had received my appointment to command HMS Kildarton from the Admiralty and it seemed no time before I was once more flying out, courtesy of British United Airways, in one of their VC10s to the barren rocks of Aden. This time everyone had been told to take their blue uniforms as well as their tropical kit. All the familiar faces were around but the situation in South Arabia seemed to be getting worse and everyone seemed a bit more tense.

It was another very proud moment in my life as at the age of 33, I was piped aboard Kildarton to begin my fourth command. No time to hang about so I went straight up to see Patricia and Bill Curtis and of course the Admiral himself, Peter Howes. Within a matter of days there were disturbances and riots in

Waiting for us on our return from the UK, HMS Kildarton, alongside Admiralty Jetty, Aden

Mukalla. Militarily, nothing was to be done about it, whilst the politicians tried to sort out a situation in which a youth had been killed and twenty four people injured. Kildarton was sent on what the Middle East Command called a mobility exercise and as we patrolled offshore, the 2nd Battalion the Parachute Regiment arrived at the nearby Riyan airport. They landed in Beverley aircraft and were escorted by noisy RAF Hunter jets flying overhead. It was, in fact, a successful show of strength, we had all left within twelve hours and hopefully everything returned to normal. I wondered!

Our next task was to visit one of the strangest outposts of the British Empire, namely the island of Kamaran at the southern end of the Red Sea, three hundred miles west of Aden. There to meet us on our arrival alongside his jetty, which was just long enough to take us, was the Commissioner, Tug Wilson, who had asked for our assistance in a number of small but technical jobs.

Commissioner Tug Wilson

224

He was a marvellous man from the West Country and an amicable eccentric who appeared to love his work as the British headman amongst three thousand happy Arabs, in this desert island, miles from nowhere. He spoke perfect Arabic with a West County drawl and his eccentricity was obvious when he drove us to the small airfield from which Aden Airways operated. The welcoming noticeboards were quite crazy and full of amusing but useless information, all in English. He showed us the work required to be done, which would involve a few engineers and electricians and it was agreed to leave it till the coolness of the next morning.

In the meantime a football match was arranged against the islanders, and it must have been witnessed by the entire male population and their children. After the match I visited Tug's

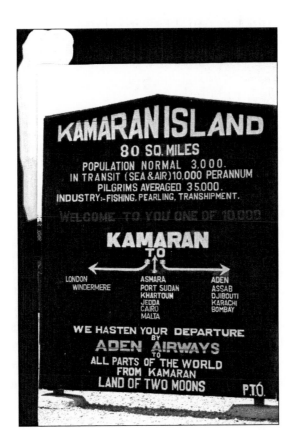

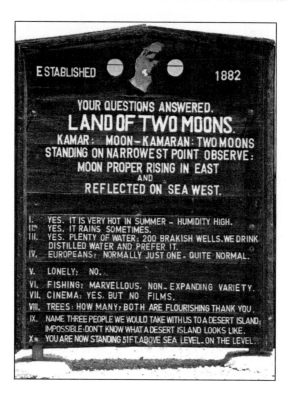

so-called residence and had a swim in his extraordinary swimming pool which was about ten feet square and had a vast depth of about twenty feet. During the excellent curry supper, he asked if we could help him produce and lay the moorings for port and starboard buoys at the entrance channel to his harbour We agreed to show him how to construct the concrete sinkers and then we would return at a later date to lay them in the exact required positions. As he drove us back to the ship, he told me to bring a rifle plus a few rounds with me tomorrow and I could go game shooting.

Next morning while the stokers and electricians did their technical work, Andy and I plus a couple of able seamen helped Tug construct two large boxes about a cubic yard in size. We told him to fill them with cement and as it was setting place in each box one of the two mooring rings which we were providing. I had never been game shooting before but nevertheless Tug insisted that

Kamaran Island Harbour with the small airport to the left

evening I went in his Landrover with two Arabs. He instructed me to aim close to the ears near the temple and off we went creating a cloud of dust as we sped across the desert to the chosen area. Within minutes a gazelle pranced across the sand, I took aim as instructed, fired, and surprisingly it was a good shot. This lovely animal rolled over and over in the sand, we raced towards it, and one of the Arabs gave it the coup de grace. It was the only living thing apart from a rat or mouse, which I have ever knowingly killed and I wished I had not done so. As we drove to the residence with the gazelle dead in the back, they indicated they would have the head cleaned up and that the next time I was in Kamaran I could collect it and have it mounted to put above my mantelpiece at home. I felt quite sick and said no thank you very much.

On our way out of Kamaran we checked on the depth of the positions in which Tug Wilson wanted his mooring buoys so that we could obtain the correct length of wire and chain required. On our return to Aden we received the following signal from the High Commissioner's Office, which had been sent by Tug Wilson:-

Grateful for your sending Kildarton here. Please express to Commander Reeder my personal thanks for all the help he gave us and ask him to pass to his crew my appreciation of the hard work put in. I hope you will be able to send this ship here again before long.

Although we had helped put on the show of strength at Mukalla in June, Kildarton had not been alongside there and it was April since Calton had last done so. They were extending the concrete jetty, where we always berthed, and James Ellis asked if it were possible for us to give a helping hand. The team went into action but it was very hard work in the tropical heat. So with a few working just for a short time each, they were able to help finish the job in two days. A couple of our lads got quite bad sunstroke so Florence Nightingale came down with some secret potion and administered unto them at the end of her day's work. Although she knew I hadn't got my swimmers with me, instead of going straight to her flat, she drove the Landrover about two miles westwards along a sandy track to a completely deserted and very long beach. She said she wanted to do something she had never done before and when she stopped she got out of the car, undressed and slowly walked towards the sea. I did the same, caught up with her, and because of my concern for sharks, kept to seaward of her in water no deeper than four feet. It was certainly very enjoyable having that part of the Arabian Sea all to ourselves. With the political situation in the East Aden Protectorate, I think she foresaw the end of her contract rapidly approaching, and thanked me for protecting her on the opportunity for her first skinny-dip.

I spent most of the daytime in the Administrator's Residence and when James wasn't busy he filled me in with the situation up country. He talked about the various regions and told me he and Joanna would shortly be spending two or three days in the Hadramaut region and I would be very welcome to accompany them. I jumped at the idea and said I was sure that the Admiral would agree to it. I hadn't forgotten the French Foreign Legion's invitation to their Bastille Day celebrations on 14th July. Also the crew were due their reward for their concrete work on the jetty. We called in at Aden for one night so that we could pick up Colin

Doland whom I had promised a trip to Djibouti and what better than for the Bastille celebrations.

The best thing about our two-day visit was the tremendous time the ship's company had in the port, as well as in the Legion's Club. Charles showed Colin, Andy and myself around the Brigades Training area and in the evening the three of us were invited to the Officers' Bastille Day Dinner Dance. The dress was Red Sea Rig which is white open-necked uniform shirts, cummerbund and lightweight black uniform trousers. Colin found it all very interesting being able to talk soldiery with Charles and I was very happy to be able to repay some of the kindnesses he had shown to me.

Another political and diplomatic problem was capturing the attention of the Royal Navy in the Middle East and that was the Beira Patrol. In November 1965 Ian Smith had unilaterally declared the independence of Rhodesia and become the country's Prime Minister. Great Britain imposed sanctions, as did the United

With Colin Doland and French hosts at Bastille Day dinner dance,
14th July 1966

Nations, but with their combined incompetence, nothing much seemed to be happening and Rhodesia was getting as much oil as it wanted. In the port of Beira in Mozambique was the terminus for the oil pipeline to Rhodesia and in order to prevent tankers disembarking oil there the Royal Navy had on 1st March been ordered to start up the Beira Patrol. There were Tribal Class frigates and other warships coming and going through the Suez Canal and stopping off in Aden for a night's fuel stop. All these ships and the patrol were under the control of the Flag Officer Middle East. The rules of engagement were both complicated and far too lax and our warships were not allowed in Mozambique territorial waters. The RN was getting no help or guidance from the government, Rhodesia continued to receive as much oil as needed and the whole thing was crazy.

Three days after our recent visit to Djibouti terrorists killed two RAF sergeants in the Crescent. Things were getting worse, security had to be tightened up and life was more tense for everyone but particularly the families. We were not allowed to be in the streets alone and had to go around in at least twos or threes. I always did the short walk from the ship to the Crescent on my own. As we already knew it is lonely being Captain of a ship and no-one wants to accompany you on a stroll ashore. We were all different age groups and had different interests. One night a Poison Dwarf, the name the Cameron Highlanders had inherited at Minden in Germany approached me pointing his machine gun roughly in my direction. "Who are you sirrrrr?" he asked in his broad Glaswegian accent. "I'm captain of that minesweeper over there," was my reply. "You know yerr no allowed to be on yerr own sirrrr, so please go back to yerr ship sirr." I phoned his colonel next morning and congratulated him on the fact that one of his regiment was the only one to have picked me up for being on my own in Aden. Whenever the Cameron Highlanders were on duty there were never any security incidents. The terrorists knew it was a good time to lie low, as they were one of the toughest and best units in the British Army. When any battalion was on duty, they were divided into three platoons, one on patrol one on stand-by and the other was off duty. In the case of the Cameronians, the platoon on stand-by, rumour had it, were checking that the off duty platoon were not getting too drunk and disorderly!

I was asked to Peter Howes' farewell party in his residence and to dine on the terrace overlooking Steamer Point and Kildarton was indeed a great pleasure. I was personally very sorry to see him leave his post as Flag Officer Middle East. He had been a tremendous boss to work for and with, and it was in no small measure due to his expertise and personality that our team in the South Arabian Patrol Vessel was able to carry out our tasks so efficiently. In the flimsy he gave me before his returning to the UK he wrote that I had conducted myself to his entire satisfaction and that:-

> *Lieutenant Commander M.J. Reeder has proved himself a most capable, forthright and efficient Captain of HM Ships Calton and Kildarton and has earned the respect and affection of both officers and men.*

Peter Howes had one more appointment before retiring and then he was Private Secretary to the Lord Mayor of London from 1968 until 1972.

The first week in October found us one thousand two hundred miles up to the north-east looking after Sir Richard Turnbull, the High Commissioner of Aden. He was in the Kuria and Muria Islands and had asked for us to take him the hundred odd miles to Salalah on the mainland in Oman. Why he was up here in another far outpost of the empire he didn't divulge. Suffice it to say there had been what was known as the Dhofar Rebellion simmering in the region since 1965, we had intercepted that Russian trawler earlier in the year, the K and M Islands were handed over to the Sultan of Oman when Aden became independent a year later and the terrorism, Marxist inspired with East German support was to continue until 1975.

Sir Richard Turnbull did not talk about any of these things but he was obviously enjoying being in our relaxed ship away from the tensions of Aden and whilst reminiscing his worldly experiences. He had been Chief Secretary of Kenya, then Governor, and then Governor General of Tanganyika before coming out to Aden in 1964. He certainly caught up the rough end of the rundown of the British Empire. The Mau Mau uprising and now the Aden Emergency A serious man but every now and then showed a good sense of humour, especially when he conjected that the British Empire would be remembered for only two things, the popularisation of football and the saying f... off. He said he had told Denis Healey, the British Defence Secretary, this when he had been in Aden earlier in the year. Sir Richard sent me a very sincere thank you letter and I was very pleased to show it to the crew.

Having just returned from Salalah, we found ourselves on the way back up there in the company of HMS Fearless and the RFA oil tanker Tidesurge. We were going there firstly as a show of strength and secondly to have some dealings with the aforementioned Dhofar Rebels. Fearless was officially called a Landing Platform Dock – sounds a bit American – but we all called her an Amphibious Assault Ship and she was capable of carrying up to a battalion of infantry plus the landing craft and/or helicopters in which to land them ashore. We went alongside Tidesurge to top up with fuel on a couple of occasions and it was good to have lunch on board and meet the Master and his fellow officers.

Maybe because I had been out there longer than most, or perhaps I was getting better known amongst the hierarchy, but I received my second dinner invitation from an Admiral within a month and a half. The security situation did not encourage dinner parties as such and most social occasions were very informal. This time the invitation was from the Commander-in-Chief and Lady Le Fanu and the dress was Red Sea Rig. Arriving at Command House which was an old colonial bungalow perched on a promontory above the Navy's Round House, one couldn't help a sense of wellbeing.

There must have been at least twenty other guests, mostly married couples, and Mike and Prue Le Fanu were perfect hosts. Dinner was out on an open air terrace surrounded with bougainvillaea, and other flowers whose names were unknown to me and I was seated beside an attractive girl who appeared to be

7th October, 1966

My dear Commander

    I should like to thank you and your officers once
again for your many kindnesses on our return journey from
the Kuria Muria islands to Salalah.

    This was a pleasant climax to an enjoyable breather
in fresher air than here, and I am most grateful for the
consideration and thoughtfulness shown to me by yourself
and all members of your ship.   It was particularly good
of you to allow me to use your cabin - I hope it was not
too much of an inconvenience.

    With best wishes to you all.

Yours sincerely

Richard Turnbull

Lt. Commander M. Reeder, R.N.
H.M.S. Kildarton,
H.M.S. Sheba,
Aden

Letter from Government House

the only other unattached person there. After dinner there was dancing to a record player and I asked my next door neighbour if she would like to participate. It all seemed surreal, another world, as we danced to such melodies as "A Swinging Safari". Down below we could see the harbour, Kildarton, the Crescent and in the distance, parts of Khormaksar, plus the inevitable military Landrovers.

June came from a naval family and had come out to Aden to work as one of the secretaries in the High Commission. As we had the last dance together she whispered that she knew of me, as she had typed the letter from Sir Richard after his trip which he had so enjoyed and had seen the signal from Tug Wilson in Kamaran. It all ended rather quickly as most people felt they should be home by midnight and as I had no car, I asked June if she would mind dropping me off near the ship. Yes, she was happy to do so, but on the way she changed plans and we went to her flat for a nightcap instead! She switched on her tape recorder and we eventually dozed off. What a perfect end to the evening it was to have been invited into the home of this lovely girl and made so welcome. Before she went to work in the morning I thanked her for everything and she said she looked forward to us meeting up again very soon.

Although I didn't know it at the time, that evening was the last occasion I saw Mike Le Fanu, who in my humble opinion was the best naval officer of the century. He was a fine seaman, a brilliant ship-handler and above all a great friend to anyone who knew him. I was fortunate enough to have served with him on three different occasions in three different parts of the world, namely Londonderry, Singapore and now Aden. He had that brilliant ability of being able to lead and encourage men with his insatiable appetite for both working and playing hard. The occasional well planned skylark, plus his tremendous sense of humour all helped.

Within four years of that dinner party in Aden he had been appointed Knight Grand Cross of the Order of the Bath and become First Sea Lord and Chief of the Naval Staff, the Professional head of the Royal Navy. He retired from that post on 3rd July and was promoted Admiral of the Fleet, the highest rank in the Navy. There is no doubt he would have been Chief of the Defence Staff, that is the head of all three services, if he hadn't died of leukaemia within four months. A tragic and terrible loss at the young age of fifty seven to the Royal Navy, all three services and the country as a whole.

My proposed two day holiday in the Hadramaut with James and Joanna materialised later in the month. I was to fly Aden Airways to Riyadh, the RAF station near Mukalla, where they would meet me to go straight off on our short tour. The Wadi Hadramaut had several small towns centred along watercourses where there were watering stations for the Bedouin tribesmen. It was fascinating to see so much greenery in the middle of the rock and desert, with crops of wheat and millet close to date palms and coconut groves. Coffee was also produced in the area.

Wadi Hadramaut

In the towns were mud brick buildings and houses and for the two nights we were there we stayed in one of them. My bathroom, like all the others, had a lavatory which consisted of a hole in the floor with sand ten feet below. Evidently an Arab servant covered everything up with shovels of sand the next day. Quite a change from civilised Aden or Florence's flat in Mukalla. When modern loos were first installed, notices were displayed telling the Arab occupants to use paper instead of stones for wiping their bottoms. Translation into another language, especially involving both words and manuscript, is always problematical with the net result that the locals used both, and wrapped the stones in paper and subsequently blocked parts of the town's sanitary system. Joanna and James were most kind in showing me around this biblical part of the world and explaining everything to me. We got back to the residency rather late but the faithful Florence was waiting to take me back to her home and my return flight wasn't until late in the morning.

This was the sixth time in about a year that I had been asked to stay at the home of this charming person and I tried to find out what made her tick. She was what people used to call a spinster and although maybe not so in earlier days, she often indicated that even if the opportunity did occur now, she didn't really relish settling down to the married way of life. She really did enjoy her work and she had plenty of that to do with all the Arab women and their midwifery problems. As we chatted in the not-so-early morning, I recited a ditty I once heard:-

> Sing hey diddle diddle
> A middle-aged fiddle
> Can still play a jolly good tune
> And always remember
> A rose in December
> Is much more fun than in June.

She appreciated it and said she was only too happy to be my December Rose! "As long as you plant me in a bed and not against a wall," she added with her usual naughty but delightful sense of humour.

It was on our next return from Djibouti and while patrolling off Little Aden, that a motor boat belching black smoke appeared from the south. At the bows was a man waving a white sheet and it became rapidly obvious that they were surrendering to us. It was a Somali Navy SDML, about eighty feet in length and built in Russia. It was beckoned alongside and an armed Leading Seaman and Able Seaman were put on board whilst my interpreter Abdi Mohamed asked questions I put to the skipper. They were Somali deserters from the port of Berbera, one hundred and fifty miles away and said they wanted to escape the Communist regime in Somalia and live in Aden. Their guns were trained vertically, the white ensign was raised on their mainmast and we towed them to our berth at Admiralty Jetty. As far as I know this was the only warship to have surrendered to the Royal Navy since WW2, and after the Aden police took it, plus the two crew, away up harbour, nothing more was ever heard of the incident.

By now Rear-Admiral John Martin had been Flag Officer Middle East for two months and the transfer of the Middle East Command to Bahrain and the Persian Gulf was beginning to gain momentum. He was a different cup of tea to Peter Howes in that he was a navigation specialist and had never actually been captain of a ship. He was more of a Whitehall Warrior and there were many admirals in the same boat so to speak! He had been awarded the DSC for steadfast courage at the Allied landings in North Africa and Italy and post war he had a number of good staff and other shore-based appointments. He was Senior Naval Officer in the West Indies, based ashore in Bermuda, at the time we in the Dartmouth Training Squadron were quelling the riots in British Guiana and he had been captain of the RN College at Dartmouth immediately before coming out to Aden.

The Sultan of Qu'aiti had died in October and the coronation of his son was due to take place in Mukalla on 1st December. James Ellis had asked if Kildarton could take part and it was while preparing for this great event that I first got to know John Martin, whom I had not met before. Amongst other things he organised for me was another minesweeper HMS Puncheston, to come down from the Persian Gulf to join in the celebrations and for us,

*Believed to be the only warship to have surrendered
to the Royal Navy since WW2*

the senior ship, to be temporarily fitted with saluting guns. Where John Martin found these guns I will never know, possibly Whale Island, but they certainly arrived at Khormaksar in time for us to do a couple of practice runs before leaving for Mukalla.

We rendezvoused with Puncheston and anchored close offshore the day before the coronation. We were going to be there for three days and it was going to be hard for the crew in the heat, with no time ashore other than a couple of dull official engagements. That evening and the other nights we were there, both ships were floodlit from sunset till midnight and at 0800 the next morning at Colours both ships dressed overall. And there we stayed, all rather dull, but the Royal Navy helping the British Government, or more importantly the British Advisor, to put on virtually the last good show of cooperation in the East Aden Protectorate and giving support to the Sultanate.

Imposing though the Sultan's Palace was, the so-called parade ground at the back was like a dusty go-cart track. The two captains plus two officers and four ratings from each ship, smartly dressed in their best white uniforms, witnessed a circus as the Sultan's Armed Forces, and the Hadramaut Bedouin Legion sauntered past their new young Sultan. It would have made the Navy's parade ground training staff at Whale Island wince. In the evening I was invited by the Qu'aiti government to a banquet in the palace and had no trouble refusing the sheep's eye which I had only been half-heartedly offered. Instead I enjoyed the curries on offer and all the delicious fruits gathered in.

The next day at noon the appropriate gun salute was fired as Sultan Ghalib Bin Awadh arrived alongside in his small launch and came aboard. He had literally arrived out from the Royal Military Academy at Sandhurst, having been previously educated at Millfield School and I felt extremely sorry for him having to take over this cauldron in South Arabia. He was extremely mature for his eighteen years of age and showed great interest in the ship and stayed much longer than expected. James and I had a quiet bet as to how long he would be residing in the palace. I gave him less than a year and I won. He was ousted by the Communist takeover the following September and later went to both Oxford

His Highness, Sultan Ghalib Bin Awadh Al Quaiti,
on the morning of his Coronation 1ˢᵗ December 1966

and Cambridge universities to gain an MA and read Arabic studies. He has lived with his wife and family in Saudi Arabia for many years.

That afternoon we were open to visitors but only those who had been approved by James. After all it was only two months ago that Pat Gray, the Commander of the Hadramaut Bedouin Legion, and his wife, had been shot right here in Mukalla. We didn't want any terrorists on board and I had a couple of sentries armed with pistols, hidden away just in case. That evening after switching off the floodlights at midnight, we quietly weighed anchor and moved westwards towards Djibouti, the crew's reward for putting on a very good show in very dull circumstances. Awaiting our return in Aden was a personal letter from the High Commissioner. It started Dear Michael, included thanks to all the ship's company and finished The Royal Navy managed as usual to add a little extra to the occasion which was duly noted and appreciated.

I had asked Peter Howes, on our return from Bahrain, if it might be possible some time for one of their squadron to repay the compliment and look out for us while we went on exercises with the Kenya Navy, and had a jolly in Mombasa. Patricia Curtis had

Invitation

I welcome on board the Sultan accompanied by James Ellis, the British Resident Advisor, and the officer in charge of the Mukalla Regular Army

Snap of a "snapper". Our photographer, Petty Officer Charles Thompson, joins in conversation with the Sultan. He volunteered to be the official photographer for the Coronation.

obviously kept John Martin in the picture because he told me before Christmas that we could do that small thing mid-January. So that was the good festive season cheer for the crew, some of whom including yours truly, were about to spend their second Christmas in Aden.

The whole atmosphere ashore was changing. Politically the British government seemed to have given up the ghost even more so after Denis Healey's visit and that of a Parliamentary Delegation in September. The NLF who were from up-country seemed to be infiltrating the Federal Army and police, whereas FLOSY supported by the Egyptians were more urban and trade unionist and because of this carried little influence outside Aden. The Navy ashore, apart from the Admiral, Bill Curtis, and a couple of others, seemed to have long ago let go both ends and were only interested in the Beira patrol, moving up to the Gulf or getting home. Meanwhile the British Army had to bridge the gap between the couldn't care less attitude of the politicians at home and the thugs on the streets of Aden who were mainly concentrated in the Arab market town of Crater. The British soldier on patrol was doing this with a remarkable amount of skill and fortitude and everyone knew that this fine maintenance of law and order had to be maintained until withdrawal date on 1st January 1968 at the latest.

Life was reasonably quiet and incident-free as we all settled down to try and enjoy what we all knew would be our last Christmas in South Arabia. Andy assured me most of the crew had enough to keep them happy with invitations to parties, five-a-side football competitions and plenty of swimming. Colin and Delia Doland seemed to have a small party somewhere every evening and insisted on me being with them. We went swimming at the Club most late afternoons and Delia laid down the law that I should join her group to climb Shamsan. After all, Mike Le Fanu had done it many times, and she said I must do it at least once to ensure I never got another posting to Aden. That was the saying of the moment.

I insisted on going to sea for a couple of days after Christmas, just to blow the cobwebs away, so we went to Djibouti for what we thought could well be our last visit. The Whitehall Warriors in the Admiralty were planning our early withdrawal from Aden, and it might be sooner rather than later. We would soon be due for refit, so it would presumably make sense to have it done in the UK Meanwhile in the post had arrived an invitation to attend an informal Hogmanay party at the High Commission. It had been sent by courtesy of June whom I had last seen on the morning after Mike Le Fanu's dinner party two months earlier. No point in missing out on that.

On my arrival she greeted me enthusiastically but after a while it seemed that she was like a honey pot, and all the bees were young officers from some of the regiments based in the colony. I chatted to some of the guys, had the odd dance, and

Delia and Stan McArdle, the Captain of HMS
Mohawk aloft Jebel Shamsan – about 1,500 ft

shortly after Auld Lang Syne and the arrival of 1967, I went to say goodbye. June pleaded with me not to go and asked me to stay a little longer and be her first-footer. Within a few minutes the place was empty, everyone had to get back to their barracks or whatever, and she invited me to her flat which I hadn't appreciated was in the same compound as we had been all evening.

She was a really delightful girl and as we relished each other's company for the second time I asked her why I was so lucky.

Because of the nature of her job and the fact she was security cleared, she knew all about Kildarton and had in fact written the other letter of thanks after the Coronation at Mukalla. She admitted she had a soft spot for me and set about proving it. After all the attention she had been receiving earlier in the evening I jokingly asked her which of the many regiments in the British Army she preferred, and she assured me none. I then advised her against the Gurkhas because, although most of their officers were white, their privates were black. She appreciated that one and thanked me for the advice! Before she took me back to Kildarton, I wrote in her visitors' book Best New Year Ever, and I meant it. On parting she said please don't keep me waiting another two months.

I had to be back on board and dressed in the correct uniform to welcome the Admiral who was paying us a traditional New Year's Day visit. That entailed Andy, the Gunnery Officer and myself dressing up in matelots gear to pipe the Admiral on board and the two youngest crew putting on officers' uniform in order to welcome him as he crossed the gangway at midday. It was good that John Martin could actually come on board for the first time in his tenure of office and have sippers of rum and meet the crew.

After our efforts at entertaining the Admiral, I felt knackered and not too interested in going out to lunch. I had been asked by the Chief Reporter of the British Forces Broadcasting Service who earlier on had been on board to interview some of the crew. It had been a good PR job and they were giving a curry lunch in their canteen for various people they had met during the year. So it had to be and although arriving a bit late, the party was still in full swing and I did my best at making polite conversation with a whole lot of people whom I did not recognise or know. Whilst indulging a curry in one hand and a beer in the other, I was tapped on the shoulder and looked round to see December Rose from Mukalla. She told me the requirement for a British Nursing Sister had ceased and she had in fact finished her contract and was flying home the day after tomorrow.

My plea that I was very tired and had to go back on board for a good sleep was rejected. She said tomorrow was a public holiday

*The Captain, Sub Lieutenant and First Lieutenant piping
the Flag Officer, Middle East on board Kildarton
for the rum issue on New Year's Day 1967*

and I could have as much rest as I wanted back in the hotel where she was staying. I couldn't refuse and felt I owed it to her for being so kind to me in Mukalla. I was awakened a good six hours later, lying on my back with Rose on my lap. She was asking me if there was anything I would like. She knew how to look after me and I think I was able to help her enjoy her last thirty six hours in Arabia. I was saying goodbye to a lovely person who had given half her life to the medical care of people at home, and in several countries overseas. Always spotlessly clean in her smart uniform, with her chignon neatly in place, she was about to return to her native Liverpool.

We had already visited several of the islands in the area, usually at the behest of the High Commission. In the first week of January it was the turn of Perim which had been British as part of the Colony of Aden since 1857. It was an island about ten square miles in size with sparse vegetation and no fresh water. We were there to relieve the police detachment. Why they were there and how they existed without water – perhaps there was a rainwater tank – I never found out, but another letter of thanks awaited us in the mail from the High Commissioner.

Next week it was back to the off-beat island of Kamaran to meet again the eccentric Commissioner Tug Wilson and complete some unfinished work. Once more we played the islanders at football and next morning Tug came on board to approve the positions in which we were about to lay his port and starboard channel buoy moorings. He went down a bundle with the crew, and stayed on board for lunch on their messdeck, plus the inescapable tot of rum. We were genuinely sorry to leave Kamaran. It was the only place in the whole of South Arabia where the natives were friendly. All the men were fishermen, sons of the sea, but it was predominantly due to their Commissioner Tug Wilson that they were so happy. There was one final and rather sad request from Tug, namely to take one of their number, a mental patient back to Aden to put in care. He was voluntarily chained to a stanchion so that he wouldn't fall overboard and meet the sharks. He was carefully watched over by one of our crew. The

The armed police garrison which we relieved
from the island of Perim January 1967

following signal was sent to the High Commissioner, for the
Captain of HMS Kildarton – from Tug Wilson:-

> *Thank you and your ship's company for all your*
> *kindnesses. Your visit very much appreciated here and am*
> *asked by islanders to request your early return. Personally*
> *am still enjoying effects of rum issue.*

The following day we were on our way for the promised jolly to
Mombasa. Although the weather was perfect, we couldn't go too
fast as we didn't want to run out of fuel and have to visit
unfriendly Somalia in the far distance. Not one other ship was
seen during our six day passage and everyone was able to recover
from the New Year festivities and really relax by playing such
games as Uckers (giant sized Ludo) and Tombola. The day before
we arrived at our destination, we approached the Equator and
carried out the traditional ceremony of crossing the line in the
presence of His Most Gracious Majesty King Neptune. None of
us had been south of the Equator before, so in due course we all

Local fishermen watch as our team demonstrates their
seamanship skills for laying two sinkers and buoys
at the entrance to Kamaran Channel

received notification that we were now sons of Neptune and were permitted to cross the line at any future date unmolested by any creature of the Deep.

The Kenya Navy knew the time of our arrival within twelve daylight hours and we were acting as the smuggler of illegal arms into Mombasa Harbour. Their ships, we did not know how many at the time, had to detect us by radar and then in a friendly manner carry out boarding party practices. It was strange for us to be on the other side of the fence. The exercise went well, particularly from the Kenyan point of view, as their Air Force had also joined in on a reconnaissance roll.

We were given place of honour alongside at Mtongwe in Kilindini Harbour, where we arrived at lunchtime having been escorted in by the KNS Simba and Ndova, our two earlier adversaries. The English language newspaper Nation gave us a good welcome and informed everyone about the joint exercise which had taken place. We were in Mombasa for a week's recreational visit so they correctly informed us all. The first five days were, in fact, going to be quite busy and it started off with us giving a cocktail party for thirty guests chosen and invited by Max Walker, the Commander of the Kenya Navy, whom I had met during my previous visit on that wonderful sick leave. Needless to say Penny was on the guest list.

Penny said she had no idea what I would be doing during the visit, but correctly assumed I would be busy during the daytime. Therefore, as she wasn't due any more leave, she told me all that she had arranged was to book the Beach Lodge on Nyalii Beach and that she had the keys in her bag. Couldn't be better as far as I was concerned and within an hour of the party finishing we were continuing where we left off ten months ago. We had had plenty of small eats at the party, we didn't want to go out for a meal and it was just great to settle down in the nest which she had already prepared beforehand. We could tell straight away that we

HMS Kildarton entering Mombasa Harbour escorted
by the Kenya Navy January 1967

hadn't lost any of the affection we had for each other and the early morning Indian Ocean swim with this golden girl was the same as ever. She drove me back to Kilindini and said she would be back to pick me up around teatime.

The next day we were to receive a visit from none other than the world famous Jomo Kenyatta, who apart from being President of Kenya was also Commander-in-Chief of the Kenya Navy and the other two services. He had on his full tribal regalia and carried his renowned fly swatter. It was truly great to speak to this man about whom much had been written. Perhaps not so well known was the fact that he spent WW2 in England and worked as a farm labourer on his own farm in Sussex. During that time he married Edna Clarke whom he left behind when he returned to Kenya in 1946. During the Rebellion he was sentenced to seven years hard labour for being a member of the Mau Mau and not for actually carrying out terrorist activities. Later he involved himself in trade unions and politics and Kenya became independent on 12th December 1963. Her Majesty the Queen remained Head of State, he asked the white settlers to stay in the country and he preached and supported reconciliation. He was the founding father of the nation and the country has never been the same since he died in 1978 at the age of eighty nine.

It was indeed a pleasure to have this grand old statesman on board, and wished he could have stayed longer. I told him about the joint naval exercise and that tomorrow I was taking the press out to sea. Would he like to come then or at any other time? He declined the offer saying it was sad but he did get seasick. I don't know whether this was a fact or an excuse but he was seventy eight years old.

The press day was a bit of a bun-rush but it did only last an hour or so as they jostled for position to get better photos than their opposition. The same the whole world over. The local hacks had, in fact, done us proud and so I was only too pleased to thank them for what they had done. That afternoon we gave a children's party and it was so enjoyed by the kids that we gave another the next afternoon, the guests being organised by the Kenya Navy from a local orphanage.

Jomo Kenyuatta, President of Kenya

Every morning after being driven back to the ship by Penny, I heard all about the great runs ashore the crew were having. How, in some cases, they had been looked after by European people and how beautiful the Jungle Bunnies were. Tours of the Tsavo National Park, other places of interest and, of course, the local brewery, had all been organised.

I took Penny out for an early meal every evening. She knew quite a few very nice little restaurants about town and I told her I could get away for the weekend if she wasn't working. She suggested we stayed in a small house near Nyali Beach that some friends said we could borrow and thought it would be nicer for a change not to be having salt and sand with everything. On our way there on Friday evening I offered to get some food in but her friends insisted we use the provisions they had left in the kitchen. So with a pair of matching sarongs Penny had bought as a present, we settled down for what we thought would be our last time together. Everything was great, we didn't go in the sea at all, but had frequent fresh water showers, which were different but equally pleasurable. On the Sunday evening she told me she was flying home on leave in February and would I like it if she flew in via Aden for a few days' stopover? Poor girl, she had obviously waited to see if our second holiday turned out equally compatible and I told her I was thrilled she was willing to spend some of her holidays with me in the danger zone of Aden. I also told her that I looked forward to it very much and that I would arrange everything.

One of the good things about being at sea is the time available for reflection and meditation. I had been lucky enough to have done at least six passages navigating my ship distances of over a thousand miles. Some of them had been under emergency conditions, others in rough weather. Now we were in the calm Indian Ocean being escorted by twenty dolphin on either bow, and flying fish were landing on deck. This ship, with its happy and efficient crew, was getting towards the end of its commission and it wouldn't be long before we would be flying our paying off pennant. And what of this crew of thirty five people mostly from Great Britain? There was also the chef and my steward from Goa, plus my Somali Arabic interpreter from Aden. The chef kept us all well fed at least three times a day every day of the week. The steward looked after me, my cabin and uniform, as well as serving meals in the wardroom and Abdi Mohamed was always there when needed at sea. I never saw him when we were in Aden and I have no idea what he got up to as he was controlled by an Intelligence Officer in an office somewhere in Steamer Point. The Chief Tiff, with his stokers and electricians, kept the engines, generators and other machinery ticking over very smoothly and the rest of the crew carried out their everyday duties, as they had often proved, in a thoroughly seamanlike manner.

When we were in Mombasa one of the newspapers had stated that:-

Britain's last patrol vessel off Aden, HMS Kildarton, is now in Mombasa where its crew is spending a week's "holiday" before returning via Aden to Britain.

Where they got that information from I know not, but as soon as we arrived alongside Admiralty Jetty everyone appeared to know we were homeward bound and also that the date of departure was 27th February. When I went to see the Admiral to report on our successful visit to Mombasa, there were obviously going to be other things to discuss as well. He was out of his office and wouldn't be back for some time.

I was therefore able to get up to date through Patricia Curtis who told me that Kildarton had to be alongside at HMS Vernon in Portsmouth by 23rd March and that she would immediately be put into reserve. Could I please make out a tentative programme calling and stopping wherever I liked, but the Admiralty wanted me to pay a three day visit to Cagliari in Sardinia en route. Evidently the British Consul there had asked for a flag showing visit by the Navy. As I left her office, Patricia with a glint in her eye, asked if I had been able to renew the friendship I had briefly mentioned to her on my return from sick leave. Well enough for Penny to be flying into Aden for a few days on her way back to the UK was my cheerful reply.

We were now only required to prepare the ship for the passage home and any other preparations we could do for its disposal on arrival. Andy had the crew vigorously doing all this and it seemed a hell of a lot of extra stores for homeward despatch were arriving on board. The situation in Aden was rapidly deteriorating and I could see there was nothing much we could do about it and, in fact, the sooner we went the better. George Brown in the House of Commons had said that the orderly withdrawal of British Forces and the establishment of an independent South Arabia should occur at the earliest possible date. We were happy to lead the way!

To say I had nothing to do for the rest of our time in Aden was far from the truth. I had to do the planning and chartwork around the only three guidelines to leave Aden on 27th February, call in at Cagliari for a three day visit and arrive at HMS Vernon on 23rd March. I naturally discussed the plans with Andy before going to see John Martin two days later. He was interested to hear about the Mombasa visit and agreed with my homeward plans. As I left, Patricia asked me when Penny was due to be in Aden. "Well, Bill and I are going to be with the Admiral in Bahrain those days, so you would be welcome to have the keys of our flat". What a kind gesture.

Other work involved writing a report of proceedings, plus other reports and sending off periodical returns hopefully for the last time. What was more important as far as I was concerned was making out lists of all the kind people ashore whom I should go and say goodbye to or write to, or invite on board for a farewell drink. Colin and Delia as always were very attentive, and nearly every evening they would be helping me to carry out these social duties. Often the farewells would be at the Officers' Club whilst drinking around the pool and occasionally back on board. Colin even arranged for a dirty chest from the Indian sub-continent to be transported on board. Joanna had offered to get me one for £5 in the Mukulla market where they were regularly shipped in by dhow. You couldn't see the beautiful artwork or brass as it was completely coated in hard mud. It was secured on deck out of sight amongst other stores and it would be a nice task to occupy me on the way home.

The morning of their departure for Bahrain Patricia and Bill Curtis came on board to give me the keys for their flat saying help yourself to anything and don't bother about any cleaning or washing up as the maid will be in every day. What a kind couple of friends they were. I met Penny at Khormaksar off her East African Airways flight and we stayed the first and last days in the Curtis flat, and for the long weekend we were asked to a party and stay with an ex-Ipswich rugby teammate who worked for BP and had a house in Little Aden. No way could we enjoy ourselves the same way as we had in Mombasa, but it was nice to take her away to the more relaxed atmosphere of Little Aden. We knew as we spent our last night, before she flew home the next morning, that it would be the last of a very short but good friendship.

At the party in Little Aden was a Colonel Colin Mitchell of the Argyll and Sutherland Highlanders, later to be known as Mad Mitch. He was getting the lie of the land prior to coming out with his battalion in a couple of months' time. I, having been born in Campbeltown, and our local regiment being the Argylls, we hit it off straight away. He could see I was otherwise occupied but accepted my offer to come on board Kildarton two days later. This he did and in the short time available for us both we agreed it was unfortunate our times in Aden did not overlap and I came to the conclusion I had been speaking to one of the best infantrymen of our time.

The last week was a succession of farewells and we had one day at sea, as a Friends Day, so that the ship's company could ask anyone they had befriended ashore out for the day. Judging by the number of grateful people who came, it was well worth it. It was our last day in Aden and it was eerily quiet. We were all ready to go, we had said our goodbyes and we seemed to be sitting around pondering if there was anything we had forgotten. There was one person, June, whom I had met twice but not seen since Hogmanay and I telephoned to ask if after work she would like to come for a swim at the Officers' Club. She said she would be down in half an hour's time and pick me up on the way.

Friends Day. A trio from the band helped with the entertainment

*The Officers' Club at Steamer Point – the venue
for many runs ashore and my last in Aden.*

After a swim, a couple of drinks, and a prawn omelette each,
she suggested it would be much nicer to have a shower at her
home rather than in the Club. She said she had known we were
leaving tomorrow, had virtually given up hope of seeing me again
and thanked me very much for telephoning her. She went on to say
that she had grown very fond of me but as she came from a naval
family she fully appreciated that I was wed to the Navy and the
sea. Could, she asked, our last night be something special? It was,
and in the morning I thanked her for everything and, in particular,
for being so thoroughly honest and sincere. I knew that what she
had said would have much influence in my decision making in the
next couple of years.

She took me back to Kildarton and it was a great surprise
and honour to see this lovely girl, elegantly dressed, three hours
later with her boss, the British High Commissioner, standing
on Admiralty Jetty. The gangway was about to be slipped, but
I hopped ashore, saluted, and thanked them for the compliment
they were paying me and the ship's company. As I jumped aboard,

the gangway was finally slipped, the ropes were let go, and as the band of the Royal Northumberland Fusiliers struck up with the Maori Farewell and Auld Lang Syne, we disappeared from Aden for the last time.

Exactly one hour after sailing, we received the following signal from the Flag Officer Middle East:-

> Your excellent services off Southern Arabia
> The cheerfulness and enthusiasm of your
> Ship's company have done much for the Navy in Aden
> Bon Voyage and a Happy Homecoming.

On the withdrawal from Aden, John Martin became Commander British Forces Gulf based in Bahrain. He was promoted Vice-Admiral in 1970 and became Deputy Supreme Allied Commander Atlantic, and from 1974 until 1980 he was Lieutenant Governor and Commander-in-Chief Guernsey.

The receipt of the signal from John Martin gave everyone on board a contented feeling of job well done and we were able to settle down to a gentle cruise home. We passed Djibouti, Perim, Kamaran, and then Massawa where we had been a year ago. This year the occasion had been upgraded to a Fleet Review. Admiral Le Fanu had been there in the frigate Nubian (stop-over on way south to Beira Patrol), and the French and Russians had tried to outdo him by sending bigger ships and high-ranking Admirals. Mike had Nubian's helicopter to give Haille Selassie a guided tour of the assembled fleet.

I began to ponder the future which appeared to get less rosy as time went on. In the space of the last eighteen months I had been given two commands, which during the Aden Emergency we would take to the Persian Gulf, then twice through the Suez Canal and Mediterranean back to Portsmouth, and also south of the Equator to Mombasa in Kenya. We had welcomed on board our ships one Sultan, one Emperor, one other Head of State and one High Commissioner. The Royal Navy had trained me for all this and given me the opportunities to take part in three conflicts, the Korean War, plus the Malayan and Aden Emergencies. Now

The Mukalla chest after many weeks of washing,
scrubbing, scouring and finally polishing

what was the Navy up to? Right in front of our eyes ships were moving south to partake in the Beira Patrol. What were they doing? Theoretically preventing Rhodesia getting oil through the pipeline terminus at Beira. While British politicians were disorganising this, together with the aid of the United Nations, the oil was being transported over land from South Africa, and the same country was delivering it by sea, keeping within Mozambique territorial waters, which was a no-go zone for the Royal Navy. It was all absolutely crazy.

A lot of this pondering was being done while I removed the dirt from the chest which Joanna Ellis had bought for me at the market in Mukalla. With the aid of buckets of salt water I softened and brushed away the mud to reveal the patterned woodwork. We were soon to transit the Suez Canal and, after fuelling at Port Said, received quite a shock to the system. Thirty six hours earlier it had been really hot and we had been in tropical kit. Now we were entering the Mediterranean, it was dark, and half a gale was blowing. By the morning we had packed away our whites and put on the blues, plus duffel coats for those on watch. I couldn't believe it but when we moored up in Malta we were the only British warship there. Two American destroyers were visiting, but it was all a sign of the times.

Cagliari was a change of scenery for us all. First night in we gave an official cocktail party for thirty guests – chosen by the British Consul. We then had half an hour to change out of uniform and get to an informal supper dance given by the local English speaking community for twenty members of the ship's company. It was a delightful evening and the organiser, Maria, was making sure everyone was being well fed and enjoying themselves. We had a dance and it turned out she had been in the Italian Navy, or rather married to an Italian Naval Officer, and they were now divorced. She was an English language teacher at a local school and spoke it very well indeed. The dance music was good quality and Lara's Theme from Doctor Zhivago, which was very much in vogue, was played.

It was being played for about the fifth time as Maria and I had a last dance together. Being unable to invite me to her home she offered me a lift back to the ship. She drove a roundabout way and parked on a headland overlooking the sea. Apologising for the cramped conditions, she made life easier by undoing the front buttons of her dress, as her car seat reclined backwards. It was a very enjoyable conclusion to my first evening in the capital of Sardinia. Poor Maria, she was a lovely woman, and we still had all tomorrow after work and all day Sunday to enjoy ourselves. I asked her if she would like to arrange a little hotel nearby and she jumped at the idea. She left me at the ship and with a cheeky 'ciao' sped off in her car.

That morning I paid an official call on the British Consul, who took me to meet Ammieaglo di Divisione Carlo Maccafuri. He was also Commandante Militare Marittimo Autonomo in Sardinia – a NATO appointment. He came on board for a few informal lunchtime drinks and witnessed the start of our ship being open to visitors – an event which had been well advertised in the local press. The ship's company was eyeing up the local talent for the night's run ashore, and several of them seemed to strike lucky; maybe with some of the girls who had been at the dance the night before.

Everything seemed to have been well organised, both on board and ashore, for the rest of our stay in Cagliari. So when

With the British Consul after official call
on senior Italian Naval Officer

Maria arrived to collect me we had a short drink and then drove off to enjoy what was left of the weekend. The owner of the fine little hotel was there to meet us. He arranged for us to have a Frutti di Mare meal in our room later in the evening and he would make sure we were not disturbed in the morning. Maria went out of her way to make sure I would not forget my three days in Cagliari. I awoke on the Sunday morning to feel her lovely warm body rolling over on top of me and later ask: "Signor contento?" I replied: "Si signora, grazie mille".

After a leisurely breakfast, we drove thirty miles or so westwards as far as two small islands Pietro and Antioco, and passed the fabulous Chia Beach. Although spring was in the air, it was only halfway through March and no way did either of us want a swim. We called on board Kildarton at about six o'clock for a farewell drink and there was only the duty watch there! It had been the same (once all the visitors had left) the night before. The people of Cagliari had been so hospitable and my crew had really enjoyed themselves: we were all very sorry to leave on the Monday morning for the 72 hour passage to Gibraltar.

Andy suggested that it might be a good idea for the whole ship's company to have a farewell dinner on our only night at Gibraltar. It would probably be the last opportunity as we would all be dispersing as soon as we arrived in Pompey and everyone agreed wholeheartedly. He fixed up a good place in Irish Town. In order that everyone could attend the party for at least a while, half a dozen of the crew left early to relieve those on watch, so that the latter could come along to join in for the second half. It was a very good end-of-commission party. Many amusing stories were retold and one new item of information was that two of the crew were returning to Cagliari, for part of their leave, to be with a couple of signorinas they had met during our visit.

The weather had not been good since we came out of the Suez Canal and we had experienced a rolling southerly sea. This southerly wind and sea pushed us home and so the five days after Gibraltar were not so bad. I had specially asked Bill Curtis not to publicise our arrival at Pompey. He had done us proud in Calton, the Army in Aden were at long last beginning to get good press, and I thought that this trend should continue. There was, however, one big drama awaiting us shortly after mooring, almost unnoticed, alongside at Vernon on Maundy Thursday.

A week earlier the Liberian registered oil tanker Torrey Canyon had run aground on Pollards Rock in the Seven Stones Reef off Land's End. She was taking a short cut to Milford Haven, at the time she was the largest vessel ever to be wrecked and her leaking cargo of crude oil was causing an environmental disaster. A few hours after our arrival we received a signal stating that Kildarton was to be duty ship and stand-by for oil clearance duties down in Cornwall. This meant we had to be at eight hours' notice for sea the whole of Easter weekend. The signal had come from the Captain of HMS Vernon who had become our administrative authority. I went storming up to his office, saw his secretary, and demanded to see Captain Bob Lloyd right now, and I didn't mean maybe.

In I went, and after introducing myself, I told him:

1. For over a year Kildarton's ship's company had been in South Arabia during the State of Emergency.
2. We had brought the ship back, under the orders of the Flag Officer Middle East, to Portsmouth for disposal.
3. It had been arranged and agreed that we would arrive today so that the ship's company could go on Easter leave and that they were, in fact, at this very moment going up the line towards the smoke and beyond.

He then butted in and said that the orders had come direct from the Under Secretary of State for the Navy, Mr Maurice Foley, and that there was nothing he could do about it. I replied:

1. Admiral of the Fleet, Sir Rhoderick McGrigor had told me when I was a cadet to get the confidence of my men and that they would follow me anywhere. That is exactly what I have been doing and I was now continuing to do so.
2. We had been mucked about by politicians in South Arabia and I had no intention of being mucked about in a completely illogical way by Mr Foley.

He could see I had plenty of ammunition up my sleeve and as he began to wilt, I said to him: "How is your wife Marjorie?" I had last seen Bob when I was a kid in Campbeltown and he had married Marjorie, who was one of the three much sought after McKersie girls who lived next door to us. Bob Lloyd was completely bemused and without answering my question said he would look into the matter. I told him that I was now going on Easter weekend leave and that along with sufficient of my ship's company, I would be back on Tuesday to dispose of the good ship Kildarton.

I hadn't actually disobeyed a senior officer's order, but I had told him I had every intention of doing so if my ship's company was called out for oil clearance duties in Cornwall. Nothing more was heard about my meeting with Bob Lloyd and I have not met up with him since. Because I knew I had so many facts in my favour, I had felt good when I had left his office. It was a strange end to a wonderful commission. Kildarton was sold two years later to an Italian oil rig company.

SHORESIDES AND ANOTHER COMMAND

I joined HMS Collingwood, the Navy's Electrical School, and largest shore establishment, which was on the outskirts of Fareham. It had been commissioned in 1940 to instruct Hostilities Only ratings of the Seaman and Telegraphist branches and also housed the Radio Direction Finding School. In 1946 it took over the training of both officers and ratings in the maintenance of all electrical and radio equipment in the Fleet. Thirty years later it was still doing exactly the same thing and it could hardly be called a stone frigate because most of its buildings were still the original wooden huts.

I was therefore, according to the Admiralty, to be responsible to the Captain, with the aid of a large staff, for the administration, employment, discipline and welfare of 3000 Royal Navy and 300 civilian personnel. Quite a challenging task which proved to be interesting, but in no way testing or any great strain on the skills I had acquired, thanks to the Navy. The training, purely technical, was instructed mainly by the Electrical and Schoolie branches in the Training Area, which was housed in more modern buildings slightly separate to the rest of the establishment. I was in no way involved with that.

One of the minor perks of the job was the availability of a red "pussers bicycle" which one certainly needed if wanting to get about the vast place without wasting too much time. I occupied my first weeks in getting to know this large staff, which was aiding me in everything I was responsible for. I think everyone fulfilling that task, both officer and civilian, was older than me, although junior in status. It was all very dull and very much smelled of a nine to five job carried out in a five day week. Everyone seemed to pour out of the gates in their cars, or on their bikes, at a considerably faster speed than they had crawled in at about 0730 in the morning. Not many seemed to give a damn for

Collingwood. The training, although of a superbly high quality, was merely seen by most individuals as a means of improving their qualifications for when they went outside.

And that's exactly what the Admiralty had told me to do as a reward for my previous years' service in the organisation which I loved. At that time the rules for officers wishing to retire were that they should give at least two years' notice – fair enough. If you wanted to qualify for the minimum pension you must have served at least twenty years, not man and boy as frequently quoted, but from the age of eighteen, which was also very fair. My earliest date for pension, therefore, would be my thirty eighth birthday on 30th June 1970. I needed to carry on appreciating the situation as taught at the Junior Officers' Warfare course at Greenwich and I was getting even more sure that the pros for staying in the Navy were far outweighed by the cons. There was a year for me to finally situate the appreciation.

I found it very hard not to think back to the real Navy, to Kildarton days, and also keep in touch with the deteriorating news from Aden. In June, the Aden police had mutinied in their Crater barracks and on 20th June the Royal Northumberland Fusiliers suffered heavy casualties and were ordered to withdraw from Crater. This was because of the British Government's policy of neutral peacekeeping and minimum force and the new General Officer Commanding, General Philip Tower, refrained from reoccupying Crater. Until, on the night of 3rd July with Pipe Major Kenneth Robinson playing Mony-musk, my friend Colin Mad Mitch led his Argyll and Sutherland Highlanders back there. By dawn, having encountered very little opposition, Colin had established his HQ in the Chartered Bank, which was immediately renamed Stirling Castle, and the Argylls continued to occupy the market town until the British withdrawal from Aden in November. The Daily Telegraph in a leading article stated: British troops have shown the combination of skill, tact and cool courage for which they are unequalled. A dangerous and humiliating state of drift, which the British Government permitted to continue for a fortnight, has ended.

Not one Argyll was killed in the whole operation. Mad Mitch had annoyed General Tower and the Ministry of Defence. Because he got very good press, which captured the imagination of the British public, his other superiors were upset and so was the Labour Government. One of the many supporters he had in Aden was the Commander-in-Chief, Mike Le Fanu, who regularly got up at 0400, asked for an Argyll escort to drive him around Crater, thereby giving the Argylls as much support as he was able without upsetting the General too much. He then climbed Shamsan and got to Command House in time for breakfast and a beer. The Navy knows a good infantryman, even if the Generals and politicians did not. Colin was not awarded the expected DSO, he was given to understand he would not be promoted and decided to leave the Army which he did on his return home from Aden.

On the sporting side, for which I had overall responsibility, we had a few sailing yachts and dinghies moored at a dinghy park at the top of Portsmouth Harbour near Fareham Creek. There was an officer in charge of that organisation and he had a Leading Seaman permanently there to help maintain the boats, their gear and personal safety equipment, etc. It was on one of my visits to the area that I first met Alec Rose. He had served in the Navy during WW2 and retired as a Lieutenant(E) RNVR. He had always been keen on sailing and the amount he did depended on how often he could get away from his small market gardening and nursery businesses.

In 1961 he bought a greengrocer's shop in Osborne Road, Southsea, which I had known for many years of living in the Portsmouth area. This enabled him to indulge his love of the sea and sailing. He was attracted to partake in the 1964 singlehanded Transatlantic Race and bought a strong, sturdy wooden yacht called *Lively Lady* in Yarmouth in the Isle of Wight. It had been built in Calcutta, but needed a few changes done in order to survive the pounding it would presumably receive on its way across the pond to the USA. He consulted John Illingworth about sails, which Peter Lucas made and then Blondie Haslar organised the fitting of the self-steering gear. I had met and knew all these fine people. Alec had sailed from Plymouth Sound on 23rd May, there was a total of fourteen contestants and he was fourth to finish at the Brenton Reef Tower near Nantucket thirty six days later.

After that he decided again to sail singlehanded, but this time around the world. He had actually set out in August 1966 but had had to retire. There followed what he called a chapter of disasters. *Lively Lady* eventually got away from the Royal Albert Yacht Club on 16th July 1967. Although there were hundreds of people there to see him off, I was determined not to miss this historic moment. In order to gain a good vantage point I joined the nearby Southsea Rowing Club as a Social Member.

On return from summer leave my attention seemed to wander once again towards South Arabia. In the autumn Colin Mitchell and his Argylls were still in control of Crater, but the Federal Government had ceased to function. Outside Aden the NLF were taking over the Sultanates and Sheikhdoms and within a month they had complete control of the East Aden protectorate. My friends James, the Resident Advisor, and his wife Joanna, had survived a bazooka attack in May and the SAS had been sent to Mukalla to protect them. Now the British High Commissioner, not Sir Richard Turnbull, who had come home, but his relief, had ordered the withdrawal of all British staff from the protectorate. A month later the Sultan, whose coronation I had attended the previous December, was ousted by the Communists and left his palace in Mukalla to reside in Saudi Arabia. On 29th November that year, the British and the NLF signed a Memorandum of Agreement and at midnight South Arabia became independent under the name of the People's Republic of South Yemen.

One afternoon in early December, while I was going through the in-tray in the office, a young Schoolie came specially to see me. He was Secretary of the Collingwood Rugby Club and wanted my permission for the team to go on a tour of Berlin in the New Year. I asked him how in the hell he proposed to do that? He informed me that a close friend of his was an Instructor Officer at RAF Benson and he could arrange for the RAF to fly the team on one of their routine flights to their base in the British sector of Berlin. And he had another ex-college friend who was a Schoolie

Colonel Colin Mitchell

The Argylls in action in Crater

in the Army based at the British barracks in Berlin and the team could be accommodated there. To quote his own words it was all virtually arranged, even the three matches against the RAF (Berlin), the Army (Berlin) and the German police.

I just could not believe it. I was almost speechless, but wanting to give him every encouragement with his plans I told him to write down a detailed programme with all the relevant information and I would have the necessary memorandum published. He thanked me very much and said the team insisted I came along as manager and coach, and "bring your boots with you, Sir. You may need to play." It was nearly three years since I had actually played a game of rugby but it was something to look forward to. I had not been to Berlin before and it was the height of the Cold War. As he was about to leave he noticed I had three metal trays, one marked In, one Out and the third LBW. He enquired what the latter one was for and I assured him his memo would not go in that one because it meant Let the Bastards Wait!

Once a month there was a Wardroom Mess Dinner and Naval tradition and etiquette insisted they should be well supported. The food was usually very good indeed, abundantly drowned with good wines and port, but it was the speeches and the high jinx afterwards that began to be on the wane with me. As a young sub-lieutenant with my fellow messmates we had thoroughly enjoyed the "High Cockalorum", "Are you there Moriarty?", Elbow Wrestling and Carpet Boat Races, etc, which inevitably ended up with a stiff shirt, if not your complete Mess Undress uniform, having to be repaired and then dry cleaned. One officer I knew once enquired as to why his mess bill at Vernon was so high. He was told a charge had been levied to dry the beer out of the piano after mess dinners. Even Trafalgar Night dinners bored me stiff. Some ancient Admiral would be brought out of moth balls, would take hours telling us how wonderful the Navy was, and then propose the toast to the Immortal Memory of Lord Nelson.

The month of December in Collingwood was virtually split in two, the first half preparing for Christmas leave and the second half taking it. Included in the first half were all the Christmas dances, not to mention the private parties. There were far too many of them with the net result that there were many people walking around like zombies. Apart from the wardroom the following groups held Christmas balls: the chief petty officers, the petty officers, the artificer apprentices, the junior rates, and the new entries. The first two were held in their messes, and the last four probably somewhere in Portsmouth like Clarence Parade Pier which seemed to be the most popular. I was very grateful to be asked to them all and always left at least three quarters of an hour before the end so that the Mess President and fellow committee members didn't feel obliged to look after me till the bitter end.

During the leave period itself I was left in complete charge of the whole establishment as the Captain and most other officers (plus all the training staff and trainees) were on leave. There was a duty officer and a small number of duty watchkeepers responsible for security and fire drills. It was all deadly boring, even more so than normal. However, it was a very good time to prepare for my next life and I was seriously thinking about joining the Merchant Navy. The first thing to do was apply to the Board of Trade to see what certification I could achieve, or what they might think of granting me. This entailed much browsing of rules and regulations and writing down all my sea-going experience, types of ships in which I had served and the positions held. By the end of the leave period I had posted the letter off and also applied to become a member of the Royal Institute of Navigation and the British Institute of Management.

I had to forego some of my leave (that was no great shakes) because of the Berlin rugby tour. We were bussed up to the RAF station at Benson, flown out to RAF Gatow in West Berlin and spent Thursday night in the British Sector Army Barracks. It was unbelievable to be in Berlin and to actually see what the Allied heads of state (Eisenhower, Churchill, De Gaulle and Stalin) had imposed on Germany at the Potsdam Agreement. After the war, the country was divided up amongst the Western Blocs into two countries. The Federal Republic of Germany (known by some as West Germany) was divided into American, British and French zones and the Russian zone was the German Democratic Republic (known by some as East Germany).

West Berlin was a political enclave which had existed since 1949 and consisted of the American, British and French sectors of occupation. Many people had read in the press about Berlin but we were fortunate enough to be going there because of Navy rugby and it was only by actually seeing it all that one could really totally appreciate what the ill-conceived ideas of politicians could do to a country.

We took our uniforms with us, as it was only thus dressed that we could go freely through Checkpoint Charlie into East Berlin and thence into East Germany. We walked along a main street in the shopping centre. There were very few people there: most had to be at work. I remember a kitchenware shop and all the pots and pans were a dull grey or black. That seemed to be the colour of most things in the shop windows – nothing colourful. We saw the magnificent Brandenburg Gate which marks the entry to Unter den Linden, the renowned boulevard of linden trees. But the pièce de résistance of the whole tour was to have gone through Checkpoint Charlie and to have seen the terrible Berlin Wall: the East Germans constructed it to stop Eastern Bloc emigration to the West. Over a hundred East Germans were shot by the border guards from their pill boxes.

One day we visited Spandau Prison in the British sector. It was solely there as a gaol for Rudolph Hess, who had been Hitler's deputy in the Nazi Party and had flown to Scotland in 1941 to try and negotiate peace with the British. He had landed near Eaglesham village south of Glasgow, became a POW, was tried at Nuremberg and sentenced to life imprisonment which he served on his own in Spandau. To emphasise the craziness of it all, the day we were there the Russian Army were carrying out the ceremonial guard on the prison. They insisted on their equal share, with the three Western countries of guarding Hess, even though the prison was in the British sector.

Being able to see all this at the height of the Cold War rather overtook the actual reason for us being there and that was the matter of a few games of rugby. We won our first two matches and then had the day off on Sunday. A long lie-in was followed by a monumental curry lunch in the Officers' Mess and then the whole team, plus a few of our Army hosts, went to the mixed public sauna baths. This was an interesting experience as such things didn't exist in most countries, but the healthy Germans were very keen on that sort of thing. What the staff must have thought when twenty rugby players arrived on the scene! There were one or two big German bouncers on patrol, but no-one batted an eyelid.

In the complex were three quite large swimming pools, one very hot, one very cold, and a warm one which I much preferred. Outside surrounded by frost-covered grass was an almost freezing swimming pool. I dived into it several times, but I wouldn't have done so if there hadn't been the warm one awaiting me inside. There were many more men there, and most of the women were at least forty years old, but nevertheless their bodies were quite pleasing to the eye. It was all very invigorating and a good way of ridding ourselves of the curry lunch effect. We travelled to and from the baths by underground, which throughout Berlin was administered and controlled by the Russians and East Germans, another fascinating scene from the Cold War turmoil. Our last evening, like the two previous ones, was spent quietly visiting the biergartens and so-called night life. It was not very exciting and we were all back in the barracks quite early. It was apparent that the average age of the population was high, because most of the younger people had gone to West Germany to find much more beneficial and rewarding work.

I played in the last match which was an easy one as one might expect, against the not very experienced German Police Fifteen. The good thing about it was that it gave me the good fortune to play on the Hertha Bundesliga Football Ground which was better known as the 1936 Berlin Olympic Stadium. We flew back to RAF Benson soon after the match and there was the Collinwood bus waiting to return us to the normality of shore establishment life.

In April I received some good information from the Board of Trade, which was in reply to my letter sent at New Year. It confirmed that I had completed sufficient service as Master of a Foreign-Going Ship and enclosed was a Master Mariners Certificate. Although not yet employed as such, I was in fact a

CERTIFICATE OF SERVICE

AS

MASTER

OF A FOREIGN-GOING SHIP

No. 79001

To Lieut. Cmdr. Michael John Reeder, R.N.

WHEREAS you have attained the rank in the Royal Navy required by Sec: 99 of the Merchant Shipping Act, 1894, the Board of Trade in exercise of their powers thereunder and of all other powers enabling them in that behalf, hereby grant you this Certificate of Service as Master of a Foreign-going Ship in the Merchant Navy.

Dated this 16 th day of April 1968

Countersigned

Assistant Registrar General.   An Under Secretary of the Board of Trade

REGISTERED AT THE OFFICE OF THE REGISTRAR GENERAL OF SHIPPING AND SEAMEN

Certificate of Service

Captain in the Merchant Navy to date 16th April 1968. As far as I was concerned I now had another career, namely in the Merchant Navy. I would still be sailing the seven seas and my situation had been appreciated in more ways than one. I informed Their Lordships in the Admiralty that I wished to resign from the Royal Navy on or after 30th June 1970.

Shortly after receiving that good news, it was announced that Her Majesty the Queen Mother would be visiting Collingwood on Tuesday 11th June. It was in less than two months' time and it naturally fell within my jurisdiction to get everything organised: of course it was the gunnery officer and his small staff of GIs (all gas and gaiters) to put on the smart parade. The training programme must naturally go on as uninterrupted as possible so all the ceremonial training had to take place first thing in the day at morning divisions.

What the public and the media don't appreciate is all the unseen work and preparation that goes on for such a visit. Due mention should be made of those who organised such things as wet weather routine and the routine in case for some reason Her Majesty had to travel by train to Eastleigh instead of the intended flight to the RNAS at Lee-on-Solent. Officers had to be organised to look after the guests such as the Lord Lieutenant of Hampshire, Chairmen of the Fareham Urban District Council and Hampshire County Council and several other people I had never heard of.

I noted the Headmistress of Roedean School was on the list of guests. I presume that was because her school had been taken over by the Navy at the beginning of WW2. I am told that on the first night all the electrics were fused. Beside each bed was a push button alongside which was written: "Press here if you require a mistress during the night"! Also on the list from the same school was the vice head girl. My mind boggled: I wondered why the head girl wasn't on the list. All these people were invited to lunch in the Wardroom and had to be seated beside their host officers in accordance with their status in life and protocol. Luckily I was freelancing, just ensuring everything was ticking over smoothly and was sitting nearly opposite Her Majesty within hearing and talking distance. As always, she was a charming guest.

*I introduce the youngest WREN, who then
presents a posy of flowers to Her Majesty*

Within the month Alec Rose arrived back in Portsmouth after completing his solo circumnavigation of the world. He had done this without the aid of any financial backing or sponsorship; within the space of a day he became a national hero. The Navy had kept their eyes on him and had helped whenever a ship happened to be nearby. On April Fool's Day, when he rounded Cape Horn, the RFA Wave Chief, based in the Falklands, was in the area and relayed messages for him. Also there, flying out from Punta Arenas in Chile had been a plane chartered by ITN News and the Sunday Mirror. On 30th June, as he approached the Scilly Isles, the Coastal Minesweeper *Litterston* rendezvoused with him and was shortly joined by her sister ship *Laleston* to escort him all the way to the Nab Tower off Portsmouth.

It was estimated that over four hundred craft had been out as far as Bembridge Ledge to escort him home and that there were over a quarter of a million people at the Royal Albert Yacht Club as he crossed the finishing line. Within a few minutes he stepped ashore from the C-in-C's barge. I was in the Southsea Rowing Club and what I was unable to see because of the crowd, I was able to watch on a nearby TV set. Within twenty four hours he had been officially welcomed home by the Lord Mayor of Portsmouth and Her Majesty the Queen had agreed to confer a Knighthood on him. He received the Freedom of Portsmouth, appeared on Desert Island Discs and after his death in 1991, at the age of 82, a pub was named after him in Port Solent marina. A true son of the sea.

One Saturday in April I had a stroke of good fortune. I was standing by the bar of the Dolphin in Old Portsmouth when in walked a mate of mine whom I hadn't seen for years. He was Lieutenant Commander Jeremy Widdecombe and what happened in the next hour was unbelievable, and to this day I cannot believe it actually happened.

Jeremy was Commanding Officer of HMS Brave Swordsman and the First Fast Patrol Boat Squadron based in Portsmouth. As we enjoyed a beer or two, he told me what he was doing and that the Navy had a problem. In 1966 his ship and Brave Bombadier had participated in the funeral of the late Chancellor Adenaur and

Alec Rose steps ashore. The view we
had from the Southsea Rowing Club

the German authorities had requested that those two boats, together with other NATO countries, return to Cologne at the end of May to commemorate that participation. Brave Borderer was still in the final stages of a refit but on the instructions of the Commander-in-Chief Western Fleet, HMS Dark Hero had been commissioned from operational reserve. The only trouble was no-one could provide the crew of fifteen to get a Fast Patrol Boat to Cologne and back; it would look very bad if we only provided one boat when the other NATO countries were supplying two each.

Remembering the Whale Island slogan "Them's what's keen gets fell in previous" I told him to say no more and that I was hereby appointing myself to be the Captain. I would select the ship's company from Collingwood and we would be there, ready, willing and able, on board Dark Hero at the chosen place and time. Jeremy and I had one more pint for the road, giving us time to bemoan the state of the Navy and wonder what on earth all the Admirals were up to. We agreed the whole thing was very much a case of the tail wagging the dog, but at least our training had enabled us to get things organised pretty damned quickly – helped of course by a few pints of beer.

On the Monday morning I told my Captain what I had tentatively arranged and he gave his wholehearted permission for me to go ahead. The organisation was simple and five weeks later, early in the morning of Sunday 25th May, I took over command of a warship for the fifth and final time. There had been no official appointment from the Admiralty and no commissioning ceremony as my crew of a First Lieutenant, one ERA, four stokers, two electricians, one leading seaman and four able seamen arrived on board.

Dark Hero was 72 feet in length, had two Napier Deltic diesel engines and had been built by McGruer & Co. of Clydebank in 1957. She was one of the first diesel engine fast patrol boats and because of the excessive black smoke made by these engines' exhausts, the hull had been painted black instead of the usual navy grey. These craft were only designed for short assignments so, on returning to harbour, the crew were accommodated in barracks or a depot ship, but in our case we were going to stay in hotels.

It was great to be back at sea again and taking part in one of the Navy's most important tasks, namely showing the flag. The first stage was a quick 250 mile dash along the English Channel to the Dover Straits and then up the North Sea to Rotterdam, which is a major international commercial centre brought about by its position at the delta of the Rivers Rhine, Meuse and Scheldt. It was the second largest city in Holland and one of the largest ports in the world. As we were only there for a night's rest, so to speak, we had a couple of drinks and a meal in the hotel restaurant before retiring for a good night's sleep.

The next day with a Dutch pilot on board, we proceeded the short distance up the Rhine to Nijmegen, where we arrived mid-afternoon and secured alongside in the centre of the town. Ten minutes after we arrived one of the crew told me there were a couple of policemen on the jetty wanting to speak to me. I invited them on board and their reason for calling turned out

HMS Dark Hero – my fifth command, May 1969, organised over a few pints of beer at the Dolphin Inn, Old Portsmouth!

to be that they had received a report of Dark Hero speeding, making too much wash and causing damage to pleasure boats further down river. They knew it was Dark Hero because we were the only one with a black painted hull. I said I was terribly sorry, but there was nothing I could do about it, as I was going at the speed ordered by the Dutch pilot and the senior officer in Brave Swordsman. I suggested they went over and discussed the matter with them, which they did and I heard nothing more about the incident. Probably the Resident Royal Navy Officer in Rotterdam or the Naval Attaché in Amsterdam dealt with the matter. Warships were used to getting those sorts of complaints, sometimes justified but usually not so.

The citizens of the Nijmegen were very friendly and particularly so in the hotel, nearby shops and restaurants. They had been liberated by the Grenadier Guards in 1944 and gave the impression of being quite pro-British. Whereas they were very anti-American, earlier in that year the USAF heavily bombed the area and killed 750 people; they thought they were bombing the German city of Kieve which was a good fifteen miles to the East.

Within ten miles of Nijmegen was the city of Arnhem, which was well known because of the WW2 battle there in 1944. The British First Airborne Division with the Polish First Independent Parachute Brigade were glider-landed and parachuted into the area in order to secure the bridge. Unfortunately they were dropped too far away and because of stiff German opposition, only a few reached the bridge itself and they were unable to secure both sides. The British ran out of ammunition, some were captured, and the remainder withdrew from the area nine days after landing. The battle was later dramatized in the film "A Bridge Too Far". A friendly Dutch couple we met in a Nijmegen restaurant drove us to see the city and the bridge which was, in fact, the third one to be built. The Dutch Army destroyed the first in 1940 when the Germans invaded, the USAF bombed the second shortly after the 1944 battle and the present one was named John Frost Bridge after the British Paratrooper Commander.

I will always remember the short journey up to Dusseldorf for one thing: a huge yellow sulphur cloud hanging over Duisburg, which is renowned for its steel industry with associated blast furnaces, pig-iron and coal mines. It also claimed to be the world's biggest inland harbour and it was home of Konig Pilsner; a most impressive place but I often wonder how many of its citizens appreciated that vast overhanging cloud and its potential health hazard.

We felt it was safer to breathe again once we had pressed on for the night in Dusseldorf, another vast industrial town in the heart of the Ruhr. One night in 1943, seven hundred Allied bombers had attacked it. Now twenty six years later, it was the heart of the West German recovery, their seventh largest city as well as an international business and finance centre. When we arrived there we appreciated it was our first stop in Germany although we might have been mistaken into thinking we had arrived in Koln. There were quite a few people from there to greet us and prepare us for our official arrival tomorrow.

We had been led to believe that we had been invited for a wreath-laying ceremony and to commemorate NATO countries participation in the funeral of the late Chancellor Konrad Adenaur in 1966. Coming on board with great welcoming smiles were the leaders or representatives of various local and national institutions such as Marine Societies, the Koln Uberseeklub, the Kolner Yacht Club, the Luftsportgruppe Frechin, the Deutsche Marinebund, and the Marinekamaradeschaft. The invitation was for a six-day Marine-Freunschaftstraffen or, in simple English, International Naval Friendship Days. The programme of events gave some indication of how determined the Germans were to ensure we had a most memorable, as well as enjoyable, time.

Four of our visitors, after a few drinks on board, took Jeremy, myself and our two First Lieutenants ashore to dinner in a local biergarten. Sitting next to me was Herr Ernst Schmidt, a middle-aged retired naval officer, who was to become a guide and close friend during our visit. We were, in fact, being entertained to dinner in a brewpub, of which there were evidently a few in Dusseldorf, a city also well known for its beer. We could actually see the delicious Altbier being brewed, using paler malts than in most other beers. Thank goodness these four men had come to

Dusseldorf that evening and pre-warned us about the busy programme in Koln.

The reception we received for the size of our ships was out of this world. The German North Sea Federal Navy Band and a Belgian Military Band were playing as we in Dark Hero secured outside Brave Swordsman – the best place to be as not so many people can goof at you and everyone has to cross the inside ship first. Plenty of officials, including the four from last night, came on board but it wasn't long before we were ushered into transports and taken to our hotels. Just enough time for a shower and change of shirt before going on our first official call – at 1730 on the Senior Garrison Officer Truppenamt. Then more or less straight on to a reception and dinner for all the officers and all four navies, which was nicely informal.

The party was given by the Koln Uberseeklub, and when we arrived at the Bankhaus Herstatt there were five long tables and there must have been a hundred places at each table. Happily we were sitting amongst our own countrymen, as well as our hosts, and the Union Jack indicated our areas of named places. I found myself sitting beside a nineteen year old German girl and her

Nearly there. On the last leg from Dusseldorf to Koln

Dinner Party, Koln

widowed mother. The meal was very good indeed, but although my next door neighbours spoke perfect English, I found it all a bit difficult at first.

The daughter seemed rather disinterested but the mother did make an effort to keep the conversation going and eventually proved good company. Heidi was her name and she was a quiet, homely sort of person. The poor woman had been widowed for about fifteen years (her husband had been killed in an accident) and she had brought up the family of two on her own. She was a not-very-active member of the Koln Uberseeclub and that was the only reason she was there this evening – helping to entertain the many visitors. Maybe the wine helped, but once the meal was over, people moved around a bit and some, including the daughter, disappeared altogether. The staff cleared away a couple of the tables and the excellent oom-pah-pah band played dance music which Heidi and I very much enjoyed.

Heidi told me this was the first real party she had been to for years. As the dancing got slower and closer, she became a bit

The Bamburger Marine Choir

sleepy and said she was not relishing the car journey home. I asked her if she would rather come with me to the hotel. She assured me she would very much like to and hoped she could rely on me to treat her gently: I promised everything would be alright. We had a small breakfast in the room before we left early next morning. I had to be on board the ship to make sure everything was in order before our first official call of the day. Beforehand I had taken Heidi to her car and suggested she might like to come out for a meal in the evening. She knew of a nice little biergarten in Koln where we could dance and then hopefully have another lovely night together.

The news on board Dark Hero was good. All the crew had been looked after very well by local families and some were at the gangway about to go on tours and receptions given by businesses in the region. All the officers left for the Town Hall in order to meet the Lord Mayor and Oberstadtdirector at 1000. This involved the usual formalities but our hosts were thoroughly welcoming and the excellent drinks and small eats lasted much longer than programmed. We had nothing further to do until the evening. When I got back to the hotel I phoned Heidi to ask her if she would like to come round for lunch, then be my guest at a reception on board the German and French ships before going to the biergarten. She soon arrived with a small suitcase and a cocktail dress for the party. Taking one look at all my clothes around the room and my suitcase still unpacked, she pushed me back on the bed where I had been on her arrival, and neatly tidied all my things away.

Looking twice the woman she had the night before, it was small wonder I didn't see much of her as she spoke her native language amongst her fellow countrymen. Meanwhile, I thoroughly enjoyed meeting the French officers and chatting with them in their own lingo. No problem in finding something to talk about, as they all seemed to be rugby players or supporters, were small-ship sailors and had been to Djibouti and all the usual places in the Far East. We all agreed that we would meet up again in the British and Dutch ships in twenty four hours' time and perhaps have a good run ashore afterwards.

The Lord Mayor, Theo Burauen, welcomes us to his city of Koln. On the right is Hugh Campbell who joined the Navy with me. He retired in early days and was now a Lieutenant Commander in the RNR.

It didn't take long to unravel Heidi from her fellow German hosts, and as we toasted each other in her chosen biergarten, she thanked me for making a grandmother so happy. She went on to explain that her son had one child aged two and another was on the way in a couple of months' time. I tried for some stupid reason to work out her age and after I told her mine she happily admitted she was eight years older. She certainly didn't look it. She was enjoying being a granny and was looking forward to the arrival of the second grandchild. She said we wouldn't be able to see each other tomorrow, Friday, as she had a weekly arrangement to babysit for her son and daughter-in-law at their home in Bonn. A smile came to her face when I told her she could have a duplicate key to my room and that she could come and go as she pleased, provided she came back as soon as she had finished babysitting. After all, it was only forty kilometres away.

Friday was to be our busiest day, and as far as I was concerned the real reason for our being in Koln. While we were having breakfast, Heidi was also fussing around getting my uniform spotlessly smart and saying that she did not want her presence to impede me in any way and I must ensure it did not happen. I took her to her car, as she wanted to sort out a few things at home, and then she would be free to come back to the hotel, after babysitting, and spend as much of the weekend here as possible.

Shortly after 1000, teams of six officers and ratings from the German, French, Dutch and Royal Navies left their ships by bus for the small village of Rhondorf. Then, after disembarking, they climbed the zig-zag path to a cemetery in thick woods above the River Rhine. There, in front of us, a lantern was burning above a plain headstone on which several generations are remembered. The last inscription above the tomb read:

> Konrad Adenaur
> Geb. 5.1.1876
> Gest. 19.4.1967

We stood in silent tribute before it and at 1100 on the dot a bugler sounded a few notes and in turn each Navy laid a wreath. I don't

The wreath laying teams

know why we were last, but it did have the advantage of my being able to place the Royal Navy's wreath in the most prominent and conspicuous position. We had been there to pay homage to the late German Chancellor Konrad Adenaur who, in 1949, had asked for ten years to get over the first hill and then proceeded to mend the broken pieces in two decades. We were all very pleased to be bearing witness to that here in this part of West Germany.

After the wreath-laying I was taken out to an informal lunch at a club by Herr Ernst Schmidt whom we had briefly met that evening in Dusseldorf. He seemed to be the ringleader, if not the Chairman or President, of the Marinekamaradeschaft, and it was perhaps because I had more campaign medals than anyone else that he was to button hole me at every available opportunity. He and many of his friends, to whom I was introduced, had been in the German Navy during the war and were now retired. They were similar to our Association of Retired Naval Officers and appeared to know by name all the captains of British wartime submarines, if they were in anti-submarine warships

Konrad Adenaur's tomb

and vice-versa if they had been submariners. The two main impressions I got from these very enjoyable meetings were that they appeared to treat the last war like a game of chess, they only wanted to destroy the warships and at no time did they wish to kill anyone, although sadly that inevitably happened. We were all sons of the sea and merely carrying out the orders of dictators or politicians.

Eventually I told them that my father had been killed in the Kelly during the Battle of Crete in 1941. They knew all about Lord Louis Mountbatten and reminded me it was not the German Navy, but the Luftwaffe, who had straffed and sunk the Kelly. We all agreed that there were many cases of British and German surface ships and submarines saving their enemies from the sea. They used to have many parties and reunions, both in the UK and West Germany, to promote friendship between the navies and hopefully the two countries. Ernst asked me one favour before we finally parted company. He said he had tried unsuccessfully on several occasions to contact Godfrey Place VC. I told him that he was an ex-shipmate of mine and that he had been my Captain at Ganges. I would try to contact him on my return to the UK. When

I rang Godfrey at his retirement home in Dorset, he admitted that he had been contacted by these people but his reply was: "Mike, if you had been treated like we were over a period of three years, you wouldn't want to have anything to do with those bastards." It was the first and only time I had heard him use language like that. He was, of course, talking about the SS and the Nazis, not German sailors.

That evening it was the Dutch and British ships' turn to give the cocktail party at 1830. It was rather typical of an official party with everyone saying the right thing and being polite, as the RAF band stationed in West Germany played their good music on the jetty. All the guests left punctually at the allotted time, 2030. It was near the end that I met up with the French guys and we shortly disappeared to our hotels to change into civvies and meet up at a nearby restaurant. The conversation deteriorated from that moment onwards as the French were informed of the bawdy English words to "La Marseillaise". They merely replied by singing their song "Merd a la Reine d'Angleterre". Then many nautical words and much lower-deck banter was translated from one language to the other and we found that we shared much more than we had previously thought. All in all, it was a very enjoyable evening.

It was well past midnight when I quietly opened the bedroom door to find Heidi sitting up in bed reading one of her English books. She was wide awake, appreciative of the situation and very sympathetic, as she tidied my clothes away and helped me to a blissful sleep. Next day, Saturday, it was equally blissful to wake up with Heidi on my lap asking if I would like her to order some breakfast. She knew I wanted to take a stroll down to the ships, which we eventually did. In the morning they had been open to the German Marine Society and when we passed again in the afternoon, the visitors were of a younger age – orphans on the British ships and secondary school children on the others.

That evening our hosts were putting on a concert at the Gurzenich Festival Hall, and as it wasn't going to finish until two o'clock in the morning, Heidi suggested we go back to the hotel for a siesta. As we lay there, we talked about all sorts of things, including the difference between Berlin with its terrible Cold War still very much in evidence, and the peaceful happiness and rapid improvement being shown in West Germany.

She had not been to Berlin so I told her about all the places we had seen during our rugby tour the previous year. I also mentioned that on the Sunday afternoon we had all gone along to the mixed sauna baths and told her none of the female figures I saw there matched up to the beautiful brunette lying beside me now. She was very happy and said she would organise a private sauna for us tomorrow and that it would be much, much better.

The concert started at eight o'clock and was one of the best I have ever been to. We had the Bamburger Marine Choir, who had entertained us the first evening; they came on periodically with their nautical songs and sea shanties. There was Heino Conty, the German TV and film star, who sang Country and Western style, plus songs of the seven seas and Matrosen-Shanties. Finally, the best known German pop star of the sixties, Heidi Franke, came on to entertain us. The last number she sang was the well-known pop song "Die Sonne Scheint Nicht Mehr Ohne Dich", or in English "The Sun Ain't Gonna Shine Any More". The next morning I was woken up by Heidi whispering in my ear that it was time for me to get up and go to the service I had been asked to attend in Koln Cathedral. She made me a cup of coffee and made sure I was smart in my uniform; then closed the door behind me and returned to bed.

Apart from the church service itself, which was very impressive, I was very pleased to have gone as I was able to see for myself yet another vagary of war. The RAF and any other Allied aircraft involved, were under very strict orders not to damage in any way Koln Cathedral Their aim had been excellent, because every building in that city, including the very close-by railway station, had been damaged, if not destroyed. The Cathedral was untouched and still in its original form. I returned to the hotel, Heidi was dozing in bed, and so I crept in beside her to enjoy our last long lie-in together.

Mid-afternoon we passed by the ships which you could hardly see for the public enthusiastically clambering all over them. They were officially open to visitors and the German police had the situation well under control. We came to a small restaurant which had on the menu something Heidi thought I might like. It was a Dusseldorfer Senfrostbraten, delicious roasted steaks topped with Dusseldorf mustard, and as it was going to be our only meal of the day, we decided it would be just perfect, enjoyed slowly with a bottle of wine.

Later, on our way back to the hotel, we went to the sauna Heidi had arranged and she made it a very memorable experience. Towards the end, as we lay on a waterproof mattress, she said she was very happy to have participated in such a special friendship, but had realised from the very beginning it would only last a week and was now quite content to be returning to her home in Bonn tomorrow. We returned to our room and she packed my things so I could get away early in the morning. I asked her if she would like to follow us down the Rhine, in her car, and have a little holiday staying at the hotels we knew from our journey up. She pondered and thought it might just prolong the agony, but she would make up her mind by the morning. Once again I woke up with Heidi whispering: "May I please follow you to Rotterdam?" How could I refuse? As she wanted to go home first to sort out some of her things, I told her I would telephone her as soon as I had settled in at Dusseldorf.

For at least an hour all the friends we had made during the week in Koln were there to say goodbye. Then at 0930, with the Belgian Military Band once again in attendance, we slipped our ropes and slowly proceeded down river. All the pomp and circumstance was now over and everyone was just enjoying the very happy memories of a thoroughly successful week provided by the German sea-going people, who were only too anxious to repair all the sadnesses which their nation had incurred during WW2.

Heidi arrived mid-afternoon for our last three times together. She guided me down the Ratinger and Kurze Strasses with all the restaurants and their electronic oom-pah-pah music for which the town was well known. For our only meal of the day we had an early Dusseldorfer Senfrostbraten, and a number of dances before returning to the hotel. This woman whom I had first met as a quiet, shy, homely person, had blossomed into a lovely lady and she finally left me early on our last morning in Rotterdam after giving me a very wonderful farewell present. She, who had so much to offer, should not have been living on her own as she had been doing for so long. I received a Christmas card from Ernst Schmidt the following year and was delighted to hear she had married a retired German naval officer whom she had first met at that ship's cocktail party in Koln.

The sea was quite rough when we poked our noses out into the North Sea, with a strong following wind and swell pushing us along. We had to be watchful with the steering, as there was the tendency to broach. All was well when we arrived back in Portsmouth and my last act as captain was to get straight into a shower, sea-going kit and all. I looked like a coal miner at the end of his shift, except I was covered in diesel exhaust.

My twelve day spell at improving and enjoying Anglo-German relationships not only proved to be my fifth and final command, but also my last days at sea with the Royal Navy. After two years ashore, my appetite to be at sea had been rejuvenated and now I was determined that my last year in the Service would be worthwhile for all concerned and pass as quickly as possible.

One pleasant task I had was acting as liaison officer with the forty or so members of the Women's Royal Naval Service, who worked as writers, pay accountants, stores assistants, victuallers, cooks and stewards, and who were accommodated in the Wrennery at Collingwood. These girls, whose ranks ranged from first, second and third officer to CPO wren, PO wren, leading wren and ordinary wren, were a great asset to the shore-based Navy. Their service was entirely voluntary, they did not sign any contract and within reasonable notice they could leave whenever they wanted. They maintained their own discipline and were not subject to the Naval Discipline Act. My contact was not one of their officers, but a PO Wren who was in charge of admin. I liaised with her before captain's monthly rounds of the Wrennery and had done so with regard to the youngest wren presenting flowers to the Queen Mother.

A very important thing that was going to keep me going for the rest of my time, concerned the Ministry of Public Buildings and Works. Collingwood still consisted mostly of wooden huts. The first two buildings you saw at the main gate were wooden and they had been there over twenty years. Most officers and chief and petty officers still lived in them and a hell of a lot of planning had to go into the reconstruction of the place. MPBW had the so-called expert architects and builders and quite a lot of finance available but they did not know how many people of different ranks were going to be stationed in the future Collingwood or the desired requirement for the layout of cabins, bathrooms, bars, restaurants, lounges and even car parking. Depending on the numbers, so many square feet were allowed per person.

I had to have regular meetings with the Wardroom Mess Secretary and Catering Officer and the Presidents of the Chief and Petty Officers Messes to discuss all the requirements and ideas and then armed with all the necessary information, we would attend the monthly MPBW meeting. More questions and amendments to previous plans would follow, we would have further talks with Mess Presidents and so it would go on ad nauseum. It was difficult to arouse enthusiasm amongst everyone, but it was a very essential job and the whole future of mess and domestic life in Collingwood depended on our constructive ideas being accepted by MPBW.

Of course, included in all this was the Wrennery and my contact once again was the PO Wren in charge of admin. She was very efficient and together with one of the Leading Wrens, we were able hopefully to sort out everything month by month, along with the rest of the establishment.

At 0900 on my last day at Collingwood I said farewell to my Captain, Philip Watson. He was a marvellous man and was always very kind and supportive of me. He was a Member Victorian Order, which is given by the Queen to people who have served her or the monarchy in a personal way. He was also a Fellow of both the Institutes of Electrical Engineers and of Electronic and Radio Engineers. He was very highly thought of as an Electrical Officer in the Navy and went on to be Director General Weapons (Naval) as a Vice-Admiral. In my last flimsy in the Navy he wrote:-

> That I had conducted myself to his entire satisfaction and that I was an officer who brings a natural enthusiasm to his duties and can quickly grasp the essentials of a situation when dealing with the many and widely varying parts of his task.

Not bad for a Barrack Stanchion who was desperate to get back to sea. Anyway, I was happy with it.

That afternoon I went to my last and very final MPBW meeting. The PO Wren stayed on at the finish to let me know she was leaving the Wrens in a fortnight's time and that she would be handing everything over to her relief starting on Monday. She told me she had been accepted for a very good job at Harrods and I congratulated her because I knew that company keenly recruited ex-Naval personnel to fill their administrative and security vacancies and that she was very capable of doing well with them. On her way out I expected to be saying goodbye to her but she asked me if I would care to partner her at the Wren's Summer Ball. She would actually be out of the Wrens by then, the dress for me would be dinner jacket, as no-one would be in uniform, and I would be welcome for a few drinks at her flat in Lee-on-Solent before going on to the Ball to be held at the Lee Tower Ballroom.

On arrival I was greeted by this comely woman who must have been at least ten years younger than me and who, for about two years called me Sir, and whom I had addressed by her rank and surname. Now she was Sonia and I was her guest at her last Navy Ball. Her record player was generating slow romantic music and in between drinks we had quite a few dances. Expecting, and hoping, for a negative answer, she asked if we really wanted to go on to the Ball. She needed a little help undoing a zip, as she told me about her brother who had been a Leading Seaman in a ship abroad and was now down in Devon going through the mill to become a commissioned officer. Before he joined his last ship, he hadn't been all that keen on staying in the Navy but the enthusiasm shown, and encouragement given to him by his captain, had completely changed his outlook. With a glint in her eyes she said that she had wanted to meet this officer, out of uniform, and that the name of the ship was Kildarton. She had known this for some time, had never mentioned it before, and now I was about to receive a grateful thank you. We ended up the best of friends and I must admit it was one of the best dances I didn't go to, and my ego had been done a world of good in more ways than one.

MERCANTILE MARINE MATTERS

It is impossible to express the feeling that hit me when I awoke on the morning of Independence Day 1970. Total loneliness could be one description. Here I was, completely separated from the only life I had known for thirty eight years. The previous day I had returned – it almost felt like surrendering – my Naval ID card, which meant I could no longer walk freely on board a warship or enter a Naval establishment as I had been doing all my working life.

I did not know what to do, so I went along to the Labour Exchange in Commercial Road, Portsmouth and joined the dole queue! In those days I was quite well paid because I would receive what was known as earnings related income, but only for six months. I was still able to do some of the educational and vocational training courses and I decided to do a six week Business Management course at Highbury Technical College. That course, although very good and interesting, served to prove one thing I had already known about the UK and that there was, in fact, very little business management as such. There were many big businesses, but to a simple sailor it was obvious the only reason our car, ship-building, banking and other major industries were failing was because they lacked management and if they still existed it was because they were no longer British owned. We were shown round the Marks and Spencer and the Johnson and Johnson retail outlets as well organised examples of successful businesses whose main interest, apart from making money, was the greatest single factor – their employees – and this we were told was the reason for their success.

In between times I visited various shipping companies as far afield as Liverpool and Glasgow and went on board several different types of ships including oil tankers, ocean liners and ferries but no cargo ships. Everyone I met was most helpful and seemed to have a very good attitude to life. However, there were three things not quite up my street. The ships were too big, they were too impersonal and the crews were not only becoming less and less British, but more importantly couldn't, and weren't required to, speak English.

I was rapidly coming to the conclusion that the great British shipyards were no longer getting the orders that they had been accustomed to and that this was partly due to the lack of support from the government. On my visit to Glasgow and the Clyde I had the good fortune to meet Jimmy Reid. He had in 1971 organised the Upper Clyde Shipbuilders Work-In.

He attempted to stop Edward Heath's Conservative government from operating the shipyards without subsidy and eventually their closure on the Clyde. In a famous speech given to the workers he said: "We are not going to strike. We are not even having a sit-in strike. Nobody and nothing will come in, and nothing will go out without our permission. And there will be no hooliganism, there will be no vandalism, there will be no bevvying, because the world will be watching us and it is our responsibility to conduct ourselves with dignity and with maturity. He received financial support from across the world, Heath backed down the following year and the Clyde shipyards received over £100 million in public support. What leadership!

In his youth, Jimmy Reid had been a member of the Young Communist League and then a full member of the Communist Party. He later joined the Labour Party and finally, in 2005, the Scottish National Party. When installed as Rector of the University of Glasgow, he gave his famous "A rat race is for rats" speech, which the New York Times reported in full and described as the "greatest speech since President Lincoln's Gettysburg address."

There was one quite big loophole and it could be seen at Southampton and Liverpool Nautical Colleges. It was the training and the decline in standards, as well as the lack of money willing to be spent on it, either publicly or privately. No longer were the big shipping lines quite so keen to pay for young cadets to climb the ladder and pass the necessary exams for Second Mate, Mate or Master.

Nautical colleges were beginning to close down, as in order to make the whole thing financially viable they needed big classes.

Already quite a few places like the City of London Polytechnic were offering instruction in boat handling techniques – in a pool. Yachtsmen were being offered the facilities when not in use by the professionals. Simulation and simulators were being used instead of the real thing and this was creating a gap which needed filling.

Shortly before Christmas, I met Spencer Smith and we discussed buying the chandlery which was for sale at Chichester Yacht Basin (at that time the largest marina in Europe). I wasn't willing to put in quite as much money as he had hoped, but we eventually agreed on our respective shares of the business. Being a retailer and owning a chandlery was the last thing I had planned on doing. However, our shop was by the water and all our customers were owners of various types of boats and presumably enjoyed life at sea. Spencer and I ran the shop on our own and on most days only one of us needed to be there. The busy occasions were, of course, in the summer and especially at weekends. After a while I got to know the boat owners, particularly those who were our customers, and I would give some boat-handling instruction; then they would start asking for more.

I quite often visited Chichester Yacht Club, which was a good place to have a snack lunch and meet up with people other than customers. I became a member and put up a couple of notices advertising theory courses on any nautical subject – plus practical training in customers' own boats. Nothing very much materialised in the first year but I could sense things were beginning to pick up as the second year progressed. Spencer and I leased part of the shop to an electronics company selling radio and radar sets as well as electrical logs, speedos and depth sounders. Our turnover began to increase considerably.

Spencer was a retired architect much older than me and we were making good money. I found no enjoyment in buying an article, putting a mark-up on it and waiting for someone to enter the shop and purchase it. I was used to a more exciting life and wanted to be back at sea. We sold up at a very reasonable profit and I started announcing my own business at the end of 1973. It was three years later than I had intended but a lot of benefit had been gained in that time. Firstly, I had got to know the different makes and types of boats, which is an education in itself, then all the requirements and capabilities of the safety equipment available and finally how to operate all the electronic equipment sold in our shop.

Into the shop on a number of occasions came a fascinating woman whom I had actually seen high-diving for Great Britain at the 1948 Olympic Games in London. She was Denise St Aubyn Hubbard and was running a sailing school. She used to call in for bits and pieces of chandlery, and inevitably we would chat. Although she was too busy to give me any physical help, she did in fact give me much advice and encouragement along the lines she knew I was obviously heading. An inspiring person she had for eight years been the only female skipper of an inshore minesweeper in the RNXS – the Royal Navy Auxiliary Service, a part-time organisation which was entirely manned by civilian crews. And in 1988, at the age of 64, she became the oldest woman to finish the Carlsberg Single-Handed Transatlantic Yacht Race. She was a magnificent sailor.

There were two couples whom I had befriended towards the end of the second year. They were Ian and Audrey Wilson, who owned a super Grand Banks 42ft Europa called "Naudia", which was berthed in the Yacht Basin. Ian was extremely interested in what I was doing and offered to charter his boat to me for training purposes. He would also help me as a part-time instructor if and when I could get him to the right standard. Lionel and Mollie Jarvis lived near the Wilsons at Lingfield and had an equally nice boat moored nearby. Lionel was very busy with his particular business in London but Mollie said, now that the children were married and the grandchildren had a nanny, she would like to learn more about navigation and chartwork. She also volunteered to do anything she could to promote my future business like having interviews with the press or any other sort of publicity.

I was now convinced that the best way I could use this expertise given to me by the Royal Navy was to pass on the knowledge in a practical way to budding or unqualified seafarers. I was also convinced that I had firstly to convince these people that they both needed and wanted this training. I would offer

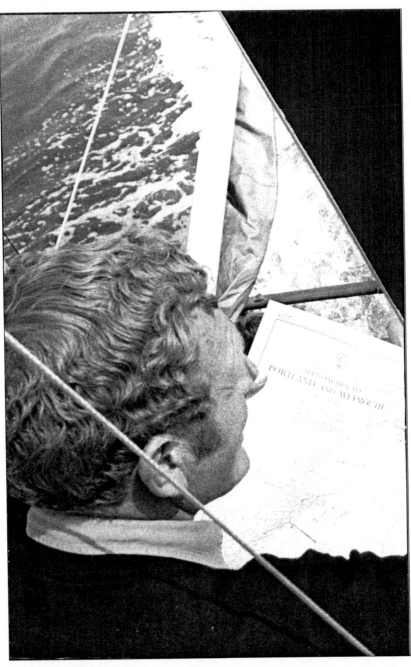

I start doing evening classes in boats from the local marinas

Practical and Theory Instruction afloat in any or all of the following subjects:-

Boat Handling	Rule of the Road	Meteorology
Safety Equipment	Navigation	Man Overboard
Pilotage	Buoyage Systems	Tides & Tidal Streams
Position Fixing	Radar	Sea Survival
VHF Radio	Diesel Engines	Night Cruising

Armed with much enthusiasm I went to the 1974 Earls Court Boat Show in London where I was kindly allowed to use a table in the corner of the Grand Banks stand. I was ably assisted by Ian Wilson and Mollie Jarvis who periodically kept me company and gave me much assistance when being interrogated by potential customers and the media. I did not have the gift of the gab or the Del Boy sales patter. Many people did come up and talk to us but very few seemed to be anxious to spend money on the particular skills I had to offer. However, by the end of the show I had been asked to give interviews to the following:-

BBC Radio Overseas with Muhlen Dahl and Jennifer Blake
BBC Radio Solent
BBC Radio Brighton
The Magazine Power and Sail

and two people had booked a Theory Course starting on 22nd April.

Over the next couple of months the interviews for the BBC and the two magazines were done and I received bookings for courses immediately after the first one already arranged in April. Ian let me use Naudia for the first as it was a Theory Course and it would only be in the Hamble area. As there were only two people booked, a father and son, Mollie said she would like to make up the numbers and learn all about navigation and chartwork.

The father and son worked hard and obviously intended to get maximum benefit from the week. As soon as the day's work

Ian Wilson on board 'Naudia', his Grand Banks 42 Europa

was finished on board, they went off ashore to view the layout of the area, visit brokers and look at boats. The Hamble River must be the most congested part of the country with marinas, boatyards, chandlers – ideal with everything to do with pleasure boating. Mollie was a charming lady and did everything to encourage me with my venture. Thank goodness she was there otherwise it would have been quite lonesome at night. We worked hard during the day, went out for a meal every evening and, in fact, had a very nice holiday which lasted until she went home on the Friday.

The next two weeks were harder work but nonetheless pleasing. My customers were Concrete Carvall, nicknamed such because he had a concrete sailboat, and Danny Clark, who later asked to be trained up to Yachtmasters standard. He was a scrap metal dealer, a Tottenham Hotspur supporter and a super guy to boot. He had to go ashore to the telephone every morning to find out the price of brass, etc and make the decision whether or not to sell. Over the years he recommended several business customers and friends and they were all from the same trade with the same Cockney sense of humour.

Mollie joins up with one of our classes in Naudia

Two couples, Shaun and Jean Kendall and Simon and Sue Gray, were the next to come on course. Shaun telephoned me a couple of years later asking if I could fly down to Lyon to join him in his Moonraker "One in a Million". He had been stranded by his friend and crewman who had had to return home. He needed help the rest of the way through the French canals and then on to the fabulous new marina at La Grande Motte. Simon and Sue went on to do a lot of cruising in their super "Fast Anchor" and Simon successfully passed his Yachtmaster exam in 1989.

With the apparent success of the Boat Show and the two good courses behind me, I had sufficient time to visit the printers and publish brochures, cards, headed notepaper and to announce the Mike Reeder School of Seamanship. I had badges produced, and through a Navy shipmate I purchased several different sized navy blue sweaters. These would be for my team of part-time instructors. At the moment my school consisted of myself as the Chief Instructor, and Ian as my sole instructor and provider of the motor cruiser.

Shaun Kendall's 'One In A Million'
moored at La Grande Motte 1974

In June, Barry Watkin, the Assistant Editor of Motor Boat and Yachting did a 5-day course with me and he wasted no time in writing an article which was published before the end of the year. In it he said:-

> I joined the party early one summer morning and was welcomed by a great bear of a man. He was the school's Chief Instructor, a former commander of one of Her Majesty's minesweepers and now responsible for installing good seamanship into his many pupils. He had that rare quality of putting everyone at ease and as he introduced the course it was clear that his infectious humour was going to be one of the chief ingredients in moulding an engineer, a company director, a chartered accountant, a mother of three and myself into an efficient crew.

Four of those pupils were on this course. There was Cynthia Goldstone, the mother of three whose husband hated boats and the sea and she had to handle the family powerboat during their annual holiday in the South of France. She said in the article:-

I was very apprehensive when I first joined the course but was soon put at ease. Being totally immersed in both the theory and practice of cruising for one week has given me confidence in my ability to handle a boat of this size. Mistakes were made by everyone but the opportunity to rectify these errors with the confident inspiring voice of Mike Reeder in one's ear is an experience no motor boat owner should miss. I look forward to the advanced course.

There was also David Munro from Bath, Anthony Roberts from Torquay and Tony Yell from Leicester who were all very complimentary about the course and I thank them all very much. Barry gave outline details of each of the days' instruction and in his conclusion said:-

Personality plays a very significant part in teaching and this genial ginger headed Scot not only inspires confidence in his pupils but puts his message across with clarity and light touch. Anyone wanting to learn the art of seamanship and navigation – or unlearn some bad habits – will be hard put to find a quicker and more enjoyable way of spending five days. I cannot remember when I laughed so much. One small criticism: I thought there was too much reliance on the automatic pilot on the first two days; this should have been introduced briefly towards the end of the course.

In August, Carl Korn asked me to guide him on what sounded like a fabulous cruise of the Tyrrhenian Sea. He had chartered a 42ft Europa called Jai Banks for a fortnight and as he had never been to sea in his life before, he wanted me as his skipper, mentor and trainer. The boat was in Port Vauban, Antibes and I should join up with him and his family at Heathrow for the midmorning flight to Nice on Saturday 10th. Carl, his wife Jean, their 12 year old daughter and his sister Mrs Weschler were at Heathrow to meet me and so began a very profitable and professionally enjoyable two weeks. Carl was an extremely clever and successful man. I was to learn a lot about him and his family as time progressed but the first thing that amazed me was his knowledge of all the equipment, both navigational and safety, which he checked before signing up for the boat and taking it over from the charterer, a Monsieur Jean Jacques Bouillant-Linet.

His family went ashore to buy the necessary provisions, probably breakfast and snack lunches as he intended to eat out most evenings when in harbour. Meanwhile he got out all the charts and told me his outline proposals for the coming fortnight. Everything he had done so far and everything he talked about made him appear to be a seasoned sailor. Yet he had never been to sea before and he had learnt everything out of books. That evening, after some instruction with toy boats on the table, we did boat-handling training in a quieter part of Antibes harbour. I always sought permission of the marine authorities before doing this. Apart from being good manners and seamanlike practice, it also gave me the opportunity of getting to know the local boating people.

Carl and his parents had escaped as refugees from Austria in 1939 and had come to England where he had remained ever since. His sister had married a Mr Weschler, a jeweller and they had somehow got down to Atlantic Spain; then by ship to Havana in Cuba where they opened up a jewellery shop. I was not told the full story but they managed to escape a second time after Fidel Castro's revolution in 1959, once again leaving all their possessions and worldly goods behind. They were now safe in Miami and once again owned a prosperous jewellery business.

On my advice, and Carl seemed all for it, we sailed early the next day. We did a couple more circuits and bumps before leaving Antibes for the well-appointed yacht harbours in Alassio, Portofino, Portoferraio, Civilavecchia, Capri, Ischia, Ponsa, Porto Cervo where, after Carl had done all the work, he took his family ashore to enjoy the sights. I would join them for the evening meal but while they were away doing their daytime tourism I called on the Port Captains and marina staff and also went on board any of the mega-yachts in harbour to try and encourage the Captains and crews to get qualified. I was spreading the gospel as much as possible and trying to promote my business.

We spent two whole nights at sea and magnificent they were in the calm moonlit waters going from Portfino to Elbe, and Ponsa to Porto Cervo. Everywhere was for one night only, except for Capri where we stayed two. I went with the family for the hydrofoil trip across to Napoli and a complete day at Pompeii in the shadows of Mount Vesuvius. One regret was the day we visited Elbe. It was a Tuesday and the only day of the week that Napoleon Bonaparte's home of exile was closed. He had been imprisoned there by the British in 1814 and had escaped the following year only to be defeated at the Battle of Waterloo. He spent the last six years of his life confined in St Helena. No escape from there.

All in all, it was an excellent fortnight. Carl hadn't yet got enough sea-time experience, none in tidal waters, to take his Yachtmaster Exam, but on the last day in Antibes he successfully passed the written exam papers for the Yachtmaster Theory Certificate. Before I flew back to Heathrow I visited Jean Jacques, the agent who had dealt with the charter. He was, in fact, Mr Grand Banks of the Riviera, a charming man and hopefully through him I would get plenty of work. He introduced me to Mike Dawes whom I had briefly known in the Navy. He owned a Grand Banks called Jan Pan in Antibes and we came to an arrangement for future chartering and training. So I now had a boat in the French Mediterranean to add to my fleet. Everywhere I went, especially outside England, everyone called me Captain Reeder, or Captain Mike, so things were continuing to get better.

It was at the 1975 Earls Court Boat Show that I first met Sir Edward Heath, the leader of the Conservative Party. He had been our Prime Minister from June 1970 until March 1974, during a time of industrial upheaval and economic decline. It was splendid when he walked up to our team and asked the reason for our being at the show. I was able to introduce them and

Ted Heath chats to the team

together we put him wise – not as a politician but as Ted, a fellow seafarer. In 1969 he had bought "Morning Cloud" and by the end of the year won the Sydney Hobart race. He captained the British winning team in the 1971 Admirals Cup (while Prime Minister) and went on to captain the team yet again in the 1979 Fastnet Race.

I was asked by a company selling Callbuoys to advertise their product with Iain Cuthbertson, the well-known actor who at that time was in Sutherlands Law on BBC Television. He was a huge man born in Glasgow with a good sense of humour. He had some fascinating stories to tell, especially about his army National Service with the Black Watch. The Callbuoy was a transistorised portable radio for distress at sea. It was fitted in a watertight plastic container capable of floating and it transmitted on 2182KHz, the International Distress Frequency.

I was most grateful once again for the help of Mollie when I was booked for interviews with John Rhodes of ITV, Susan Pritchard of Vogue, Geraldine Waters of Signature and Geoff Morgan of She magazine. In August I was very happy to repay some of that help by assisting her and her husband Lionel in

With Iain Cuthbertson, the well-known actor,
advertising an important item of safety
equipment Earl's Court 1975

getting their boat from Chichester to the Port of London. Lionel wanted to use it to entertain business customers during the Pool of London Regatta.

Jeremy Eadie from Air Bearings, a Hovercraft company in Gosport telephoned to ask if I knew anything about hovercraft. I told him I knew about the great British inventor, who had been educated at Christ's Hospital and quite a lot about hovermanship; I had never driven one nor did I have my wings. He told me about his company, that they built small hovercraft, that the Hamburg Fire Brigade had bought one and they had given one to King Hussain of Jordan – in the hope they would get orders from the Middle East.

They did not produce enough craft to warrant a full-time instructor, but could I quote them a price to make myself available

Hovercraft

as a part-time instructor if they trained me to a sufficiently high standard? A deal was struck and I started my course in the first week in February and received my Wings on the 12th. For the practical work most of the time was spent at the top of Pompey harbour going up and over mud flats trying to avoid small broken stubs of wood tearing the skirt. We went out of the harbour towards the Isle of Wight to practice getting over the hump, moving at speed, and returning to the displacement mode. All very interesting and it must have cost the parent company a lot of money. The Fareham branch ceased trading within a couple of months and I was never able to put into practice my newly acquired skill.

In April of that year two Scotsmen who owned boats at home came to do a course with me in the Solent and from that week Charlie Lyle and I have been the greatest of friends. Charlie had been born in Rothesay and was the son of a publican who owned the Harbour Bar, a watering hole I knew very well from my days in submarines. His father who had also played professional football for Morton in the Scottish Football League died in 1966, and Charlie had to help his mother with the family affairs and responsibilities, not to mention the pub which was not doing very well. He sold it very quickly and bought a run-down one called The Suez Canal in Largs, a lovely seaside town overlooking the River Clyde in Ayrshire. Working every hour of the day, he cleaned the place up, changed its name to the Clachan Bar and by encouraging women to accompany their menfolk into a family section, soon had a very successful business.

He loved boating and when I first went with him it was at two o'clock on a Sunday morning. I had helped him count up all his day's takings (most of which went to the taxman) and lock them away in a safe, before driving up to Kip Marina where his 33ft Norseman was fuelled up and ready to go. Charlie's forty hour weekend of boating ended when he opened up the pub again on Monday evening. One of the first people we met was Malcolm Wightman who was the other Scot with Charlie on the course.

We heard all about Malcolm, who was a retired civil engineer known locally as "The Hoogel". He had, on one occasion, when he had overindulged his favourite dram, referred to some rowdy people as a "Bunch of Hoogelans". The stories continued – one about him and his friend Jim Clark who during WW2 had survived the hell of a Japanese prisoner of war camp. One night after a good run ashore together the dinghy in which they were returning to their yacht, capsized. They both managed to swim to a navigational buoy where they hung on till daybreak. I was informed that the next day they bought 200 cigarettes and a bottle of whisky and put them in a watertight bag, which they tied to the buoy – in case the same thing should ever happen again!

Charlie knew plenty of people in the west coast of Scotland who would want training and he would help organise them for me. If ever I needed a boat, his would always be available. We immediately had the official opening of the Mike Reeder School of Seamanship, Scottish Branch, on board "Mareel", and adjourned to the Castle Hotel for the luncheon. Being travellers, we had no problem with the Sunday licensing laws.

Later in the month Meriel came down from her home near Liverpool to do a Solent course. She was married to a doctor who

Charlie's Norseman 33 'Mareel' anchored off Colintraive

for several reasons didn't accompany her. He was very busy at his surgery and was also much more interested in model steam trains, some of which he had built himself. Meriel really enjoyed boating and anything to do with the sea. She owned a dinghy and preferred sailing but as the family also owned a 36ft Grand Banks berthed at Port Dinorwic in Wales, she wanted to learn about navigation. She so enjoyed the first course that she paid to come down three more times and asked me if she could help with the school in any way. She was a small redhead and although a bit weak physically – when it came to steering large boats with the associated heavy rope and fender work – she was very good at explaining the theoretical side of things. I was sure there would be work for her especially at sailing once I had got the business going a bit more. She also said she would like to do a course in Scotland some time.

I now had many courses in the Solent area, mostly in "Naudia" and ably assisted by Ian Wilson. One involved a Mr Monty Black who in earlier days had been a tailor in the

East End of London. After he married his wife, Celia, they built up their business together. They now had at least one factory in Lancashire producing Burberry, traded within the House of Fraser and had other outlets abroad. At the end of the course he said he would need me for further training in the boat they were purchasing in the Mediterranean.

A stroke of good luck came the school's way. Stuart Ross, a Fellow of the Royal Institute of Chartered Surveyors, and his friend John Cockburn-Mercer who had served in the Royal Navy, booked a five day course in Naudia. They seemed to appreciate it and in July employed me to help deliver their 34 foot motor yacht "Yacoba" from Cherbourg to Royan. Apart from learning the practical art of navigation, and moving their boat to a new cruising area in France, they also wanted to enjoy visiting as many places as possible on the way down. So the trip took longer than necessary and we had a most enjoyable cruise of North Brittany accompanied by Stuart's son who was on his summer holidays from College. Within a month we received the following most

Ian Wilson about to give me a rest and take over the instruction!

welcome unsolicited letter from Stuart. Needless to say we used it many times in advertising, and later on our website:-

Letter from Stuart Ross, Portugal

Then in October I was asked by a Mr Fred Booker from Barnsley to help him take his rather ancient motor-sailor from the Solent up to his native Yorkshire. We did, in fact, motor it all the way, making short overnight stops at Newhaven, Ramsgate, Wolverstone and Great Yarmouth before reaching South Ferriby. Accompanying us was his rather old father-in-law who was suffering badly from chronic bronchitis after many years working down the coal mines. When I could understand his strong Yorkshire accent it was fascinating to hear his impassioned tales of community life down and around the pits.

I told Meriel I was doing a course in the Clyde in November. I knew she would like to have come on it but it was on the customer's own boat and as he was bringing three mates along there just wouldn't be enough room. She said she would like to come up at the end of the course so that she could look around with a view to moving their boat "Dawn Seeker" up there.

The customer's name was George Curran, a veterinary surgeon who lived in Ayr and owned a Jupiter twin-screw diesel motor cruiser berthed at Kip Marina. His three mates were Ernest Blackadder, George Margetty and Ian McKenzie, and although the weather as one might expect at that time of the year was pretty dodgy, we had a fabulous five days, visiting such places as Rothesay, Lochs Goil, the Holy Loch and Millport. Most days we would see the SS Shieldhall going down the Clyde as far as Arran, turning round and then retracing its track back to Glasgow. For free it would take organised groups of up to eighty passengers, who perhaps could not afford the railway steamers fares. They would sit in the restaurant enjoying a cruise "doon the water", blissfully unaware they were on board what was known as the "Clyde Sludge Boat" – a marvellous steamship which had been built in 1955 by Lobnitz and Co. of Renfrew.

SS Shieldhall on the River Clyde

Meriel arrived in the Inverkip Hotel in time for our end of course lunch at about half past one. I introduced her to everyone as my part-time sailing instructor, whose family owned a Grand Banks in Wales and a cheerful session ensued. I didn't see George again but I used to hear regularly from Charlie how much he enjoyed the course, how much it had helped him to continue to relish his boating and how he had progressed professionally to become Head Veterinary Surgeon of Ayrshire.

Feeling really tired, unwashed and damp from the wet weather we had endured over the past few days, Meriel told me I needed a damned good bath and that I could have one at her hotel in Wemyss Bay where she had booked in for the night. I told her I had arranged to go down to Charlie's and she said we could do that later. On arrival at the hotel she started running the bath water and in the most delightful way, stating that neither of us possessed anything we hadn't seen before, she slowly undressed and stepped in. As she washed, she continued talking and told me she hadn't slept with her husband for years and she knew that anything we might do certainly wouldn't bother him. She did not want to upset any relationships that I might have and asked that there should be no strings attached to anything we might do. I got undressed, put all my dirty clothes in a plastic bag, and hopped in beside her.

I was due to be at Charlie's that night but I remembered little – except a lovely feeling of satisfaction – until we were having bacon and egg breakfast in the hotel room and discussing my immediate programme. I told her I had a course starting in the Hamble on Monday, that I had a flight booked back down south tomorrow and that today I wanted to meet the owner and some of the staff at Kip Marina. She telephoned the Erskine Bridge Hotel, which was nearer the airport and using her Gold card booked a room for the night. She had already said she wanted to look around Kip with a view to bringing their boat up to the Clyde and we arrived there about eleven o'clock feeling very well refreshed.

Kip Marina was Scotland's only yacht harbour and was owned by a shrewd Yorkshire man called Derek Holt. In 1961 he came to the area and built two very successful caravan sites, both overlooking the Clyde at Cloch Point and at Skelmorlie. With the expansion of boating in the south of England as well as other areas of the world, he foresaw the same thing about to happen in the west of Scotland. He bought a plot of land, again overlooking the Clyde, near the village of Inverkip and employed two people to work full time literally digging a hole. When the hole was big enough both in area and depth, he drove in a few piles and between them attached a couple of pontoons. He scooped open an entrance to the Clyde, in came the sea water, plus his first few customers, who secured their yachts to the said pontoons. Whatever the state of the tide, the tiny harbour was always deep enough for the boats to gain access and remain afloat.

Rumour has it that Derek got early warning of the fact that the Scottish Electricity Board wanted to build a power station nearby. One day an employee of that organisation called on him and enquired what he was doing with all the aggregates he was excavating as it would be useful for building the power station and its very high chimney. Derek said he had already received several enquiries but if the SEB were willing to pay him so much per ton, plus the charges for him to deliver in his own lorry, a deal could be struck right away. It was, and so Derek got paid twice for doing the one job.

The initial marina with over 250 berths had been officially opened in 1971, and was very much a going concern when I walked into Derek's office and met the man for the first time. I told him about my past, my qualifications, exactly what I was up to and also what I had been doing this last week. It was great to talk to such a successful man and he told me he would give every support to my project and that I should go and talk to his yachtbroker this afternoon. He did say before I left that he had seen me in his marina on Monday and again yesterday afternoon.

I walked across the road and, as arranged, met Meriel for lunch at the Inverkip Hotel. Being a Saturday the place was buzzing but we managed to find somewhere for a quick drink and a plate each of their marvellous, very fresh haddock and chips. She said she wanted to have a scout around the area and would pick me up at five o'clock.

The yachtbroker, David Cook, was awaiting me in his office and it was obvious that Derek had talked to him while I was having lunch. We chatted and I learnt a lot, but the main point of interest was that they intended becoming agents for some of the better quality makes of boat. Also they were negotiating the import of some Taiwanese trawler yachts and becoming their British agent. He was sure there would be plenty of work coming my way and he would do all he could to encourage it. He did, however, state that Derek Holt expected ten per cent of all the monies I took from customers operating out of Kip Marina. I agreed on all this, we shook hands and, with a smile on his face, he said Derek was a thoroughly honest and shrewd task master who spends a lot of his time in his office from where he could see all that was going on. I already knew that! Incidentally the power station only functioned for a few weeks but the chimney was a very good navigational mark, close to the entrance of Kip Marina for many years to come. Just steer towards the lum Jimmy!

At my request, Meriel stopped on our way to the hotel so I could buy a bottle of Malt and some small eats. We wanted to have a quiet evening in her room discussing the week's events. After she checked in I opened the bottle and she proposed a toast to our business friendship. I told her about the meetings with Derek and David and that the prospects were good and she said she definitely wanted to bring Dawn Seeker up to Scotland. It was very convenient to have the boat near their home, but it was a bit restricted and she felt it was time for a change. It wouldn't be for at least another year, but in the meantime, I could use the boat any time I wanted to arrange a course in Wales, and she didn't want any money. Just pay for the diesel and also she would try and get me some customers. That night, we enjoyed each other's company to the full. On my flight south I reflected that this had been a successful year and that due to the great kindness of four people I now had the availability of high quality boats in the Solent, Clyde, Wales and the Med, as well as an agent in Scotland, a part-time instructor down south and a sailing instructor who also wanted to be my Welsh agent.

However, the year had not quite finished as awaiting me was a message from Monty Black asking me to go down to the fabulous new marina at Puerto Banus, forty miles north east of Gibraltar. He had a 36ft Grand Banks called Sea Banks berthed there and he wanted me to instruct him for his Yachtmaster Theory after Christmas. I flew to Malaga on 27th December as Terry and Leslie were also on board there was obviously no room for me. So he told me to book in at the luxurious Andalucia Plaza Hotel. The arrangement was rather like being a schoolteacher as opposed to being an instructor. In other words he only wanted me between nine and four. I soon found out how boring hotel life can be when you are on your own, even though he was paying for all meals and expenses at the hotel.

The first four evenings I took a stroll around the marina and met various people. The capitan of the Puerto in his turret-type building at the entrance to the marina was very interested in what I was doing and said there was nothing like that in Spain. Another evening I went to visit the few yachtbrokers there were in the office block. While passing his fabulous looking red Spanish fishing boat, I talked to the owner, Alan Maden, who told me his life story. He was from Halifax and for tax reasons he had come down to the Med and worked in one or two mega-yachts. In the last one he had been captain. He had got a bit bored with that, had bought this boat and was doing quite well, taking out customers, most of whom came from the local hotels and holiday camp. We went along to the marina bar and had a couple of drinks, and I joined him there the next evening to meet some of the local boating guys. Every evening I delayed going back to the hotel, because all I did was read a book, magazine or paper, while slowly eating a fabulous meal, and then retired to bed.

My last night was New Year's Eve and I asked an attractive blonde, whom I had noticed sitting by herself at dinner every evening if she would like to join me for the celebrations. Her name was Stella, she was Italian and she recently arrived from Sardinia to work as the PA for the hotel manager. There was a short cabaret which included a Flamenco dancer. In between times we danced a lot and after Auld Lang Syne everyone disappeared to go off to other parties. As she didn't drink very much and as we both had to work in the morning, she asked me up to her suite for just one more dance or two. It was probably my quietest Hogmanay for a long time, but the one during which I was to find out that blondes aren't necessarily blonde everywhere!

After such a wonderful Italian start to the New Year, I was very pleased to have a quiet day invigilating Monty doing his Yachtmaster theory papers. He passed all right and after he had given me a wad of pesetas, I strolled up the hill to the hotel, picked up my suitcase and Stella very kindly drove me out to Malaga airport. Her final words were a request that I should come and see her next time I was in the area.

Shortly after the Earl's Court Boat Show Charlie contacted me to say he had two customers who wanted five days' training in the Clyde and that I should use his Norskerry. Charlie and Malcolm came along for the first two days to make sure I knew the boat all right and they set the tone for all Scottish courses. Some of my customers owned boats, some were doing a course before buying, they all enjoyed boating and were willing to work hard at their training. We tried to go to a different place every night so that they knew how to approach and handle their boats in and out of the various harbours. This week we visited Tarbert, Millport, Loch Goil and Rothesay before adjourning to the Clachan Bar on the Friday evening for the end of course celebrations.

A couple of weeks' later Meriel telephoned to tell me there was a middle-aged couple who had just bought a Grand Banks the next size up from them and it was moored nearby in Port Dinorwic. She gave me their telephone number as they had indicated they would like some training. I telephoned and they agreed my fees for a five day course in the North Wales area. It was dark when Meriel picked me up at Bangor rail station and drove me down for the first of many nights and days I was to spend in Dawn Seeker. She put a homemade fish pie in the oven and for a toast to our continued business success she produced the

Charlie's next boat, a larger Norseman 38 'Norskerry'.
Guess where? The Kyles of Bute.

remains of the Islay Malt we had enjoyed at Erskine six months ago. Before we fell asleep she asked me to spend the weekend at their home in Barmouth.

My crew of three, the two parents and their 23 year old son, were complete beginners. They had to be taught all about their boat but the initial task was to make sure all three of them could handle it in and out of the marinas. The next subject of importance, particularly in north Wales, were the diversifications of the tides; the accessibility of each place they wanted to visit would depend on the time and height of high water.

Every day they did the necessary chartwork and workings out of the tide to visit Conway and travel through the magnificent

Menai Straits to Pwllheli and back to Caernarvon for the last night. I told them that by leaving early on tomorrow's tide we could use the same tide to get back into Port Dinorwic. By now the family was working together as a team and they told me, quite correctly, that we would be back in their home port just in time for an afternoon cup of tea. We did some more boat-handling before leaving Caernarvon and then to finish the week off all three in turn brought the boat back into their marina berth. Meriel, smartly dressed in her navy blue sweater with my business badge suitably sewn on, was most impressed and told them so as she walked on board for the final cup of tea and general discussion on the week's events.

Meriel was full of welcoming chatter as she drove the forty odd miles to Barmouth. Their house, overlooking Cardigan Bay, was most impressive with quite a large garden and two big diesel tanks hidden away behind bushes. They both had diesel cars and the central heating was oil-fired. She showed me her sailing dinghy which she loved so much and we were greeted by two lovely dogs, one Labrador and one Retriever. Upstairs she showed me to the spare room and then started running the bath water. As we got in she asked me why I was grinning so much. I instantly replied that "When you introduced me to your two dogs you said you didn't like cats – yet you have a cute ginger pussy!"

The local yacht club was the place to informally relax on a Friday night. Meriel seemed to know everyone there and introduced me to many of her friends who were only too keen to swap nautical tales whilst enjoying a beverage or two. When we got home I was quick into the new bed, while she locked up the house and then jumped in beside me.

The rest of the weekend was spent driving around marinas, meeting harbourmasters, generally spreading the gospel and partying at one or two yacht clubs. When I left her on Monday morning I thanked her for the wonderful weekend and for being such a great agent and friend. As the train sped southwards I knew I had a very contented Welsh agent. She had asked me to her home which she had organised so that she could enjoy her love of the sea and boating.

In June Monty Black asked me to take him and his crew back down to Puerto Banus. Earlier he had got a professional team to deliver the boat back up to the Hamble and they had managed, in rough weather, to cave the front windows in. Terry and Leslie, who were in fact his best shop fitters, had helped him completely refurbish the boat and it looked very luxurious when I joined them for what resulted in a perfectly smooth return to Banus. It took a week with one stop at Vigo for fuel.

Immediately on arrival he gratefully paid me off with the customary wad of pesetas to cover my fees plus hotel and flight home. Firstly I went to Alan Maden to check that it was still okay to shark fish tomorrow as he had insisted I should stay on an extra day for that reason when I was next down. I told him I would be on board at 1000 in the morning and went up the hill to the Andalucia Plaza. Stella seemed genuinely pleased to see me and said she hoped we could have as good a time as we had had on New Year's Eve six months ago.

Alan Maden's shark fishing boat 'Flamingo' moored in Puerto Banus.

There were about ten of us on board the shark boat as we moved out of Puerto Banus to the rendering of "We Are Sailing" by Rod Stewart. When we arrived at the area, Alan showed us how to bait our rod and lines, at the end of which we had different coloured balloons. The movement of a balloon would indicate whose rod the shark had taken, and mine was the only catch of the day. I hauled it in to about six feet of the stern. It was tugging and flapping all over the place so I handed over to Alan who eventually got it on board. We were well out of harm's way, higher up around the wheelhouse, as he pummelled it to death with a wooden mallet. The whole process took about half an hour, and his party trick was to slice open the dead mammal from jaw to tummy and take out its heart, over which he poured some Fundedor Spanish brandy, and it started beating again.

On our return, Stella was waiting to take me to Malaga airport or at least that is what I thought she was going to do. As soon as I got in the car she said she had reorganised my flight for midday tomorrow and that she had booked a room for us at a nearby airport hotel. I was delighted with the change of plans; all of which she had arranged through the Andalucia Plaza. Our night together started with a nice warm bath – necessary for a rather salty sailor back from a day at sea. She had beautiful long legs which led me to comment that there was something funny about them – there was an equally beautiful bottom at the top! This lovely Italian woman was truly molto simpatico!

I was very pleased when Alan Maden arrived in the UK to be trained for his Yachtmaster Certificate. At last, after two years, I was instructing my first professional so that he could become qualified to be captain of a mega-yacht. Ian and I did the course in Naudia and on Saturday 20th November Alan became the first professional I had trained to become a qualified yachtmaster.

Within a very short time a Welshman called Bill Davies telephoned me from Lymington to book a course in his own Moonraker. He brought a couple of friends with him and the four of us had a very successful five days' training. At the end he told me he would be delighted to charter me his boat called Myfanwy and we agreed on a very reasonable price. I would pay for the fuel but he would provide it, as through his business he could get it much cheaper. He had a demolition business in Cardiff – you know the sort - with a heavy metal ball swinging on the end of a crane which he used to demolish things like old houses and old railway bridges. He would bring down some 40 gallon oil drums full of fuel to the marina, roll them along the pontoon and pump the stuff into his boat's tanks. Was it really worth the strain? Anyway, thanks to his kindness I now had another boat available in my fleet, this time in Lymington. I used it about six times in two years until the owner of the marina saw him transferring his fuel in the middle of the night and banished him forthwith. He moved Myfanwy down to Dartmouth but unfortunately it was of no use to me there. It was a sign of the times that marinas could throw customers away.

Early December, when most people were preparing for Christmas and I thought my season was over, I received a call from a Mr Gordon in Scotland telling me he was buying a boat at Malahide near Dublin and wanted me to help him bring it back to Kip Marina. He was in a hurry and wanted to get the boat out of the Irish Republic and back to Great Britain before our Chancellor of the Exchequer imposed a rumoured 25% luxury tax on all imported boats and associated equipment. He agreed my terms; within an hour Charlie Lyle telephoned with an almost similar request. He had just purchased a Grand Banks 42 and wanted assistance with the delivery to Kip. I reprimanded him for not having contacted me earlier and suggested he call Mr Gordon to come to some business arrangement with him.

On 9th December I arrived at Dublin airport ten minutes before Mr Gordon walked off his plane from Glasgow, followed by none other than Charlie and his crew of three, namely The Hougel, Alan Paton and Kenny Trythall, his engineer. We had two great days in Malahide getting the boats finally fitted out and prepared for the passage to Kip. Malahide is a coastal suburban town to the north of Dublin and was a seaside resort for the wealthy of the Irish capital. All day long canned Christmas carols were being played. I think they only had one record and not much choice, so you knew exactly which carol was coming next. This did nothing to stop our enjoyment of the general hospitality of Mr Stafford the ex-mayor of Dublin and Myles Stapleton. On the last day we carried out successful sea trials and spent the night at Howth where there were better facilities including the excellent Howth Yacht Club.

For some unknown reason Charlie in his Cobra sailed four hours before us. Mr Gordon still had a few financial matters to settle and preferred to have a really good yacht club lunch before we departed Howth in Gordonia.

At about 1945 I heard on the VHF radio the motor yacht Cobra calling Belfast Coastguard on Channel 16, and reporting his position as being in Belfast Lough. I knew because of his speed and the fact he was only four hours ahead of us that he was nowhere near there. I got onto Channel 16 and told Cobra to stop calling the coastguard, who luckily hadn't heard him and to speak to me on an inter-ship channel. I then asked The Hougel, who was acting as Charlie's navigator, if he could see any lights. Yes, he could see one to the west. What are its characteristics? Hold on a minute. It is quite bright and flashing twice every so often. I then told him the light he could see was St John's Lighthouse near

Charlie in his Grand Banks 42 'Cobra',
which we escorted up from Dublin

Ardglass, which was exactly where I had calculated him to be by DR navigation.

I told The Hougel it was unsafe for him to be navigating in the dark and that they should wait where they were until midnight when we would arrive and guide them the rest of the way to Kip. When we arrived in the area we saw Cobra coming out of Ardglass where Charlie had decided to go for fish and chips and a couple of bevvies rather than waste four hours in the middle of the Irish Sea.

Four months later Charlie had arranged for four customers to do a course in Cobra. They were Douglas Lamont, John Wilkie, Peter Hart and Alastair Douglas. I travelled up early and spent the weekend with Charlie to make sure we had all the necessary equipment on board as well as just having a good time. On the first evening we were at Tarbert, then Loch Goil and on Wednesday we were back at Kip because they wanted to drive up to Glasgow and watch Scotland play Sweden at Hampden Park. Thursday night we had to be in Rothesay as Charlie had asked me to join his party at the Licensed Victuallers Ball in the Glenburn Hotel. It had been a busy day and we were a bit late. I wonder if I am the only person ever to have driven a 42 ft motor cruiser alongside Rothesay Pier wearing a dinner jacket, ready to hop off and get into his host's car patiently awaiting him.

There was a club called the Argyll Naval Officers Association and having been born in the county I had become a member. By sheer coincidence, the annual dinner happened to be on the Saturday and so for the first and only time I went along to the hotel near Easdale where it was held. The guest of honour was none other than Admiral Henry Leach, an ex-shipmate of mine. We naturally recalled happy memories of earlier times in the Far East, but I remember well the after dinner story he told:

While inspecting a NATO warship at sea I asked a lone sailor on the after deck what his job was. "I am the lifebuoy sentry, sir," he replied.
"What," I enquired "would you do if you saw one of your messmates floating past in the sea, having fallen over the side?"

Without hesitation he answers: "I should shout Man Overboard, I should seize the nearest lifebuoy and throw it over the side and I should ring up the bridge and inform the Officer of the Watch." Professionally correct but almost too glib, so I probed him further as to what he would do in those circumstances if it was one of his officers.

He paused for a moment and then looking me straight in the eye, said:

"Which one, Sir?"

One of the many customers I was very pleased to train was a young Scot called Coco. His real name was Ian Belford and he had been working as a deckhand in the Mediterranean. He preferred life in Scotland and wanted to better himself in the shipping industry. I remember on one of the days of our course him saying: "Here comes the Clyde Banana Boat". He was referring to the MV Garroch Head which had taken over from the Shieldhall on the daily sludge trip to Arran and back.

In 1977 the Shieldhall was bought by the Southern Water Authority to carry sludge from Southampton to an area south of the Isle of Wight. For many a year she was seen by our school's courses in the Solent area, until the late eighties when increasingly tough European Union regulations on sewage disposal brought the practice to a halt. The Shieldhall was taken over by a preservation society, the Solent Steam Packet Limited, which operates as a charity. All work is carried out by unpaid volunteers, she has been restored to seagoing condition and is now listed in the National Historic Fleet, Core Collection.

Meanwhile, Coco went on to become a skipper of the Largs-Millport ferry and then for many years was Master of a Caledonian MacBrayne ferry in the Kyle of Lochalsh. He swallowed the anchor and continued to be successful as the manager of a French-owned refuse company, then Manager of the Highlands and Islands Housing Department in Inverness. Recently retired, he is able to enjoy his love of the sea in his motor cruiser which he has moored in the marina at Inverness.

An architect called George Horspool from East Kilbride went to the 1977 Earl's Court Boat Show with the express intention of buying a boat. To all the agents he expressed two requirements. There must be enough room to stand up as he was a big, tall Scot and there must be two engines in case one broke down. He bought a Princess 37 called Charlotte of Rhu, which he kept at Kip Marina, and I had a hardworking but most gratifying week with him cruising to Loch Goil, Ardrishaig and Campbeltown before returning to Kip where he could practice going in and out of her berth ad nauseum. He did admit to having had a few earlier mishaps with his boat-handling but hopefully we had cured him of those problems. He went on to become a very successful architect and I last saw him a couple of years later proudly standing on his new Grand Banks 49 called Alaskan Star, which I'm told he still owns to this day.

Early in the year Ian and I did a course for three people and also in the crew was Norman Cuthbert from Boat Magazine. In his article he stated:-

The middle of March was, if you remember, full of gale warnings in all areas – this included the Solent and Chichester where on a Monday morning with three others I joined the Mike Reeder School of Seamanship in the motor vessel Naudia owned by Ian Wilson who is a navigation expert and accompanied us as assistant instructor. My companions were Tom who runs a shop fitting business in London, Phil a printer from Luton and John a solicitor from Ireland.

He said that Mike, a man of great experience and a first rate tutor is the Principal and Chief Instructor to students from every continent in the world and that all his instruction is carried out on board the suitable craft he charters in many sailing areas around the British coast or in the Mediterranean. He went on to describe each day's programme of instruction and near the end of the course he disclosed to his companions his reasons for being aboard and asked for their impressions. Their written replies were:-

Phil: The course synopsis in the brochure was abbreviated and I was surprised how much more comprehensive the actual course is – full of unexpected topics. I didn't realise before I took this course how much there is to seamanship.

Tom: I've learnt more this week about practical navigation than I did in six months trying to study it at home on my own. I came to do navigation but I've also learned a lot of basic seamanship which cannot be picked up from a book or in inland waters.

John: I could have taken a course in navigation at a shore establishment or by correspondence course. Here I have been able to combine seamanship and navigation, theory and practice on one week on a seagoing vessel. The course has combined comfort and convivial company and yet the instructors haven't allowed things to deviate too far from the main task in hand.

Norman himself finished off by writing that, although about half of the ground covered was not new to him, he certainly learnt a lot and felt that much more confident and competent. The instructors were there at all times to assist and answer questions. They not only knew the sea but enjoyed teaching people about it.

Naturally I was very pleased with everything and also thanked Ian very much for helping to make it such a success. What pleased me most was the emphasis on the teamwork we were building up and the frequent use of the word seamanship. The Shorter Oxford Dictionary describes the word as the art or practice of managing a ship at sea and that is exactly the reason why I set up the school, to teach that fine art which I had been taught in the Navy.

At Easter time three Belgians telephoned me and asked for a week's instruction in the Mediterranean. They wanted a working holiday lasting a week and wanted suitable training pending their purchase of a motor cruiser. I immediately called Mike Dawes in Antibes and he assured me Jan Pan would be available and ready on 7th May. My customers' names were Johan Peeters, his wife Lucie and their friend Patrick Merckx. We left Antibes on the Saturday and with quite clever customers, we were able to do all the necessary training and still have a good time visiting La

Johan, doing his boat handling in 'Jan Pan' at Antibes

Napoule, St Tropez, Port Grimaud, Cannes and Juan Les Pins before returning to Antibes for the last night.

In 1978 Ian Wilson told me he had, after much deliberation, decided to sell Naudia. He was in no hurry but he was determined to get the good price he knew the boat was worth. In October he telephoned to say he had sold it to a German called Hans Verner who ran a charter company in Yugoslavia. Part of the deal was for Ian to get the boat as far as Gibraltar for which Hans would pay the delivery charges. And then he would be able to do the easy part and get the boat the rest of the way. Ian realised he could not do this and so asked me to organise it. How much should we charge? I told him that in November it could take us weeks because we could be holed up in some harbour gale-bound and waiting for the weather to improve. In the end I suggested my normal fees of so many hundreds of pounds, added ten per cent and then doubled it. I telephoned my friend Danny Clark, who had offered his free services for the opportunity to come on any long passage like this. He needed the experience, like Ian, for the Yachtmaster exam for which I was preparing him.

It was all over and dusted in a week. I made out a watchkeeping rosta which we disregarded from the word go. We got on so well with our general chatter, risqué stories and rude jokes. Above all it was our tremendous sense of humour which kept us going through the long hours of darkness across the English Channel, down the Bay of Biscay and along the Iberian Peninsula with never a ship in sight. There were always two of us up keeping each other awake whilst the other slept. We never saw the sun, it was overcast all the way and we only had to take refuge from rough weather for one day. That was at Leixoes, the large man-made commercial harbour sticking out into the Atlantic near Porto. We topped up with fuel and had a good run ashore before a fine weather forecast enabled us to get an early start for our last dash to Gibraltar, where we arrived at 1030 on Remembrance Sunday. There was a full military wreath-laying ceremony taking place at exactly the same time as at Whitehall. We kept our two minute silence, watched the march past, and then reminded ourselves of Navy days in Main Street before catching the evening plane back to the UK. It was sad to say farewell to Naudia, but luckily Ian was still around to help me.

One of my less successful ventures, due entirely to bad weather, was the attempted delivery of Ron Read in his Princess 41 from the Solent to Puerto Banus at the end of May. It took us a week to get as far as Jersey, where we moored up close to the St Helier Yacht Club. I have never seen the morale of our people, Ron and his three friends, go downhill so quickly, as every shipping forecast, one after the other, spoke of southerly force sixes, sevens and gales. I did theory instruction every day until early afternoon and then we would adjourn to the club and enjoy their excellent hospitality at the bar and restaurant. Most time was spent playing snooker, billiards and table tennis, just passing the time away until the next miserable forecast.

It was during these recreational periods that I was able to find out, mostly from his crew, what an amazing person this quiet unassuming Ron Read was. He had been a Squadron Leader during the war and was awarded the DFC for courage of the highest order when flying Halifax bombers over the industrial Ruhr. After the war he managed airports in Cardiff, Bahrain, Stansted, British Guiana and in Jersey. Then he was appointed to lead the development of the former RNAS at Abbotsinch, which I knew from Navy days and which opened in 1966 as Glasgow Airport. He had written to me from Riyadh and he was with me whilst on leave as the British Aircraft Corporation's Chief Executive in Saudi Arabia. He was about to retire when the Waste Management Corporation beckoned him back to Riyadh to be their Chief Executive. What a man, and it was fantastic to spend a week with him in Jersey while the foul weather prevailed. He had to get back to Riyadh and his crew to their normal working tasks, so his boat eventually arrived in Banus in the care of a delivery team.

Before they finally left Great Crosby to reside in Barmouth, Meriel, Pat and the two sons moved Dawn Seeker up to Kip Marina. She was able to spend more time helping out at the Merioneth Yacht Club and she became very interested in the Three Peaks Race, the first of which was held in 1977. The race was inspired by the adventures of the climber and sailor Bill Tilman and was the brainchild of two local doctors Rob Howorth and Merfyn Jones. It entailed three sailors and two runners sailing from Barmouth to Fort William and stopping en route at Caernarfon, Ravenglass, and Fort William itself to climb the highest peaks in Wales, England and Scotland, namely Snowdon, Scafell and Ben Nevis. Crews were limited to five and the use of engines was not allowed except when entering or leaving harbour.

Seven teams took part in the first race and it is said it took those entrants five days to sail 389 miles, climb 11,000 feet and run or walk 7.3 miles. By 1979 the race was becoming more and more popular, it needed more supervision and the media had become more interested. The committee decided they needed a comfortable motor boat to cover the last stages between Crinan and Fort William, and so Meriel offered the use of Dawn Seeker, skippered by me. Everything had been agreed on business terms and although Meriel was not making any money out of the deal, she was acting as my agent ensuring I would be paid and she knew she would enjoy the racing.

I flew up to Glasgow Airport on 17th July, was met by Meriel who had driven up from her home and we joined Dawn Seeker at Kip Marina. She had brought up a huge stew and while it was slowly cooking we made up for lost time, as it was well over a year since we had last worked together. The appetiser had to last us a few days and we then settled down to the superb pot mess and with the inevitable bottle of vino we began our work.

The weather forecast was great so we decided to leave at the crack of dawn and proceed round the Mull of Kintyre where the tidal stream would be favourable and arrive off Crinan that evening. So that we could save the large quantity of remaining stew we went alongside at Crinan and had a super snack at the Seafood Bar, and then back on board for a good night's rest before yet another crack of dawn departure, this time for Fort William. Although we were ahead of the race leaders, the moment we arrived alongside the town pier we were descended upon by committee people and their friends. Meriel seemed to know them all and was very good at doing the introductions and keeping the business-like atmosphere going.

I put out planks between our fenders and the piles on the pier, because although only a slight breeze was blowing it was bound to increase as would the movement with all the boats due to come and go. The leaders soon started coming in and every arrival was greeted by friends or family coming on board. Many brought bottles of booze and cans of beer so the boat began to resemble a bar and it entailed quite a lot of washing and tidying up. Everyone was happy and cheerful and very grateful for our presence. This went on for the best part of two days so we didn't get much sleep. Shortly after the last boat crossed the finishing line on Thursday, we moved Dawn Seeker over to the Sea Lock at Corpach at the entrance to the Caledonian Canal. This was where the final finish of the Ben Nevis Run, and therefore the Three Peaks Race took place, and it offered a quiet and safe mooring for the night.

Meriel had booked a room at the Grand Hotel where the Three Peaks Supper was being held. We got ashore early in the afternoon and were able to enjoy the welcome hot bath and have a siesta before the evening's celebrations which went on until the wee small hours. We were able to have a nice long lie-in, as we had a day to spare before getting back to Kip and my next job, which entailed crossing the North Sea.

I had been asked to help and train a Dutch couple to get their Princess 37 from Great Yarmouth across to Holland where they wanted to cruise the Dutch canals for their summer holidays. I always insisted on being paid in advance and they wanted five days. I arrived on board and straight away it was obvious he could handle his boat very well due to his inland waterway experience going up and down the Rivers Ouse and Trent. So we concentrated on chartwork and tidal streams in preparation for them taking their boat across the North Sea. Including checking all the safety equipment and that they had done the engine checks correctly, this took two days. On the third day, with a good weather forecast, they navigated us the hundred miles across to Scheveningen where we arrived as the sun was about to set.

As the woman had never handled the boat before, the next morning I taught her how to steer a compass course and how to turn her twin-engine motor cruiser on the spot. Then after a short break for coffee and with her husband tending the ropes and fenders, I taught her how to bring the boat alongside, both forwards and backwards. This took most of the morning and we agreed another few turns tomorrow should be fine. We then went ashore for lunch in this charming fishing town and from that moment he seemed to lose interest in learning any more, but concentrated on contacting friends and arranging their holiday. The name of the town was extremely difficult to pronounce unless, of course, one was Dutch. I found out from some older locals that they had used the name Scheveningen as a means of catching German infiltrators during the war. Even the Germans had a problem saying the word correctly.

They kindly asked me to a fabulous fish restaurant that evening with about six of their friends. Many different drinks were tasted and he was obviously intent on enjoying himself and was getting delightfully inebriated. Shortly after returning on board I was lying on my bunk in the forward cabin when the woman gently slipped in beside me. She said she was there to thank me for the kindness and patience shown during the morning's boat handling instruction. She had on a short loose-fitting nightie and when I enquired about her husband she assured me he was sound asleep in the after cabin and we could actually hear him snoring. I felt I could not refuse her as to have done so would probably have caused too much of a commotion!

In the morning he once again didn't seem interested in further training but I gave her some more of the promised boat handling instruction. Then they went ashore together to arrange, amongst other things, my flight back to Heathrow where I was due to be flying later that day. Meanwhile I went to the market and, for the third or fourth time, indulged in the super raw herrings doused with onions and sweet vinegar. When the couple returned I was informed that they had reserved a table at the same fabulous restaurant as last night and that I was booked on a flight back to the UK tomorrow morning. I couldn't possibly ask them for an extra day's payment when I was in for the same super fish meal and, judging from the glint in her eyes, another reward from this very attractive Dutch lady!

The next week I was doing a course in the Clyde and when we visited Troon I was beckoned by David Cook into his office where Mr and Mrs Jan de Wilde from Zwyndreht in Holland were in the process of buying a Moody 33 sail boat. It was called *Dutch Treat* and I thought to myself that I had two of those last week! David introduced me to them and it turned out that they were taking a year off work and wanted to sail their new boat down the Irish Sea, along to Moody's Marina in the River Hamble and then across to Le Havre and through the French Canals to the Mediterranean. They wanted sufficient training to be competent at sailing the boat before they left England.

I told them I personally couldn't do it as I was fully booked, but my sailing instructor, whom I would introduce at the weekend, would fulfil all their needs. I told Meriel, who was thrilled at the idea, she came dashing up and booked in for the weekend. On the Saturday we met the de Wildes who agreed my terms of so much per day for the instruction plus Meriel's travelling expenses. The three of them discussed an outline programme, they knew how to contact Meriel when required and they paid me a deposit of half the estimated total cost. All quickly agreed upon and Meriel and I retired to the hotel to reflect. I wanted to satisfy myself that she was willing to accept the responsibility. She assured me she was and furthermore insisted she only wanted paying her reasonable expenses.

She telephoned in November and said the boat was safely at Moody's and because of all the administration required to clear customs for VAT etc, and the length of time required to be at sea getting across to Le Havre, could I be there to do what they estimated would take three days? We duly arrived on the Monday morning and Meriel showed me to our single side-by-side bunks at the very stern of the boat. The owners still had a few things to do including some stores to collect but there wasn't much time as we had to clear customs at their quay in Old Portsmouth and we must be there by 1800. We were there in time but it must have been the coldest night of the year and no way were we going to be able to sail the ninety odd miles across to Le Havre. There wasn't a breath of wind, there wasn't a cloud in the sky and it was, in fact, a beautiful but freezing moonlit night.

Jan and I sat by the wheel all night long while Jan did all the chartwork and navigation. We were occasionally fed cups of soup by the women who very sensibly kept warm and possibly had the odd nap, down below. I lost count of the number of sweaters I had on. The temperature seemed low enough to freeze the balls of a brass monkey. The history of this good old naval expression originated in the days of sail, when cannon balls were piled on a tray, known as a monkey. In cold weather the brass tray contracted more quickly than the iron cannon balls and so the pyramid collapsed. We arrived at about 1000: all four of us went into the nearest French "greasy spoon" and had a monumental fry-up before returning on board. In our cold, cramped after cabin Meriel and I snuggled close and had a good four to five hours sleep.

Quite late in the afternoon we started to organise them for their inland waterway trip to the Mediterranean. There was an area where north-bound transitters of the canals left their "no-longer-required" canvas sheets, rubber tyres and wooden planks. We were therefore able to show them and help to fit the fendering equipment, which they would need permanently in place for their next few weeks' transit of the canal system. We went ashore for a farewell dinner and they paid me the remainder of the monies owing plus, of course, our ferry fares back to the UK. Instead of catching the intended ferry we booked in to a nearby hotel and indulged ourselves in a very well earned night's rest.

I told Meriel how expert she had been as my sailing instructor and that having earned me a lot of money I was tomorrow going to hire a car and give her a few days' holiday in the Cherbourg Peninsula. The weather continued to be perfect for that time of year, sunny by day and freezing by night. We visited the D-Day landing beaches in Normandy but spent most time in the sailing areas I knew she would enjoy at Deauville, St. Vaast and Barfleur.

We did the Three Peaks Race once more the following year and it was great fun as always. I remember the morning we took the press out from Crinan to meet the race leaders. We sailed at 0400 and it was a beautiful still day and we had to wait at anchor. By 0700 it was so hot that I dived into the invigorating cool, deep water of the Sound of Jura for what proved to be my last ever swim in UK waters. Meriel organised a nice warm shower before cooking the usual vast breakfast.

I first met Richard Crouch in October 1977. He had owned a small sports cruiser and had hired a so-called expert to help him deliver it to Poole. When proceeding westwards down the Solent his expert thought Hurst Castle was a merchant Ship and then went too close inshore and ran the boat aground on rocks clearly shown on the chart near Hengistbury Head. Richard decided he had better learn how to do things himself, so joined up with two others for a course in the Solent area on board *Myfanwy*. We became the best of boating friends after that course and I did several short courses with him when he purchased a Powles 37 named *Miss Barbados*.

He was visiting one of the Earl's Court boat shows at which I was working. He asked me to meet him at the Savoy for dinner that evening at 1830. When I arrived, he was immaculately dressed, as always, but apologised for the fact that we would have to go somewhere else: he had a roll-neck sweater on and no tie. I nipped into a taxi, rushed back to my digs in Philbeach Gardens and recovered a spare tie I had in my grip. All was well and we had a fabulous evening in the Savoy Grill. There seemed to be a fixation about the wearing of ties those days – even amongst the clergy where I had heard that:-

> With heaving breast the Dean undressed
> The Bishop's wife to lie on
> She thought it crude done in the nude
> So he kept his old school tie on!

Richard's story is one of a bit of luck, much generosity and sheer hard work. He came from a poor family and started work as a coal delivery truck driver. He changed to delivering oil. If he hadn't played village cricket these events would have never come about. In the same team was a bank manager who, without any security, lent him £4,000. With this he bought a second hand bowser, filled it with oil, sold the oil and with the profit bought more oil, and so it went on. He drove the lorry himself and by the time I met him he was a very wealthy man and had his own oil distribution depot in the Dartford area of Kent. Because of this business and not knowing how long, due to possible weather delays, it would take to deliver *Miss Barbados* to the Med, he asked me to do the job.

It was a fabulous trip all the way, having to stop every night for fuel. There was one delay – a complete long weekend – in Ribadeo on the north west coast of Spain. There was a fisherman's fiesta on and no fuel was sold because the attendants were away on holiday.

In September of that year I joined him, his wife Lesley and their two friends Marlene and Douglas for a week's cruise along the coast from Alicante. Then the next year, in March, we had a

Right to left: Richard and Lesley Crouch, with their friends, Marlene and Douglas on board 'Miss Barbados' in Southern Spain

week, mostly in Andratx, followed by a three-week cruise to Ibiza and around the whole of Majorca. I think we got to know every bay and marina in the islands and we had great fun everywhere we went. Richard was very generous and paid me my full fees every time, as he appreciated it was my livelihood.

Then, with a view to buying a bigger boat, he wanted to sell his Powles where it was berthed in Majorca. As there was so much expensive gear and equipment in the boat, he decided he and I should drive in his Landrover down through France and Spain to Barcelona. Then across in the ferry to Palma, de-store everything and bring it home for his new boat in England. It was a very busy but worthwhile trip.

On the second and last balmy evening there the peace was shattered by a loud American shout and high revving of engines. It was a Grand Banks Alaskan 49 whose owner was unsuccessfully trying to moor his boat at the marina. Richard and I went along and asked if we could help in any way. "I guess you sure could,"

Instructing Marlene the use of a sea-fix for radio direction finding.
The bustenhalters hanging out to dry are hers!

was the owner's reply with equal nods of agreement from the two females on board. When I reached the flying bridge I explained that I was a Seamanship Instructor and asked if he would like me to instruct him how to moor the boat, or actually do it for him. "We've come all the way from Barcelona, so I'd be grateful if you did it, because we're a bit tired." I asked Richard to do the ropes and fenders and we had his boat moored stern to on the jetty in a few minutes. "I guess you guys would like a drink," he said as he ushered us into the lounge which was well adorned with tennis trophies and memorabilia. He then said "Mah name's Boyd Browning and this is mah wife Francoise Durr." He introduced the other woman and we all shook hands. Luckily I had heard of the French tennis player so I was able to make all the right noises as we enjoyed some Scotch on the rocks.

Francoise Durr was born in Algeria in 1942. She won 26 singles titles and over 60 doubles titles during her career which had been at its best in the 60s and 70s. She was also well known as the tennis player who travelled the circuit with her dog "Topspin", who carried her racquet on and off the court.

Boyd enquired as to what we were doing in Adratx and when I explained that I was a Master Mariner and navigation instructor he said: "I'm an airline pilot and don't need any of that crap". The two women disagreed, said that's exactly what they all needed and maybe next year we could arrange something. Next morning Richard and I were up early to catch the first ferry back to Barcelona and nipped down to "Good I.D." as the American boat was called. We knocked on the gangway and there was no answer. We could see right through the boat to the forward cabin whose door opened as we knocked for the second time and out came all three. "Hi guys. Welcome aboard and have a coffee or fresh juice." As the three of them sat down in the lounge we accepted a quick fruit juice and, explaining we were cutting it a bit fine for the ferry, departed never to see them again.

By late in the summer we had started moving *Dawn Seeker* from Scotland down to the South of England and had got it as far as its old berth in Port Dinorwic. Meriel asked me if and when I had a quiet spell, say in November, I could help her take it the rest of the way. She would as always be happy to pay my fees. Shortly after my arrival at her home and the usual lovely welcome, we went to the Saturday evening party at the yacht club. In the morning we had to make an early morning getaway in order to catch the tide. It was all a bit rushed but we had plenty of time ahead of us to get to know each other again and catch up on each other's news. A short overnight stop at Fishguard and, as we approached Land's End, the weather began to deteriorate and the forecast worsened.

The coastguard gave us no encouragement whatsoever, so we put into St Ives Bay for the night and anchored on the leeward side of a group of hills. In spite of this, it turned out to be, I think, the worst night ever at anchor. Motor cruisers never lie well in breezy conditions let alone in very rough weather. I was up every half hour or so to check we were not dragging and possibly let out more chain of which we did seem to have ample. Every time I returned aft, there was Meriel to dry me out and keep me warm.

The next morning the coastguard told us the harbour master was refusing entry to St Ives harbour as it was so rough: waves crashing over the breakwater. The best thing for us would be to wait for the tide at lunchtime, and then go into Hayle until the weather moderated; they reckoned that would be in a couple of days' time.

I could not weigh the anchor. I tried from all angles but it appeared that, with all the jamming and yawing, we were well and truly dug in. As I was preparing to let go the rest of the anchor chain (and mark it with a couple of large fenders for recovery by a diver) a privately owned Scottish fishing boat came to our rescue. With his derrick he was able to lift our chain and anchor on board his vessel with ease. We followed him into Hayle and went alongside to collect our property. His fees were a bottle of the best malt whisky, which we helped him and his wife consume over the next couple of storm-bound days! Hayle was not the best place in the West Country to be holed up as there was much poverty in the area after the mine closures. So we bought some stewing meat and vegetables and made a huge pot-mess. This kept us well fed between long enjoyable spells keeping warm in bed.

Towards the end of our trip round Land's End to Newlyn one of the engines started overheating. I could not find any leaks within the fresh or raw water cooling systems or anything else wrong and so Meriel telephoned her husband, who organised for Patrick to come down. He was a skilled diesel engineer and managed to have the problem sorted in no time at all.

Newlyn is a large fishing harbour with some good pubs and restaurants. Chart users will know that its Ordnance Datum is the reference point used to line up the chart datum of British harbours in the Tidal Level section of Admiralty charts. We enjoyed it there and stayed on an extra night before continuing on our way to East Cowes. There we secured alongside the berth Meriel had booked for a year.

It had been good to meet up again but unfortunately we both seemed to be getting less work for each other and felt it might be some time before anything else cropped up. Before she left to go back home she gave me the keys of *Dawn Seeker* and told me to use the boat any time I wanted. Hopefully she would come down to help every now and then. We actually saw each other twice more and as always it was fun. We had had a very happy business friendship and I was very grateful to her and her family for all they did to help me.

As the beginning of the eighties approached, signs that our school was doing well began to come from unexpected directions. They had started off with our de-storing of *Miss Barbados* and then Harry Poole contacted me to persuade me to join the Federation of Sailing Schools. He was the Secretary. Then an elderly Canadian couple, Wardon and Audrey Evans contacted me. They called themselves Canada's business attaché in Europe. I'm not sure if that was their official title. They had a new Broom 30, which they had bought at Brundal in the Norfolk Broads and wanted me to help them deliver it to Calais and give them sufficient training to enable them to take their boat on their own through the French canals and then down to a port near Torremolinos where they had their home.

With them was a friend, Bill Shepherd, who was a circuit judge in Canada and whose last and only visit to Great Britain was as a young officer in the Royal Navy during WW2. His story was hard to believe but at the age of 19 with the war just started he decided it was no use fighting it from Canada. Best to get over to the front line in England and instead of joining the Royal Canadian Navy he joined the Royal Navy. Like a lot of people, including yours truly, he found the best time in his life was his time in the Navy. Similarly he realised it was a young man's life and, in times of peace, rather dull, so he returned to Canada and became a legal wizard. Training Wardon and Audrey was great but when not occupied doing that, Bill and I were as thick as thieves, recounting our naval escapades. In spite of his lengthy time ashore back in Canada he hadn't lost any of his navalese.

Then a chest specialist at a London hospital, called John Swithinbank invited me to visit him at his luxury flat overlooking the Fulham FC ground alongside the River Thames. The poor man had congenital respiratory problems and therefore could only be at sea in his Ranger 36 for very short periods. He wanted me to take it down to Castets at the beginning of the Canal Lateral a la Garonne and Canal du Midi. It would be necessary for me to go gently, as there would be a heavy cargo of at least six large oxygen bottles on board which he needed for his own medication.

I asked Charlie Lyle if he would like to help me and he jumped at the idea. We left Chichester Yacht Basin on the glorious first of June and very soon we were going through the Alderney Race. Charlie, as we know, had been boating for many years but had never been south of the Isle of Wight and I think he was quite impressed with the seamanship required to traverse the tidal races. A sailboat trying to accompany us abandoned the idea and went the longer, less rough, way round the Casquets.

We were delayed by fog for one day in Guernsey. That was good, because our day of arrival was a Sunday when the important shops selling duty free goods were all shut. Nothing else prolonged our journey along the north Brittany coast and down the Chenal du Four (another impressively tidal area) with nightly fuel stops at Port la Foret, Port Haliguen and Royan. Then proceeding up the River Gironde past Bordeaux to the first lock in the canal system. We left the keys hidden in an agreed place for John to take over his boat the next day.

Whilst travelling northwards along the River Gironde by train in gorgeous weather, I spared a thought for the twelve Cockleshell Heroes. After a series of disasters at the beginning of Operation Frankton in 1942, only four of the original team remained. Those four Royal Marines, in the middle of the night, in the depth of winter, planted their limpet mines on the enemy merchant ships moored in Bordeaux harbour and only two came back alive, Blondie Hasler and Bill Sparks.

A distinguished Royal Marine Officer, this was one of the many events in which Blondie partook during the war and which ultimately led to the formation of the Special Boat Service. He was awarded the DSO and also recommended for the VC but was not eligible because his actions were not in the face of the enemy. After the war he became known as the father of single-handed sailing and he invented the first practical self-steering gear for sailboats.

As previously mentioned, it was great to meet him a few times while Sir Alec Rose was doing his single-handed sailing in the sixties.

No sooner had I got off the train from Bordeaux than Richard Crouch wanted to be accompanied on his maiden cruise in his new Hatteras 51 called *Miss Barbados* – like his previous one which we had recently decommissioned in Andratx. It was July, the weather was good and we spent the first three days making sure everything was in perfect working order and that we had all the necessary spares and provisions for a three and a half week cruise. After three very good runs ashore at Guernsey, Camaret, and Port Haliguen we arrived at Pornichet where sadly Richard had to return home, leaving me in charge of the boat.

During that week every evening the head waiter in the nearby marina restaurant, which we had visited first night in, gave me a vast helping of Moules a la Marinière at the starter's price of £1. Included in the deal was as much bread and butter as I wanted – this went down well with the fantastic creamy winey oniony soup that was left after I had eaten the moules. I had all other meals on board while watching the Olympic Games in Moscow and seeing Alan Wells, the Scot, win the 100 metres Gold Medal. Richard returned in time for us to have further runs ashore at Le Puliguen, Concarneau, Douarnenez, Jersey and Alderney before securing alongside the berth in Lymington. We had a memorable cruise even if we hadn't visited all the places intended.

Earlier in the year there was a telephone call from Alex McMullen, the new editor of Motor Boat and Yachting, to tell me they were doing an article on courses for cruising and that the magazine was willing to pay half my fees for their reporter Shane Kelly to do a five day course in the Clyde. I told him I had a course for a married couple from Cumbria starting in August and thanked him for his offer which I willingly accepted without mentioning that his magazine had already done an article on my school six years earlier.

Shane was a young Kiwi who had emigrated to Australia and was over in Great Britain for a few years gaining experience as a journalist in the boating world. The customers were Frank, a pharmacist from Carlisle and his wife Jennifer, and they were planning to buy a Princess 32. Shane started his report:-

> We met for the first time on a Monday morning at Kip Marina on the Firth of Clyde in Scotland. We were welcomed by Mike Reeder aboard the floating classroom *Cobra*, which was perfect for the task, and had been fitted out with superb equipment. Mike is no stranger to the job. He joined the Royal Navy when he was 13 and spent 25 years in Her Majesty's Service. He has crewed and navigated aboard submarines, instructed other sailors and commanded a minesweeper.

Shane described each day's instructional activities and mentioned that the Clyde was a beautiful cruising area and an excellent place to conduct our type of course. He went on:-

> Mike's style of tuition suited us well; he let the crew get on with the job unless information was sought and no-one ever seemed afraid to ask a question. Navigation is one of the more popular topics of the course, though I suspect it is the simple way it is taught that makes it so. Mike claims it is his naval training that has given him the ability to present a comparatively complex subject in a simple way. He was never irate, nor did he ever seem to worry about anything.

> His personality and relaxed teaching style play a large part in the success of his courses. The atmosphere is relaxed and excellent for absorbing the information in the lectures. Mike has the ability to instil a lot more than straight learning – a respect for the sea and common sense among other things. By the end of the week we were all good friends, and came away convinced that it was money well spent.

That evening, needless to say some of us adjourned to Charlie's at Largs for our end-of-course celebrations. Amongst many of the revellers a few ex-customers including Ian Harrison and his family who were staying at a local hotel. I had spent a fabulous fortnight in his Fairey Spearfish on their maiden voyage from Glasson Dock near Preston down to the Scillies and back. That had been three years ago and so we had a few nautical yarns to tell and went down to his boat *Say No More* for a night cap.

Whilst in Scotland I met up with the Nardini family. I did some training with Pete and Ricky in their boat *Delfino* and also Mario Giovanacci in his Sea Kip 40. Pete runs what is possibly regarded as Scotland's most famous café restaurant and ice cream parlour and the following year joined our crew taking the Hatteras down to Cannes. We met his elder brother Aldo and his wife Sandra at their home and also at a fabulous meal in their restaurant later in the week. They celebrated their 50th wedding anniversary in 2011, and Aldo reached the ripe old age of 80 the same year. Their daughter Daniela Nardini is the well-known actress who was to win BAFTA best actress awards for her role in the BBC TV series This Life and later opened a pet grooming shop in Largs called 'Cutz and Mutz'.

Then a Mr Azar from the Lebanon bought a Princess 41 in Lymington and asked me for five days' training in the Solent area. He was an architect and property developer and his home was in a town called Jounie to the north of Beirut. At that stage of the civil war he said it would be very unusual if he and his family didn't hear gunfire every day. Like one or two other Lebanese I had met, he was making preparations in case he had to take refuge and move his family from their beautiful country. During the week we discussed how I could get the boat to Larnaca. I suggested he organised for it to be land-transported to the south of France, and that our school would do the rest.

Three weeks later, having caught an evening flight down to the Riviera, we spent the night on board and left early next morning calling at Ajaccio in Corsica before stopping at the Costa Smeralda in Sardinia. There Porto Cervo must be the ritziest of yachting harbours. Lovely wealthy mega-yachts and yet its shops and restaurants all too expensive even for the average boat owner. We asked a passing RIB where the nearest bank was and the crew said five miles away, because everything closed down here yesterday. It was now 1st October. We asked the marina office for a weather forecast and they showed me the one, which was already two days out of date. The forecast for tomorrow – when they eventually found it in a drawer – was good NW force 3. Armed with this good news we set off yet again at the crack of dawn.

After a very pleasant early morning start, and as we progressed on our easterly course of about 150 miles towards the island of Ponza, the weather got worse and worse from astern in the west. Dark, thick brown clouds began to appear and long ago we would have turned around if it had been from any other direction. However, by now we were half way, and beyond the point of no return, and beginning to broach. We took over hand steering as the auto-pilot couldn't cope with the stern sea. We were averaging between 8 and 22 knots as we settled down for the next five hours with Ponza clearly visible ahead, when we were on the crest of the waves. The harbour was full of vessels taking refuge from the same gale. They all seemed to have had the same duff forecast as us and, with difficulty, we found a space in which to safely anchor.

We were weatherbound there for two days. The next vivid memory of the cruise involved rats at Reggio, the huge commercial harbour on the toe of Italy. They were the size of cats, seemed domiciled and walked freely around the area. This necessitated keeping all the doors, windows and port holes on board firmly shut, which was not too agreeable in the hot climate. We got out of there as soon as possible and crossed the Bay of Squalls to Corfu and Corinth.

Mr Azar had arranged to join us for the rest of the cruise at Zia Marina in Piraeus, and we had telephoned him from Reggio to confirm our date and time of arrival. After a good night in the town of Corinth and the usual spectacular passage through the canal, we went on to meet the next drama in Piraeus. Our arrival in a cheap little forty one foot boat did not please the deputy port captain of Zia Marina. He wanted to be filled up with much larger and wealthier boats. "Go away," boomed across the harbour, from this vast ape of a man, before I even had a chance to explain we were only stopping to pick up the owner by prior arrangement. He wouldn't listen to me and repeated his nicety three times before we retired speechless from the scene to find a more amiable welcome elsewhere.

This we found five miles or so further along in Athens itself. It was a much more upmarket, privately owned marina with restaurants bordering on the sea. Mr Azar, who had witnessed the events at Zia, was there to meet us and bought us the best meal for a long time at one of the superb restaurants. The rest of the cruise, ably navigated by the owner, to Nascos, Rodhos and from Pathos along the south coast of Cyprus to Larnaca was enjoyable and uneventful – until we walked into the travel agents to book our flights home. They informed us the first flight direct to London was in a fortnight's time. I could not believe this, and after much discussion with the Indian lady who was serving me, she indicated that if we went out to the airport tomorrow early and spoke to the ticket clerk we could well get on a plane straight away.

Our evening meal at an open air restaurant by the marina further endeared us to Cyprus. The place was inundated with wild cats scavenging for food. All they got from us were fairly well aimed salt and pepper pots with which the waiters kept us adequately supplied. After a while the animals seemed to prefer other tables. The airport resembled an ex-RAF wartime base, which is exactly what it was, and had no modern offices or facilities. Whenever a ticket clerk appeared on the other side of the long counter there would be a mad rush. This is where my rugby training and experience came in and we got the first plane out of Larnaca. We had first class seats in a Cyprus Airways plane to Heathrow via Zurich.

Evidence that our School of Seamanship had a good reputation came before Christmas when I received a dubious accolade in the form of a letter from the Royal Yachting Association. They asked me if I would be willing to serve on the working party and committee looking into the formation of a National Motor Cruising Certificate and the production of their Cruising Logbook G18/83.

The person who had proposed me was Bill Anderson, a retired naval officer whom I had met only once since we both left the Navy. He was doing great work virtually in charge of the RYA in a dingy office in Buckingham Palace Road in London and later from slightly more upmarket places, firstly in Woking and then Eastleigh – all far removed and out of touch with the real boating areas like the Solent, West Country and Scotland. In spite of this Bill did a magnificent job, aided by a small staff, in setting up the Yachtmaster Scheme.

As regards the committee and/or working party, the trouble was that the meetings were in London during working hours and on weekdays they expected a very busy Principal and Chief Instructor to do this for free and pay his travelling expenses as well. Welcome to the real world!

In my real world of the moment the response of the professionals, namely the captains, first mates and deck hands of the mega-yachts, was causing a bit of bother. Their attitude was that they could all drive and manage their yachts perfectly well, and they had very good references from their owners to prove it. But they rarely went out of sight of land, or out when it was rough. In the Cote d'Azur, all the crews knew about the mistral. It was a strong mountain wind which originated in the Alps, swirled down the Rhone Valley and caused rough seas in the Golfe de Lyons and as far east as Genoa. Some of the charter crews, when it was rough, used to shoot lines about the mistral to their charterers, and encouraged them to visit the other harbours in their nice comfortable cars, thus avoiding the risk of seasickness. More importantly, as far as the crews were concerned, it would save their boats getting covered in salt, their engine rooms getting dirty and the ships' sides getting smothered in exhaust fumes. Their boat could then qualify for the battered trophy presented to the charter yacht which had the most customers and did the least sea-time in a season!

In spite of this slight antipathy amongst captains and their crews, of whom eight had by now come to us for training and their Yachtmasters, I knew things would change and it was just a matter of time. After all, owners would want well qualified captains to take their vessels further afield, across the Atlantic and even possibly around the world. Maybe the insurance companies would insist on better qualifications.

FALKLANDS AND HEAPS
OF HIPS

On Friday 19th March 1982 a group of Argentinian scrap metal dealers, including a few of their marines, occupied a disused whaling station in South Georgia and raised the Argentinian flag. The British Defence Secretary at the time was John Nott, who in the previous year's defence review was proposing the withdrawal of the Navy's Ice Patrol vessel, HMS Endurance, from the South Atlantic, the scrapping of HMS Hermes, the sale of HMS Invincible to Australia and the phasing out of our two assault ships Intrepid and Fearless. All this had sent a signal to the Argentinian Junta that the British government was unwilling, and would soon be unable, to defend its territories and subjects in the Falklands.

But luckily we had three admirals, all of whom I was fortunate enough to know and with whom I had been shipmates in the fifties and sixties. The first was Admiral Henry Leach whom I had last met at the Argyll Naval Officers' Dinner in 1976. He was now First Sea Lord and Chief of the Naval Staff. On hearing John Nott was undecided what to do, Henry went straight to the House of Commons and told Margaret Thatcher that if the islands were invaded Great Britain could and should send a Task Force. He considered it would be the Navy's job to recover the islands.

On Wednesday 31st March the Argentinian fleet set sail and Henry Leach sent orders to a Royal Navy Force carrying out exercises in the Mediterranean to be prepared to sail south. He had already told Endurance to sail from Stanley to South Georgia. Two days later the Argentinians invaded the Falkland Islands and Henry Leach told Margaret Thatcher that in three days' time the Task Force would be on its way. The nuclear submarine Conqueror sailed southwards on the 4th and the two aircraft carriers Hermes and Invincible, in the company of escort vessels, left the next day. Whilst on a Mediterranean cruise the SS Canberra was requisitioned and on its return to Southampton was quickly refitted. On 9th April she left with the Royal Marine Commando Brigade and the Parachute Regiment embarked. The whole Task Force eventually comprised 127 ships, 43 warships, 22 Royal Fleet Auxiliary ships and 62 Merchant Navy ships. In the face of public anger at both himself and the Foreign Secretary, John Nott offered his resignation but it was not accepted by Margaret Thatcher. In the end it was Galtieri, not Nott, who prevented the Invincible being sold to Australia.

Meanwhile, a Turkish owner had asked me to be captain of his brand new 61 foot Hatteras and sail it from the Hamble to Piraeus in Greece. He wanted his future boat keeper, Mustaffa, who had been a petty officer submariner in the Turkish Navy to be on board for the experience, otherwise our school had to provide the crew. I immediately asked Charlie if he would like to be my first mate and replying very much in the affirmative, asked if Pete Nardini and Ivor Tiefenbrun could also be in the team.

So the crew totalled five and we all joined on Monday 19th April with the intention of leaving the next morning. The ship was brand new, the bedding and furniture still had its plastic covers on; there were still half a dozen workmen and women from the boatyard doing various additional fittings of electrical equipment, extra cupboards and lockers, etc. Everyone seemed to be in everyone's way as we the crew sorted out our cabins and personal gear.

Pete Nardina, as we knew, ran his very successful restaurant in Largs and so his job was obviously to be the chef and ensure the fridge and deep freeze were full of plenty of good food. Charlie busied himself going round and finding out where everything was and ensuring it all worked. I was doing most of this with Charlie but my main concern was my conviction that no way was the workforce going to be finished, cleaned up and out of the boat with all their gear by knock-off time that evening.

Remembering my Navy days and experience with dockyard mateys and their desire to prolong a job as long as possible, I spoke to the foreman and told him I would give him one more day and that I was leaving at 1700 tomorrow – I did not mean maybe.

Although there was a mad rush at the end, I started up the engines at 1650 and at 1700, with only the intended crew on board, we left the pontoon and went round to the fuel berth to top right up with diesel. My ultimatum to the foreman had worked, we remained in the Hamble for the night and left at my usual crack of dawn next day.

Everything went fine, as the team settled in to their cruising routine and we arrived alongside the fuel berth in Jersey to top up again. The reason this is mentioned is because I was very concerned about the fuel consumption and the fact that the Hatteras agent had said there would be no trouble crossing the Bay of Biscay; the full 350 miles extremity from Rade de Brest to Corunna at the recommended cruising speed of 16 knots. I worked out exactly how many litres we had used to travel the distance from Hamble to Jersey and my first impression was that we wouldn't make it. I could get just one more statistic to help me and that was the number of litres used on the second leg to Douarnanez. My worst suspicions were confirmed, we followed the coastline to Pornichet, fuelled up again and then did the 250 miles across to Bilbao.

We arrived in north Spain well after dark and there seemed to be no empty berths for our size of boat. I found a post sticking out of the water and invited Charlie to secure to it for the night. He refused and probably just as well, because we were told the next day that it was the flagpole of the roof of the Club Nautico, which had been blown away in a recent gale! Eventually a local marinero whistled at us and guided us into a suitable vacant space. Having successfully crossed the Bay without running out of fuel we had the Sunday as a day of rest in Bilbao. We celebrated the good news from the South Atlantic that we had put the Argentinian submarine Sante Fe out of action and recaptured South Georgia.

Leaving early on the Monday morning we pressed on as far as we could until near nightfall and, as we were entering San Estaban de Pravia, Charlie asked me the time of high tide. I told him it was three hours ago. He replied that it said in the Pilot Book that it is dodgy to enter three hours after high water because of the tide rips and the narrow channel. I had, in fact, read the book beforehand while choosing a place for the night. According to Charlie, two people clapped on the shore, as we successfully beat the rapids! There was nothing good about this former coaling port, which looked like Transylvania with its dimmed street lights. There were no attractions ashore, so Peter produced a super meal, and we all had a very good night's sleep moored alongside a dredger – built by that well known Scottish builder of dredgers, hopper barges, and tugs, Simons and Lobnitz. As we left, at the same time as the dredger in the morning, we noticed at the top of the harbour a rusty old British Sealink ferry. Apart from being a dirty former coaling port, it was apparently a breakers yard. Not a place recommended for posh yachties!

Next stop La Coruna which is a most attractive place, with a very welcoming Club Nautico and restaurant close by in the marina. As we approach Cabo Finisterre the weather roughens up. Helping me with the decision to take refuge is the Turkish crewman, Musty, who has been continually complaining about the roughness of the sea and predicting that it is going to get much worse. So we took refuge in a lovely little fishing village called Camarinas. There was no room for a large 61 foot gin palace, so we moored up on the inside of the outer breakwater where there was a concrete jetty. By the next morning Musty had found out how he could get a bus to the airport and a flight back to Turkey. Poor guy, he was certainly a fair weather sailor and he was neither enjoying the cruise, nor of any use to me. So I decided the only sensible thing to do was give him the necessary money from the owner's fund and let him go.

We were weather-bound in Camerinas for three nights. The place was so small and there were no freshwater taps at our jetty. Charlie and Ivor persuaded two Spanish kids, who should have been at school, to fill up two dustbins with drinking water and pull them on a cart along a rickety old path to our boat. Half the water was spilt on the way, but those kids, apparently happy with their financial reward, did many return trips.

On the second day a local official told us we would have to go, as a large fishing boat was having to take refuge from the weather and would be coming in where we were lying, in about half an hour's time. We had no intention of leaving the safety of the harbour, but went alongside the Spanish trawler on its arrival from Cadiz. None of us could speak the others' language, but we got on extremely well as fellow sons of the sea. Bottles of whisky went one way, bottles of red wine the other and when they were cooking their fabulous fresh fish, they always cooked enough for us as well. Pete told the trawler's skipper that when we left the jetty to allow them in, a couple of our brand new ropes had been stolen. By our last day there, he had recovered them for us – from underneath the tarpaulin on a local boat.

One of the several memories of the quiet life ashore in Camerinas was the sight of oldish ladies sitting by their front windows making lace. Having sheltered there from the storm, the rest of the journey to the Mediterranean was fine. Every day we kept up to date with the news of our Task Force going south towards Ascension and beyond to the occupied Falklands. Ivor was our master tactician and forecaster as to, if, when and how, we would successfully re-take the Islands. The Argentinian Air Force was being very brave and competent and even their Navy was beginning to leave harbour.

At the time I was saying that we had the best three admirals of the day running the show. They were all seafarers and leaders of men, and not your stereotypical Whitehall warriors. Henry Leach had already proved himself to be Margaret Thatcher's knight in shining gold braid by despatching the Task Force so quickly and efficiently. He had John Fieldhouse as Commander-in-Chief of the whole Fleet and he had been out to Ascension to organise things when he wasn't doing it at Northwood. The man in charge of all three services our Chief of Defence Staff was none other than Admiral of the Fleet Terry Lewin. He had been in New Zealand when the Argentinians invaded, but within 28 hours he was with the War Cabinet. He had direct access to Margaret Thatcher and quickly won her confidence. Small wonder I frequently took pride in repeating they were all ex-shipmates of mine.

We were at Vilamoura in the Algarve when we heard that Terry Lewin had persuaded the Prime Minister to change the

Rules of Engagement and had given Conqueror the order to sink the Belgrano. The warship was, in fact, 44 years old and was the ex-USS Phoenix which had survived Pearl Harbour. It had a crew of at least 1100 and more than 350 were killed. Very sad, but after that the Argentinian Navy was not seen again.

On our way through the Gibraltar Straits it was getting a bit choppy. We had the flood tide with us heading into a Laventar wind. We had to slow down and as we were going to be a bit late in Gibraltar, we decided to have supper on board. I switched on the generator and some time later Pete the chef asked if I had, in fact, switched on because his cooker wasn't getting hot. Net result, the Onan generator wouldn't start and so all the luxuries of cooking, washing, machines, fabulous hot water showers, etc, were denied us until we could get the problem repaired, hopefully in Gibraltar tomorrow.

The mechanic who came on board in the morning found the problem but could not solve it. The generator had been flooded with salt water, presumably because the clapper valve on the exhaust system had failed to stop sea water entering as our bows dipped into the head sea. Cannes was the nearest place with Onan Generator distributors so it was decided we should go there instead of Piraeus. I might have been seen walking back from the shops carrying a £40 camping gaz cooker so that we could boil a kettle, or cook some bacon and eggs, on board this luxurious near-million pound pleasure yacht.

Gibraltar was a beehive of activity, especially at night time, with arms, ammunition and stores being transferred from Great Britain to Gibraltar and onward to Ascension for our Task Force. One good thing: it was May, it was warm in the Mediterranean and we were able to cope without the luxuries normally provided by the generator. As we rounded Europa Point, on our way east from Gibraltar, poor Peter had to feed the sharks with most of the contents of our deep freeze.

Puerto Banus was no way the same as ever and had changed significantly. It was six years since I had last been there and the Costa del Concrete had well and truly expanded in all directions, especially inland. You could no longer see the Andalucia Plaza

Hotel or the bullring from the marina. We stayed close to the boat and had a fantastic meal at, of all places, the Argentinian Steak House before moving on to Almeria where we were weather-bound again for three days. Our jetty was close to where builders' aggregate was stored for the ever advancing urbanisation. Banus, being a luxurious area, was very international but Almeria was truly Spanish and perhaps naturally there was a pro-Argentine feeling amongst some of the locals. They appeared to take a certain amount of delight in telling us that the Sheffield had been sunk in the South Atlantic. One afternoon we were sitting in a café and asked the waiter if anyone worked in Spain in the afternoons. The reply we got was that it was in the mornings that no-one worked. In the afternoons they had siesta!

As soon as we arrived in Cannes, an Onan mechanic came on board to look at the generator. He then took me into the board-room to meet Monsieur le Directeur who told me straight away that Onan accepted full responsibility for the failure of their equipment. The next morning the head Hatteras man in Europe, Mr Antonio from Rome, came on board. He was already in Cannes for the film festival. He reiterated what the Onan man had said in accepting full responsibility and that they would make good the problem there in Cannes. All the way from Hamble, everywhere we went, our Hatteras 61 was the posh boat. Now we were moored up in Port Pierre Canto and appeared like a dinghy amongst all the mega-yachts there. We had a few days' holiday awaiting the arrival of the owner so that we could give him his boat.

I was soon down to the Mediterranean yet again. A Yorkshire couple owned a very nice two-bedroomed apartment built into the hillside in a small quiet bay called Binibeca in Minorca. They had a fast 26 foot Sea Ray which they used for water-skiing; they also wanted to go day cruising. We had a fabulous five days' training around the island as far as Ciudadela and anchoring off the beautiful beaches. They had a couple of friends staying with them for the week: as the apartment was a bit small, I spent all day and meals with them before disappearing after dinner. I would row the short distance and spend the night alone in their boat secured to a mooring buoy in the small bay.

Back in the UK, needless to say the talk and our thoughts were very much about the Falklands. As the build-up for the recapture of the islands was taking place, my previously stated confidence in the three Admirals achieving final victory was still there. This was supplemented by my admiration for many of the officers and men with whom I had joined the Navy, or helped train at a later date, in the Dartmouth Training Squadron or at HMS Ganges. There was Rear Admiral Sandy Woodward. We were not great friends as I think we only had three things in common. We joined the Navy on the same day, we were in the same submarine training class and neither of us were volunteers for submarines. He was a fine officer, possibly just the man for that kind of conflict, and deserved all the accolades that came his way.,

Having got the Task Force to the Falklands, Sandy, in his flagship Hermes, remained out at sea and out of Argentinian Air Force range. On Friday 21st May the Amphibious Task Force, under the command of Commodore Mike Clapp, started landing at various beaches around San Carlos. First to go was 3 Commando Brigade of Royal Marines and Paratroopers, with Brigadier Julian Thompson RM in charge. I had met up with Mike and Julian during various stages of our training and I knew everything would be okay with their leadership and planning.

On the same day HMS Ardent was sunk, followed three days later by the sinking of HMS Antelope. But the next day, the 25th, was probably the worst day of the lot, when HMS Coventry was sunk and the SS Atlantic Conveyor was hit. The latter had been able to transfer eight Sea Harriers and 6 Harrier Jump Jets to the carriers Hermes and Invincible, when out of range of the Argentinian Air Force; all but one of the Chinooks were lost when Atlantic Conveyor was hit by Exocet missiles in Carlos Water.

Atlantic Conveyor was a container ship requisitioned under the system known as STUFT – Ships Taken Up From Trade – and was a great loss. Twelve men died, including Captain Ian North, who was a real old seadog, a tower of strength, and much loved captain. He went down with his ship, which eventually sank while under tow three days later and he was posthumously awarded the Distinguished Service Cross in recognition of gallant and distinguished service during operations in the South Atlantic.

I agree it is easy enough to be a simple sailor at sea in the Solent when such situations occur, but one of the main lessons we were taught, when appreciating the situation at the Junior Officers' War Course at Greenwich, was not to put all your eggs in one basket. Our tutors quoted the example of, during the Crimean War in 1854, all the Army boots being sent to Balaclava in one ship, which was sunk. So the poor soldiery had to fight in their socks! Some 128 years later, all the Chinooks were in one basket called Atlantic Conveyor, so the Royal Marines and other PBI - Poor Bloody Infantry – had to yomp. Surely there was another merchant ship, the Conveyor's sister ship, Atlantic Causeway, for example, that could have transported half the number of Chinooks or even more.

At long last the breakthrough I had been seeking for a long time came in the form of some of the more experienced mega-yacht captains. Firstly, there was Jim Billingham whom I had met several times, both in the Solent and the Mediterranean, and Jeff Marsh, who was David Bowie's captain. Then Graham St George came with Mike Insull, who was captain of the well-known "New Horizon L" owned by a Dutch publisher with the marvellous name Prince Leon van Leeuwen of Lignac.

It was during the week that Graham and Mike were passing their Y/M that the QE2 returned from the Falklands and it was marvellous to escort her up Southampton Water and join in the patriotic emotion. The next day HMS Glamorgan was hit by an Exocet missile killing 13 and wounding 14 of her ship's company. We had been hearing a lot about Glamorgan and her brave activities in the South Atlantic. I was particularly interested because she was commanded by a great guy who had joined the Navy with me, Captain Mike Barrow. I knew how much he must have felt about this tragic event. Those 13 dead shipmates were buried at sea and it had all happened two days before the Argentinian surrender. The ship itself was quickly repaired and returned to the UK. Everyone was delighted to hear Mike had been award the Distinguished Service Order. Exactly a month later, the "Great White Whale", as the SS Canberra was affectionately nicknamed, sailed into Southampton to an even greater welcome in which we were able to partake from on board Dawn Seeker.

Our next trainee was a fascinating character who lived in Glasgow and owned a chain of garages. He wanted instruction in his 32 foot Princess at Troon Marina and when I telephoned to say my friend Charlie Lyle would be meeting me at Glasgow airport, he said he needn't have bothered as he also owned a fleet of taxis. I went up a second time, as shortly after my first visit he exchanged his Princess, plus £25,000 for a 41 foot Puget Sound trawler yacht "Feeoleen the Third".

Every night he went home to Eaglesham. In the mornings we would meet for breakfast at the marina restaurant. On most occasions he had some gruesome story to tell. In his garages he ran a breakdown service with recovery trucks and he was frequently called out to help at some nasty road accident. He seemed so traumatised at some of the overnight scenes he had witnessed that it took him a good couple of hours, with many cups of tea and cigarettes, to finish breakfast, and get down to the business of learning about seamanship.

1982, which I am sure will always be remembered as the year Argentina invaded the Falklands, came to a close and memories began to recede into the distance. I realised that just as a happy and efficient warship's crew must change, so had our team and its area of responsibility. I felt sure one thing was not going to change and that was the continual flow of HIPs (Highly Interesting People) whom we hoped would continue to seek our tuition.

The Yachtmaster candidates were coming through quite quickly: most of them in small groups of two or three because they wanted personal tuition and they or their owners were willing to pay for it. The training for most took a fortnight, that is a week's theory and a week's practical. When it was getting a bit too much I asked David Strang to join the team and do the classroom work for me. David was ex-Navy, had been a few years ahead and, although a large man, a midget submariner who specialised in X-Craft in the mid fifties. He ran the Lymington Seamanship and

Navigation Centre for a few years before closing it down and retiring to the Isle of Wight. He was an excellent seaman and had just the right personality for training these young professionals their theoretical syllabus. Meanwhile, I would be taking others for the practical in Dawn Seeker and by the end of 1982, we had successfully trained 27, including Mark Souter, our first Australian.

For the 1983 Boat Show the magazine Motor Cruiser in an article on "Buying a Motor Cruiser", Iain Allen suggests that you must ensure, after you have purchased your boat, sufficient money is left for a course on seamanship and navigation. He goes on to show two photographs of a mixed group studying coastal navigation and carrying out boat handling aboard Mike Reeder's School on the Clyde. Three boat shows later the same magazine in its article "Learning the Fundamentals" gave pictures of our school instructing yet again in the Clyde.

During the third week in January I was in fact back up in the Clyde, not in Charlie's boat this time, but Ivor Tiefenbrun's marvellous Southern Flight which he had bought from Neville Duke, the WW2 RAF fighter ace and famous Test Pilot. The last time I had seen Ivor he was stark naked flat out on the flying bridge of "UMB". Not a very pretty sight, especially as one of his heels was very close to the port engine stop button, which he had succeeded in pressing when we were crossing the Bay of Biscay. I thought the engine had stopped because we were getting short of fuel, my main worry while crossing the Bay. Evidently Charlie had to stop me jumping up the ladder from the wheelhouse and throttling him – when I had been told the real reason why the engine stopped!

It was much colder weather when I joined him and his brother Marcus, in a Scottish January at Kip Marina for what proved to be a most enjoyable week. Having been rather upset with Ivor six months earlier, I was able to find out this week what an interesting and wonderful guy he really was. He was the elder of two sons born in Glasgow seven years after his father had arrived there as a refugee from Austria. He developed his engineering and business skills in his late father's company, Castle Precision Engineering and then in 1972 founded Linn Products, manufacturers of hi-fi, audio and home theatre equipment. His product Linn Sondek LP12 remained an industry benchmark for at least two decades and in 1992 he was appointed MBE.

Later in the year, amongst the Yachtmaster candidates were an Italian, Daniello Cruciani, and Graham Hooper, the captain of Heinekens yacht. Graham had owned a photographic business in Devon and when someone absconded owing him a few thousand pounds, he was so disillusioned he sold up and took to his small boat "Killestre" with his wife and two young daughters and sailed down to Antibes. His family all learnt French and his daughters grew up bi-lingual and running successful businesses, one of them a hairdressing salon. It was during this year that Freddy Heineken was kidnapped and released, three weeks later, for a ransom of 35 million guilders. Graham was an extremely hardworking captain who used to do a lot of the deckwork and maintenance himself. Every time I went down to Antibes I made a point of meeting up with him. He very kindly recommended a lot of the crews, including his own, to be trained by our school.

Spoke to one of the country's eccentrics when we did a course for a Mr Jones, his wife, and her father in their 43 foot Horizon from Brundel in the Norfolk Broads. They owned three retail

Southern Flight

shops in the area, and had this very nice boat, "Miss Melony", in which they liked to do short trips on the Broads. If the weather was suitable, and with longer periods away from work, they wanted to go further afield in the North Sea. During the few days on board, we went from Great Yarmouth down to Wolverstone near Ipswich on the River Orwell. On the outward and return journeys we passed an old wartime artillery Fort Roughs consisting of two steel-reinforced concrete towers spanned by a 6,000 sq ft iron platform, which Roy Bates in 1967 had declared as the Independent Principality of Sealand.

On leaving school, Roy had gone to Spain to fight in the Spanish Civil War. In WW2 he was an Infantry Major and saw action in Africa, Italy and elsewhere. Wounded several times, he survived malaria, sandfly fever, frostbite and snakebites and a stick grenade smashed his jaw and showered his face with shrapnel. After the war he imported meat from Eire to Ulster, rubber from Malaya and then built up an inshore fishing fleet, and a chain of butchers shops in Essex. And as the stories go on, so you believe what you like. He called down to us from his independent state, situated a mile or so outside UK territorial waters, while we hovered 100 feet below in the calm North Sea.

He gave himself the title of Prince Roy of Sealand which he claimed as the world's smallest sovereign state and had created its own constituency, flag, passports, stamps, currency and national anthem. When accused of being a bit extraordinary, he evidently replied that he liked a bit of adventure, that it was an old British tradition, and there's still a lot of us about. I hope he was right. There were certainly plenty around when I first joined the Navy, but I think the world, not only Great Britain, has changed and that there aren't too many Roys about these days.

I felt very embarrassed that I hadn't even heard of our next three customers. The first, Trevor Horn, had a small Sunseeker which he had recently purchased and kept in the boatyard at Poole. The course was mainly for boat-handling and sufficient navigation to be able to take his wife and two young kids boating locally in the bay. At our first lunch he drank a Coke while I had a beer. He wasn't at all surprised that I hadn't heard of him, or his business. I was far too old! In a nutshell he was a musician and a record producer. He married his business partner, Jill Sinclair, in 1980 and he said that he had formed the Buggles Group two years beforehand and, at that time, smoked and drank anything that was on offer. If it hadn't been for Jill, who took charge of him and made sure he behaved, he wouldn't be where he was now. And where was he? He had achieved probably his greatest commercial success with the Liverpudlian band Frankie Goes to Hollywood, and he went on to receive literally hundreds of awards and was appointed CBE in the 2011 New Year's Honours for services to the music industry.

Next we received a letter from an address in Harrow and signed Frederick Forsyth. I wondered who he was and was told probably the well-known best-selling author. Freddie turned out to be one of the most interesting and well-travelled people I have met and told us, without boasting in any way, his early life story. He had had a good education at Tonbridge School, had become fed up, left early and went to Tangier for a prolonged holiday. He was in the RAF, became a jet fighter pilot, and then decided to become a journalist. He joined Reuters in 1961 and then the BBC for whom he reported the Nigerian Civil War. After six months the BBC were no longer interested in Biafra and wanted him home.

Freddie stayed on in Biafra, as a freelance journalist and wrote his first book "The Biafra Story" in 1967. Two years later, at the age of 33, he wrote the international best seller "The Day of the Jackal". He told me he spent much time in the country about which he was researching his next novel, and used the same techniques as in journalism to produce a successful book nearly every year. I enjoyed listening to his political views, and particularly admired his patronship of Better off Out, an organisation calling for our withdrawal from the European Union.

Bernard McNicholas was a marvellous Irishman, the son of Michael and nephew of Patrick, two brothers who left County Mayo to start contracting businesses in the post war London area. In 1949 they worked almost exclusively for British Telecom. Bernard came to me for training because he owned a 56 foot

Baglietti moored in the marina Baie des Anges, near Nice and wanted to be able to control the boat without having to rely on a professional crew.

In 1957 Michael and Patrick had split up but they, and various cousins, although strong competitors in the contracting business, were still good friends out of the office. Bernard was Chairman of McNicholas plc, with a multi-million pound turnover and one half of a contractors dynasty. He hoped that one day they would all trade under one roof, but in the meantime they were to get contracts for cable TV and much overseas work including emergency power lines in the Falklands, the concrete concourse and pavement at Disneyland, and the ring main round Baghdad.

The mid-eighties brought about quite a change in our fleet. The owner of a 31 foot Birchwood called "Sucram 2" said he would like us to charter his boat. And over the horizon came a Fairline 36 Turbo owned by an American couple who worked for the Printronic Corporation. We had trained them a couple of times and on a third occasion we helped out with the charity "Ending World Hunger". Batons were being relayed from Geneva to Santa Monica in California and we were asked to transport the seven batons plus seven runners by sea from Calais to Brighton. The rest of the relaying would be by land, except of course across the pond from Heathrow to New York by air. They very kindly said we could use their boat, "Artisan 3", at any time except of course when they were using it.

Then Meriel telephoned to say that they weren't getting much use out of Dawn Seeker in the Solent and asked me to help Patrick take her back up to Port Dinorvic. It was the end of a very happy era – I fully realised that, when I stepped ashore from Dawn Seeker for the last time.

I had another communication from Alex McMullen, the editor of Motor Boat and Yachting, to ask if his new Features Editor, Alan Harper, could do a course in November. They wanted to do an article about learning afloat, and I just couldn't believe how kind and attentive Alex and his staff were being. The third time in ten years was indeed a piece of good fortune for the business. I used "Artisan 3" for the course and the crew consisted of Alan and two Johns, Towle and Dennis from Yorkshire and Humberside. Alan gave a blow by blow account of the daily syllabus and also wrote:-

> *"Mike has the air of an ex-rugby playing naval officer and that is exactly what he is. His approach seems relaxed and easy going until you realise that most of what he says ought to be written down because, come Friday afternoon, he's going to expect you to know it."*

That week was the first time I met Lester McCarthy the superb photographer who worked solely for Motor Boat and Yachting or IPC Media. He arrived on the Wednesday morning just to take a few shots, and then disappeared. I got to know him and learn more of his skills at later dates. I have seen him up very high masts, and being rolled over in dinghies as he was passed intentionally by fast speed boats whilst he took his superb photographs. Alan went on to be editor of MB&Y and after that to write more articles for the boating press.

That edition of MB&Y was the first published after the 1985 Boat Show and by coincidence heralded the beginning of the

Alan Harper being instructed at boathandling

Alan Harper between John Dennis and John Towle,
very attentive at instruction

Yachtmaster rush which was to go on for at least another ten years. Every training session or course was different and every person had an interesting story to tell about his or her experiences at sea. The Yachtmaster candidates were getting younger and less knowledgeable. That did not matter in the slightest as it was merely a greater challenge for us all. I think we all had at least three things in common, enthusiasm, a love of life especially at sea, and a sense of humour.

Some of the more experienced ones helped to produce one of the happiest and amusing weeks. They were Felix Robinson, Steve Morrison, Paul Bechman, and David Ryder. It was a laugh a minute with everyone, including the examiner, helping things along to a successful conclusion. Felix was undoubtedly the star turn and being a keen golfer told the story of the visitor who dashed with only a towel into the empty ladies' showers. The men's was full up and he was in a hurry to get to his next appointment. When he came out of the shower there were three women sitting at a table between him and the entrance. So that he wouldn't be recognised, he decided to put the towel round his head rather than his middle and in answer to their similar query as to who it was, the three females replied thus:-

> "I have no idea", then
> "It certainly wasn't my husband", and the third said
> "I can assure you he isn't a member of this club."

Apart from the essential theoretical and practical subjects which had to be taught, our main emphasis was on the development of the seaman's eye, to be observant as to what's going on and pick out the most important things first. Each of these electronic gadgets is an aid to navigation and could well give the wrong assistance if it is not tuned correctly, set up correctly, the wrong information is fed into it or the person operating it is a tosser. One of our first problems was the RYA Examiners. They were all competent at sailing but I had to teach most of them how to handle motor cruisers.

An American called Max telephoned from London to ask if we could give him a navigation course as soon as possible. He and his wife were on board within four days and this was possibly both the most intriguing and extraordinary course I did. Max and Dorcas were abattoir owners from Yuma, Arizona and this was the first time they had been out of the United States. They had landed at Heathrow the day before they telephoned me and to this day I do not know why me, and why they wanted to do a navigation course. They were fascinated by London, its buildings and the fact that very few of its avenues or streets were straight – they all seemed to be curved.

They had come to Europe for a year's vacation and they had no plans. Very little navigation was done and the whole week seemed to be taken up with suggestions and proposals, as to what they would do for the rest of the year, and whether today was a good day to change dollars into sterling. I was not only a simple sailor but a financial wizard as well! Of German descent, they couldn't speak a word of German and they had no desire to visit Germany.

Long story cut short, I arranged for them to buy a second hand Profile 33, a slow displacement boat and cruise in it down the French canals and back. They could then sell it for virtually the same price they had paid, before returning to the USA. I was able to give them boat-handling and rope work instruction before they went on their way rejoicing. They were a good couple and it was very interesting to hear about their life on the farm, which they had bought after inheriting the slaughter house from Max's father. Dorcas was a big woman with strong biceps caused by humping carcasses around the place. I didn't see them again, but I heard that they had reached the Mediterranean and had had a successful holiday. They asked the broker from whom they had bought the boat, which was now at the southern end of the canal system, to sell it and remit the money to them at their home in the United States.

The opportunity to demonstrate the worries, concerns and terrible responsibilities a trainer can have, especially in a customer's own boat, occurred in May when Robin asked me to take him and a chum Colin in his Solent 35 on a cruise to the Channel Islands. The first evening was spent in St Peter Port where both were keen on seeking female company for the evening. I told them that Guernsey was not likely to be a successful hunting ground. The next day Robin invited his girlfriend to fly out from the mainland and she arrived that evening with her daughter aged about six.

The week's tuition and cruise progressed very successfully until Thursday at midday when the weather forecast for the morrow was northerly force 6. I advised that, while the weather was still good, we returned straight away to the safety of the Solent where their tuition and cruise could be finished off. He said he would like to stay another night and sail in the morning. I grudgingly agreed provided we left at first light. I was up at 0530 to hear the latest forecast which was Gale Force 8 later, which meant probably in 12 hours' time.

He and girlfriend eventually got up at 0800, we went ashore for a full monty breakfast and they stayed until well after nine o'clock so that he could buy her a tax free gift. On their return he decided we had run out of beer, so off ashore again to replenish stocks and we eventually left at 1100. Now the problems began. As we proceeded further north towards the Alderney Race the sea state got rougher and rougher. Robin and girlfriend were on the flying bridge while the young girl and Colin were below with me in the lounge. There I could keep an eye on the chart and radar and the general safety of the boat and the crew of five, all wearing lifejackets since before we left Guernsey.

Every time the boat bashed into the waves I told Robin to slow down, and the little girl became more and more frightened. Eventually, I told the mother that as I was a seamanship instructor and not a babysitter she must come down below and look after her daughter. Within a short space of time both the mother and daughter were huddled together on the lounge floor frightened out of their tiny minds. There was only one thing to do and that was order Robin, who appeared in his macho sort of way to be enjoying driving his boat, to turn round and go to the nearest place of refuge, namely Cherbourg. With the wind and sea behind us it was no problem covering the short distance to the marina. Because he did not heed my professional advice, Robin had to pay for accommodation in the night ferry to Portsmouth for all five of us, his mooring fees at Cherbourg marina, and the return trip for his crew to pick up his boat at a later date. I am sure his girlfriend would never go boating with him again.

Bernard Matthews was my next customer. He started his business in 1950 by buying the dilapidated Witchingham Hall in Norfolk and filling its rooms with turkeys. Thirty years later he started advertising on commercial TV his own turkey breast roast as being "bootifull". I almost recognised his strong Norfolk accent when he telephoned to book his skipper on a Yachtmaster's course. He told me about his mega yacht which he called Bellissima – Italian for Bootifull – and that it was moored in an Italian marina near Genoa. He also told me that although his skipper was Lebanese he had in fact arranged for him to become an Italian citizen with an Italian passport.

I joined a Hatteras 58 in the Mediterranean called "Lucayan Chief", and was welcomed aboard by an Israeli family Ben, Moshi and Carolina Shemesh, and their friend Avinoam Heller. They lived and worked at Swiss Cottage in London. Ben had his pilot's licence and had interesting tales to tell about his conscription time in the Israeli Air Force. He wanted to run this quite large boat without professional crew and he and his young, fit family seemed well capable of doing so. We spent most of the time in and out of Antibes where his boat was due to be permanently moored but did have one run ashore in Monaco.

Changes of scenery cropped up quite often and we continued to get what we advertised as delivery with instruction, that is training the owner to deliver his boat himself with some supervision. On one such occasion my friend David Cook told me he had sold a Grand Banks 42 called "Jay 4" to Brian Bateman who wanted help in getting it from Hull to Kip. He told me to telephone Brian at his home in East Kilbride and make the necessary arrangements direct with him. I joined him and his two crew, George and Mark, a week later in Hull. Firstly, I made sure we had all the necessary navigational and safety equipment on board and that Brian knew how to handle his boat. Then, having done sufficient tuition for the crew to navigate the vessel as far as Inverness, off we went on what proved to be a good and worthwhile seven days.

The first two nights were at sea and on the third morning we entered the Caledonian Canal and spent the next night in harbour enjoying a few bevvies at Muirton, where David Cook joined us for the rest of the voyage back to Kip. It was one of those typical rainy days in Loch Ness and we couldn't see either side as we steered down the middle for a very welcome lunch at Fort Augustus. Overnight we moored up at a pleasant little spot with its own wooden jetty at Loch Lochy. Next day we descended the well-known Neptune's Staircase. The eight locks enabled vessels to "drop down the 64 feet" to Corpach, where we left the canal and progressed southward to round the Mull of Kintyre to Kip Marina. It was great to meet David again. A very experienced full

*Brian Bateman keeping a watch in the gloom
(note the model of Nessie on the windscreen)*

Neptune's Staircase

member of the Association of Brokers and Yacht Agents, he had worked with many well-known marques in the yachting world, including four years in America. I was pleased to hear in 2009 that he had set up his own business, David Cook Yachts, at Fairlie Quay, a mile south of Largs Marina.

On return from Scotland I bought a motor cruiser. It wasn't quite like that as we had been looking for some time and of course money was not no object. We took a fancy to a 36 foot Swedish motor cruiser with an after cabin. It was not the most comfortable boat in the world but it was well constructed and most importantly of all, a very good sea boat. It had a GRP hull but a lot of the teak and mahogany woodwork around the windows was rotten. Every time I went on board I found more rot, so the potential cost of repair went up and my offer to purchase went down. I almost felt sorry for the vendor, as he would have to pay to get the work done, but on 12th November he preferred to accept my lowest offer and I became the owner of Royal Dram.

It was shortly after purchasing "Royal Dram" that I first met James Powell at Yachtmail, his chandlery at the town quay in Lymington. Obviously a lot of my safety equipment, etc, needed replacing and/or updating. He was always friendly and when

Royal Dram

I took my customers into his shop he was always willing to give them a fair deal.

In early 1988 he had suffered the loss of his brother, who with two other crew members had foundered in the fishing vessel Southern Enterprise" off Littlehampton. No trace of the terrible accident ever came to light. James has been very successful in buying and selling other chandleries as well as a clothes shop and a bar/restaurant but most of his working life has been in Yachtmail. My only complaint was that he was always too busy – impossible really to get to know him. In 2012 he won the Boating Business Website award. Having learnt to sail at the age of four, he has always had a love of the sea and now enjoys sailing his Jeanneau 42 around Greece.

Later on I had the most unexpected, but interesting, request for training and it was from a young, newly promoted Lieutenant Commander in the Royal Navy, who wanted boat-handling instruction in a twin-screw motor cruiser. He explained that he had been appointed commanding officer of one of the patrol boats in the Hong Kong Flotilla and that the only training the Navy would give was one day in a civilian manned MFV in Portsmouth Harbour, and that had been cancelled. He said he was only too willing to pay out of his own pocket, whilst he was on weekend leave, to get good training!

One of the more magnificent boats I have been in is the 52 foot Silver, called Sea Lass, owned by the well-known architect Roger Zogolovitch. It had been built in 1932 by the Silvers Boat Yard at Roseneath, and Roger had bought it in rather a run-down condition. He spent a lot of money having it restored by Classic Boats and when I first went aboard in the River Beaulieu to give Roger and his wife five days' seamanship training, I almost felt I was stepping back in boating history. Sea Lass was a classic and you could tell the way Roger had had it lovingly restored that it was the architect in him. He was Chairman of Lake Estates and Solidspace and went on to be a board director of the Royal Institute of British Architects. Perhaps of more interest to us seafarers, who very occasionally visit London, he helped design the Riverside Restaurant.

Roger helming his 'Sea Lass' in the Solent

Malory Maltby, the well-known television broadcaster, director and cameraman, told me he was producing two videos for Freetime Television Ltd on a Yachtmaster series for Motor Cruiser Owners. Alex McMullen, the editor of MB&Y had recommended that I should be the instructor. Richard Yonwin would provide the boat, a Princess, plus the crew consisting of Russell, his sales manager and Dawn, his secretary. It was a most enjoyable three days and intriguing to watch Malory, always acting as a one-man band, doing several jobs, including filming, recording and announcing, at the same time. He said he would make a film star out of me and that our school would flourish as a result of his work. I know he was correct by the number of potential customers saying they had seen the videos. I think he also flourished judging by the number of shops one saw selling them!

Very soon afterwards, I was confronted by film cameramen again, this time for the BBC who wanted to use one of our boats to film rough weather for their Armada film. Sod's law, but for the two days they chose to do the filming there was only a slight breeze and the sea was flat calm. We did manage to film a bit of rough sea by dangling the cameraman upside down on the bathing platform and highly magnifying some minor overfalls near St Catherine's Point at the south of the Isle of Wight. Having the director and producer Alan Ereira on board was very stimulating, especially when we were told the reason why we had to do some filming of Hengistbury Head at sunrise. It was there and then that they could film some shots that resembled the part of Spain that he wished to insert into his film. We were very pleased to hear he won the 1988 Royal Television Society Best Documentary Series Award for his Armada. We had perhaps helped a tiny bit.

A bit of light relief occurred when I joined a couple of reasonably competent and cheerful guys in their 40 foot C-Kip trawler yacht for five days preparation prior to taking their Coastal Skipper exam. We returned to Lymington the first two nights. The next night was at Shamrock Quay and on the Thursday we called in at the Camber in Old Portsmouth for a pub lunch. Afterwards they arrived on board a little after me in the company of two girls they had been eyeing up in the pub.

As it was a beautifully warm summer's day, they said they would navigate the boat back to Lymington from the flying bridge. I stayed down below as I watched them manoeuvre the boat out of the harbour and it wasn't until we were off Cowes that I went up top to enjoy the sun. The two girls were lying flat on their backs completely naked – a most pleasing sight for a Thursday afternoon. I left the boat as soon as we arrived alongside, and when I came down on board in the morning there was a note to say they were driving the girls to Portsmouth and wouldn't be back till about 1000. I have heard some people say a bit of nooky is good before an important fixture, whether it be sport or a Coastal Skipper exam. Anyway, in this instance, the saying proved correct and they passed their exams later that day.

Salim Hassan Macki held a master's degree in petro-chemical engineering and owned a Grand Banks 42 in Muscat. He held numerous executive positions and was also Ambassador for the Government of the Sultanate of Oman whom he represented at

Omanis Salim and his son Basil on course in the Solent

the United Nations. It was fun to be training such a well-travelled and interesting person. I gleaned he didn't enjoy the political side of things and later noted he had managed to slip out of that responsibility. He was able to focus on his very strong and talented oil interests and was later appointed as non-executive director of Heritage Oil in America. Basil, his son, also on course, became a director of Gulf Hotels (Oman).

My first visit to Ireland since I left the Navy came as the result of an unexpected telephone call from Phil Myett. He asked how he should get his Princess 35 from the Lake District to Cork. You would have to put it on a lorry was my cheeky reply! He laughingly said that he knew that would be the initial requirement but he proposed the lorry should get it to, say, Liverpool Marina, and that he would like me to help him the rest of the way by sea to Crosshaven Marina in County Cork. He would then like to have a couple of days' further training on arrival.

A superb week followed starting with the passage in glorious weather from Liverpool through the Menai Straits, across the Irish Sea to Arklow. Once in Ireland things became even more amusing, friendly and thoroughly entertaining. At our evening meal in the local hotel I heard an American visitor ask the waitress where the nearest pharmacy was, and her reply was to go down the main street and when you get to the bottom you'll find it there on your left or right! The next day, another calm trip to book in at his new permanent berth at Crosshaven Marina. Nearby is the oldest yacht club in the world, the Royal Cork Yacht Club, where we spent a couple of evenings with the extremely friendly locals. We were told the story about the man from Dublin who telephoned someone in Cork:

"Hello, is that Cork double two double two?"
"No, it's Cork two two two two," was the reply.
"Oh, sorry to have troubled you," said the Dubliner.
"It's quite alright, the telephone was ringing anyway."

A big event which heralded the end of the eighties involved professional Yachtmasters. There were so many in the south of France wanting to do their training with us. We decided to charter a trawler yacht in Antibes in November and it proved to be an excellent floating academy for the theory instruction. We had four five-day sessions each with four guys – a total of sixteen. These sixteen, including a Canadian, an American and a Turk, came to the Solent before Christmas to successfully gain their Yachtmaster Certificates and so end a very happy year for us.

It was also the end of a happy decade for us, as over 200 candidates had received their Yachtmaster certificates and we had been booked for plenty of different types of tuition in a variety of different places. We were hopeful this success would continue for at least another decade. Our fleet, some of which we hadn't yet used, but was nevertheless still available to us, consisted of Royal Dram, Artisan 3, Sucram 2, in the Solent, Jan Pan in the Mediterranean and Charlie's latest boat in the Clyde.

The nineties were going to be heralded in with three recent maritime tragedies very much in mind. On 6th March 1987 the modern RoRo ferry, Herald of Free Enterprise, capsized moments after leaving Zeebrugge for Dover, killing 193 passengers and crew. She had left harbour with her bow doors open and within minutes was lying on her side in shallow water. The incident caused the highest death rate of any post war disaster involving a British ship.

The following year HMS Southampton was in collision with the container ship Tor Bay whilst on Armilla Patrol near the entrance to the Persian Gulf at the Straits of Hormoze. Whatever the circumstances Southampton was crossing the bows of Tor Bay, was badly damaged and was towed back on a barge to the UK.

In August a year later, the pleasure boat Marchioness, built in 1923, and a Dunkirk Little Ship, was run down by the gravel dredger Bowbelle upstream of Canon Street railway bridge. Both vessels were proceeding down river and what proved to be one of the River Thames' worst tragedies resulted in the loss of 51 people being drowned. Luckily there were 80 survivors from a ship which sank within a few seconds after being hit by an overtaking vessel. In the Marchioness incident lookouts were blamed for not keeping a proper lookout but I know there were several other instances of the International Regulations for Preventing Collisions at Sea being broken. The Marine Accident Investigation Branch of the Department for Transport was carrying out one of many enquiries, most of which would probably go on well into the turn of the century.

NAUTICAL NINETIES AND
MARINERS' MISHAPS

In the English Channel the nineteen nineties started off with a storm. In Lymington there had already been the worst floods in seventy three years and it was impossible to take the car down to your boat as the nearby road and car parks were several inches under water. Royal Dram was in no trouble as she was well secured alongside a pontoon and once the flooded car park had been negotiated, was easily accessible. However, one of two marinas on both sides of the Channel did suffer, notably Cherbourg, where the pontoons and boats were literally blown up into the far north east corner. In one Plymouth marina the pontoons were lifted by the rising sea level above the piles and with the attached boats blown towards the leeward corner.

Two Frenchmen, Patrick Simon and Michel Touille, had arrived in England fresh from their New Year celebrations at home, ready to take the Yachtmasters tuition and exam. Usual routine with the theory first and then during the second week in Royal Dram, we were able to visit all the harbours in the Solent and do all the necessary practical work by the Wednesday evening. By this time the weather, which had been deteriorating every day, had now reached gale force. We had been mooring the boat every night in the protection of the Southampton marinas, and first thing on the morning of the exam it was actually blowing the South Westerly Force 10 which had been forecast.

Luckily Ken Burgess was the examiner. There is no doubt he was one of the best; he owned a Moody sailboat and had been a navigator in the RAF. He was now an instructor at the Warsash School of Navigation, was no fool and knew a candidate could be examined much more thoroughly in an estuary or harbour rather than out in the open sea. At the time he was one of the few RYA examiners I did not have to instruct in the art of handling a twin-screw motor vessel. We stayed within Southampton Water all day, never going past Calshot, and the two Frenchmen were a credit to their country in handling the boat extremely well in very windy conditions and doing everything else required of them.

One of my favourite and certainly most talented customers was Akira Shimabukuro, who was Japanese and who, five years before we met, was a seaweed fisherman in Okinawa. Nigel, a previous Yachtmaster, had met Shimmy out there and told him to stop wasting his time – he could earn much more money working in the mega-yachts in the Mediterranean. Shimmy was a very competent seaman, a very hard worker and was probably the most sought-after crewman in the Mediterranean. He wasn't content to live in the crew's quarters for the rest of his life and so began – for him – a very important fortnight in England. When he left Okinawa, he couldn't speak a word of English and here he was, five years later, speaking the language perfectly. He assured me he had picked it up from his shipmates, and did not attend a single lesson or class. He had all the necessary Japanese

Shimmy ashore with his mates

technical books and for any of the few problems that popped up, we referred to them.

Being a very competent seaman, and having owned his own fishing boat in Okinawa, he passed his exam with flying colours. He immediately became captain of a Japanese owned vessel in Singapore. Seven months later he sent along a fellow countryman called Kiyokakasu Shirado, alias Kiyo, who had been a deep sea fisherman going as far south as Australia and sometimes the Falklands. Kiyo worked equally hard, and passed. Shimmy came back to England a year or so later and took a sailing course with us. The last I heard of them Shimmy was captaining super-yachts in the United States and Kiyo had become an American citizen and was captain of a US coastguard cutter. I am extremely happy to have started the training for two such very nice guys who deserved to do well in their careers.

Udo Danzer, a German, telephoned at the beginning of the last week in March to ask if I was available to fly down to Nice on Saturday. He was at the airport to take me down to his boat, a Princess 46 Carrera, moored at Port La Napoule. He had taken delivery of it that morning, in exchange for the 36 foot Riviera he had used as a day boat for about a year. Now he wanted to go cruising in the Mediterranean and that is why he had asked me to give him the necessary training.

That afternoon I made sure he knew everything that went on underneath the floorboards. It is quite amazing how many people purchase a boat and, provided everything appears to work, the curtains and carpets look nice and the bunks are comfortable, that's it. If a boat owner knew how water and other liquids operated in a boat and how to get rid of leaks, he would be saved a considerable amount of money, as well as inconvenience. It involves being shown the fresh water, the engine cooling, and bilge pump systems, where they are, and how they work.

This lesson was brought home the very next morning after breakfast, when although the bilge pump itself couldn't be heard, I was aware of too much water being automatically pumped through an outlet into the marina. I lifted a floor hatch near where we had been sitting for breakfast and there we could see at least a foot of water in his new and clean forward bilge. Udo thought his boat was sinking and wanted to get out and arrange for Arie de Boom, the agent from whom he had bought the boat, to fix it. Luckily I was between him and the door and wouldn't let him escape. I tasted the water, it was fresh, and therefore I knew it was coming from within the boat and that the problem was small. After a bit of searching it was found that the hose leading from the fresh water pump to the bottom of the cold water tap in the forward hand basin was loose. It had not been secured with a jubilee clip.

I switched off the fresh water pump (thereby relieving pressure in the system) and no more water was pumped into the bilges. I called it a "Friday afternoon job". Udo said that in Germany they called it a "Monday morning job". We went ashore to tell Arie de Boom that all that was necessary was his assistance with a screwdriver and a one inch jubilee clip.

Udo Danzer was President of Mercedez-Benz in Kuwait at the time. Not only was he responsible for selling the cars to the

With a German customer from Kuwait in a British
Motor Cruiser at La Napoule in France!

Kuwaitis, but importing other merchandise as well. We happened to meet up when Perrier were having problems with their bottled water and he was importing Highland water instead. I told him that it was a fine thing to be selling good Scots water, instead of the French stuff. His reply was that they imported Highland water because it was owned by Arabs! He was a thoroughly clever and well-informed man, and it was a delight to be training him in his super new boat, "Conquisita". Because of the Iraqi invasion of Kuwait, I heard no more of him, but gather that he is now living in Mandelieu-la-Napoule where he had been purchasing a house at the time of our course.

I was down in France again very soon with a Dutchman, his wife, daughter and her boyfriend. They had acquired a 1965 van Lent, steel hulled, 42 feet in length and it was moored in Le Vieux Port in Cannes. When we arrived on board it had a very strong, but pleasant, smell of coffee. He was the manager for the main distribution depot of Douwe Egberts based in East Anglia. That week we had the choice of every form of coffee; but only Douwe Egberts. He wanted the boat to finish up at the new berth he had booked at Port Grimaud and during the week we did coastal navigation to La Napoule, St Raphael, Port Frejus and St Maxime. At all these harbours we practiced extensively the art of mooring stern-to.

On the last Friday we visited St Tropez, he let go the anchor and secured stern-to at the Quai Jean Jaures. We stepped ashore and had a magnificent farewell lunch. After weighing the anchor, he informed me that both engines were stuck in slow ahead and that he was unable to get them out of gear. He walked away from the controls leaving them to yours truly. I told him to get on the bows and shout at any boat that threatened to get in our way that we had mechanical problems and couldn't stop. When we were safely clear of the harbour and out in the Gulf I found that it was only the port gear that was stuck. As we approached Port Grimaud he stopped the port engine and took us alongside the long quay by the office of the Capitainerie – using the starboard engine only. While he arranged for a mechanic to come down and sort out the gearbox problem, his wife took me out to Nice airport for my flight home.

A successful alongside at St Raphael

The year had started well with three foreigners and, as it continued in that vein with many British customers, we felt we were truly entitled to be called Europe's leading sea school. Someone had already named us that.

We were doing a course in the Clyde on 22nd November and were actually in the Kyles of Bute when we heard there had been a terrible accident in Bute Sound. At two o'clock in the morning the nuclear powered submarine Trenchant had snagged the nets of the fishing vessel Antares. She had four officers undergoing the Submarine Command Course – the well-known Perisher – and had surfaced to find a trawl wire on the casing. The subsequent search of the area found the missing Antares on the sea bed. We felt stunned and quite sick when we arrived in Loch Goil that evening to hear on the BBC news that all four of the crew had gone down with the Antares.

The next year turned out to be the year of the press. In February The Times telephoned to ask if Barry Pickthall, their yachting correspondent, could do a boat-handling course with our school. I asked John Milsom who had passed his Yachtmaster

Deep freezing in Port Solent

earlier in the month to come along with his wife June. It was fun even though there was still snow on the ground at Port Solent. Barry Pickthall was also managing director of PPL Ltd and was a well-known sports writer and photographer, who covered many Round the World races as well as Americas Cups and Olympic Regattas.

In April there were two Yachtmaster candidates. Barry Cross was first mate of a 193 foot yacht called "Capella C" and had been a leading seaman in the Navy. Barry was with us for two weeks and we were joined for the second by Michael. He owned a Humber 38 in Lymington and had taken his theory earlier on with David Strang. When we arrived back in harbour, after successful completion of the exam, Michael asked if I was available to go out into the Solent to have a photo taken of Royal Dram. He said he was doing an article on his experience with my school for Motor Boats Monthly. I couldn't believe it, and wondered if there was any coincidence in the fact that Alex McMullen was now Consultant Editor of the magazine, having recently handed over to Alan Harper at Motor Boat and Yachting.

Everything comes in threes or so the pessimists are inclined to say. This optimist was very pleased to receive his third communication of the year from the press. It was from Graham Bailey, the assistant editor of Motor Boat and Yachting, who wanted to sign up with our school to take MB&Y's motor cruiser "Prospector" on a relaxed training cruise of the West Country. I met up with him plus Susan Mark, who worked for IPC Magazines Ltd and Lester McCarthy at the Breakwater Restaurant in Brixham Marina for supper on the Sunday evening. I hadn't met the first two before but Lester, the ace photographer, and I had met up several times.

The plans for the week were detailed to me there and then and as Graham said in his report, with every glass of red wine these plans became more ambitious. The first two nights were at Dartmouth and Fowey and then on Wednesday we had lunch at

Graham Bailey guiding us into Mevagissey Harbour

Mevagissy before going on to Falmouth and securing alongside the Visitors Yachthaven at the Town Quay. There are several privately owned marinas in various parts of Falmouth harbour stretching from Penryn to Mylor to Pendennis, but ours was owned by the local council and was near the centre of town. The Yachthaven staff were very welcoming and told us the wash places were unisex and a short walk over the other side of the square.

Whilst the others went to have a look round and decide on the late evening entertainment spot, I went for the early shower. I arrived behind two middle-aged women who turned out to be off a French yacht. As there were only two showers they went on ahead and I sat down to read some magazines in the small waiting area.

A very short while later one of the women popped her head round the door and indicated her shower was vacant or that's what I thought. I didn't appreciate she was actually inviting me to share it. Her English was not good but I was enjoying chatting in French. "Chantal, venez ici, regardez le Coq Sportif," she called across to her friend and I knew she wasn't referring to the national symbol of France! Chantal came over and the three of us were sharing the same bar of soap in the one shower room. They were enjoying my French, particularly when I called each one in turn "Ma Belle Minette". I don't know what they might have called our brief encounter – possible a douche a trois – but for me it was French frolics, all good fun and did the entente cordiale a power of good!

The team had just arrived back on board when I returned. We discussed the plans and did the navigation for tomorrow and then went for a super meal at a fish restaurant they had found on their earlier reconnaissance. The next day we went to Newton Ferrers on the River Yealm and after lunch ashore in the pub, prepared for our night passage to Plymouth where we arrived at 0200. The team was quite tired after the night navigation so straight to sleep in preparation for our last day and return to Prospector's mooring in Brixham.

I thought Graham Baily's article, which was conveniently published in time for the next Earl's Court Boat Show, was very good. He wrote sufficiently about the tuition but was particularly good in his brief description of each place we had visited both for the lunch, and the nights, in his so-called West Country cruise. This was to be the last article about us in MB&Y and I am extremely grateful to the various editorial staff Barry Watkin, Alex McMullen, Alan Harper and now Graham Baily for all the good things they did supporting our school well into the Millennium and beyond. Customers were continually quoting the articles in MB&Y.

I have always admired people who had been poorish at the start of their working life and by sheer hard work and determination managed to make a good fortune out of their lives. Dick Ballinger was one of them. He told me that he and his mother had a very small farmhouse, with a few apple trees near Weymouth, and one day, shortly after WW2, someone called and asked if they could park their caravan in the field for a few nights. They asked the price, Dick didn't have a clue how much to charge, but suggested a few bob per night. The next night someone else asked to take up the only other available space. And so it went on for many days during the rest of the summer right up until October. The attraction was the closeness of the beach at nearby Bowlease Cove.

That winter they bought the field next door and so on until the local council told them they must provide suitable washing places and toilets. This they did and instead of sending their campers to the nearest shop which was some way away, for their bacon and eggs, etc, they decided to open a shop on site. And so it snowballed and by 1991 he had built the Prebendal and Waterside caravan camps, a few miles to the north east along Weymouth beach and made them into the vast Waterside Caravan Park, which now has all the 5-star amenities one would expect of it.

It was in May that I joined him in "El Sueno", his two year old Birchwood 37, which he had just bought in my favourite small marina at Saint Jean Cap Ferrat. Teaching him about his boat and the navigation he required, for the small amount of cruising he was going to indulge in, was no problem. Sadly, his wife was physically impaired on one side, could move only slowly and use one hand. So most of the week the challenge was to teach him to handle his boat and prepare all the ropes and fenders for easy use once he had manoeuvred stern-to between his two neighbours. On one occasion the boat owner on the other side of the jetty came to help us. I thanked him and in my very best French explained that my owner was being instructed by me on how to do everything singlehandedly, and therefore would he please not help us. "Why don't you speak bloody English mate?" He was an Australian living and working in London!

Dick and his wife were a great couple and were in the process of retiring, having sold the caravan park the previous year. He was a very modest guy and could not explain his success other than it had all happened at just the right time, immediately after the war, with the subsequent expansion of caravan and camping holidays. He had had no business training and did everything by intuition.

With the expansion, both in numbers and size, of the large yachts, authorities were beginning to take note of the quality of the vessels themselves and the training of the crews. It was impossible to keep track of the new regulations that were being promulgated and when they were to finally come into force. As regards the yachting industry, in 1991 the Professional Yachtsmen's Association was formed. Jeff Marsh, who had been to our school ten years earlier, was one of the founder members, and the Hon Treasurer. The PYA has been involved with the MCA's yacht policy since the beginning.

On 7th August 1992 the QE2's hull was extensively damaged when she ran aground off Cuttyhunk Island near Martha's Vineyard. The Marine Accident Investigation Branch report stated that the leak was contained within deep and double-bottom tanks with no effect on stability. The depth of water was less than shown on the chart, the height of tide had been over estimated and the effect of squat was underestimated. Nevertheless, she was still doing at least 23 knots in shallow water. A sounding taken immediately after the accident was only two metres more than her draught.

What has happened to the excellent RN officer training? The superb Dartmouth Training Squadron was disbanded in 1972 to be replaced firstly by the Intrepid and then Fearless, and then the guided missile destroyer Bristol. Several times I even saw a large fishing trawler being used in the Solent as a means of training young officers to command men and the small warships of our future Navy. Merchant Navy training for big ships was nearly all done ashore and in simulators. As early as 1976 they were offering simulator facilities to yachtsmen at the London Polytechnic.

The International Maritime Organisation (IMO) had drafted in 1978 the Standards of Training Certification and Watchkeeping (STCW78) though it had little impact until 1995. All these regulations, as always, seemed terribly complicated and smelled of red tape but as far as super yachtsmen, who wished to be captains, were concerned, it basically meant passing Master Class 4. Deck hands had to qualify as OOW (Yachts) if they wished to be employed in such vessels and be eligible to keep a watch.

By sheer coincidence, or was it, I had a letter from Bronwen Emerson in the Cote d'Azur enquiring about the prices and other details of our Yachtmaster courses. I telephoned her to ask if she had the necessary qualifications and when she would like to do the course. Her replies were very non-committal and sounded unenthusiastic. Very soon I found out, by the grapevine, that she was the wife of Steve Emerson, who had been with a sailing school in Plymouth and now they were starting up a school called Freedom Yachting in Antibes.

I had already been aware of Blue Waters Yachting starting up a couple of years earlier, and had spoken several times with Peter Bennett, John Wyborn and Philip Holden. We had agreed to cooperate; so did Steve and Bronwen Emerson once they had got going. At that time they could only teach potential yachtmasters the theory, as a lot of the practical training and the exam itself had to be held in tidal waters. It was good to have these two schools in the Mediterranean because they were at the front door of most professional yachtsmen, and our school was beginning to find it hard to stem the flow.

Then training had to be looked into. The requirement for someone to qualify as captain of a commercial yacht up until now had been only the Yachtmasters Certificate. The Maritime and Coastguard Agency (MCA) brought in the extra necessity for a commercial endorsement, which meant you had to do a Sea Survival Course and pass a medical fitness test. These very good rules, finalised in 1994, made it almost impossible for an uncertified captain to get command of a yacht over 24 metres in length. It was in this year that I took the medical test and have been lucky enough to pass it every five years since.

We were still getting those who needed practical tuition and wished to take their final exams. We also began training those who wanted their Class 4, which we found enjoyable because of the higher standard. More were requiring their Yachtmaster (Ocean) which involved astro-navigation and worldwide meteorology. David Strang had by now retired to the Isle of Wight so I asked Nigel Thomas who lived in Brockenhurst if he would like to take some of the Oceans on, and he was very willing to do so. At the same time Philip Jackson, who had taken his Yachtmsters with us in 1976 and owned a 40 foot Dutch steel motor sailor said he would like to help in any training. Although we had lost David, two more were added to the team and we were now training mariners from complete novice to Merchant Navy Class 4, and thoroughly enjoying it.

Out next customer came not from Europe but Australia. Her name was Anthea Monger and at the time she was bosun in a 35m Fiendship. Because of her job her seamanship was good and I was very pleased because she was the first woman to become a Yachtmaster, commercially endorsed for power-driven vessels.

Then came an unusual call from the Ministry of Defence. I think it was a retired Royal Marine officer asking for a quote to train five MOD policemen in the Clyde area for their Yachtmasters. I had seen these people coming out of their comfortable offices, getting into the Nelson motor cruisers and warning approaching yachts to pass more than 150 metres from protected Naval shore installations at Faslane and Coulport. I knew the boring job they had from my submarine days and also whilst instructing courses in the area, I did not particularly relish the task, quoted my normal fees, and received the expected reply that he had had to accept the cheapest quote. I didn't bother to ask why the Navy couldn't do the task themselves.

The year 1995 was an important one in many ways. The Global Positioning System (GPS) whose signals were first broadcast in 1977 would be declared fully operational in July. Also the new Masters Certificate Class 4 under STCW95 came into operation. On April Fool's Day an unusual invitation came my way when I was asked to be guest of honour at the Middle Thames Yacht Club annual dinner and dance. My host was the Commodore, Bill Taylor, who with his wife Alex had done what they called an absolute beginners class during the summer of 1987 in Royal Dram.

Bill and Alex in their "Findon Lady"

With the invitation they sent a photograph of their "Findon Lady" taken on the Ostend-Brugge canal. On the back of the photo they had written:-

"This is your fault."

Four years, thousands of pounds, and several nervous breakdowns later, we made the continent this summer.

Whilst earning my dinner and replying on behalf of the guests, I quoted a saying I had heard from John Hodson, a civil engineer, who lived next door. It went like this:-

> One evening in October when I was one third sober and taken home "a load" with manly pride, my knees began to stutter, so I lay down in the gutter, and a pig came up and lay down by my side. Then we sang "it's all fair weather when good fellows get together." Until a lady passing by was heard to say "You can tell a man who boozes by the company he chooses." And the pig got up and slowly walked away!

John was no sailor but he had to know all about tides and tidal streams when he was John Mowlam and Co.'s "head man" constructing the new London Bridge during the years 1967 and 1972. Road traffic had to continue both ways during building and as an extra job he had to oversee the meticulous numbering of each stone from the old Rennie's bridge. It was sold to Robert McCulloch and shipped via the Panama Canal to Long Beach, California, and then trucked to Lake Navasu City.

Later that month I took Ian Fairfield CBE in his meticulously maintained Broom Ocean 50, "Gwenna IV" from the Solent to Gibraltar. I now knew Ian quite well as I had trained him for his Yachtmasters eighteen months earlier. He had been in the Navy at the end of the war and had owned various boats since then. When I first met him his boat-handling and navigation were already ace, but his theoretical knowledge was poor. His attitude to Rule of the Road was that he kept well away from all other vessels he could see during the day and from all lights he saw at night. I gave him some books and sent him away to learn all about the collision regulations and the lights and symbols and improve his knowledge of meteorology. When he came back for the exam he was marvellous and passed with flying colours.

Since the war he had been chairman of a group of companies, mostly to do with the sea and including Pains Wessex, McMurdo and the yacht clothing company Splashdown. He also chaired an organisation which produced anti-missile chaff. During the Falklands war the taskforce was running short of chaff because of the Argentinian Exocet attacks being so numerous and successful. His workforce went into full production twenty four hours a day; because of this he was awarded the CBE.

I asked him why he needed my assistance to get to Gibraltar and he replied that his wife would be joining us in Gibraltar when we arrived and his two sons, who worked abroad, would join him later. He told me he was going to be the engineer and that I would be the captain and do all the chart work and navigation. We had excellent weather all the way to Camaret, and then across the Bay to Gijon. Every morning before leaving harbour, he would meticulously check the engines; they, the bilges, and the whole of

Gwenna

the engine room were kept spotless. On our way along the north coast of Spain he found a tiny diesel leak at an L-shaped joint in the fuel system leading to the turbo-charger on the port engine. He considered it a fire risk and he did everything he could but was unable to stop the leak. We arrived at Corunna on the Sunday evening and he telephoned the MD of Brooms in Brundle straight away and ordered two of the spare parts one for each engine. They were ordered from Ford Mermaid in Hampshire at 0900 the next morning, they travelled by DVL to Corunna airport and they arrived on board, by Spanish despatch rider, at 1100 on the Tuesday. Marvellous and it only cost Ian £36 for the speedy delivery. It was interesting to note that the items had been slightly altered with a curved corner; they had obviously had a similar problem before and had rectified it without telling the owners. Our next ports of call were at Leixoes, Lisbon, Sines and Lagos in Portugal.

Sines was the only one of the four places I hadn't been to before and it was a fascinating little fishing harbour. No one spoke a word of English except the receptionist in the hotel. She was very helpful as our tourist guide. Several explorers, of what was then regarded as the New World, came from this part of Portugal situated on the western edge of continental Europe. It was the area in which Henry the Navigator had operated at the beginning of the 15th century. He set up a school of navigation at Sagres and from here with the aid of cartographers and astrologers he set about forging trade routes to India via the Cape of Good Hope. Vasco de Gama was actually born in Sines about the same time as Henry died and we saw his monument in the town. Vasco was reportedly the first sailor to travel from Portugal to India, via the Cape of course.

After our cultural visit to the western part of the Algarve, next stop Gibraltar. Ian was driving his vessel on the last stage of the passage and I was crewman as we secured alongside the wall in the new, but not yet completed, marina at Queensway Quay. A rather portly harbourmaster took the ropes which I passed to him and he told me that I probably incorrectly thought that, as we were now in the Mediterranean, that there were no tides in

Gibraltar. He told me that today was actually spring tides, that it was now high water, and that I should leave enough slack on the ropes to allow for a metre's fall in tide.

I met up with him later in the marina office and thanked him for the tidal lecture: it was similar to the one I had been giving to potential yachtmasters from the Mediterranean a fortnight ago in England. I explained my situation and he told me he had been a chief petty officer in the Navy, his last job had been shore-based in Gibraltar and he so liked it that he had decided to retire there. He joined us for a few beers in Irish Town before Ian and I went off for our farewell meal. Although I saw "Gwenna IV" a few times back in the south of England, it was the last time I was to see Ian Fairfield who sadly died towards the end of 2008.

No sooner had I flown back from Gibraltar than I was back down again this time with Gavin Barlas in his Trader 41+1 called "Kaywana". As crew he had his son Simon and a friend Brian on holiday from Zimbabwe and he had asked me to captain the boat as far as Gibraltar. At Lymington he showed me round his boat, we checked all the safety equipment and I suggested he secured the dinghy to the davits more thoroughly – otherwise it would probably come adrift in choppy conditions. Then followed a very instructive and enjoyable passage with Gavin doing all the work, assisted by his crew, under my supervision. We called at Camaret, Santander, Corunna, Leixoes and the penultimate stop was Lagos on the Algarve.

We had three nights at sea and the last 120 miles to Gibraltar we did overnight, with Gavin and Brian doing the first watch, and Simon and I doing the dreaded middle. I was turned in my bunk, with as always one eye and one ear open, when at about 2230 there was a shout from Gavin calling my name. I was in the wheelhouse in a flash – covering my eyes to maintain my night vision – while he told me that he had lost a radar contact approaching on the port side and that he couldn't visually see anything. I went outside and there coming towards us, without any navigation lights, was a fast black vessel with the word "Aduana" painted on its side. It was a Spanish customs boat and, after asking us where from and where to, politely allowed us to proceed. I had warned Gavin and his crew about all the on-board lights in the vicinity of the steering position impairing one's night vision, and this was a good lesson nearly "rammed home".

As happens quite often in the Gibraltar Straits, with the Laventar blowing from the east into an east-setting tidal stream, we had a severe dose of wind against tide and had to slow down. It seemed hours before we got past Tarifa and were able to turn north-easterly towards calmer waters and Gibraltar. Gavin wrote a short article in Motor Boats Monthly describing the trip down. He and Simon took the boat on to Torrevieja on the Costa Blanca and then down to Calad'Or in Majorca for the winter.

Possibly the last five years of the century were to prove the most varied and successful of the school's existence – certainly the busiest. Early on a South African requested a fortnight's personal tuition leading up to his taking the yachtmasters exam; two weeks which proved to be thoroughly satisfying in every way. Juan Koegelenberg only spoke Afrikaans when he left his home town of Brakpan on the outskirts of Johannesburg five years beforehand. He went down to Cape Town and became very competent at scuba diving and similar activities. He suffered an accident which prevented him continuing in that sport. Like a lot of Afrikaaners he went to Saint Marten in the Dutch West Indies and started working in the luxury yachts.

I gave Juan the nickname of Yarpie which is a mildly offensive Afrikaans word – the one we gave to all South Africans with whom we trained in the Navy. He was very happy to be called such and he frequently telephoned me from America to give me some more yachtmaster trainees and always started the conversation by saying: "Hello, Mike, it's your favourite Yarpie here". After leaving us, he straight away became captain of a yacht and I heard in 2010 that he had recently circumnavigated the world as captain of the 50 metre yacht Jemasa. It belonged to Jemasa Holdings in Los Angeles and as far as I know he is still there.

By sheer coincidence our next customer, Richard Tickle, was also South African, but because he was now resident in Malmo it gave me my first opportunity to visit Scandinavia since the good old Dartmouth Training Squadron days thirty odd years ago. It was an extremely enjoyable week teaching navigation in the calm waters of the Oresund, the southern part of the Kattegat, and visiting lovely little Swedish fishing harbours. I had not heard of them before and they had such names as Barsebackshamn, Limhamn, Landscrona and Dragor.

On the last morning Richard arrived with two Swedish friends carrying several crates of empty Carlsberg bottles and announced that we were going to Copenhagen, as Carlsberg beer was much better than the Swedish beer; though you could buy it in Sweden it wasn't quite the same, and more expensive. So we had a very worthwhile navigational plan passing under the 8km long Oresund Bridge whose construction had only started in 1995. After our farewell lunch in Copenhagen's Nyhaven the replenished stocks of concoctions were being indulged by the crew long before we left Danish waters. I was able to enjoy plenty of my favourite Akvavit, after we had arrived safely home in Malmo.

Dominic May at Berthon's telephoned to ask me to be coxswain during the trials of the Harwich Lifeboat which was nearing completion at their yard. It necessitated doing a few hours' engine trials at maximum speed on about ten different occasions. The good thing was that these trials took place in the summer months and therefore I spent all the time up on the flying bridge, out of everyone's way, whilst the engineers and RNLI inspectors carried on with their work down below. The bad thing was that there were many yachts, fishing boats, and other small craft around, and I had to try and keep well out of their way so as not to cause too much wash whilst maintaining our 25 knots. It was great at first to see and use all the up to date equipment fitted in these lifeboats, but after a couple of days it became a bit boring – charging down to Portland and then back around the Isle of Wight all in half a day. I don't think we sank anyone with our wash; in fact, everyone was waving at us in a friendly manner, such is the popularity of the RNLI.

In September Alan Gough telephoned as he wanted me to go to Corunna and bring his boat back to Falmouth. Three years earlier I had trained him in the Solent for his Yachtmasters. Since

Trials Coxswain of New Harwich Lifeboat

then he had part-exchanged his Trader 41 "Jemma Jane", for a 58 foot Trader "Edana of Mann", which he had taken down to the Mediterranean for a couple of years. He was now returning to the UK and on arrival at Corruna he received an urgent call to return to Douglas, Isle of Man, where he was to act as barrister in a very important case.

I rang Charlie who had now sold his pub for a very reasonable profit. We both flew down to Corunna and on board was Alan's father-in-law, a marvellous character whom we had met a couple of times before. Alan called him "The Major" as he had been in the Army during WW2, but his sole claim to nautical fame was that he enjoyed cooking, doing the ropework and steering the boat. In other words a bloody good chef/deck hand.

Unfortunately the weather forecast for the Bay of Biscay was not good, so we decided to creep along the north Spanish coast where there were plenty places of refuge should the weather be too bad. Ribadeo was our first nights stop and on the next day we reached Santander. The weather instead of moderating decided to deteriorate so we had three days there. We could get forecasts

Alan Gough on board his 'Jemma Jane'

from BBC Radio 4 on the Longwave and from the Santander Port Authorities. Also Alan was relaying faxes from the UK – all bad news – so we endeavoured to enjoy some of the local hostelries.

On the first evening there the friendly harbourmaster had taken us to a local restaurant Taberna Vicente who was a Maestro Asador and his steaks were delicious. Vicente also claimed to have been the world paella champion and showed us pictures of him and his staff producing some in cooking pans which must have been a good five metres in diameter. His smaller ones were very good, as we sampled them the following night. He couldn't speak a word of English but was very proud of the fact his two daughters could: they had been to Aberdeen University and had qualified as vets.

There were water problems on board in that one of the tanks leaked. However, the other was okay and was sufficient for us (provided we kept it topped up). Another problem was the radar which hadn't worked since we switched it on in Corunna and engineers in Santander were unable to repair it. Never mind, the SS Canberra had sailed most of the way to the Falklands with its radar switched off to avoid detection by the Argentinian Air Force.

After three days in Santander the forecast for the Bay improved and so we decided to sail the next morning. As we listened to the forecast we were all aware of a foul smell in the boat. Poor Charlie rustled around and found that the sewage holding tank was not only full but had sprung a leak. I checked and the two way indicator showed that, when the toilets were pumped, the discharge went to the holding tank. This proved incorrect and when the pointer was moved to holding tank the toilets pumped to sea. We left the pointer in that direction and it was now okay for us to use any of the loos, but once a holding tank or toilet has leaked, it takes ages to get rid of the smell. What amazed us was that the owner had apparently survived without any of these problems for at least two years in the Mediterranean. He must have used the marina facilities.

I was up before 0600 the next morning and the forecast for the Bay was okay, but by sheer luck, or perhaps good nautical training, I listened to the Santander Port Authority forecast (given firstly in English and then Spanish). It initially gave a gale warning for the sea area Cantabria, which covers out to approximately ten miles along the north Spanish coast. Then in more detail it said that westerly winds force 4-5 were going to increase to gale force by 1000, it would be raining between that time and 1500, and then the winds would slowly die down to force 4 by 1800. It was actually more detailed than that, and every item proved to be correct. We decided to leave at 2000 after an early meal at Vicente's and by the time we got out into the Bay the sea would have hopefully calmed down.

We cleared harbour, everything was okay and the sea state, as one would expect after the gale, was a bit choppy. We were on auto-pilot and as we were about to settle down to our watch-keeping routine I was aware of the boat veering over to port. The auto-pilot had packed up and we found that its compass, under a forward bunk, had come loose and was tumbling all over the place. I had taken over hand steering to at least maintain a reasonably steady course, but the dim light on the compass was useless. I could not see to steer anything like an accurate course, which I would have to have done for the next eight hours of darkness. There was no alternative but to turn back to the berth we had departed from in Santander four hours earlier.

The next day, Thursday, decisions had to be made. Here we were in a boat whose radar and auto-pilot didn't work and whose steering compass could not be seen at night. There seemed no prospect of getting anything repaired in the next few days, and time was running out. Charlie needed to get back and I had a fortnight's course starting in England on the Monday. Flights from Bilbao to London were not all that plentiful, but we did get the last two seats left on the Friday evening.

On Christmas Day 1996 we were told that Pete Goss, who was competing in the Vendee Globe non-stop single-handed round-the-world yacht race, had heard a Mayday call. It was a distress signal being relayed by the Australian Marine Rescue and Control Centre and it had been originated by a fellow race competitor, Frenchman Raphael Dinelli, whose position Pete plotted to be 160 miles astern and to windward. The conditions were atrocious. However, Pete, who had served nine years in the Royal Marines, mostly "sailoring" as opposed to "soldiering", knew that the tradition of the sea stated that when someone is in trouble you go to their assistance. He instantly ruined his own chances in the race by turning into hurricane force winds and the sea state that only the southern ocean can produce. On the morning of 27th December with the help of an area search carried out by a Royal Australian Air Force rescue plane, Pete went alongside the life raft and pulled Raphael out to safety.

Pete spent the next few days "nursing the Frenchman back to normal life" and landed him in Hobart, Tasmania, before continuing in the race. They had become, and continued to be, the best of friends. Pete was awarded the Legion d'Honneur, France's highest award for gallantry, which he received from President Chirac, and was best man at Raphael's wedding.

The year 1997 was due to be quite an historic one as far as the Commonwealth was concerned. Firstly, Her Majesty the Queen went to Newfoundland for the quincentenary celebrations of John Cabot's landing from the sailing brig "Matthew" and becoming the first discoverer of North America. A replica "Matthew" was built that year and we were asked to train the skipper for his Yachtmaster (Ocean) certificate and the bosun for his Yachtmaster theory. As both lived in Lymington and the good ship "Matthew" was moored alongside the Royal Lymington Yacht Club, at the time it was a very interesting experience.

The new "Matthew" was designed by Colin Mudie, the well-known naval architect, and built in Bristol of all the good timbers. It had a few extras unavailable to Jean Cabot, namely radar, GPS, satcom and an engine. Cabot was actually Italian, but was commissioned by King Henry VII of England. It was another famous son of Italy, Colombus, who became the first European to set foot on mainland America one year after Jean reached Newfoundland. It was on July 1st 1997 that China resumed sovereignty over Hong Kong thereby ending over 150 years of British colonial rule.

Shortly after "Matthew" sailed out of Lymington to start its epic journey, so did Royal Dram leave for County Cork in Ireland. Yes, I had decided to sell her after ten very worthwhile and enjoyable years. Many more of my customers wanted to be trained in their own boats and although we were still getting the same amount of work we were beginning to use Royal Dram less and less. Although it costs a lot of money to maintain, run, insure, and moor a boat in a marina, I was able to sell her for the same amount as I had paid. We had a lot of fun with her but there is a saying that the second best day in a sailor's life is the day he buys a boat. The best day is the day he sells it, and I think this was true for us.

Another strange case of the Royal Navy's lack of training ability occurred when the Royal Marine Special Boat Service at Hamworthy near Poole, sent me, on two separate occasions, a total of five candidates for Yachtmaster tuition. It was all invigorating stuff. I do not know that they were tremendously

MATTHEW
ALL SHIPSHAPE
AND BRISTOL FASHION

Matthew alongside at Royal Lymington Yacht Club

enthusiastic about the job in hand. It was probably just another task, the necessity for which I was unable to find out. They all arrived with their brown paper bags of pusser's sandwiches, they were obviously good seamen from their small boat training, but the most work involved the teaching of the theory. It was great to talk with them about life in the present-day Navy – and Royal Marines – and one thing that certainly hadn't changed was the fine sense of humour.

One of my most hoped for weeks came early the next year when I finally succeeded in persuading Charlie Lyle to take his Yachtmasters. With him were a South African, Bryan Pridgeon, and an Australian Adam Goes. For Charlie the time was just a formality, and so it should have been for someone who had been boating as a hobby all his adult life. The other two, both young enthusiastic professionals, took it in turns to be captain and helmsman. On the first day out the captain, after telling the helmsman to steer 090 for a while, told him to steer 080. He put the wheel to starboard and I said nothing, as he eventually got us on to the correct course. The next alteration of course was to 100 and he put the wheel to port. I then pounced and had both of them altering course all over the place to make sure they knew which way to put the wheel when changing compass courses.

This wasn't the first instance but I was rapidly coming to the conclusion that these guys had never steered anything bigger than a dinghy. In the larger yachts they got the automatic pilot to do all the work – and thinking. They might know a lot of the theory and have sailed the world, but they were nearly all lacking in basic seamanship skills. We were there to remedy that. The week which Charlie later described as the best in his life, flashed by with the continual banter between a Yarpie, an Oz and a Scotsman helping all three progress towards a successful conclusion.

It was about now that people were beginning to mention an International Certificate of Competence. Holland and France were complaining that boats from the British Isles were entering their coastal waters and marinas and then proceeding into their European canal systems without any experience or certification. They were particularly concerned about bareboat charters. So in

1998 the Department of Transport through the MCA appointed the RYA to issue the certificates known as ICC. They included an endorsement which a captain was required to have if he wished to navigate on most European waterways. It was known as the Code European des Vois de la Navigation Interieure (CEVNI).

My first ICC customer was one of the country's best known sculptors. He was Philip Jackson and I had been with him a couple of years before when he owned a small Falcon 22. Now he had a more substantial Grand Banks 36 which, like the Falcon, he kept in Chichester Yacht Basin near to his studios in Midhurst. A quiet, unassuming man, he had mentioned his being commissioned for the Bobby Moore sculpture at Wembley Stadium when he gave me his card. It was only after I had finished the course in "Sissal III" that I began to find out what a skilled perfectionist he was at his job. He has been commissioned by royalty, the armed services, the church, the Football Association and Manchester United. To us mariners possibly the best known of his sculptures were those of King George VI at BRNC Dartmouth, the Jersey Liberation one at St Helier and the Yomper, the 4.60m high bronze, unveiled in Portsmouth in 1992. Philip received many awards, the most recent of which was when he was appointed Commander of the Royal Victorian Order in 2009.

My last course of the year and the century was for Douglas Patterson, a New Zealander who was taking both his Yachtmaster and Ocean tickets. One day we were coming out of Portsmouth and over by the Nab Tower we could see, apparently aground, a large merchant ship. It turned out to be the 10,000 ton Dole America, a refrigerated cargo vessel carrying mostly bananas and pineapples. Evidently at 0300 in the morning it had hit the Nab Tower, had been holed in three places, one above and two below the waterline and so it began to take on water and list. The master let his ship take the ground intentionally on the Horse Tail Bank.

The good news was that a couple of days later the Kiwi passed his exams and so ended another period of good teamwork at our school. We had now trained over 450 owners, captains, mates and crew for their Yachtmasters and we could now happily celebrate the Millennium. After a temporary patch-up, "Empire

Dole" was taken into Southampton for full repairs, and was still there ten days later. I asked myself how a modern ship like that with an experienced Norwegian master, and all its sophisticated equipment, managed to hit the Nab Tower which was 100 feet high and had been a well-known landmark for sailors since 1920. I am sure the answer was the modern blind reliance on global navigational satellite systems.

FINGS AIN'T WOT THEY
USED TO BE

The last few years of the old century, like the first of the new, brought much concern as to the capabilities of those manning the warships and merchant ships of our once great seafaring nation. It appeared as though the time and the amount of money being spent on training were decreasing considerably and so was the quality. It was also beginning to emerge that mariners were being trained to use GPS as a means of navigation as opposed to its intended use as an aid to navigation. Also too much time was being spent in simulators instead of hands-on instruction in boats or ships. This made us, in our school, even more determined to continue our training in boats so that everyone received as much practical tuition as possible on the water, and in tidal conditions.

A good assignment was a visit to a lovely little harbour in Holland called Monnickendam in the south west corner of the Zuider Zee and about 15 miles by water from Amsterdam. The owner was a well-known Swiss businessman, Peter, who had in earlier days been a Swissair pilot. He had recently bought "Laertes", a Dutch steel trawler and wanted help with delivering it to St Katherine's Dock in London. On the first day I made sure he knew the layout of his boat and we did all the usual checks: the engines plus all the navigational and safety equipment. Then we did our chart work for the passage across the North Sea to the Thames Estuary. I showed him the well-marked dangerous exclusion zone 200 metres from the approach Channel to Sheerness. Fifty seven years ago the SS Richard Montgomery had dragged its anchor, gone aground and broken its back. It was one of over 2000 American liberty ships produced to carry supplies – in this case for the Normandy invasion. On board were one and a half tons of TNT high explosives – still considered to be deadly.

The second day we took a nice slow trip from Monnickendam down to Amsterdam, then to the end of the Noordzee Kanaal where we secured to a jetty in a quiet little town not far short of Ijmuiden. We had hoped to go straight out into the North Sea and do the 150 miles across to England by breakfast next morning. However, there were south-westerly gale warnings in force, not only for the next twenty four hours but for much of the coming week.

Needless to say the gale warnings were still in force when we got up early the next morning and there were pictures in the Dutch press of a large merchant ship aground, having apparently broken down and been blown onto a sandy beach up to the north of us at Texal. And so began one of the worst days the modern world has known. After breakfast, because of the weather situation, we requested a berth for at least one night in Ijmuiden's Seaport Marina. We were asked to wait a while as they needed to prepare a berth for a boat of our size. The wind was certainly stronger the nearer to the North Sea we progressed,

Laertes near Monnickendam

414

and Peter manoeuvred us into the berth they had organised for us late forenoon.

He immediately tidied everything in the lounge and the moment he switched on the television we saw aircraft crashing into the twin towers of the World Trade Centre in New York and bursting into flames. The date was 11th September 2001 and here before our very eyes we were witnessing the tragedy which became known in the USA and the rest of the world as 9/11. With this terrible news plus the bad weather forecast, we decided to leave "Laertes" in Ijmuiden, go home and come back another day.

One of the many signs that standards in training were starting to slip came from the RYA in 2001 authorising examinations for Coastal Skipper and Yachtmaster to be conducted in the Mediterranean and also the Baltic Sea. Now, although they had to answer theoretical questions on tides and tidal streams, and enter in their logbooks experience of tidal waters, in fact they need have had no practical experience whatsoever of tidal streams or other currents. In March the next year I received a letter from the RYA. They had apparently just woken up to the fact that an American company called International Yachtmaster Training had been running yachtmaster courses in Florida.

For several years I had been in touch with IYT. Juan Koegelenberg had told me about it, because several of his boating friends still preferred to come to England and our school for tuition: although it was much more convenient for them to be doing it in Fort Lauderdale where many of the super-yachts are based.

For a while our attention was drawn towards local seafarers. We had recently heard of the death of Maralyn Bailey, who worked at a garden centre in Lymington. She and her husband Maurice had in 1968 sold up their home in Derby, bought a 31 foot yacht "Auralyn" and over the next four years spent every penny they earned on fitting her out. They then set forth from Southampton in June 1972 with the intention of sailing to New Zealand and starting a new life.

Their voyage across the Atlantic and through the Panama Canal to the Galapagos Islands went well. Then, on 4th March the following year they collided with a whale. A huge hole appeared below the waterline. The water rushed in. Hurriedly they had to abandon ship and slip into their liferaft and dinghy (which Maurice had roped together). They wrote the whole story in their best-selling book "117 Days Adrift", a signed copy of which I own. They were true son and daughter of the sea. Undaunted they bought another sailing boat and for a further four years they sailed the seas until, in 1980, they retired in Lymington.

Maurice teamed up with a colourful character called Tim Bacon, who was born in Melbourne, Australia. The family returned to England when he was 18 months old. In 1992 Tim bought the lease of Yot Grot, a marvellous glory hole which, as the name implies, sold useful and useless yachting paraphernalia. The shop became derelict and "due for demolition", so he closed it down forever in 2002. He then took on the lease of a small pub at Hamptworth about 15 miles north of Lymington. He suffered leukaemia, lost his battle with the dreaded disease and died at the young age of 59. Only a few weeks beforehand, we had enjoyed a few pints of his delicious beer, as well as his company, at his aptly named Cuckoo Inn. Every year he used to run a beer festival and gave us one of his pint glasses on which was inscribed "If you're drinking to forget, please pay in advance!" His sense of humour, as well as his personality, are very much missed by all who knew him.

At the beginning of the war a near neighbour called "Cyclops" was a sergeant pilot in the RAF. He was commissioned in 1942 and a year later his Spitfire was hit by a German bomber approaching Leicester. His windscreen was shattered and the splinters caused severe damage to his right eye, which surgeons were unable to save. He was fitted with a clear blue false eye, which he would sometimes remove, ask someone to "keep an eye on it", and place a black patch over the socket! He later wore the patch permanently and returned to operations as a fighter pilot. After the war he became a test pilot, was awarded the

AFC, appointed CBE and retired as Air Commodore. A dedicated and skilful yachtsman, he was appointed Commodore and later Admiral of the RAF Yacht Club in the Hamble. In later years he bought a small motor cruiser and wanted to visit the waterways of Europe.

Also nearby were Bill and Isabel Buckoke. In 1941 Bill went to Dartmouth as a Special Entry Cadet and spent his first year at sea as a midshipman on surface ships. As soon as he was promoted to sub-lieutenant he joined the Trade. A potentially successful career in the Submarine Service was curtailed when he failed the medical for the world famous "Perisher Course". He was found to have TB and was discharged from the Navy in 1951, the year he married Isabel, who came from a naval family, had trained as a Coder in the WRNS and had worked in a tunnel at Newhaven for D-Day. After the war she hated working in an office (I sympathise with her!) and inserted the following advertisement in The Times:-

"Ex-WRNS would like employment as Deck-Hand
in Yacht."
"(Can cook – qualified shorthand-typist)".

She was taken on by Brigadier Noel Blandford-Newson who was fitting out a converted Scottish fishing boat in the River Hamble. He and his wife Joan, known as the Mate, were taking "Nyala" to Germany where Noel was to supervise, on behalf of the Control Commission, the destruction of the U-Boat pens.

Bill qualified as a chartered accountant and went on to become a director of Gillette and the German company Braun (bought by Gillette) in Kronberg, West Germany. He used to thoroughly enjoy reminiscing his time in submarines and attended as many reunions as possible. In his retirement he had a good time sailing with friends and so that they could visit the continental canal system, both he and "Cylops" passed their Cevni tests with our school.

Another near neighbour who had a boat was Leslie Dartnell. His real love was cars but for a while owned a Sunseeker which he kept at Bray Marina. He worked as a designer with Saatchi and Saatchi the global advertising agency, when it was founded in London. Leslie later kept his boat moored between two buoys on one of the River Stour's trots at Christchurch. A very talented member of the Lymington Art Group, two of his paintings I am particularly pleased to have are of Honfleur Harbour, and one of a fishing vessel laid up at Mudeford.

Unfortunately, 2002, especially the second half of the year, I will remember more for the mishaps involving the Royal Navy rather than the continued varied tuition given by our team. On 7th July HMS Nottingham went aground on the submerged, but well charted Wolf Rock, near Lord Howe Island in the north Tasman sea. The findings of the Board of Enquiry made interesting but very distressing reading. Despite poor chart preparations and inadequate precautions, it was stated, Nottingham had anchored safely in the afternoon.

Then at 2057 she gets under way whilst the captain is ashore having dinner. He arrived back on board by the ship's Lynx chopper at 2153 and was not on the bridge nine minutes later when the ship grounded on the Wolf Rock at a speed of 12 knots. The Board of Enquiry also stated that at no time did the Executive Officer or Navigating Officer refer to the chart or take a fix, that the Wolf Rock had not been identified as a hazard and that inadequate standards of navigation, planning and chart preparation had contributed directly to the grounding. The Navy certainly had a major PR crisis to deal with.

Ten days later HMS Trafalgar, which had already grounded near Skye in 1996, grounded there again, this time on the islet of Fladda Chuain. On board she had a Perisher Course of three and at the time was doing 14½ knots at a depth of 50 metres. The Board of Enquiry's findings were later released and stated the grounding was because of human error, that the chart work was untidy and inaccurate and that insufficient attention had been paid to the strong tidal streams running at the time - all very basic stuff. They went on to report that tracing paper overlaid the navigational chart to protect it from being written on and thereby obscured vital information! I had never ever been trained to use, or actually used, or even heard of anyone else using, tracing paper overlays until now. The Board of Enquiry strongly discouraged their use in the future.

As a result of the Nottingham and Trafalgar incidents, and also others reported in the media, it appeared there were more mariners determined to receive the hands-on basic skills training still provided by our school. One such customer wanting personal instruction was the master of the 6,000 ton diving support vessel "Terschelling". Although from Harlingen in Holland the ship was registered in Panama and we were able to ensure the master obtained the necessary qualifications.

One of Hays Ships Ltd

Then followed the managing director of Hays Ships Ltd from Aberdeen, who came on course for a week. His company operated a small fleet of survey, research and patrol vessels for the wide variety of clients. He was already quite experienced, so in the space of that week we were able to organise the qualifications he required. Coincidentally the MCA Examiner on both occasions was Robert Avis, a chum of mine, who was the Commanding Officer of HMS President the London HQ of the Royal Naval Reserve.

Robert had risen from Ordinary Seaman to Captain in the RNR and been appointed a Fellow of the Royal Institute of Navigation in recognition of his contribution to the safety of navigation in pleasure and commercial yachting, with a particular emphasis on the understanding and use of modern radar systems. Before that, in 2001 he took on the thankless task of controlling the Royal Yacht Squadron's temporary landing stage at the America's Cup Jubilee in Cowes. Then, after successfully directing the 100th anniversary of the RNR in 2003, he was awarded the OBE.

The year 2005 got off to a fine start when Ellen MacArthur, all 5ft 2ins of her, broke the singlehanded Round the World sailing record by 14 days. She had done it in "The B&Q", a 75 foot trimaran and was to hold that record for three years. She was honoured and became "Dame Ellen". Not long after, the following letter was evidently received by the B&Q Services Department:-

Dear Sir/Madam,
My congratulations to you on getting a yacht to leave the UK on 20th November 2004, sail 27,354 miles around the world and arrive back in the UK 72 days later. Could you please let me know when the kitchen I ordered 96 days ago will be arriving from your warehouse 13 miles away?
Yours sincerely,
John Roberts.

In June we were to witness the largest fleet review that has ever taken place. Altogether 167 vessels from 36 countries and over 25,000 sailors took part. The ships had been arriving in the Solent for days, together with thousands of spectator yachts. The largest ship was the French nuclear powered aircraft carrier Charles de Gaulle. It took the Queen, embarked in HMS Endurance, two hours to sail up and down the lines of anchored ships. After the review by Her Majesty, there was a sail-past of tall ships and then hundreds of small yachts. The latter was all magnificently organised by Robert Avis. It was a tremendous loss to the maritime world when he died of cancer a year later at the young age of 54.

Shortly after the fleet review I met a Frenchman, Gerrard Fiske and his English wife, Kay. They had owned a few sailboats, but were now getting to a less energetic age and had purchased a Nimbus 380 called "Alouette". Gerrard had already done the Yachtmasters theory. All he wanted from me was tuition and guidance in getting used to handling his new twin-screw motor cruiser and getting to know various places in the Solent with which he was not familiar. He kept the boat in Port Hamble and I went out with him about ten times before Christmas. It was all very good fun and as time passed I tried to persuade him to take his full Yachtmasters exam.

He eventually agreed and the great event took place early in 2006. As soon as he had passed, he asked me to organise the transportation or delivery of Alouette down to Port Grimaud in the Gulf of St Tropez. They had a house there, as well as one on the Thames at Richmond. They reckoned they were going to spend more time, especially in the summer in France, so that was the reason for the boat's move. I suggested it would be stupid to have it delivered by sea or put on a lorry and that it was a golden opportunity for them to slowly cruise southwards through the French canals. They could stop off and moor the boat up for spells if they wanted to return to London for special family occasions or whatever.

As a result of my persuasion I was to have a most enjoyable five days helping them to get across the English Channel and start on their journey through France. The passage across was good in fine weather and there aren't many small places to spend a night better than the Vieux Bassin at Honfleur. Nice cafes to sit out and watch the world go by and at least two superb fish restaurants for the evening meal. The next two nights, after busy days boating, were spent in quiet little villages – Port de Poses and Port St Louis – before arriving in the centre of Paris. I had not been to it before but there was this marvellous marina called Port de Paris-Arsenal, right in the centre of the city, close to the Place de Bastille.

There I showed them the best way to fender up, with the use of tyres, for the remaining 250 or so locks on their way south. Some friends were going to join them for the next stage of the journey. After a splendid farewell dinner in the Boulevard de la Bastille, I had one last night in their luxurious boat, before catching the early morning Eurostar from Paris Nord to London Waterloo. They sent a card to say they had arrived safely on 18th May 2007. It had taken them over a year to enjoy their slow boat to Grimaud.

In June 2004 it had been announced on Iranian television and on the BBC News that Iran had seized three Royal Navy boats crewed by six Royal Marines and two sailors, while inside its territorial waters in the Shatt Al-Arab waterway. The Navy personnel who were shown blindfolded on Iranian television were filmed making an apology and released three days later.

I am sure the most humiliating day in recent Royal Navy history occurred three years later on 23rd March. A boarding party consisting of fifteen sailors and marines from HMS Cornwall were searching a vessel suspected of smuggling cars into Iraq. As the search was being carried out, Iranian Navy patrol boats detained the boarding party and their two RIBs – having accused them of being in Iranian territorial waters.

For the next few days we at home, as well as the rest of the world, witnessed these fifteen Royal Navy personnel, including one female leading seaman, being paraded on Iranian television. British politicians made their usual useless statements, including one from the Foreign Secretary, Margaret Beckett, demanding their immediate and safe return. We watched this going on for thirteen days. Every now and then the Iranian President Mahmoud Admadinejad would appear to shake hands and smile cheerfully with the captives smartly dressed in their Iranian-provided suits. When they were released, most agreed that they had been well looked after.

The First Sea Lord, according to the Guardian newspaper, described it all as "one bad day in our proud 400-year history." We were to hear a retired Admiral on BBC News:

> *"The boarding parties have GPS and they have a system which allows communication. It means they know where the mother ship is, and the mother ship knows where they are. GPS means they know their position exactly. It's not like the old days when they went away in a boat and didn't really have a clue where you were."*

He later added:

> *"We try to down play these things. Rather than roaring into action and sinking everything in sight, we try to step back and that of course is why our chaps were effectively able to be captured and taken away."*

Someone wrote "it seems the further the Brits move their Admirals from the sea, the more they are paid and the closer their brains get to their pockets"! It certainly seems that this century we no longer have the likes of Sir Roderick McGrigor who knew how to lead "the greatest single factor" and not "chaps who were effectively able to be captured and taken away".

What were the "old days"? Perhaps when Lord Louis Mountbatten was in Malta on board HMS Liverpool as C-in-C Mediterranean. The US Sixth Fleet entered harbour and his friend, the American Admiral signalled "Good morning, Dickie. How is the second largest navy in the world?" Lord Louis replied "Fine thanks and how is the second best?" Or perhaps it was during the Korean War when the United Nations were having difficulty demolishing a target close inshore. They would send for HMS Belfast, the most accurate gunnery ship in the fleet. Or maybe it was when our three Admirals, Terry Lewin, Henry Leach and John Fieldhouse prevailed upon Margaret Thatcher to victory in the Falklands.

Now began the real humiliation with statements coming eastwards across the pond from the United States. To mention a few:-

"Why didn't the Cornwall provide any support?"

"Sure sounds like someone in command dropped the ball ... in a big way."

"The incident in HMS Cornwall calls into question whether there is very much fight left in the dog that is the Royal Navy?"

"The Royal Navy is hardly a shadow of its former self."

"The disgrace suffered by the Cornwall will give the British people the courage to demand a Navy as courageous as the sailors who serve in it."

Liam Fox, the Conservative MP, and shadow Secretary of State for Defence even admitted:-

"This fiasco seriously damaged the reputation of the Royal Navy and the standing of this country abroad."

There was an horrific accident involving a speedboat in Tarbert that year. Very early, at 0045 one Sunday morning, three married couples left the hotel at which they were staying and went in their "Sea Snake" the short distance round to Stonefield Castle. It was too dark to do anything so they returned to Tarbert and crashed at high speed on rocks near the inner harbour entrance. What seemed a good idea at the time resulted in three of them losing their lives, and the other three being seriously injured. Post mortem toxicology tests on the bodies of the two who had been helming showed that both were nearly 2½ times over the drink-driving limit for motor vehicles.

Mentioning speed, for a number of years more and more fast rubber dinghies, with hard bottoms, and fitted with up to four outboard engines, were appearing on the scene. They were known as Rigid Inflatable Boats (RIBs) and were classified along with other boats, which do not normally provide accommodation or cooking facilities, as powerboats. The owners of this type of boat could receive training for Powerboat Levels 1 and 2, then Intermediate and finally the Advanced course.

I am not a great admirer of these machines and I met a super guy called John Burgess, who was an enthusiast, had become a very competent instructor, and was willing to join the team. John had been commissioned in the Royal Corps of Signals, Territorial Army and had retired with the rank of Major. He has been in market communication for thirty years and formed his own advertising and PR agency, Burgess Brook and Honess Ltd. Powerboating was a hobby of his, but he always managed to organise his work to allow time to instruct any of our customers coming through!

By sheer good fortune I was next asked to instruct a farming family and yes, their names were Robert and Denise Farmer! Robert wanted to be able to manoeuvre his Sunseeker Martinique

John instructing a powerboat Level 2 course

"Elysian" forwards and backwards, in and out, of all the marinas in the Solent area. Once he had mastered that he insisted their two sons William and Sam learnt not only how to handle the boat, but also the theory and practical work up to ICC level. They then sent one or two of their business friends on course and very kindly let me use "Elysian" for some of my other courses in the local area.

They were only a mile or so out of Lymington and it was fascinating to watch the family working together looking after buffalo, cattle, pigs and poultry. At the same time they were building up the very successful Hurst View Leisure complex providing static caravan homes, a mews of cottages, and an open camp site for tents and touring caravans. With their open way of life they were always very welcoming and radiating good humour. After the first few weeks I didn't see too much of Robert as he was always commuting down to Swanage to build up a similar leisure business – and attract more "chancers"!

Next I was asked to train Richard and Katherine Ward for their Yachtmasters. They had a Sealine S34 called "Res Ipsa" berthed between two mooring buoys and alongside a small wooden pier in the River Avon at Christchurch; it was a very attractive area on the other side of the river opposite the Priory. These two, and particularly Katherine, had done other courses and all the necessary preparation. It was a pleasure to teach them and there was no bother when it came to passing their exam. They then toyed with the idea of buying a bigger boat. They wanted to call it "Lazi Daze" after their dog Daisy, who was lazy and had cruised with them all her life. At the 2011 Southampton Boat Show an agent on the Sealine stand suggested they buy a three year old SC38 with a part exchange offer for "Res Ipsa". Katherine asked the name of the SC38 and, when they were told it was "Lazi Daze", they couldn't resist going through with the deal.

Following on fairly soon was another real boating enthusiast Colin Chamberlain. He owned a Humber 40 and had so far enjoyed all his boating on inland waters. After two days' classroom instruction, mostly on chart work and tidal streams, we embarked on a four day cruise of South Wales: we visited Penarth,

Who is that doing a RIB course between the QE2 on her last visit to the Clyde, and the 'Waverly', the last ocean-going passenger steamer in the world?

Richard and Katherine Ward with their new dog Summer Daisy on board "Lazi Daze"

Swansea and then Portishead before returning to the inland waterways at Sharpness. He now has "Perche No" (Italian for "Why Not") at a mooring in Cardiff Bay, where I spent a very pleasant couple of days cruising and anchoring in the area. That winter he visited the boat many times from his home in the Midlands and even spent Hogmanay on board watching the fireworks and celebrating the arrival of the New Year. In spite of many attempts at persuading him to take his Yachtmasters, he seems in no hurry, but I am sure he will do so in due course.

A welcome return visit to the Emerald Isle came in June. Scots hotelier Michael Moylan had a house and a 43 foot Aqua Star at Kilmore Quay in the south east of Ireland and wanted to take his Yachtmasters. It was a lovely, small fishing village and the port had been developed and completed ten years earlier. It now had a 55-berth marina, and continuous deep water berths for fishing vessels. The main place ashore is Kehoe's Pub Parlour and

Right to left: Colin, his wife Dev, and their friends Sharon and Steve on the flying bridge of "Perche No" – plus, of course, Dylan the dog.

Maritime Heritage Museum which, as the name implies, portrays local marine history.

Living next to Michael was his boating companion Johnny Moore, who had received a bad back injury whilst minesweeping as an Able Seaman in the Irish Naval Service. The very first day I found out that neither had enough previous sea experience or knowledge to take the Yachtmasters but this did not worry them. All they wanted to do was to learn as much basic seamanship as possible and enjoy a good cruise navigating the Irish coastline. The first week we went westwards to Waterford, Dunmore and Kinsale. The latter is a fabulous place which I already knew, and needless to say we enjoyed all the Irish banter and hospitality amongst the locals. Although we didn't meet her, we very much enjoyed the story about one pub:-

> On the barmaid's chest in Kinsale
> Were tattooed the prices of ale
> And on her behind
> For the sake of the blind
> Was the same information in braille.

We were, after all, near Limerick! On the way back we visited Crosshaven and of course the oldest yacht club in the world, the Royal Cork.

Johnny worked at Kilmore Quay in the RNLI station and he introduced me to their coxswain, Brian Kewell. He knew I had been Trials Coxswain of the Harwich Lifeboat so let me take over at sea on one of their weekend exercise runs. A thoroughly competent seaman, he told me he was having problems with the tide and tidal stream questions for his certificates of competence that he was taking at the RNLI HQ in Poole. I willingly gave him some tuition before partaking of a couple of pints of Guinness in the local!

The following week we went northwards to Wexford and Malahide and past the wind farm out in the Irish Sea. All the time Michael was happy to relax and let me concentrate on Johnny getting his Coastal Skipper Certificate. At the end of the enjoyable

On exercises with the Kilmore Quay lifeboat

fortnight I was once again able to appreciate that there were several words in the Irish lingo, similar to the Spanish "mañana", but none of them conveyed the same sense of urgency!

Time was catching up with me and I was beginning to think seriously about swallowing the anchor, but my customers wouldn't allow it. With the two schools flourishing in Antibes, as well as the IYT in Florida, it is true that the number of Yachtmasters coming our way was decreasing. But there was still plenty of work to keep an old seadog happy. More and more people seemed to want the personal tuition which our school provided.

Angola would possibly be one country in the world from which one would least expect to receive an email. So I was suitably surprised and pleased to hear from Ian Jack who had been in the Army and was now Security Manager for Hughes Sub Service Engineering Ltd at Porto Amboim in Angola. As there was no system of maritime instruction or certification in that country and he was in charge of several boats, he wanted to receive as much instruction as possible. Our school had been recommended to him and could I therefore make out a proposed programme with all the costing so that he could get his company's approval to go ahead?

He arrived in July, Angola's mid-winter, for a fortnight's hard work on his part and we managed to get him his Yachtmasters Theory, Advanced Powerboat, Diesel Engineering, Radio, and First Aid certificates. He obviously learned a lot, seemed to enjoy it and on his return to Angola sent a message saying: "Thanks to you and all who assisted in the course. It was both very informative and enjoyable."

I found it very informative to learn what his company was doing in Angola. HSSE had only been formed in 2005 and had contracts in the UK and other countries. At Porto Amboim they were literally pouring concrete into the Atlantic Ocean and forming a vast fabrication yard to build offshore structures. This would allow for the conversion of former very large crude oil carriers to become floating production storage vessels. At the seaward end would be a 460 metre quay wall and further out to sea a 630 metre breakwater.

It was at about this time that the RYA announced that the Coastal Skipper certificate would be changing its name to "Yachtmaster Coastal" as from 1st January 2010. The syllabus would remain the same and current holders of the CS certificate could change theirs to the new Yachtmasters. Was this solely a name change or a lowering of training standards? Many people thought the latter.

The last week in October will be one I don't think I will ever forget for a number of reasons. It started off on the morning of Monday 18th May with me flying up to Glasgow being met by Charlie, being driven down to a smart Sealine 52 in Largs Marina, and introduced by Charlie to the owner Jim Pierce. Jim had been boating before and had got his Powerboat Level 2 in Loch Lomond. He needed some more tuition and a helping hand in his much bigger "Golden Sign" in Clyde estuary waters. I was to be with him for three days, the first of which we spent in harbour doing the usual things: checking all his safety equipment; ensuring he knew the layout of his boat and doing the necessary chart work for a visit to Campbeltown.

The next day we did a few "circuits and bumps" before leaving the marina. As we progressed further south it was getting rougher and I knew it would be more beneficial if we diverted to calmer water. I got Jim to do the chart work and then he turned the boat round and we proceeded northwards towards Tarbert. There was no vacant pontoon large enough to take us, so we left and went across to the fabulous new marina at Portavadie on the eastern side of Loch Fyne. This was the first time I had been there, although thirty years ago I had watched from afar as an oil-rig construction village and basin were being built at great expense to the British taxpayer. Not one oil rig was ever constructed, and the village lay empty and deserted for many years.

There is now an extremely pleasant complex – consisting of a modern marina with restaurant and shops, which serve holiday and timeshare villas and apartments – all tucked away in a quiet corner of Argyll at the south-western end of the Cowal peninsular. After lunch we navigated back through the magnificent Kyles of Bute to Largs.

Since I first met Jim I had been trying to persuade him to bring his wife along. On the third and last morning she said she would like to join us provided we could go up to the Braehead Shopping Centre in Glasgow. He told me it had its own pontoon on the river right in the centre of the city. I immediately encouraged him together with his wife to do all the planning chart work and handling of the boat to get us up there and back. I would stand well out of their way and watch them, only stepping in if and when they needed help or an emergency occurred.

When we reached Greenock and the beginning of the buoyed channel I suggested they went up to the flying bridge and conned the boat from there, whilst I sat below and kept a gentle eye on them. They took the large scale chart plus pilot book with them and steered the boat the correct side of the buoys, marks and beacons before taking us alongside the Braehead pontoon. In the nearby BAE Systems shipyard at Govan and Scotstoun you could see the two Type 45 frigates HMS Diamond and Dragon nearing completion.

As we walked ashore in the shopping centre Jim told me his company had built most of the steelworks. I already knew he had made the new stand at Hamilton Academical Football Club and I soon found out that JD Pierce was reputed to be the foremost structural steel fabrication and erection contractor in Scotland. They recently won the contract to redevelop Haymarket Railway Station in Edinburgh. Charlie was there to greet us when we returned to Largs. We had a few celebratory drinks at Scotts Restaurant and then he drove me to the airport for the last flight home.

That was the good news for the week. On the Friday morning radio and television reports were coming through that Ross McKerlick in Skye had said: "When I woke up this morning and looked out of my window I could see a submarine. It was about a mile from my home and appeared slightly tilted." He said it was in an area of shallow water where he would not risk taking his yacht, and he was surprised how close it had come as there are good navigation buoys several hundred metres from the shore. The newscaster went on to say that the channel that runs under the Skye Bridge had red and green buoys, known as lateral marks, to make sure vessels do not run aground. He confirmed that the submarine was several hundred metres from the buoyed channel in an area where Admiralty charts show submerged rocks.

The Ministry of Defence confirmed that the submarine "Astute" had "run into difficulties" off the Isle of Skye and a Royal Navy spokesperson said the vessel had been grounded on silt and was re-floated at high tide. They did not mention that the tug "Anglian Prince", which had come to tow her free, had been in collision, which resulted in damage to Astute's starboard foreplane.

The next day the newspapers reported that "The world's most advanced submarine has run aground on rocks off Scotland causing considerable embarrassment for Navy chiefs". On 27th October the Navy announced that the captain had been relieved of his command and on 20th November stated that he would not face court martial over the embarrassing blunder.

What were we all to think about this very expensive and totally unnecessary situation? The Board of Enquiry's findings would presumably come out in due course but to me it could all be summed up in a few of the statements which the media had circulated. A month earlier the Astute's commanding officer had said on the BBC: "We have a brand new method of controlling the submarine which is by platform management rather than the old conventional way of doing everything by using your hands. This is all fly-by-wire technology including only an auto-pilot rather than a steering column.

It was this system which had presumably got the Astute to an area where Ross McKerlick said he would not risk taking his yacht. John Ainslie who was co-ordinator of the Scottish CND said: "Enquiries into previous incidents have shown appalling lack of common sense and basic navigation skills on these high-tech submarines."

On the afternoon of Saturday 22nd January 2011 I was really delighted to receive an email from a long lost boating friend Richard Crouch whom I had last met in 1984. Briefly, he had suffered cancer, had had one or two nasty operations, had been cleared by the medics, and now wanted the necessary licence to captain a super-yacht over 24 metres in length. I telephoned him the next day and three weeks later he booked into the Master Builders Hotel at Bucklers Hard for a week's preparation for his latest boating ambition. He was determined to buy a Hatteras 85 and had found two such craft, one in Florida, and one on the Pacific coast of Canada.

Between 1977 and 1984 we had done much training and boating together in the south of England, and had visited most ports down to the Mediterranean and as far as the Balearics. By the end of the week he had his radio and first aid and refreshed up to Yachtmasters standard, which would have been all that he needed to qualify for a vessel under 24 metres in length. Poor Richard spent the next four months purchasing his dreamboat "Three C's", which was 25.9 metres in length berthed at Ford Lauderdale. He was also, of course, having scans and appointments with the medics who were able to keep him in reasonable order.

I joined him plus a couple of friends at the London City Airport for our flight to Toulon where "Three C's" was due to

*Dockwise Yacht Transport, the vessel in
which Three C's crossed the Atlantic*

The super-yacht "Three C's"

arrive next day by Dock Express. Richard was obviously excited and looking very well and we stayed at the luxurious Kyriad Prestige Hotel in La Sayne sur Mer. When we arrived on board we were not prepared for the first shock, which was that the starboard propeller was bent. The thoroughly efficient Dutch female dockmaster assured us it had arrived in the dock like that and signed an official letter to that effect.

The boatyard at Beaulieu-sur-Mer was the only yard willing to lift us out and do the repairs straight away. So my last captaincy of a vessel in the Mediterranean began slowly, as we didn't want to cause any vibration or further damage to the boat. We made passage with a Sunday night stop at Frejus, before being lifted out of the water on the Monday at Beaulieu. The prop was taken away for repair at Antibes. No-one seemed in too much of a hurry to get "Three C's", and her impatient crew, back in the water. The prop did arrive back lateish Wednesday afternoon but, by the time the yard had re-fitted it, those responsible for lifting and returning boats to the water had gone home. C'est la vie, it would have been the same in the UK.

The next morning we were back in the water and after Richard had paid a vast bill, hopefully retrieved from the vendors or their insurance company in the USA, we were able to start our intended cruise towards Barcelona. After three days and nights aboard the boat in the yard at Beaulieu it was great to stroll ashore in Porquerolles, one of the Iles d'Hyeres. It is under the protection of the Cros National Park and is one of the loveliest ports of call on the coast; marvellous in low season but much visited in the summer.

Thus ended our six nights in France. We then crossed the Golfe du Lion into Spain and called at Port de Roses and Palamos before securing alongside in the vast Marina Port Vell in Barcelona. We had a few very relaxing runs ashore and then I left Three C's for a fortnight. Lesley and Richard had a couple of friends joining them for a holiday and Richard wanted to get some work done on the boat with the aid of spare parts being flown out from the US.

My return was met with some very gloomy news. Throughout the time I had been away, including that while their friends were on board, the sea toilets had been completely blocked up. Also the fuel and electrical systems seemed to have gone haywire. In short, Richard, because of his very bad cancer, had been unable to go out to Florida during any stage of the boat's purchase. He had left the whole thing in the hands of agents, brokers, salesmen and engineers who were supposed to know the boat inside out and who were in Richard's employ. Somewhere along the line (and the boat had been surveyed) he had been let down very badly. The boat smelt like a public lavatory because a new macerator had not been fitted and pumps did not work.

There is no doubt that fortnight set poor Richard back a bit; all he wanted was to get the boat, in suitable condition, to Majorca, and give his family and grandchildren their promised holiday during the month of August. In spite of all these problems, we managed to leave Barcelona the next day and secure stern-to on the pier in the town of Andrax that evening. We then had three more days in the fabulous marina at the Club de Vela, during which time Richard and I were able to re-live happy memories of previous visits to the area over 27 years before. I returned to the UK with the intention of flying back when his family holiday was over, but as I said goodbye I knew inside me that it would be for the last time.

The year 2012, apart from my surfeit of years and the expected tragic news of Richard's death from cancer, was the one in which I finally decided to swallow the anchor. In 2012 also, in addition to confirming all that we already knew, the Board of Enquiry's findings into the grounding of HMS Astute became public – about a year and a half after the event.

The Officer of the Watch was responsible for Astute's safety and navigation and the fact he had no radar echo-sounder or chart, and made incomplete preparations before going on the bridge were the major causal factors in the grounding.

I am quite sure that most of the recent collisions and groundings, including that of the Astute, would not have occurred but for this dreadful dependence on Global Navigational Satellite

Systems. Mariners should perhaps follow the advice of Portsmouth Poll in the Boating Business Press: that is, throw away their GPS and radar. They should get a Two Point Navigation System which looks attractive on any vessel, is twice the fun, and can be mounted anywhere!

Two Point Navigation System

ACKNOWLEDGEMENTS

Firstly and foremost I wish to acknowledge the part played by the Royal Navy of the 20th Century in the excellent training they gave me and it is for that reason I have dedicated this book to that wonderful organisation. Because of the training, I was able to take part in three conflicts, for all of which I volunteered, visit over sixty different countries, and meet so many people. Amongst the very interesting people I was lucky enough to meet, I owe most thanks to those who helped me start up my life in the Merchant Navy and form my School of Seamanship.

The enjoyment was due to the hundreds of talented customers whom I had the pleasure of helping to instruct, and this instruction could not have been given without the support of the Team. The longest serving member is my greatest chum, Charlie. Also in that team, in order of joining were Ian, Molly, Meriel, David, Nigel and John.

My ability to write this book came about because at a very early age I was encouraged to keep scrap books, newspaper cuttings, photograph albums and diaries. These gave quick reference to all the exciting things I was able to experience in my lifetime. Of my thousand or so photographs, there are about 150 in this book – some dating back seventy years. Most were produced by myself, given to me by the individuals concerned, or by Royal Navy shipmates and photographers. In particular, I wish to thank Petty Officer Charles Thompson, our man in South Arabia. Also the editorial staff of Motor Boat and Yachting and Motor Boats Monthly, and their photographer Lester McCarthy for their tremendous support in the first twenty years of our School of Seamanship.

Most helpful in publishing – in fact I could not have managed without her, has been Rebecca. She has her day job and her own secretarial business to run. In her spare time in the evenings

ACKNOWLEDGEMENTS

and at the weekends she edited my transcript, scanned in the photographs and proof read before presenting the completed work (to the publisher) for printing.

Finally, it may be because you asked not to be mentioned in the manuscript, but to anyone I have neglected to include, a massive Thank You.